A History of the English Church

Edited by the Very Rev. W. R. W. STEPHENS, B.D.,
Dean of Winchester,
and the Rev. WILLIAM HUNT, M.A.

III

THE ENGLISH CHURCH

IN THE FOURTEENTH
AND FIFTEENTH CENTURIES

THE ENGLISH CHURCH

IN THE FOURTEENTH AND
FIFTEENTH CENTURIES

BY

W. W. CAPES

AMS PRESS
NEW YORK

Reprinted with the permission of
Macmillan and Co., Limited
Originally published in 1900

AMS Press, Inc.
56 E. 13th Street
New York, N.Y. 10003

Manufactured in the United States of America

INTRODUCTION

INTEREST in the history of the English Church has been steadily increasing of late years, since the great importance of the Church as a factor in the development of the national life and character from the earliest times has come to be more fully and clearly recognised. But side by side with this increase of interest in the history of our Church, the want has been felt of a more complete presentment of it than has hitherto been attempted. Certain portions, indeed, have been written with a fulness and accuracy that leave nothing to be desired; but many others have been dealt with, if at all, only in manuals and text-books which are generally dull by reason of excessive compression, or in sketches which, however brilliant and suggestive, are not histories. What seemed to be wanted was a continuous and adequate history in volumes of a moderate size and price, based upon a careful study of original authorities and the best ancient and modern writers. On the other hand, the mass of material which research has now placed at the disposal of the scholar seemed to render it improbable that any one would venture to undertake such a history single-handed, or that, if he did, he would live to complete it. The best way, therefore, of meeting the difficulty seemed to be a division of labour amongst several competent scholars, agreed in their general principles, each being responsible for a period to which he has *devoted special attention, and all working in correspondence through the medium of an editor or editors, whose business it should be to guard against errors, contradictions, overlapping, and repetition ; but, consistency and continuity being so far secured, each writer should have as free a hand as possible. Such is the plan upon which the present history has been projected. It is proposed to carry it on far enough to include at least the Evangelical Movement in the eighteenth century. The whole work will consist of seven crown octavo books uniform in outward appearance, but necessarily varying somewhat in length and price. Each book can be bought separately, and will have its own index, together with any tables or maps that may be required.*

I am thankful to have secured as my co-editor a scholar who is eminently qualified by the remarkable extent and accuracy of his knowledge to render me assistance, without which, amidst the pressure of many other duties, I could scarcely have ventured upon a work of this magnitude.

W. R. W. STEPHENS.

THE DEANERY, WINCHESTER,
   20th July 1899.

According to present arrangements the work will be distributed amongst the following writers :—

I. The English Church from its Foundation to the Norman Conquest, by the Rev. W. Hunt, M.A. Ready.

II. The English Church from the Norman Conquest to the Close of the Thirteenth Century, by the Dean of Winchester. Shortly.

III. The English Church in the Fourteenth and Fifteenth Centuries, by the Rev. Canon Capes, late Fellow of Queen's College, Oxford. In the Press.

IV. The English Church in the Sixteenth Century from the Accession of Henry VIII. to the Death of Mary, by James Gairdner, Esq., LL.D.

V. The English Church in the Reigns of Elizabeth and James I., by the Rev. W. H. Frere, M.A.

VI. The English Church from the Accession of Charles I. to the Death of Anne, by the Rev. W. H. Hutton, B.D., Fellow of St. John's College, Oxford.

VII. The English Church in the Eighteenth Century, by the Rev. Canon Overton, D.D.

CONTENTS

CHAPTER VII

CHAPTER VIII

CHAPTER IX

CHAPTER X

CHAPTER XI

CHAPTER XII

CHAPTER XIII

CHAPTER XIV

CHAPTER XV

CHAPTER XVI

CHAPTER XVII

APPENDIX I

APPENDIX II

CHAPTER I

THE PRIMACY OF PECKHAM

King Edward I., 1272–1307.   Abp. Peckham, 1279–1292

THE thirteenth century was an age of constitutional growth and conflict ; an old social order had passed away, and organising genius was required to build up a new framework within which the vital forces of the nation might act in harmony together.   Popular rights were often vehemently reasserted both in Church and State against despotic influences within or aggression from without ; the lines of a new Civil Order were drawn by firm and cautious hands ; but the ecclesiastical problems were found very hard to solve, so great was the complexity and conflict of the elements involved.

The ecclesiastical problems of the age.

To adjust the relations of the clergy and the Civil Courts, of the powers of Church and State, of the Papacy and the Crown : to reconcile the national requirements with the apparent interests of the Church at large—this was a task which called for courage and forbearance on both sides, and progress in the work was slow and fitful.   It required statesmanship of no mean order ; it was impeded alike by the self-interests of short-sighted rulers and the claims of resolute Churchmen ; administrative weakness often sacrificed what wise legislation had secured.

The following pages have to deal with the various phases of this struggle.   At the opening of the period, though the difficulties were many, the outlook might seem hopeful, but the prospects were soon clouded over.   Misrule and pestilence, foreign war and civil strife demoralised the national temper; Wyclif's uncompromising tenets, followed by the Lollard propaganda, stirred a strong movement of reaction, and turned the rulers of the Church into resolute opponents of reform; the unprecedented statute *De hæretico* ushered in melancholy times of spiritual stagnation; and the Middle Ages closed in scenes of discouragement and gloom for the religious interests of the nation.

Edward I. was a born ruler of men and a great organiser, but he was confronted by resolute archbishops, watchful to maintain the privileges of the Church, eager often to extend them, and to resist his schemes of legal definition which limited the wide authority they claimed. Conflict was unavoidable between antagonists of such a stamp. It went on in various forms all through the reign till it ended in the discomfiture and degradation of the prelate, who was deserted in his hour of need by the Papacy which he had served better than the Crown. To meet the possible dangers of such conflict, as well as from affectionate regard for faithful service, Edward tried and tried again to secure the primacy for Robert Burnell, his chancellor, who was a great Minister of State, if a somewhat questionable Churchman.

Edward failed to secure the primacy for Burnell.

When the archbishopric was vacant in 1270, the monks of Canterbury turned a deaf ear to the suggestion that Burnell should be elected. Edward, on his way already to the Holy Land, hearing that they were in no compliant mood hurried back to Canterbury, and bursting into the Chapter - house where they were seated, charged them at their peril to disregard his own and his father's will. The stiff-necked monks braved his displeasure, and elected their own prior, Adam de Chillenden, but he was set aside by the pope in favour of Kilwardby, a preaching friar, who was of high repute for sanctity and learning. When he was made a cardinal a few years later, perhaps because his administrative powers had disappointed the hopes which had been formed, and a stronger hand was needed in the Papal interest, the Chapter, now mindful of King Edward's wishes, elected Burnell, who had been raised meantime to the See of Bath and Wells. But Pope Nicolas III., in spite of pressing letters from the king,

delayed and finally refused to sanction the appointment (1278),
"nor could be moved thereto," says a chronicler of Waverley,
"by prayer or bribe."

What the reasons were we are not told.   It may have
been on moral grounds, for we read of grave scandals in the
private life of the Minister, and these were doubtless   Whose in-
brought to the knowledge of the court of Rome.   It fluence was
is more probable that the influence of the great   mistrusted.
statesman was too well known and feared ; the policy of the
Crown might seem threatening to the interests of the Church ;
many religious houses were being stripped by judicial action
of privileges which they claimed ; the Statute of Mortmain *De
religiosis* (1279) was soon to limit their further growth by
prohibiting the assignment of landed property without the
consent of the feudal superior under whom the lands were
held, in disregard of the plea urged by the monastic writer
that "the defeat of the Amalekites of old was due to the
prayers of Moses rather than to the prowess of the men of
Israel."   The clerical advisers of the Crown who inspired or
carried out the large-minded policy of Edward were not
likely to find favour in the eyes of the Churchmen of that
day, whose feelings found a vent in many a bitter phrase and
Scriptural allusion, such as that of Cotton, who says that the
Treasurer, John de Kirkeby, was a "forerunner like that
other John in Sacred History, but he came to prepare the
way of his lord, not to a kingdom of heaven on earth, but to
a limbo of hell."

Ecclesiastical preferment was regarded at that time as
the natural reward for the trusted servants of the Crown ;
the Chancellor and Treasurer were nearly always dignitaries
of the Church.   Edward was acting within his rights and
strictly following precedents when he urged that Burnell
should be raised to the vacant See of Winchester (1280).
But the monks were scolded by the pope when they proceeded to elect him as their bishop.   They were told that
the preferment which he had already was enough.   The
electors had shown scant caution or respect when they
ventured to choose a man whom the Apostolic See had
already disapproved of.

John Peckham, who was raised to the primacy in 1279 in

spite of the wishes both of the Chapter and the king, was a

Peckham, the pope's nominee. Franciscan friar, highly skilled in all the knowledge of the schools. Not perhaps a "vigorous satellite of antichrist," as "foul-mouthed" Bale would have it, he was at least "a creature of the pope," as he humbly styled himself.

But he was somewhat disenchanted by the experience of his relations with the Papal Court. The necessary forms, the complimentary visits to the cardinals were very costly : to meet them, together with the expenses of his journey home, he had to borrow 4000 marks, and he applied in vain for help to pope and friendly bishops and religious houses. For many months the loan weighed heavily on Peckham's mind ; the Italian money-lenders pressed for payment, and archbishop as he was, he feared to be excommunicated for default.

Assertion of ecclesiastical privileges. One of his first public acts was to preside over a synod summoned by him to Reading in July 1279, to deal with urgent and weighty business.

Besides the abuses of plurality and non-residence, which will come before us in another chapter, the main topics were the intrusions on the privileges of the Church. Here the bishops trod on dangerous ground, and the king had Peckham summoned before his Council in the Parliament which met in Westminster at Michaelmas, and forced him to withdraw formally the threats of excommunication levelled at certain interferences with spiritual courts and persons, as also the order to the clergy to post up in cathedral and collegiate churches the Great Charter which asserted the liberties of Church and State. The glove which he had thrown down had been taken up at once, but the dispute was of long standing, and was not soon or easily to be disposed of.

Two years afterwards another synod met at Lambeth, and again the king interposed, but this time beforehand, with the warning that there must be nothing done in it to prejudice the dignity and interests of the Crown. It is possible, as is implied in some accounts of it, that bolder schemes were laid aside after the royal mandate, but it is certain that the obnoxious resolutions framed at Reading, which were then withdrawn, were in the main repeated in so many words at Lambeth.

It was the old question of the anomalies and conflicts caused by the Conqueror's separation between the ecclesiastical and civil courts.   The sphere of competence in each case had not from the first been logically Disputes of jurisdiction. defined or rigidly maintained.   The archbishop, bishop, and archdeacon had each his separate court and representative official—to say nothing of the chapter of the rural dean—each his apparitor and system of citations, principles of Canon Law, methods of purgation, penance, excommunication, distinct from the experience and procedure of the ordinary courts.   Besides the questions of doctrine, ritual, and clerical obligations, which were of course reserved for spiritual tribunals, they had also cognisance of immoralities to be dealt with in the interests of moral discipline for the good of the delinquents, though lay courts had punishments for some of them as wrongs or crimes.   They had also special competence in matrimonial cases, to which a sacramental character attached, and as in days of ignorance the clergy often had to make men's wills and prove them as executors, they acquired in course of time large powers of probate and testamentary administration.   The sphere was wide and ill-defined ; efforts were made often to extend it further, while "the benefit of clergy," which had been conceded since the days of Becket, was frequently assumed to cover a variety of cases in which the interests of spiritual persons were concerned.   The lay courts on their side were watchful to repel aggression ; writs of prohibition issued from them which became a standing grievance with the clergy, and we hear the echoes of their discontent in the records of their synods.

The legislative genius of Edward, and the statesmanship of his advisers, were turned to the problems of these overlapping jurisdictions.

The first Statute of Westminster (1275) provided that the clerk who was held guilty of felony, and handed over to the Ordinary on his demand, should not be released without sufficient evidence of witnesses in his favour (*sans due purgation*).   On this point there were often grave misgivings that criminous clerks were let loose again upon the world.   The second Statute of Westminster regulated the procedure of the king's courts in dealing with suits about advowsons, attempts to evade the laws of mortmain, to alienate ecclesiastical property in land, or ignore the obligations under which it was conveyed, and to extend exemptions enjoyed by the military orders.

Meantime, in spite of the king's rebuke already mentioned after the synod of Reading, and his warning before that of Lambeth, the bishops on their side prejudged the question of disputed jurisdiction by excommunicating any who might venture to stay ecclesiastical proceedings by writs from the lay courts, or violate in any way the rights of Holy Church as established by the Great Charter.

It is likely that some remonstrance from the Crown called forth the bold and lengthy letter in which Peckham asserted the paramount claims of spiritual authority when confronted by the civil power (November 1281). For the liberties of the Church and for the authority of the Canon Law he found no lack of scriptural arguments and illustrations, drawn indeed from conditions wholly different, and he pointed to precedents from the history of the Church in British, Saxon, and Norman times to substantiate the claims. The "oppressions" which he complained of were indeed of early date, and the sainted Becket had chosen to suffer martyrdom rather than confirm the "illicit and damnable" articles which were contrary to the canons of the Church. He trusted that the monarch would be wary and not be deceived by "impious advisers," whom he hoped that the Most High would scourge with such temporal chastisement as might save their souls. But the days of Hildebrand were over, and the high-flown appeal fell somewhat flat. It was followed in 1285 by a manifesto from the bishops, in which they detailed their grievances as to suits about tithes, libel, sacrilege, and usury, and attacks upon their privileges where actions in their own courts were stayed by writs from the royal chancery. It was to be feared, they urged, that on these grounds more people were *ipso facto* excommunicate in England than in any other land.

There was much need of further definition, and the writ *Circumspecte agatis* (1285) was issued by the king, with primary reference to the See of Norwich, but it was regarded afterwards as a statute defining the uses of writs of prohibition. Cases

Claims of spiritual authority.

of purely spiritual correction for mortal sin or libel, sentences of excommunication for assault upon a clerk, punishments inflicted for neglect of church repairs or churchyards, claims of tithe withheld, oblations and mortuaries, were decided to belong to the ecclesiastical department, and were not to be interfered with by lay courts.

But while stoutly maintaining the prerogatives of the spiritual tribunals, Peckham was well aware of the shortcomings of their officials. He and his successors speak in strong language of the " horrible frauds " caused by the " presumption of ignorant advocates," of the disloyalty of others who obtained writs to stay proceedings, of the extortions of archdeacons, of false certificates and forged proxies and clandestine inquiries, of the " plague " and " damnable presumption " of apparitors, and the " diabolical craft of rural deans." But it seemed a point of honour to regard their claims as sacred, and the battle of the rival Law Courts still went on. Among the deeds discovered by the industry of Prynne in the White Tower, where they had been long buried in dust and cobwebs, there are many which tell us of the fines and warnings needed to repel the ecclesiastical aggressors, who would overstep the limits of their province, as also of the clerks rescued by their ordinaries from the hands of civil justice for purgation or a bishop's prison, and freed sometimes, as it was urged, without due care.

But it was not only in these relations of Church and State that more definition was required; within the Church itself on every side there were the signs of conflicting privileges and jurisdictions. Rivalry be-
tween Canter-
bury and
York.

1. There was the age-long rivalry between the Sees of Canterbury and York, one familiar symbol of which was the claim of each prelate to have his cross carried erect before him in the other's province. A chronicler of this time called it "a frivolous quarrel long out of date." It was two centuries old already, and it lasted well on into another. Wickwaine of York sent a piteous letter to Nicolas III. in 1280 to complain of sorry treatment, how the official of Canterbury, "with Satan and his satellites," made a furious assault upon him on his way and dashed the cross to pieces, and when the archbishop had another carried in its place, he hardly escaped

with life from the insults of a multitude of men of war.
Peckham took up the quarrel and wrote to forbid any offers
of hospitality or signs of deference to the northern primate,
if the obnoxious symbol of authority were flaunted.   The
jealousy lived on in their successors ; kings interfered ;
popes remonstrated ; but to no effect, till in 1352 Archbishops
Islip and Thoresby at last agreed to lay the question finally
to rest by mutual concessions.   A like contention, but less
known to history, went on awhile between the Archbishops of
Dublin and Armagh.

2. The Courts even of the same province were not
agreed as to their several spheres.   In 1282 the southern
bishops drew up a list of twenty - one gravamina

The Court of Arches and Diocesan Courts. against the Archbishop's court ; they complained
of his arbitrary bearing, of slights on their jurisdiction,
of frivolous appeals encouraged, of inordinate delays,
and many points too technical to be here stated in detail.
Peckham seemed in no yielding mood at first, but he saw
reason to appoint a commission of inquiry consisting of men
of special experience and learning.   Their report was on the
whole in favour of the bishops, and implied aggressions and
innovations on the part of the official of the Court of Arches.
It had become a court of first instance, not a court only of
appeal, for all litigants who lived within the province, besides
its special sphere of action in the diocese of Canterbury.   On
the other hand, Peckham had repeatedly to rebuke the malpractices of diocesan officials, to whom he wrote in very
trenchant style.   The bishops, when they screened them, were
promptly called to order.   Even the saintly Cantilupe of Hereford, who declined to enforce the sentence passed by the
archbishop, was first angrily rebuked, and finally obliged to
quit his diocese and go before the papal Court, to further his
appeal against the excommunication levelled at his head.

3. But the disputes and heart-burnings connected with the
rights of visitation were of much more general interest and
took many different forms.   The primate journeyed

Disputed rights of visitation by archbishops from time to time through his whole province, the
bishop through his diocese, holding inquiries in
cathedral   chapters,   religious   houses,   collegiate
churches and elsewhere ; listening to complaints, dealing with

faults to be corrected ; the archdeacons and the rural deans made their rounds more frequently in their narrower districts. It was no slight burden to provide for the reception of these visitors with their retinue and officials ; it was found needful to define the length of stay to be allowed, and the legal amount of procurations. The Lateran Council of 1179 had ruled that the archbishop must not have more than forty or fifty horsemen, the bishop only thirty. The archdeacon should be content with five to seven, and the rural dean with two. Attempts were often made to resist or evade the onerous visit, sometimes with open defiance or strange shifts, backed up by much chicanery and quibbles.

In 1280 Peckham issued a solemn warning against certain " sons of iniquity " who threatened to oppose, in their " rash and malicious presumption," his visitation of the diocese of Lichfield. At St. David's he swept aside with a strong hand the pleas and demurs of a discontented suffragan.

York, again, had nearly always a contumacious suffragan at Durham, who towered above his metropolitan in secular dignity and wealth. The haughty Antony de Bek flung into prison the notary and clerks who had presumed to serve on him the citation of John le Romayne. An excommunication followed in due course, but the bishop was in attendance on the king, who resented it as an insult to himself, and a fine of 3000 marks completed the discomfiture of the archbishop.

Still more often do we read of troubles connected with the diocesan's visits in his own See. The monastic chapter looked upon the bishop as an intruder in his own Cathedral, and resisted all inquiry on his part into their management of their trust, and the conduct of their daily lives. In Peckham, as he says, the monks of Canterbury found no " reed shaken with the wind " : he would rather die than expose himself and his successors to " infamy " by weak concessions. At Durham in 1301 the chapter had an undoubted grievance when Antony de Bek, who could brook no opposition, met their appeal to Rome by imprisoning their prior, besieging the convent, stopping up their aqueduct, and sequestering their estates. On the other hand, the violence or insults

came more often from the other side.   Beverley in 1282
prevented its diocesan by force from preaching in its minster.
At a later date, when the Bishop of Rochester visited his
Cathedral, one of the monks preached with insolent language
in his presence, being bribed, we are told, with a flagon of
wine to spend his wit upon their chief.   To the monks of
Rochester, the chronicler goes on, "it seems a natural instinct
to backbite and assail their bishop, so he must always have
a stick at hand to keep them in their places."

4. The visitatorial power of the bishop extended in
theory to all the churches and religious houses in the
Exemptions diocese, but there were many recognised exceptions
of royal to the rule, and many which were matters of
chapels dispute.   The royal chapels of Wolverhampton,
Stafford, and others had been included in Peckham's round
through Coventry and Lichfield in 1280, but over them the
king claimed absolute control and forbade episcopal intervention.   The doors were closed, the chaplains would not
appear even to claim exemption, excommunications followed
in some cases and appeals to Rome.   Though Peckham
boldly reasserted his authority, the king claimed further
independence for the chaplains and clerks engaged regularly
in his service, and here again Peckham was not backward in
his protests.

Edward before and after this repeatedly forbade interferences with his chapels, warning off time after time archdeacon, bishop, and archbishop.   But the dispute was not
easily laid to rest.

5. Jurisdiction over religious houses in general was
asserted vigorously by Peckham, much of whose time and
and convents. correspondence was taken up with the correction
of abuses and drafts of fresh regulations for their
guidance.   They were some of them in a state of anarchy,
monks quarrelling with their prior, as at Canterbury where
Peckham went to settle a "great trouble and perilous
dispute," or at the alien priory of Lewes where the French
prior had little influence over English monks.   Episcopal
registers elsewhere point to a like supervision of the convents,
not limited to the larger questions of morality and administration but dealing with homely details of daily discipline, such

as the pocket-money of a prior who had resigned his office,
or the number of "honest and convenient dishes" to be
served up for dinner, or the disuse of chess-playing as too
exciting or frivolous for ascetics.

But there were wealthy and important monasteries which
by special Papal privilege were exempted from such visitations, and these were ever on the watch to defend and
enlarge their rights. Peckham could not even as an invited
guest enter St. Augustine's, Canterbury, with his cross erect
before him, without a pledge in writing that the form carried
with it no pretensions to authority within the convent walls.

Even the celebration of mass at Westminster by the
primate had to be formally explained as without detriment to
the exemptions of the house. At the Council of Lambeth
(1281) the abbots of Westminster, St. Edmund's, Waltham,
and St. Alban's disregarded the summons to appear, "like the
children of Reuben who abode among the sheepfolds when
the Lord's people went forth to war," but the resolute
prelate gave orders to sequestrate their impropriated churches
and they speedily submitted. Peckham might well call some
of the exempt "wild asses," so hard was it to tame their
stiff-necked spirit.

6. The monks hugged their privileges and kept the
bishops, if possible, at arm's length. But they looked with
no kindly eye upon the friars, whom they thought
pushing and insidious rivals. Matthew Paris had   Monks and
friars.
complained of the wiles by which the friars
gained what was supposed to be a temporary shelter on some
convent land, and celebrated mass upon a portable altar, and
then enlarged their action till it was too late to eject them.
Their reputed sanctity made them formidable rivals. In
1298 the Earl of Warwick on his deathbed desired to be
buried in their precincts, and not in Worcester Cathedral
with his sires. Proud of the triumph, "they paraded," says
the indignant chronicler, "with the great man's corpse
through market-place and streets, and laid him to rest at last
in ground which had been in my memory a kitchen garden."

Peckham, as a friar himself, had a natural sympathy for
his own brethren, and often wrote to intercede for them, as at
Coventry and Reading, with the monastic landowners, who

either refused to give them a foothold in the neighbourhood, or leave to breathe freely when they were cooped up in narrow and unhealthy quarters.   When he thought they were unjustly treated, as at Scarborough, he spoke out vehemently against the "demoniac monks," and spared no pains with the higher powers in their behalf.   Yet the monks' jealousy was not without some reason.   It was hard to see close by the Abbey gates the offerings of the pious diverted to the bold intruders, and to find that people were flocking to confessors whose learning and piety they thought sometimes that they had reason to mistrust.   Thus at St. Alban's, when a friar applied for permission to act as confessor within the jurisdiction of the abbey, he was examined and dismissed—not without some jibes perhaps—as a presumptuous ignoramus.

7. The parish priests had little cause to love either of the two rival classes.   The monks had steadily encroached and robbed the parishes of their tithes, first by securing Parish priests and friars. the advowsons from lay patrons, and then by moving the powers of Church and State to let them appropriate the churches.   It needed all the authority of the bishop in each case to secure even the pittance needed for a vicar.

Disputes arose as to the fees and the oblations.   Pensions were left unpaid.   The Cistercians and other privileged Orders whose home farms were tithe free tried to claim exemption even for the lands they rented, and a Bishop of Lincoln appealed to the Chancellor Merton (1272) to redress this grievance in the King's Courts.

The friars for their part pushed into the parishes; as revivalists and popular preachers they humbled and discredited the local clergy; they boasted of the Papal sanction —confirmed repeatedly by Peckham—which conferred the right to act in the confessional, with or without the leave of parish priest.

To these more general and widespread classes of contentions we may add a great variety of local claims and privileges, which were matters of debate and of heart-burning, Other matters of debate. often out of all proportion to their real importance.

The Chapter of Canterbury urged many claims which were not always readily conceded, as that suffragan bishops of the province should be consecrated in their cathedral. Monks and canons might have equal shares in the election of a bishop, and cases are recorded in which the monks ignoring the canons elected their own prior, and the dispute was only settled after appeal to the papal Court. There were quarrels about the rights of burial in chapels which were not parish churches; there were old-standing claims of parishioners and monks to different parts of the same church as at Leominster and Rochester.

Finally, the University of Oxford was a long time in settling its relations to the See of Lincoln on which it was at first dependent. The bishop had agreed to let the chancellor have cognisance of immoralities which would come before the courts Christian elsewhere, lest the scholars should be drawn away from Oxford, but in 1284 Bishop Sutton had such cases cited before his court. Peckham wrote to remind the bishop that at Paris the scholars enjoyed privileges which he was now curtailing. But when the University claimed rights of probate and others not included in the earlier concessions, Peckham would not support the "customs contrary to common law," nor sanction the protest of discontinuance of lectures.

Collision and debate in many of such cases were largely due to the natural, often unconscious, tendency of officials of all ranks to strain their rights and extend their jurisdiction. The claims were often based on Official tendencies. customary law, where the evidence was not conclusive, and the pleas seem fanciful enough at times, as when the archbishop's visitation was resisted on the ground that he ought to visit his own See the first, or that he should take the others in a certain order, or that he must visit in person —a claim contrary to all the analogies of mediæval usage— or visit once only during the tenure of his office.

Documentary evidence might be forthcoming, but not be above suspicion. Peckham wrote that there were countless forgeries to attest privileges that had been never granted, and in papal letters there are often references to such cases.

One main cause of the conflict was the irregular system

of exemptions which disorganised Church discipline and administrative action and introduced confusion and jealousies in all departments. The ambition of every religious house was to free itself from episcopal control : of the dependent cells to shake off the tutelage of the convent : of the bishop to defy his metropolitan : of the chaplain or servant of the king to escape the bishop's order to reside upon his benefice : of the archbishop to obtain the Papal Bulls which dispensed with restrictions of Canon Law. All these privileges were to be purchased for a price. It needed only a long purse and friendly cardinals and a diplomatic agent. Ecclesiastical machinery might be put sadly out of gear thereby, but there were good times at Rome. It was far indeed from being only the result of cupidity or weakness at the papal Court. Royal favour and caprice, and the anomalies of feudal usage, have also to be taken into account. Bishop Bek of Durham was a Lord Palatine, and in attendance on the king, and not to be lightly excommunicated, like any humble clerk, as Romayne of York learnt too late, to his cost. The disciplinary measures and the pompous rhetoric of Peckham were alike fruitless before the barred doors of the royal chapels. Fine phrases about pluralities fell idly on the king's ears, when with an empty treasury he needed rich benefices to reward his servants. The great officers of State meantime, the Treasurers and Chancellors, steadily used their influence to increase the wealth and importance of their Sees by the grants of royalties and feudal privileges, but, urged Prynne, "to the great impairing of the rights and revenues of the Crown, as the Charter and Patent Rolls abundantly evidence."

The occasional conflict between authorities of Church and State thus caused was of quite trifling moment as compared with the general disorganisation and discredit of ecclesiastical machinery, brought about by the privileges procured from Rome.

The highly centralised system of the Papacy had its great advantages in theory. There was a high court of appeal before which every important question might be brought, and every doubt be laid to rest. Ecclesiastics need not expose their differences before the scornful criticism of secular courts,

Irregular exemptions.

but could go straight to the fountain-head of justice. That was the ideal picture. The sad fact was that in every part of Christendom the powers of discipline were weakened and the hands of administration paralysed by the special appeals or general exemptions which withdrew individuals, convents, orders, even bishoprics from the inquiry and control of those immediate superiors, who would else alone have had the knowledge and the authority to correct possible disorder. There could be no finality in such a system, and little apparent consistency of purpose. An impetuous Boniface could by one sweeping order repeal all the "dispensations, provisions and concessions" of the years immediately past, and replace them with a different set.

The example thus set at the centre was a tempting one to follow. The episcopal Registers of the fourteenth century abound in illustrations of licences given or sold, to the sad weakening of Church discipline. Archdeacons were allowed to go abroad for a few years to acquire some knowledge of Canon Law. Boy-rectors were sent to the University to gain a little learning to fit them for Holy Orders, while their parishes were farmed out for them, and vicars were provided for the Churches.

The frequent conflict of authority, as well as the hopes of possible exemptions, made appeals to Rome, or to the pope wherever he might be, a constantly increasing practice. The Curia was, in its judicial aspect, *System of appeals.* not merely a high court of appeal, dealing with important questions brought up after due inquiry made in the earlier stages of procedure, but a court of first instance for Christendom at large. The pope could be moved to take direct cognisance of any matter brought before him, or listen to complaints from every quarter. The delegates appointed by him, suggested it might be by the petitioner himself, could have instructions sent to them to hear the case at home, superseding officials of a higher rank, or treating them even as defendants in the suit. From every part of Christendom royal couriers and special messengers were speeding to the papal Court. Bishops and abbots elect seeking confirmation, but perhaps with hostile deputations close upon their heels: letters of complaint from minister or

king against some presuming prelate: litigious priors armed
with bulky documents and copies of old charters: stiff-necked
parish priests or runaway monks with the story of their
personal wrongs: proctors and "Rome-runners" of every
kind were always on the road, to provide fresh work for the
chancery of the Holy See.

The first thing to be done was to secure a friend at court,
or an agent who would expedite the business in hand.
The bishops and the religious orders had each a proctor
regularly retained to further their interests and keep them
well informed as the currents of rival influence flowed
to and fro. There was much correspondence too with
friendly cardinals, with one or more of whom standing relations were kept up and confidential messages exchanged.
Humbler petitioners had to content themselves with agents
of low degree, unless armed with introductions to some
great man's clerk or servant. All this was no mere labour
of love. Even wealthy prelates found it often a heavy
drain on their resources. Proctors must have retaining fees,
their "refreshers" when there was much work to be done,
their pensions or promises of good livings when they came
home. They were not always to be trusted, in spite of the
oath they had to take that they would advance their patron's
interests, not their own. One Pudlesdon in 1290 took the
oath and broke it, gaining for himself what he had been
commissioned to secure for Bishop Swinefield of Hereford.
The cardinals expected complimentary visits, in which the
applicant must not come empty-handed. Peckham indeed
names without disguise the amount which he can offer to a
cardinal his correspondent. The Holy Father too will surely
not refuse to accept some offering from his grateful children.

With such golden showers descending on the officials of
the Curia, or the influential personages who pulled the
strings, and with so much business always on hand, it was
not likely that appeals would be always dealt with very
promptly. The delays were enough indeed to tire out the
patience of those who had to wait through weary months at
great expense for personal audience; they were at times
inordinately long, as in one case that we read of, a suit
brought by a certain Langon against Cantilupe, which lasted

on for years. It was brought before six popes, and when at last it was decided in the plaintiff's favour, the defendant and others interested had long since passed away, and executors merely were concerned.

Turning back from these general features of the times we note that at the Council of Lyons in 1274 magnificent prospects opened out before the minds of sanguine dreamers. The noble-minded Gregory X. ruled over Christendom, which, thanks to his unremitting efforts, enjoyed a breathing space of peace.

Prospects after the Council of Lyons.

Representatives of the Greek church were at the Council, by their emperor's desire, to be a visible sign of the re-union of the Greek and Latin churches, for which the pope had yearned and laboured. What might not come of the influence of a great leader of men, with so lofty an ideal, who in two short years had worked such wonders, and who hoped to fire a united Christendom with some of his own enthusiasm for the Church's mission? Himself a Crusader at the time of his election, he longed to see the nations of Europe drop their fratricidal strife and combine once more with all their undivided energies to rescue the Holy Land from unbelievers. The generous unselfishness thus fanned into a stronger flame must surely react on the home life of the Church and purge it of its sordid vanities and inveterate scandals. But the good pope had but a few months more to live, the "vision splendid faded into the light of common day." It is idle now to ask how much might have been realised if he had been given a few more years of life.

The prospects of a grand Crusade were the most shadowy and unreal of all. Edward himself was almost the last of the Crusaders, and his work in that respect was done before he was seated on the throne. The death of Gregory was fatal to the movement for

Crusading hopes.

which the enthusiasm of the Council had been stirred; the union of Christendom for which he strove was instantly disturbed, and rival monarchs busy with their selfish schemes of conquest, or hard pressed in self-defence, had little time or energy to spare for what had now become a hopeless dream. It was not entirely shelved, indeed. The resolution of the Council to raise funds for the Holy War by

ecclesiastical taxation was carried out in England persistently enough. There was a show from time to time of
making special preparations, and of using the funds thus
raised, which were made over for the purpose to the king.
Despatches pass frequently to and fro upon the subject.
Now it is a letter to some prince in the Far East, who is
thanked for proffered help. Now it is a question whether
Edward will start himself or send his brother Edmund.
Then the pope writes pressingly to urge an early date, and
to say that the King of Tartary is ready. But there is
always something in the way: the raids on the Welsh
frontier; threatened hostilities with France; disturbances
and war in Scotland; one or other of like causes taxes the
king's energies and makes it impossible to organise the
general movement. There was much talk of it, indeed, on
all sides, but rather as a form of penance to be undertaken
after mortal sin, or as a last resource of bankrupt credit,
than as an outburst of spontaneous zeal.

Meantime the tidings from the East grew more and more
depressing. The Christian possessions in Palestine had long
been little more than isolated garrisons in the
midst of unbelievers. The stronghold of Acre,
with its dependencies of Tyre, Sidon, and Berytus,
and a few outlying forts alone remained, and all the last
hopes of the Crusaders were centred on the great en-
campment where the military orders and the friars and the
trading states of Italy had each their separate quarters.
But the Sultan Khalil Ashraf brought up a vast army to
the siege; Europe sent no succours; the King of Jerusalem
and Cyprus sailed away on the day of the assault, and left
the gallant defenders to their fate. After an heroic struggle
Acre fell (1291); Tyre and Sidon were instantly
deserted; Berytus surrendered, and the flag of the
Crusaders waved no longer in the Holy Land.

Tidings of disaster.

The fall of Acre.

A thrill of grief and shame passed through Europe at the
news. It was a humbling thing to read the threatening and
vainglorious missives in which the Sultan boasted to the
Christian ruler of Armenia of the progress of his conquering
arms, which had left no tower or wall erect in Acre or in
Tyre, and had glutted the birds of prey with Christian

corpses.　A Bull of Nicolas IV. dwelt in piteous terms upon the "cup of bitterness which had been drained." The Bishop of Tripoli—which had also fallen in 1289 before Malek-el-Mansour—came over to England at the pope's desire to spread more widely the details of the ignominious disaster. Here and on the Continent provincial synods met to debate the measures to be taken to retrieve the honour of Christendom and recover the lost ground.　They could do no more than urge the scheme of Gregory — the election of a strong emperor who could dictate peace to Europe that she might concentrate her strength on the Crusades, expedients to raise money, proposals to tax those of the laity who would not fight, and to merge in a new union the rivalries of the two Military Orders.

But these had been mostly tried before and failed.　Peckham had already done his best in 1290, and nobles had started with Thomas Bek, Bishop of St. David's, to give help that came too late to rescue Acre.　Lists of preaching friars were drawn up, and they went to and fro to awaken slumbering zeal. Masses and processions were ordered for that end (1295); urgent letters came from Pope Boniface in favour of the Templars who were guarding Cyprus as a stronghold against the Moslems, and for succours to the King of Armenia, hard pressed by the infidels not far from the borders of the Holy Land.

Nothing came of these appeals, or of the oft-repeated prayers that Edward and Philip would lay aside their quarrels, and Scotland acquiesce in English rule—without which nothing could be done.　There was a passing gleam of hope when the news came that the chief of Tartary and the Armenian king had gained a victory over the Soldan of Egypt, as Boniface announced in jubilant terms, but again the clouds rolled over the prospect, and another Bull deplored the melancholy condition of the Holy Land and the triumph of the unsavoury Turk (*fœtidæ nationis Turchorum*). Henceforth it was but idle talk and shadowy schemes; expedients for ecclesiastical taxation; matter of reproach to be banded to and fro by jealous kings, each of whom would volunteer for the holy war, if it were not for his rival's plots. Enthusiasm flickered up once more, but in a short-lived, ill·

concerted movement in 1309, which was doomed to failure from the outset.

If it was a far cry to Palestine, and there were memories of ignominious failure there, something might be done at least at home to quicken zeal and humble The Jews in England. unbelievers. The expulsion of the Jews from England in 1290 might seem to express in part such feeling. But it was no mere act of bigotry to be explained alone by the intolerant spirit of the age. For the Jews had not settled here merely as honest shopkeepers and traders ; they were not, as might be thought perhaps, the pioneers of English commerce ; they were money - lenders, brokers, bankers, representing classes needed in the later developments of civilised life, but often odious in the earlier stages. They were only usurers to English eyes, and usury was hateful to the people as well as forbidden by the Church. It was legalised for one class alone. The Jews, who were exempt from ordinary rates and customs, but tallaged by the king at his good pleasure, were allowed to get such interest as they could from the necessitous —limited, however, to twopence weekly in the £ for Oxford scholars—with the prospect that the king might wring it out of them again when he so pleased, as water from a well-soaked sponge. Prynne reflects the earlier feeling, when he calls them "the king's most absolute bondsmen and exquisite villeins." Men eyed askance the strong stone houses in the Jewries, such as few mansions in the towns could rival, talked of the wealth amassed by cruel extortions, of the estates mortgaged to these money-lenders, which by collusion passed through forms of law into the hands of greedy nobles ; of their sneers and jibes as Christian processions moved about the streets, passing even at times into bold profanity and outrage ; of the arm of St. Oswald, held by them in pawn from Peterborough, and the sacred vessels of St. Edmund's Abbey ; of dark deeds of horror done here and there by them in secret, such as credulous fancy has imagined in many a later age.

Edward was inclined to severer measures from the first against them, under no pressure from the rulers of the Church. They thought rather of conversions. The provincial prior of the Dominicans insisted that sermons should

be preached to them, to which they must "listen gently
and attentively without blasphemous words or wrangling."
A refuge was provided for the converts (*Domus
conversorum*, afterwards the residence of the Master   Hopes of con-
of the Rolls in Fetter Lane), and the Crown   version.
allowed for their support much of the proceeds of the
poll-tax and the fines levied on the Jews. Peckham, when
he finds that the law permits them to rebuild their old
synagogue—though not to erect a new one—contents himself with saying that it should not be much decorated, since
any place was good enough for them to "beat the air in
with their abject ceremonies." Some years before, indeed,
what was called their "howling" at their prayers in their
chief synagogue disturbed so much the devotions of the
"Friars of the Sack," who lived next door, that the king
ousted the noisy Jews from their fine house, and gave it
to their jealous neighbours. Meantime, the bishops did
their utmost to discourage the presence of Christians as
servants or as guests in Jewish households.

The conversions did not go forward fast enough, and
Edward and his people grew impatient. Already in 1275
he had forbidden the "unbridled license of their
usury," and ordered them to wear a special badge Impatience of
shaped like the tables of their law. He tried to   Edward.
make them turn to honest trade or manual work, allowed
them even to take lands to farm, but they could not change
in a day the habits which centuries had formed, and took
by stealth to usury as of old. In 1278 many of them were
put to death for tampering with the coinage. A few years
later numbers were imprisoned, then let out for a heavy
ransom. They had been already driven forth from certain
towns where their presence gave umbrage to the local
magnates, or provoked the impatience of the townsmen at
the anomalies of municipal control.

At last in 1290 came the final order of expulsion; the
people were well pleased to hear of it, and gave a subsidy of a tenth in consequence, and as no Jew
turned Christian, in a few months over 15,000 Final expul-
exiles left. The country was content to see them   sion.
go. Theirs was hard treatment certainly, but in 1376 the

citizens of London demanded that the Lombard usurers
should be banished from the land. Long before they had
been as keen against the Caorsines of Southern France, and
from the same cause; there could be no spice of religious
bigotry in either case.

What really distinguishes church life during the few
years that closed the thirteenth century is the movement

Peckham's zeal against Pluralists. of Reform, the serious and persistent effort in
high places to sweep away some of the worst
abuses of the past. It was no movement from
below; it was no endeavour of the State. Archbishop
Peckham was intensely earnest in the cause; to judge only
by his letters, there were few who shared his hopes. He
referred indeed in his first public utterance at Reading to the
instructions which Nicolas III. had given him on the matter,
on which he felt so deeply. It was to enforce the decree
of the Fourth Lateran Council (1215) against incumbents
who held more than one benefice with cure of souls. A
constitution of Othobon the legate had in 1268 dealt,
though not quite in the same way, with the same abuse.
But the popes were the worst offenders, for they dispensed
with the rule for their own favourites, and the example had
been followed on all sides. Peckham acted in grim earnest,
calling the pluralists "sons of Belial, sacrilegious usurpers
of benefices." He affected indeed to temper mercy with
vigour, allowing the pluralist to retain the last benefice to
which he had been presented, though Othobon had decreed
that it was *ipso jure* void. But he made even the haughty
Antony de Bek of Durham disgorge some of the plunder,
and give up five of the benefices which he had held. He
refused entirely to accept De la More, the bishop-elect of
Winchester, because he was a pluralist—a ground of objection almost unknown before. He did the like at Rochester,
and refused for a time to sanction the promotion of John
de Kirkeby, the king's treasurer. He protested at the
king's indifference to the abuse; ordered sequestration in
other cases, expostulated even with cardinals and popes
because of the favour shown to an offender whom he had
deprived.

To non-residents again he would have no mercy shown.

Roger Longespée, Bishop of Lichfield and Coventry, was peremptorily told to attend to the duties of his See. Though as a foreigner ignorant of English he " could not feed his flock with the word of preaching, he could at least make some provision for the poor." Deaneries and chancellors' livings were to be sequestered in default; canons were to be fined for every day's absence; rectors were summoned home without delay. Even the king's clerks engaged on business of State were not to be excused at first, till Edward sternly interposed. But it was not enough merely to reside, the customary duties must be done. Another bishop was old and blind, a coadjutor must be named to do the work. Certain parishes were being neglected, so large amounts were ordered for the poor at the incumbent's cost. And as disciplinarian.

To prevent abuses in the future more care was to be taken by the patrons who presented. For himself the archbishop would not give a benefice even to a cardinal's protégé who could not speak a word of English. The Abbot of Shrewsbury, and the Prior of Lewes were warned to be more careful in the future. To the latter, indeed, he sternly said that he had scarcely ever known a presentation made by the convent on conscientious grounds. Strict disciplinarian as he was, he showed anxiety to protect the parochial clergy from the exactions of officials. The Archdeacon of Hereford was to be sharply warned, as also the Bishops of Coventry and Lincoln, to exact no more than their legal dues. Abuses were sternly disallowed, like that by which a pension for a bishop's cook was charged on the prior of a convent.

Visitations conducted in that spirit must have been a terror to evil-doers. The penances assigned by him were no trifling matters. Sir Osbert Giffard for the abduction of two nuns was to doff his knightly trappings and be flogged three times in Shrewsbury market, and three times round Shrewsbury and Wilton churches, putting on afterwards a sheepskin and no shirt, and then to go and fight as a crusader for three years. Religious houses took up no small measure of his time, for letters of rebuke and drafts of new regulations are given in his register with unusual fulness of detail.

In later years Peckham's tone grew more and more desponding.   There was more reason now for what had His despondent tone. seemed at first the petty affectation of dating official deeds by the years—not of his promotion but his bitterness (*amaritudinis*).   The abuses in the Church were to his fancy like the seven vials of the Apocalypse.   Not to repeat what has been said already about points discussed above, he deplored the weakening of episcopal authority by the encouragement of appeals from its decisions, and the interminable delays in the procedure of the Papal Courts.   Evils were allowed to remain long uncorrected, while a mastery of the technicalities of the Canon Law was thought a better title to promotion than ability to preach the Gospel in its simplicity and power. Writing to a cardinal he darkly hints his fears that the unwary pilot will overturn the bark if he allows sinister influences at court to betray for a platter full of florins the vital interests of the Church.   Had he not vainly striven to recover the treasures of ecclesiastical art belonging to the See which had been carried by Kilwardby to Rome, together with the official registers which have never been replaced?   No one was more devoted than he was to the Roman See, yet no one had more often been undeservedly dishonoured by it. One of his last letters, written to the Chapter of the Grey Friars assembled at Oxford, dwelt in gloomy terms on the desolation of the Church, for "nothing appeared more contemptible to some than that for which Christ offered Himself a sacrifice upon the Cross."

AUTHORITIES.—For the whole period covered by this book the proceedings of provincial councils and the constitutions of the bishops may be found in Wilkins' *Concilia Magnæ Britanniæ*, fol. Lond. 1737.   The petitions or proceedings in Parliament relating to the Church are contained in the *Rotuli Parliamentorum*, fol. (Record Com.).   Royal writs and correspondence with the Pope and foreign Powers are given at length in Rymer, *Fœdera, conventiones, et literæ*, fol. 1704-35.   Our knowledge of the history of Edward I.'s reign is drawn mainly from the following sources : Walsingham, T., *Historia;* Rishanger, W., *Chronica*, in *Chronica Mon. S. Alb.*, ed. H. T. Riley, 1863 ; *Flores Historiarum*, vol. iii., ed. H. R. Luard, 1889 (Rolls ser.) (often quoted as Matthew of Westminster) ; Cotton, Bartolomæi de, *Hist. Angl.*, ed. H. R. Luard, 1859 (Rolls ser.) ; Hemingburgh, Walteri de, *Chronicon*, ed. H. C. Hamilton, 1848 (English Hist. Soc.) ; Chronicle of Henry Knighton, ed. J. R. Lumby, 1889 (Rolls ser.) ; Chronicles of Reigns of Edward I. and Edward II., in the early parts of the *Annales Londinenses* and *Paulini*, ed. W. Stubbs, 1882 (Rolls ser.) ; *Registrum Epistolarum* Fr. J. Peckham, ed. C. T. Martin, 1882 (Rolls ser.) ; *Literæ Cantuarienses* (Letter Books of Monastery of Christ Church, Canterbury), ed. J. B. Sheppard, 1887-89 (Rolls ser.). Writs of prohibition from the Civil Courts and many documents of interest are published by Prynne in his *Exact History of the Pope's Intolerable Usurpations*, fol., Lond. 1670, and the statutes referred to may be found in *Statutes at Large*, ed. O. Ruffhead, 1769. Illustrations of the disputes of authority and jurisdiction referred to in the text are scattered over the pages of the monastic chronicles, of which a fuller list will be given after Chap. XIV.; it may be enough at present to refer to those contained in Wharton's *Anglia Sacra*, 2 vols. fol. 1691, and the *Chronica Mon. S. Alb.*, ed. H. T. Riley (Rolls ser.), 1863-73.

CHAPTER II

King Edward I., 1272–1307.   Abp. Winchelsey, 1294–1313

THE struggle between Edward and the clergy under the guidance of Archbishop Peckham had turned chiefly on questions of jurisdiction, or on what each side regarded as the aggressions of rival courts of law. *Taxation of ecclesiastical estate.* Peckham, as has been seen, stoutly defended the privileges of the Church, and in theory at least would abate no jot of her pretensions, but Edward had succeeded in defining strictly the province of the spiritual courts, and in resisting the efforts made for the extension of their powers.

The struggle was now to be renewed but on a lower plane ; it concerned not the spiritual pretensions, but the temporal possessions of the clergy.   These were matters in which Peckham had shown little interest.   Even the Statute of Mortmain (*De religiosis*), which called forth such vehement protests from the chroniclers, was scarcely noticed by him in his letters, and as a friar true to the spirit of his Order, he laid little stress on the endowments of the Church.   During his time of office, and in the few years preceding it, the king had lived mainly "on his own," and for national purposes the burden of taxation had been far from heavy. The clergy, under pressure from the pope, had in 1273 contributed a tenth of their income towards the king's expenses in the Crusade, and another tenth for the king's brother Edmund.   The Council of Lyons in 1274 had voted a tenth for six years for the Holy War, not without some protest from Richard de Meopham, Dean of Lincoln, on the ground of poverty and the heavy burdens to be borne, but the "great philosopher," as he was styled, was summarily silenced by the pope. In 1275 there was a promise of a voluntary grant from the Spiritualities, and in 1280 Convocation voted a tenth for two years in York, and a fifteenth for three in Canterbury, but in 1283 further aid was refused in the Council of Northampton on the ground that the parochial clergy were not represented. In response, however, to a new vow of Crusade, Edward obtained in 1288 the sanction of Pope Nicolas IV. for a grant of a tenth for six years, and the like in 1291, while an ecclesiastical tenth was also specially voted for the Crown after the expulsion of the Jews.

In connection with the grant of Nicolas a new valuation of ecclesiastical property was set on foot, called the "Taxatio," superseding earlier assessments. The work was carried out by the bishops of Winchester and Lincoln, Valuation of
Nicolas IV. and complaints were loudly urged at the stringent action of the assessors, who "incomparably exceeded the insolence of the old officers, valued property more heavily than it was wont to be rated, and even thus could not extinguish the inextinguishable avarice in the heart of the king." "The Egyptian priests," says another chronicler, "were freer than we are now, for Joseph took all the land of Egypt except that of the priests, but Pharaoh now has us and ours." A third reports that Nicolas himself was thought to be lodged in hell for it, "according to the prophecy of Joachim." It was said that the assessors fixed the valuation at two or three times the amount returned on oath, and certainly it was in many cases raised to that extent above the earlier assessment.

Of the money raised for the Crusade much, doubtless, had been used for ordinary calls, though the treasure seized throughout England in 1283 by the king's order, which called forth a vehement expostulation from Straits of
the Crown. the primate to Burnell, and from the pope to the king himself, seems to have been afterwards replaced.

But the banishment of the Jews—who before had been always tallaged at the king's pleasure—had cut off one sure

source of income. The quarrel with Philip of France
had made war inevitable, and further troubles both in
Wales and Scotland were soon to intensify the financial
strain. War was decided on in 1294, and money promised
readily. But none had come from the clergy before September 21, when both Provinces met at Westminster by
royal summons. They had been alarmed already by the
search made in July in all cathedral, collegiate, and monastic
treasuries, in obedience to letters patent from the Crown,
and the record made of all that was there found, "an
execrable scrutiny, horribly sacrilegious, the like to which
has never been in ages past." "Even the house of St.
Edmund they violently profaned with their scrutiny," says a
writer of that convent.

Edward appeared in person before the assembled clergy
and set forth the requirements of the State and the justice
of its claims upon them, apologising for arbitrary
acts, like the inventory just taken, of which he
threw the blame upon his agents. The Bishop of
Lincoln begged for an adjournment of three days, and at
last they made an offer of two-tenths. Edward, in fierce
anger at the inadequate response to his appeal, threatened
to withdraw protection, and put them under the ban of
outlawry if they did not pay one half. Resistance speedily
collapsed. The Dean of St. Paul's, preparing to address the
king, had died suddenly in his excitement, and now there was
no further protest, though an ineffectual attempt was made to
get the Statute of Mortmain repealed as the price of their submission. The demand seems exorbitant, indeed, and in marked
contrast to all that we hear before during this reign. We
need not be surprised, perhaps, at the claim that was thus
made on the monastic and episcopal estates, which formed
so large a part of the landed property of England, for the
charges on them for all national purposes had not been
heavy for the last twenty years, and they were often eyed by
the laity with jealous looks.

It is of interest, however, to inquire what was the position
of the parochial clergy, and how far their means can have
enabled them to bear this heavy burden. The actual value of
their benefices is given in each case in the "Taxatio" of

Burden laid on the clergy.

Nicolas, but it is difficult to find a multiple which can be agreed upon to translate the figures into the currency of our modern times.   This has been variously stated as from twelve to twenty-four, but it must in fact depend upon the social grade concerned, or rather upon the nature of the commodities consumed. Their means and power to bear the demand.
It would be one thing for the bare necessities of life, and quite another for what were then luxuries, imported and of high price, though now to be found in the most modest household.   But though the purchasing power of the sums at which the benefices were assessed may be a doubtful quantity, and it varied certainly from time to time, yet we can get some idea of the relative value of rectorial incomes to the spending powers of other classes.   Five marks, or £3 : 6 : 8, are often mentioned as the usual stipend of a chaplain, and the provision secured by the bishop for a vicar amounted commonly to nearly twice this sum.   On incomes below ten marks no tenths were charged by pope or Crown, and in this way nearly half the parochial benefices escaped the payment of the moiety exacted from the rest.

Thorold Rogers, who made a long study of the economic conditions of the Middle Ages, calculated that in eleven manors on the estates of Merton College, whose accounts he could thoroughly examine, the average receipts of the rector of the parish from each estate were rather more than two-fifths of the income of the lord.   But the estimate which he gives of £15 as the average is certainly much higher than the returns of the taxation warrant.   He also calculated that with meat at about a farthing a pound, and wheat averaging six shillings a quarter, £3 would have sufficed to provide the whole family of a yeoman with a liberal amount of bread and meat and beer, and leave some little margin for the home-made clothes.   It would seem, therefore, that even the pittance of the chaplain was not less than was absolutely needful for a yeoman's family, and that no benefice was taxed which was not at least twice as large.   But in most deaneries there were several valued at a much higher figure, rising in exceptional cases even to £60 or £100. A large number, indeed, of the estimates were very low, and we can hardly doubt that many of the clergy must have

lived as plainly as the rural population round them, and
have had little to spare for the charities expected from them
by the poorest of their neighbours.   But the rectorial
income was higher relatively to the means of the unbeneficed
clergy than in our times, and the pressure of taxation must
have been certainly less felt by the poorer clergy.   A considerable number seem to have been quite well endowed, with
private means in many cases also, for the best preferments
were doubtless secured often by the higher social classes.

And we must remember also that it was, in theory at
least, a celibate clergy.   Such permanent unions as did
exist were not recognised by Canon Law, and were sternly
discountenanced by episcopal regulations.   Retrenchments
to meet the sudden call of an exceptional tax were, of course,
far easier in the households of an unmarried clergy.   The
rates and taxes have usually amounted in our days to at least
one-fourth of the professional income of the beneficed clergy.
The demands of Edward, though occasionally large, were
commonly much lower, and left, therefore, some margin for
an exceptional call.   It is true that the requirements of the
popes were not so modest, and that when nuncio, legate, or
bishop *in partibus* was sent on special errands, allowances
were made on a very liberal scale by papal order, and many
a groan upon the subject breaks from the indignant
chroniclers.

The whole sum thus raised by Edward's unprecedented demand upon the ecclesiastical resources of the
country seems to have been £105,000, including of course
the contributions of the religious houses which formed
a large part of the whole.   Many of these were in debt
already, and could not easily reduce their expenditure to meet
the sudden call.   The consent of the synod was followed
by a writ in which the king, referring to the "liberal and
hearty" contribution of the clergy, secures them from any
exactions of his agents, after which he graciously acceded to
some requests as to the details of payments.

So far there had been no resistance ; the archbishopric
of Canterbury was vacant by the death of Peckham, and the
leaderless clergy submitted without a protest.   But the expenses of the campaign in Wales, and the preparations for

the impending war with France, obliged the king to ask for
further aid.   He was so hard pressed indeed as to beg one
of the cardinals to secure from the pope a grant Further need
of the first-fruits of all English benefices that from the
might be vacant in the three years following, the strain of war.
cardinal of course to share the profits.   He laid hands also
on the income of the estates which belonged to foreign
convents.   The cardinals of Albano and Palestrina, sent by
the pope to negotiate a peace, had come and gone meantime,
with no result except the further burden of their maintenance.

It was at this critical season that the step was taken
which completed the representative character of Parliament, and defined the constitutional elements of
Convocation.   Provincial synods, consisting chiefly Convocation and the
of the dignitaries of the Church, had been "*præmuni-
entes*" clause.
often summoned by the archbishops to treat of
purely ecclesiastical concerns ; these had grown more
representative in the course of the thirteenth century.
First proctors of the cathedral and conventual clergy were
included ; then archdeacons were furnished with letters of
proxy from the parochial priesthood, or the bishops were
bidden to bring with them three or four of their principal
clergy ; and at last in 1283 a writ of Peckham prescribed
the method of appointment in the Southern Province of
two proctors for the parochial clergy of each diocese, and
one for every cathedral chapter, together with the heads of
the religious houses.

Meantime diocesan as well as the provincial synods had
been often separately consulted on taxation, and even sub-
divisions of the diocese had acted independently in making
grants ; it was desirable to enable the two provinces to act
together, and to supersede for national objects the anomalies
of divers councils.   Writs were issued for a Parliament to
meet in November at Westminster ; the prelates in the writ
of summons were reminded of the principle that " that which
touches all shall be approved by all," and it was prescribed
that the archbishops and the bishops were to bring the deans,
archdeacons, one proctor for each cathedral chapter and two
for the clergy of each diocese.   In 1294 the king had already

summoned the clerical estate to Westminster, but some weeks before the meeting of the lay estates. The lords, clergy, and commons were to be now combined as three estates of the realm in one assembly. The parliamentary representatives of the clergy were to be part of the National Parliament, and the king's writ was addressed to the several bishops and directed the attendance of the proctors by the clause *præmunientes*. Convocations as ecclesiastical assemblies might meet at London or at York, but for national objects the clergy were to be represented in a National Parliament.

They met November 27, 1295, to discuss the king's request for aid. Robert Winchelsey, a scholar and divine of high repute, sometime Rector of the University of Paris,

A tenth accepted.

and Chancellor of Oxford, was now archbishop of Canterbury, by general consent of chapter, king, and pope. He had discussed already with his suffragans at St. Paul's the conditions of the times, and taken measures to improve the machinery of the spiritual courts. He now offered a tenth, with the promise of further aid till peace should be secured, but, to use the fantastic language of the chronicler, the king sent a "captain of fifty" with a flat refusal to accept the offer. The archbishop and the clergy held out firmly. Another "captain of fifty" was sent to demand a third or fourth, but at last the offer was accepted, and "Israel returned to its tents."

The war in Scotland in which Edward was engaged during the spring and summer, while his brother was in

Further demands.

Clericis laicos.

Gascony, drained the treasury, and Parliament met in 1296 (November 3) at Bury St. Edmunds to give further aid. The laity made their grant, but a new element had been brought into the ecclesiastical debates by the issue, earlier in the year (February 24), of the famous Bull of Boniface VIII., known as *Clericis laicos*, by which under pain of excommunication the clergy were forbidden to give, and the secular authorities to receive, any grant of aid from ecclesiastical resources. Winchelsey laid the new Bull before the clerical estate, which included representatives of all orders of the clergy, and he discussed the requirements of the national crisis caused by the hostility of France, their promise of a subsidy, on which the king laid stress, together with the strain on their means caused by earlier demands. After a debate which lasted several days without result, the king, at the request of the archbishop, allowed them to postpone their final answer.

On St. Hilary's day (January 13, 1297) the Convocation met after due summons at St. Paul's. The president in urgent terms appealed to it to devise some course of action which would save them from disobe- The subsidy withheld. dience to the pope, or possible disaster to the State. A message from the king was laid before the meeting, and the bearer of the message, to whom the papal Bull was read, warned the clergy at their peril to disregard his master's pressing need. The various aspects of the question were long and anxiously debated, and at length the primate returned answer that they would send to the pope, and beg his leave to obey the king's demands. The messengers declined to carry back this answer, in their fear of the king's passionate resentment. Three bishops and others were deputed to lay before him the grounds of their decision. His reply was brief, "As you have not kept faith with me, I am not bound to you in any wise."

A few days afterwards the Chief Justice of the Common Pleas gave public notice that the Court would hear no pleas in favour of any prelate or ecclesiastic, and that no redress would be given when they were The clergy outlawed. wronged. "Unheard of horror," cries the chronicler, " Mother Church, which was wont of old to rule her children, is now reduced to bondage, nay, trampled under foot." All their lay fees were seized at once. The king's servants were encouraged to stop upon the road any well-mounted monk or cleric, and make him change horses with them on the spot, Outlawed as they were, they might look for even rougher treatment, and many suffered in this way from sturdy knaves. Some instantly submitted and bought the protection of the Crown. After a Parliament had met at Salisbury (February 24), to which only the laity were summoned, agents were despatched to every county to offer such protection to all who would redeem their property by payment of one-fifth. Few accepted the terms at first, but at a synod at St. Paul's (March 26), after lawyers and preaching friars had counselled submission to the temporal power, the archbishop advised the clergy to act as each best could for his own safety. With few exceptions all redeemed their goods and paid the tax.

Winchelsey stood firm. He had excommunicated all who acted in defiance of the Bull, and "made up the hedge for the house of Israel to stand in the battle." But all who published his sentences of excommunication were lodged in prison and detained there for some time. His own lands and household furniture were seized in the king's name. No one, under pain of forfeiture, might offer him a home ; his horses were taken from him on the road as he sought an interview with Edward ; and for a while he sought a shelter in a country parsonage and subsisted on the alms of the villagers to whom he preached. We cannot but admire the resolute composure with which he braved the storm, deserted by nearly all the bishops, while the preaching friars even turned against him and made light of his censures.

Winchelsey braved the storm.

Winchelsey's wisdom as a statesman and a patriot must be otherwise regarded. He had long known about the Bull which was published almost a year before, and was believed to have used his influence to have it issued. He might surely have foreseen that Philip of France was not likely to submit to it, and indeed it was soon explained away in deference to his outspoken protests, but of this again Winchelsey took no heed. For England itself, however, it was a fatal policy to support. The need of the State was very pressing. The Crown had an undoubted claim upon the loyalty as well as the self-interest of the whole Order, which owned so large a proportion of the land and contributed in other ways so little to meet the national burdens. There were already angry comments on the wealth and power of the Church ; the criticism was to grow more bitter still ; it would be dangerously loud in face of obstinate resistance to taxation. Again, it was clearly not the true policy of a National Church to appeal to the authority of the pope against the Crown in the questions of temporal possessions. The direct claims of the State could be freely discussed in Parliament ; the action of the Government could

Questionable policy.

be controlled by the power of the purse. But the experience of the last reign had shown what evils of misgovernment could go on without a check if popes and kings combined to share the plunder and silence a defenceless Church. A Stephen Langton united all orders in the State in the cry for the Great Charter; Winchelsey, if successful in his stand for what he called the Church's freedom would have sundered fatally the barons and the commons from the clergy.

It is strange, again, that he had so little insight as to put any trust in the old forms of spiritual censures, which were fast becoming rusty weapons out of gear for such a conflict. They had been shapes of terror once; they were now materialised and degraded by the appeals to the civil power to enforce them. The thunders might roll unnoticed over the heads of the obstinate or unbelieving till the writ of arrest (*literæ captionis*) carried the delinquent to the gaol. But these writs were frequently refused; the sentences themselves were forbidden by the Crown; then they were idle and ineffectual to defy its power. Excommunications were always in the air. They passed to and fro between ecclesiastics in high places; were expected even by Peckham when he could not pay his debts; they were flung broadcast at times like the curses of a scolding tongue; were hurled even at a saint like Cantilupe, who died perhaps unabsolved; were licensed even for a schoolmaster to curb unruly boys. Could it be thought that a strong man like Edward, pious and reverent as he was, would submit to censures so grossly discredited and abused?

Edward had been entirely successful in his quarrel with the clergy, and had "crushed the cockatrice in the shell," to use the strong terms of Prynne. But it was followed by a struggle with the chief barons, Reconciliation. growing out of the constitutional question of the claim on them for personal service out of England. This was not so easily disposed of. It was a conflict quite distinct indeed in character, but the resentment of the clergy made the barons' protest much more threatening, and Edward found it politic to be reconciled with the archbishop, and restore the lands that had been seized, and even to throw himself publicly in touching terms upon his loyalty before his own departure for the wars. Winchelsey was moved to tears, but when appeal for further aid was made, the difficulty of the Bull was raised again, and once more it was announced that the aid, if not freely given, must be taken.

Straitened as he was for funds, and provoked by opposition, Edward had been hurried into arbitrary acts of forced taxation which he had reason to regret. These perhaps suggested to Winchelsey the demand for the confirmation of the Charters, which for some time was a rallying cry among the barons. Yet the whole spirit of the age was utterly unlike that of the times in which the Great Charter of English liberties was signed. Edward's policy had been to educate and train the temper of constitutional freedom. His life-work had been largely that of legislation. He had developed parliamentary forms. It was pitiful to see him treated with ungenerous suspicion, as if he were a wilful tyrant; and salutary as the check was in the unfolding of our national life, assuredly he had no cause to love the man whom he regarded as the chief author of an unworthy slight.

Demand for confirmation of the Charters.

During the urgent crisis of the Scotch war, while the king was away in Flanders, the archbishop reconciled it to his conscience to allow the clergy to vote a tenth for the national defence, but later on he recurred to his former attitude of resistance to taxation on the old ground, though Boniface himself had, in fact, withdrawn or explained away his Bull.

It was unfortunate for so strong a partisan of papal power that the haughty pontiff put forth his sweeping claims in such uncompromising terms. The pretensions which he made to Scotland as a fief of the Apostolic See, and with which he interposed between the combatants, naturally provoked an outburst of passionate protest throughout England. The arrogant message was laid before the king by Winchelsey, who at much sacrifice of dignity and personal comfort had made his way through hostile country to the camp in Scotland. The papal arguments were gravely met and answered, and some time afterwards at the Parliament of Lincoln (1301) a spirited remonstrance against the "marvellous and unheard of" pretensions was drawn up in the name of the English

The pope's claim to Scotland.

baronage, but Winchelsey withheld his name from the
national protest.

He gave far worse offence by his action at this Parliament.
He appears, by the statement of his admirer Birchington,
as also in a letter of the king, as the prime mover
in a Bill of Twelve Articles, in which the dis- Further
            offence in
affected nobles paraded their grievances and Bill of Twelve
            Articles.
pressed for immediate redress, and that in language
which Edward called " outrageous." The impatient and
suspicious temper in which they pressed their claims, together
with the attack made on his ministers and servants, seem to
have stung him deeply, and the archbishop, whose hand he
saw in it, was never afterwards trusted or forgiven. His
policy may well have seemed unpatriotic, as he induced the
barons to support his claims that ecclesiastical property
should not be taxed without the pope's consent. Yet the
clergy were not to escape so easily. A tenth was demanded
of them for three years, for Rome exacted and bestowed
upon the king what the Crown forbore to take.

There were secondary causes also, which helped to strain
still further the relations between the archbishop and the
king. Winchelsey almost from the first had been Relations
at variance with Walter de Langton, the king's with Walter
favourite minister. The latter, when elected Bishop de Langton.
of Coventry and Lichfield, had been consecrated at Cambrai
in 1296 by special wish of Edward, and soon afterwards tried
to free himself from his metropolitan's control by liberal expenditure at Rome. This was of course resisted and resented.
The petition of Parliament to remove him from his post
as treasurer met with no success (1301), but he was soon
suspended by the pope from his office in the Church, and
summoned to Rome to meet certain grave charges which were
brought against him. Edward wrote in strong terms in his
favour, protesting at the sinister action and intentional delays
of his accuser, John de Lovetot, who was flung into prison on
his return. The case dragged on, though Langton spent his
money freely. At length he was sent back for trial on further
evidence in England, and Winchelsey reported to the pope
that after regular inquiry he had been acquitted by the help
of thirty-seven compurgators of all the charges brought against

him, which included witchcraft, adultery, homicide, and
simony.   He was again restored to his office in the Church,
but he did not love the archbishop better after the troubles
and humiliations, in which higher influence may well have
been suspected.

Besides the rivalry with Langton, Winchelsey's resolute
and uncompromising self-assertion brought him often into
collision with the royal prerogative, or the jurisdiction of the courts of justice.   Writs of prohibition frequently were issued to restrain him, or his
officials, from exceeding the rightful exercise of his authority,
as when he excommunicated the Constable of Dover Castle
in a secular dispute, or sued a sheriff for executing a royal
writ.   He gave great offence by his persistent efforts to visit
and exert authority over royal chapels, ignoring the rebuffs
experienced by Peckham.   In spite of repeated warnings his
agents insisted on visiting the free chapel in the Castle of
Hastings, and the Canons petitioned the king in Parliament,
in 1303, to have their wrongs redressed.   Winchelsey was summoned to appear in person to answer for the "insolence and
wrongs which the king could no longer bear with patience."
He was not likely to find much favour at court when he
ousted from the benefice of Pagham, in 1298, Theobald de
Bar, brother-in-law of the king's daughter, who had been
presented to it when the See was void.   A royal writ was
served on the agents of his nominee, when they attempted to
take possession of the church, and appeal was made also to
the pope.   The case dragged on for two years.   When it
went against him he forbade the Bishop of London to execute
the sentence, but notwithstanding he was excommunicated
publicly himself in London, and the rights of Theobald were
confirmed.

The opportunity soon came to do something more than
thwart and mortify the haughty prelate.   Boniface, whom he
had served so faithfully, had passed away in 1303,
heart-broken at the ignominious outrages heaped
on him by Philip's ruffian bravos.   In 1305 the
contemptible Bertrand de Got, Archbishop of Bordeaux
and Edward's subject, became pope as Clement V., and it
was no hard thing to influence by sordid motives his self-

Winchelsey's self-assertion resented.

Abandoned by Pope Clement V.

seeking will, so far as even to degrade the strongest papal partisan in Christendom.

On the occasion of the pope's coronation at Lyons (November 14, 1305) Edward sent an embassy, in which Bishop Langton was included, with instructions to them to treat of matters which their royal master had "much at heart." Among these were the requests that the pope would absolve him from his oath to observe certain additions made to the Charters in 1297, and would prohibit any spiritual censures that might be used in their defence. Langton succeeded in both points, and doubtless improved the occasion further by outspoken or suggested charges. Meantime at home there had been stormy scenes. Edward thought the time had come to take steps against the men who had conspired to thwart his policy in 1297, and humbled him in 1301. In the case of the barons he was content with heavy fines. But this was not to be enough for the chief actor in what seemed a treasonable movement, though a heavy penalty of £6000 was said to have been demanded for neglect of writs of prohibition and other offences. At an interview which followed the king upbraided him for his defiance of repeated warnings, his rebellious spirit, and oppressive and ungenerous action towards all who thwarted him. As there were none present probably at the interview, we need not credit the chronicler's account of the confusion and abject submission of the prelate, which seem at variance with all we read at other times of his unflinching and consistent courage. Still less need we accept the highly coloured picture which Thorn, his bitter critic at St. Augustine's—full of the petty rancour of his convent quarrel—paints in still more striking colours. In his account the archbishop grovels in the dust, and owns by silence to a treasonous plot to depose Edward from the throne in favour of his son, on the evidence of a letter which the king produces on the spot. In the State Papers of the time, in Edward's own language, which is strong enough, there is no trace of such a plot, and the rebellious temper which is mentioned seems to signify the thwarting of Edward's policy, and the defiance of his warnings.

The blow was soon to fall. In 1306 a papal letter suspended him from all his functions, and summoned him to

appear before his judge. The insulting language used, "the
venerable prelate, if venerable he be deserving to be
called," showed that he was prejudged already.
He went to the king's presence for leave to cross
the sea, and was told publicly that he might go, but
with Edward's leave, at least, return no more. Repeated
letters were written to the pope with bitter complaints about
his action in the past, and urgent requests that he should not
return to endanger union and peace. The chronicler of St.
Augustine's goes on to tell us further that not only was all
the property of Winchelsey seized in the king's name, but
that the monks of Christ Church were severely punished
for the passing hospitality which they gave him. Woodlock,
Bishop of Winchester, who interceded for him, calling him
his lord, incurred the heavy displeasure of the king for pity
shown to such a traitor. At the papal Court Winchelsey
found only scornful treatment; he was not allowed even to
plead his cause, for judgment had been given against him.

And scornfully treated in exile.

But the pope's price had to be paid. He claimed to
appoint a guardian of the temporalities of the See, and to
have the patronage of its vacant benefices, and in
this Edward, after a brief resistance, acquiesced.
He also sent his nuncio Testa to collect all that
could be scraped together, by fair means or foul,
as tenths, or Peter's pence, or first-fruits, or offerings of other
sorts. To indulge his resentment against Winchelsey, the
king required the pope's support; he was now obliged to
countenance aggression which in earlier days he would have
instantly repelled. It was a return to the bad traditions
of his father's reign, when the Crown and Papacy conspired
together to further their selfish interests at the expense of
England. The degradation of the papal partisan at Canterbury left the Church a defenceless prey to worse exactions.
The issue proved how mistaken was the policy of Winchelsey
throughout. The control by the State which he resisted
meant also a defence against a foreign despot. The control
itself was limited and counterbalanced by the power of
the purse acting through constitutional forms. Edward's
was the true policy of the well-being both of Church and
State; but he threw it to the winds in a moment of vindic-

The pope's support dearly bought.

tive passion, and was compelled to temporise and make concessions even to a weak pope like Clement, whose base
compliances had to be dearly paid for.

Clergy and laity alike grew impatient at the burdens
put upon them by their foreign taskmasters.   At the Parliament of Carlisle (January 20, 1307) a document
mysteriously passed from hand to hand, and the   Resentment of Parlia-
smouldering fires blazed up at once.   It professed   ment of Carlisle.
to be a letter to the Church of England from
Peter, son of Cassiodorus, and in high-flown rhetoric, with
many pearls of Scriptural quotations strangely strung together,
it deplored the piteous condition of the Church, oppressed by
the Scribes and Pharisees who sat in Moses' seat, and who
bound the heavy burdens grievous to be borne, and laid
them on men's shoulders.   It compared the chief pastor
who did not feed his flock to the Assyrian king who laid
waste the temple of God and carried off its vessels of gold.
It called on kings and nobles to rise up and resist the aggressions of the spoiler.

A petition was drawn up without delay, setting forth the
various grievances, which were intensified, as it was thought,
by the sinister activity of Testa and his agents.   These—to
state them in detail—were : "the unbridled multitude of
apostolical provisions," which discouraged men of birth and
learning from undertaking spiritual duties ; monastic funds
diverted from their proper uses ; cathedral offices and important benefices held by cardinals or foreigners who, being
non-resident, neglected the duties of their charges.   First-
fruits were greedily exacted ; moneys left for the Crusades
were withdrawn for other uses ; the numbers of the papal
agents multiplied, and their maintenance made a heavy charge
upon the English Church.

It was decided in this Parliament, with the king's assent,
to warn Testa that his action was illegal, and to instruct the
sheriffs to proceed against his agents when they were guilty
of such conduct.   This was followed up by a remonstrance to
the pope to like effect.   Meantime a cardinal legate, Peter of
Spain, came to Carlisle on the business of the marriage of
the king's son with Isabella of France, and to treat of peace
between the rival powers.   At his request Edward withdrew

the instructions issued to his officers to enforce the decisions
of the Parliament, and allowed the Nuncio and his agents to
proceed with their exactions, only warning him that he was to
do nothing "to the prejudice of the Crown or of its lieges."
But when, on the strength of that withdrawal, the agents of
Testa persisted in acting as before, the Council at Westminster decided that the saving clause inserted implied that
their action was not warranted, and that the prohibitio
of the Parliament was binding still.   It was a pitiful conclusion to a great king's reign, for he died a few months
later.

Yet in the main Edward's attitude towards the Church
had been statesmanlike and loyal.   In her true interests he
defined more strictly the limits of her jurisdiction,
Edward's atti-
tude towards and asserted the rights of the Crown to contribu-
the Church. tions from her for the national defence, while he
checked the increase of her property in forms prejudicial to
the State.   By so doing he arrested the growing jealousy and
impatience of the laity, which might else have clamoured for
more drastic measures of reform.

There was much to be said too at that time for his desire
to reward his ministers with ecclesiastical preferment, and to
relax the rules of discipline in their behalf.   Only in their
order could he find the trained lawyers with the literary skill
that he needed for his work.   His own resources were too
scanty to reward them fitly, and the influence among the
clergy of experienced statesmen with large knowledge of the
world tempered the narrowness of professional training and
encouraged the spirit of national independence.   What Rome
thought of it, or felt instinctively, may perhaps be measured
by the unwillingness she showed to allow preferment to his
trusted servants, by the rebuffs of Burnell, and the suspension
and trial of Langton.

While pressing the just claims of the Crown he stooped
to no personal exactions.   He asked, indeed, for the
customary compliment of a benefice for a royal clerk from
each newly-appointed bishop, for a corrody or pension from
each religious house for an old soldier or worn-out servant, for
the palfrey and kennel-house of a deceased abbot, but not for
gifts such as earlier kings had wrung out of reluctant givers.

He watched over the interests of decaying convents, and came forward in the moment of distress to protect them from the results of their own want of good government or thrift. It was necessary to provide that the life-holders of monastic property should not alienate their estates, and by the Statute of Westminster (1285) lands so aliened were to revert to the donor or his heirs, while the purchaser lost all claim to the purchase money paid. But one of his first cares in an earlier statute (1275) was to warn off the greedy nobles who might burden the hospitality or abuse the weakness of their monastic neighbours. He was scrupulous in restricting the license of his own agents who might else have distressed the religious houses on the Welsh frontiers by the demands for food or means of carriage for the wars, such as those which long made the name of "purveyors" odious through England, and no less than seventeen Commissions to his Justices in the year 1282 were found by Prynne to inquire into supposed violations of this Statute.

Almost to the last he calmly but persistently defended his royal prerogative in its relations to the Church against the constantly repeated aggressions of the pope. Thus he objected altogether to the Bulls which touched the questions of civil rights with which his courts were competent to deal, just as his writs of prohibition repeatedly warned off the ecclesiastical officials from like cases, and heavy fines at times chastised obstinate aggression of the kind. Bishop Bronescombe of Exeter was prosecuted for damages of £10,000, and another bishop was fined 1000 marks for the offence of his archdeacon and his clerks. Edward jealously defended the right of the Crown to issue the *congé d'elire* for the elections of the prelates, and insisted on his sanction as an indispensable condition. An Abbot of St. Augustine's who accepted office in neglect of this was heavily fined, and only pardoned after intercession by the Chancellor Burnell; while the chapter of Dublin, which presumed to elect without his leave, was prosecuted at his suit in 1305, and the damages were laid at £20,000. The temporalities of the Sees were in other cases kept for some time in his hands to mark displeasure at the irregularities of the appointment. It needed many flattering letters from friendly cardinals to intercede for John of Pontoise,

who gained Winchester by provision only of the pope.   In
other cases he refused to restore the temporalities till the
bishops had publicly renounced in the papal Bull confirming
their election certain clauses which seemed to him derogatory
to the interests and dignity of the Crown.

AUTHORITIES—To the authorities mentioned in Chap. I. we may add
Thorn in *Anglicanæ Historiæ decem scriptores*, ed. Twysden, fol. 1652 ; *Memo-
randa de Parliamento*, 1305, ed. F. W. Maitland, 1893 (Rolls ser.) ; *Taxatio
ecclesiastica auctoritate P. Nic. IV.* 1862 (Public Records).

CHAPTER III

King Edward II., 1307.   Edward III., 1327.   Abp. Reynolds, 1313.
Meopham, 1328.   Stratford, 1333

THE period of the reign of the second Edward is one of the
most depressing in our history, discreditable alike in the affairs
of Church and State.   Pestilence and famine for
long years, inglorious defeats and destructive forays   Reign of
on the northern borders, corresponded closely to   misrule.
the scenes of confusion and anarchy at home where, in the
lack of guiding principles of truth and honour, the only
motives to be traced were those of sordid self-interest and
party strife.

A startling catastrophe at the beginning of the period
gave a shock to the whole religious world.   It was with
bewilderment and wonder that men heard that the   Downfall of
great military Order of the Templars was charged   the Templars
with dark deeds of horror done in secret within   abroad.
their convent walls.   It was soon told that on one day the
whole brotherhood in France was seized by order of the
king, and hurried off to wait in prison for their trial for the
blasphemy and obscene rites of which they were accused.
The trial, indeed, was but a mockery of justice ; the downfall
of the whole Order was complete.

The worst features of the strange and pitiable story belong
to the history of France, and happily we need not dwell
upon the agonies of gallant knights tortured in their dungeons
till some sort of confession was wrung from them, to be
disavowed again when they came out—mangled wrecks of

life too often—into the light of day to face their judges. The cruel scenes of the Inquisition are pictures that have been often painted, but it would be hard to find among them a more pathetic tragedy than the fearful doom of the grand master and his brave comrades, on whom men had looked but lately with admiring envy, now given to the flames as relapsed heretics, sacrificed to the jealous greed of a merciless king, and to the sordid self-interest of time-serving prelates and a crafty pope, who owed that king his papal crown and dared not thwart his aims.

The secular historians of the age are in the main agreed as to the causes of their ruin. Philip of France coveted their wealth, was jealous of their military power and strongholds, was impatient of a debt not easily to be repaid, and was determined to crush a rival influence that even the Crown might find too strong. The Order itself was little loved, though feared and honoured. It had done gallant deeds of chivalry in defence of Christian pilgrims, but all that was over now that Acre had fallen and the Holy Land was given up to unbelievers. At home their privileges were odious, for they had ceased to have a meaning ; their houses and lands were exempt from episcopal control, paid no tithe to parish priests, were free from ecclesiastical taxation, while their pride and wealth and stately bearing often offended their lay neighbours.

In England the charges against them were not credited at first. Letters were written in the name of the young king to the French monarch and the pope to express the general surprise. Their honour was unquestioned here. It was but lately that Church councils had proposed the fusion of the Templars and the Hospitallers as the best hope of rescuing the Holy Land. But the answers were pitiless, the pressure urgent, and the chiefs of Church and State decided to arrest the Templars in obedience to the papal Bull, which denounced any who might venture to give countenance or help to the accused, while it lavished fulsome praises on the royal defender of the faith, whose motives had no taint of covetous desire, since he had no wish to profit by their fall. Papal inquisitors arrived—an unprecedented thing—to conduct the proceedings at the trials which

And in England.

were held at London, Lincoln, and York. The bishops sat
with the inquisitors. Witnesses were encouraged to appear
before them, and a curious medley of evidence brought
forward, such as would be swept aside at once in any modern
court; wildly improbable in its details, full of blasphemies
and indecencies of idiotic type, with some few darker shades
of mystery and horror.

Except in the case of a few apostates of ruined character,
who seemed willing to avenge themselves on those who had
expelled them, or here and there of some half-witted prisoner
dazed by the strain of long suspense, little was avowed
beyond the facts of secrecy in the ceremonies of admission
to the Order at the dead of night, and questionable rites
of absolution. As this was not enough, the use of torture
was sanctioned in their trials, though King Edward and the
northern prelates formally protested that it was contrary to
the common law of England. It was not, however, to be
carried so far as to cause the maiming of limbs or violent
shedding of blood. It is hard to say how far it was enforced;
the accused in their despair submitted to abjure their errors
and do penance; their English homes were broken up,
the inmates distributed among the religious houses, where
they were not always welcomed, and pensions were provided
for their maintenance out of the proceeds of the lands that
had been seized. The whole Order was formally dissolved
by the authority of the pope in 1312, while the Council of
Vienne was sitting.

The downfall of the Templars, notwithstanding all their
proud traditions, was a dangerous precedent for unsettled
times, and the pope strained every nerve that kings and
nobles should not reclaim what their forefathers had given to
the Order. But the hoarded treasures had disappeared,
and when the estates in England were given over to the
Hospitallers, they were weighted with such heavy costs and
royal dues that they were for long years of little value to
their owners.

In the ruin of the Templars the Papacy had played a
most ignoble part, had flung away its interests as well
as truth and justice. The Order which it had betrayed
so meanly was its own special champion in the cause

which it professed to have at heart. Clement had already deserted Winchelsey, who had served the Papacy not wisely but too well. Who could feel security or pride

Papal policy, as French, odious in England. in loyalty to such a master? He had transferred his court from Rome, with its long traditions of dominion, to take up his abode at Avignon, where he was overshadowed by the Monarchy of France. His cardinals became French in sentiment and aims; his policy perforce determined by the influences that were dominant around him. To English eyes, already keen to criticise ecclesiastical abuses, the Papacy itself seemed to take the wrong side in the long national struggle, and Peter's pence to be but a disguised form of strengthening a rival power. Yet England still remained "a garden of delights and well that never failed," as a pope called it. While France had, through its Pragmatic Sanction, secured by the action of St. Louis, limited the interference of the popes in the elections of the clergy, and denied their right of ecclesiastical taxation, here year after year they claimed more and more frequently to appoint bishops at their own free will, to quarter their legates on the English Church, or make the best benefices serve as pensions for the families or hangers-on of cardinals or pope. The so-called Monk of Malmesbury breaks out into a passionate invective on these abuses of his day: "Of all the lands of earth it is England alone that feels the burden of its papal lord. His legates come and strip us bare. Others armed with his credentials demand our prebends. Rules of residence are abolished for our deans. Canons are rarely to be seen. Lord Jesus remove the pope from off our backs or curb his power."

The papal correspondence fills a large space at this period in the pages of Rymer, and the crafty Clement writes now in hectoring vein, now in terms of bland authority to claim concessions which earlier rulers would have resisted at all costs. His Bull in 1309, soon after the young king's accession, bitterly complains of the officials of the Crown who had interfered with the agents of the cardinals, and enforced the regulations of the Parliament of Lincoln. It speaks of the "laymen glorying in their malice, potent in iniquity, who forbid the legal processes and sentences of the

courts in favour of any applicants who claim by title of provision."

The weakness of the new government gave a good opening
for aggression, and the opportunities were not neglected. The
young king broke at once with the traditions of his Weakness
father's policy. One of his first acts was to have of the new
Winchelsey recalled, to give more dignity to the government.
ceremonial of the coronation, in which, however, the
archbishop was not well enough to take part. Another was
to degrade the late treasurer, Walter de Langton, who had
checked his earlier extravagance, and brought upon him
the grave displeasure of his father, when the prince in his
petulant folly trespassed and hunted in the bishop's woods.
The disgraced minister was thrown into prison, his lands and
ample treasures were seized in the king's name; " no man
in England," so Knighton tells us, " dared say a word in
his behalf," and even four years afterwards we find the
northern Bishops pleading for his release from his imprisonment at York.

The first Edward had vainly pressed for the promotion of
his favourite servants, after election by the chapters in due
course, and had seen their claims ignored at Rome. His son
was differently treated. His nominees inspired no fear, carried
no weight as statesmen, and were for the most part appointed
readily enough after heavy payments had been wrung from
them or their patrons. They represented the shifting currents
of court influence in England. The letters written in their
behalf to Avignon were signed in the king's name, but
dictated by queen or favourite or party leader. The bishops
themselves were ambitious partisans, and the king writes to
the pope more than once, bitterly regretting the part which he
himself had taken in their favour, and complaining of the
treachery of his agents at the papal Court, who disregarded
his instructions and used their opportunities of backstairs influence to push their own fortunes and defeat their master's
schemes. It is a melancholy picture, as we look behind the
scenes, and few of the actors in the drama could have won
men's confidence or respect.

Winchelsey indeed for some few years still towered in
moral stature above the rest. His name carried great weight

at court and with the barons, and when he passed away in 1313 it seemed to the writers of the times that

Contrast be-
tween Win-
chelsey and
others round
him.

"sudden darkness clouded over the clear light of day." With a chorus of many voices they raised the monument of praise to the man of indomitable courage, "strong as a lion," "unshaken as a wall," who was "called by Providence to rule the spouse of Christ." They told each other of the tokens of divine displeasure at his treatment in high places; that Edward I. heard of a disaster in Gascony on the same day that he treated Winchelsey so roughly; and that his accusers before the papal Court soon met with sudden death, while the monarch's decease was revealed by supernatural means to the exiled primate at Bordeaux.

By the contrast of the meanness and self-seeking of the prelates of a later day the proportions of his character grew more heroic; men began to revere him as a saint, and at his shrine at Canterbury rich offerings at first flowed freely in, to drop, however,—so short-lived is fame,—to seventeenpence in 1375.

His lifelong rival Langton remained a few years more upon the stage, but with no gain to his good name. After long disgrace the Ordainers, who were appointed as a Commission of Reform, demanded in 1311 that justice should be done him and restitution made; but he speedily deserted the barons' cause—perhaps because Winchelsey was at its head—and revealed their plans to Gaveston, "playing the part of an Ahithophel, to the great dishonour of his name."

He became treasurer once more, the trusted servant of the king, who begged him to stand firm against the censure of the barons and the thunders of the Church. He was sent on errands of special trust to Avignon, and Edward wrote pressing letters to beg that his business might be soon despatched, for he had urgent need of him at home.

Meantime the archbishopric was vacant, and a very different man from Winchelsey stepped into the empty place.

Thomas Cobham, the elect of the chapter of Canter-

His successor
Reynolds.

bury, for sanctity and learning called the very "flower of Kent," was set aside, and at the urgent request of Edward, backed up by lavish gifts, his old tutor, Walter Reynolds, was nominated by Pope Clement. We find in the chroniclers a fearful catalogue of his shortcomings. "A wanton son of Belial," of "infernal avarice," "teaching by example the doctrine of Balaam," "so illiterate that he could not spell his own name aright"; such were the flowers of rhetoric with which they decked his memory; and certainly there are few signs of dignity or wisdom in his guidance of the Church in those dark days of trial. He spent his money freely in the papal Court. A royal letter speaks of the "intolerable outlay" required of him at Avignon to defray the costs of his translation from the See of Worcester, and he paid doubtless heavily for the various privileges of jurisdiction which he afterwards obtained.

The bishops of that age were, for the most part, of low repute. Lewis de Beaumont, a kinsman of the queen, became Bishop of Durham in 1318, thanks to the influence of the royal families of France and England, and of vast sums spent in bribery. "He was crippled in both feet," says Murimuth, "like many Frenchmen, and if the pope had seen him, he might never have been bishop." It was more to the point that he knew so little Latin that he could not even read aright the formula required of him at his consecration, though he had been learning it for days beforehand. He stammered and stuck at the word *Metropoliticæ*, and said at last, "Let it be taken as said." Another time, in the ordination service, he found the phrase *in ænigmate* so hard that he muttered in the hearing of those who were standing near, "By St. Louis, he is an ill-mannered fellow who put in that word here."

Hereford was given in 1318 to Adam of Orleton, who was prominent among the episcopal intriguers of the age. We shall hear more of the "great bustling in the world," as Fuller called it, of this factious schemer in the interests of the Mortimers of Wigmore, to whom he owed his rise despite the opposition of the king, who had good reason for mistrusting one who proved a bitter and unscrupulous traitor. William de Ayermin, a clerk of the Treasury, went on an embassy to France, and there he deserted his master's cause, and intrigued with the queen's party, by whose influence with the pope he was nominated to the See

The bishops.

of Norwich, though the chancellor Baldock was the choice of the electors (1325). So angry was the king, says the monk of Norwich, that he sent soldiers to arrest the bishop, who hid himself in his cathedral till the storm was over. The temporalities of the See were long withheld, nor were they indeed restored till after the fall of the Despensers, by whom his treachery was bitterly resented. Walter of Maidstone, "notorious in England for his dissolute behaviour," was promoted in like way to Worcester. The bishopric of Lincoln fell to Henry de Burghersh, a nephew of the powerful baron Bartholomew de Badlesmere, though he was but four-and-twenty and his learning very slender. The chronicler or so-called Monk of Malmesbury breaks out in a long jeremiad as he thinks of the "dumb idols," the "sounding brass and tinkling cymbals," an "illiterate fool lording it in the Church of Christ," the "ridiculous presumption of the young bishops who have learnt nothing yet are ambitious to be teachers." "Let the miserable prelates take good heed, when they mount unworthily the pastoral throne, lest they be hurled headlong with Lucifer to hell." Irish archbishops, too, are charged in papal letters with the grossest scandals.

There were, indeed, a few good men and true in the high places of the Church, like Archbishop Melton of York, who "by God's grace kept his purity untarnished, like Joseph in Egypt and Daniel in Babylon," while he waited in Avignon two years for consecration, and came unscathed out of that furnace of temptation, but his appointment as treasurer was bitterly resented by the incapable and jealous Reynolds. Gilbert de Segrave, Bishop of London in 1313, was a man of "noble character, and specially odious to the pseudo-primate." John Dalderby of Lincoln was thought by many worthy to be canonised. But such men were to be found more often among the rejected candidates.

To the credit of the chapters, however, it may be said that they sometimes elected the best men of the times, and persisted in the freedom of their action, though the court and nobles did their utmost to influence the electors and turn them from their conscientious choice. The chroniclers give curious pictures, with

The action of the chapters.

much local colour, of scenes at the elections, which look
like unconscious mimicries on a petty scale of the intrigues
at papal conclaves. Thus William of Dene the notary tells
us that at Rochester in 1317 the archbishop used his
influence for his own chancellor, and Lady Badlesmere
for another candidate, but the monks chose their own
prior, Haymo le Hethe. Formal difficulties were raised at
Avignon, and though letters from the king were sent in
favour of the bishop-elect, the queen, supported by the
royal family of France, pressed for the appointment of her
own confessor. After much debate among the cardinals,
and large expenditure on bribes all round, and many letters
from men of influence in England, the election was at length
confirmed in 1319. The bishop, who had been brought
almost to death's door meantime by sickness and anxiety,
pledged his credit to pay the necessary outlay, and returned
home so poor a man that the clergy of his diocese had to
subscribe twelvepence in every mark out of their incomes
to maintain him for the first year of office. His lot was cast
in evil times, when self-seekers were climbing nimbly up
the ladder of promotion, and playing fast and loose with
principles and causes, but he was true and loyal, though
he had no easy course to steer amid the troubles caused by
intriguing prelates, mutinous monks, and riotous disturbers
of the peace.

It cannot be supposed that much progress would be possible with such spiritual guides. The complaint on all sides
was of a demoralised society. "The English people,"
said a chronicler, "surpasses every other in three *Society demoralised.*
features, in arrogance and craft and perjury. Juries
are corrupt. Rancour and malevolence abound in high
places. Rapine makes its infamous gains at the expense
even of the ministers of God." The standard of Church
government was lowered. Restrictions on non-residence
were relaxed, and complaints were rife of extortionate fees
exacted by archdeacons.

The clergy in their Convocations were still busy with the
old questions of privileges and rival jurisdictions. It would
seem that the concessions of 1285 had been ignored in the
anarchy of the present reign, for the articles put forth in

the Parliament of Lincoln in 1316 (*articuli cleri*) mainly reaffirmed the old provisions.   They insisted on the privilege of non-residence for beneficed clerks engaged Complaints in Convocation. in the business of the State, but they guaranteed, though ineffectually, the freedom of ecclesiastical elections against all pressure from without, and limited the power of the sheriffs to distrain on the possessions of the clergy.   The courtier Reynolds exerted all his influence to get liberal grants to meet the royal needs, but in 1314 his method of procedure had roused the suspicions of the clergy. Technical irregularities were pointed out in the writ which directed him to summon his provincial synod, and objections raised to the presence of the king's councillors deputed to discuss the subject of a subsidy.   A later mandate was issued by him in due form for a Convocation, but the tenth granted by it came in slowly, and when he pressed in 1316 for more liberal help, another tenth was given with reluctance.

They had been heavily taxed by the pope, they urged, and in the hard times of agricultural distress from which they suffered there would be nothing left to be given to the poor. On all sides there were complaints of the exactions of the papal Court.   Letters signed with the king's name dwelt on the "horrible abuses of the Camera."   Parliament refused to confirm the grants made to the pope's relations.

The bishops for their part made a formal protest against the mode in which the prohibition of pluralities had been enforced of late.   John XXII. had condemned The Bull "*Execrabilis.*" them, as also the dispensations bought at a heavy price in what was called Clement's market, which had made of no effect the legislation of the Fourth Lateran Council of 1215.   His constitution of 1317, known from its first word "*Execrabilis,*" ruled that all clerks who held more than one benefice with cure of souls should within one month after notice resign all but one of their benefices, or else all were to be void.   He "reserved" for himself all the benefices thus vacated, and one or two historians were bold enough to urge that the pope did so in his anxiety for the well-being of the Church of England, that "the vine of the Lord of Sabaoth, which was bringing forth wild grapes, might bear sweet fruit."   In fact within a few months he was busy

filling up in England some fifty of them, and the chronicler of
Bridlington says that he gained thereby "a countless store of
treasure." But even so he did not act rapidly enough to
deal with the crisis which he had caused himself. The
bishops, writing to him on May 30, 1318, complained of
churches left without a parish priest, or only with an alien
who knew not "the bleating of the flock," of faithful laity
estranged, of buildings falling into ruin, and begged for
authority to fill the vacant benefices, if the pope would not
present from a list to be submitted by them.

There are few bright traits to relieve the darkness of the
picture, as painted by the writers of the times, but in the
north of England it was more lamentable still.
For a whole generation the Scotch wars spread   Piteous
insecurity and havoc far and wide. Moss-troopers   plight in
                                                   northern
overran the border lands. Marauding expeditions   counties.
carried desolation far down in Yorkshire. Ill - organised
levies, hard to keep in hand, were often on the move. The
chronicler did not feel secure even in his convent cell. Had
not the canons of Bridlington seen the king leave them
in hot haste at the tidings of a hostile foray? Were not the
canons of Bolton driven from their ruined home, and boarded
out for four marks apiece in friendly monasteries?

But suffering and danger called out the better qualities
of the churchmen of the North. There is little trace in
them of the factious spirit and self-seeking policy of the
southern prelates. King and nobles were quarrelling in the
camp before Berwick (1319), and making little progress with
the siege, while the invading Scots were ravaging Yorkshire at
their leisure, but the archbishop and chief abbots gathered
such hasty levies as they could, and tried, though ineffectually,
to drive back the enemy at Myton on the Swale. They were
routed hopelessly, and the archbishop's standard only saved
as by a miracle. Men mocked at the strategy of clerics, and
called it "the white battle," in allusion to the surplices of the
men of peace who took part in the fray; but at least they
bravely risked their lives, while the men of war spent their
time in paltry feuds, and let the plunderers go by.

Another time, not on the field of battle, but in the council
chamber, they showed true patriotism, while they rebuked the

narrowness of party spirit. In 1321 the attitude of the great
Earl of Lancaster was neither that of peace nor open war
with Edward. With bold assurance he summoned
a sort of parliament of his own, both clerical
and lay, at Sherburn in Yorkshire. Bishops
and clergy met in the Rectory-house, after the opening of
proceedings in the church. They agreed to help in any
measures of resistance to the invasion of the Scots, but
they prayed that "for reverence and honour of God and
Holy Church, the salvation of the realm, and the quiet of
the people," there might be forbearance from threatening
movements, and that in the next Parliament concord and
union might be brought about by peaceable discussion. The
northern clergy interposed, that is, on what seemed the eve
of civil war, in the interests of peace, and for a while their
effort was successful.

The council at Sherburn.

It may be said to the credit of the Holy See that they
followed the example set them by Pope John XXII. His
correspondence contains in the *Secreta* many letters
addressed to king and queen and nobles, in which
in every variety of tone he urges the interests of
union and peace. He implores Edward to be more frugal in
his household, more wary in his choice of councillors, more
self-restrained in his relations with Thomas of Lancaster and
others, more mindful of his royal dignity and the welfare of
Church and State. He trusts that Rigaud of Assier may,
as bishop of Winchester, have influence with him for his
good. If wholesome advice could have availed, the king
would not have fallen, for few rulers have had more of it.

Good advice from the pope.

After long years of misrule and dearth, suffering and discontent were very general throughout the realm, and they found
forcible expression from the clergy in a provincial
council held at Lincoln (January 1323). They refused
a further subsidy after the tenths which the pope had
levied for the king. The pressure of dearth was very urgent ;
the exactions of court and nobles were bitterly resented. Few
dared to speak out plainly, but pamphlets were flung about
which were full of angry lamentations. The state of England
was most critical ; wars were ruinously mismanaged, irreligion
rampant, no consistency or honour in public men, party spirit

The synod of Lincoln.

stifling the sense of common weal. 'Shame on the bishops that they are dumb and raise no warning cry. They should bethink them that God raised them from the dust to sit with princes that they might be as watchmen set on high to bear witness against the people's sins."

How sorely the need of some true champion had been felt we may judge from the reverence shown for the memory of Lancaster, and the wish to make a saint out of such a questionable hero. He was coarse, wanton, and vindictive, it was owned, but at least he seemed to die for the constitutional liberties of Church and State which were assailed by the extravagances and caprices of the court. Miracles were reported even at his tomb at Pontefract, but "the king like Pilate had guards placed to bar the access to it." Reverence for Lancaster.

The excesses of misrule which could not be mended were to be ended soon, and in the closing scenes the bishops took a prominent and a discreditable part. Some of them, though raised to their Sees a few years since by royal favour, were involved in the factious movement of the Mortimers. John Hotham of Ely was attached and fined. As to John of Drokensford of Bath and Wells and Burghersh of Lincoln, the king feebly deplored in letters to the pope his own part in their promotion, and would have them, if possible, banished from the realm (1323). Against Orleton of Hereford his resentment was still stronger. Charged with the guilt of treason, the bishop appealed to his Order to stand by him, and before the trial began they appeared in a body to escort him from the Hall of Justice. So the temporalities only of the See were seized. Irritated but not crushed they only intrigued with more bitterness against the king. John of Stratford, who had betrayed his trust as agent for the king at Avignon, and supplanted Baldock the king's nominee for the See of Winchester in 1323, resented the displeasure of his master, and his abilities and knowledge of affairs strengthened the opposition to the ruling powers. Some or all of these bishops shared the queen's hatreds, or affected sympathy with her wrongs, advised her in her schemes abroad, and joined her standard when she landed to march against the king. Intrigues of bishops.

A few indeed were faithful, and gathered at Lambeth
round the irresolute archbishop, who in his
folly had hoped to keep London quiet by a
papal Bull against invasion that had been issued long before
against the Scots. For two days they talked of mediation,
but had not nerve to act. On the morrow the rebellion
broke out in the city. The loyal Bishop Stapeldon
of Exeter, to whose custody the city of London was
entrusted, but whose official acts as treasurer had
made the Londoners hate him as " fumische and without
pite," was surrounded by an excited mob while he was riding
towards the Tower, and beheaded in Cheapside with a
butcher's knife. His head was set on the pillory, and then
sent to the queen at Bristol. The body was left in St. Paul's
churchyard all day, and was carried afterwards to St. Clement
Danes, near the bishop's new mansion in the Strand, but
only to be refused admission by John Mugg, the timid and
ungrateful rector, who owed his benefice to the murdered
bishop. It was hastily covered with a ragged cloth given
by a woman's charity and was huddled out of sight in a hole
among the ruins of a deserted church hard by, where it
remained for months uncared for, till in calmer days it found
decent burial at Exeter. Bishop Gravesend of London, we
are told, would have shared the fate of his brother of Exeter
if he had fallen into the people's hands.

A loyal few.

*Murder of
Bishop
Stapeldon.*

Meantime the sounds of the tumult in the city were plainly
heard at Lambeth, and warned the archbishop that it was
not safe to stay where he was loved so little. He fled away
in hot haste, borrowing without leave the horses of his neighbour, Bishop Hethe of Rochester, who sent early to the
Palace, but only to find the primate gone, and had to steal
away on foot as best he could, at some risk and with much
fatigue, and so after some days to Rochester. He was well
aware of the danger that he ran, for he had already warned
his brethren at Lambeth that " the bishops were generally
hated, for their fatuous ignorance and sloth were thought to
be the cause of all the ills of England."

While the timid adherents of the king were taking ineffectual counsel, other bishops flung themselves eagerly into
civil strife. Orleton of Hereford joined the queen at once,

and preached at Oxford before the University on the text,
"My head, my head" (2 Kings iv. 19), which he took to
point the moral that the body politic was sorely sick for want
of better guidance and a change of rulers.   Or, if we accept
a different account of what was perhaps a second sermon, he
preached with even more audacity upon the text, "It shall
bruise thy head" (Gen. iii. 15), which was explained to typify
the triumph of the queen, who would crush the serpent when
the Despensers were laid low.   Events moved fast ; next
month the king was taken and his cause was hopeless.

Then even the archbishop deserted his old pupil, to whom
he owed so much.   Bishop Hethe tried vainly to dissuade
him, but he "feared the queen more than the King
of Heaven," and with servile acquiescence to the
new regime, he preached before the Parliament
upon the theme, "The voice of the people is the voice of
God."   It was no wonder if the citizens who were assembled
at Guildhall to see the bishops take the oath to defend the
rights and liberties of London, or "to sacrifice to Mahomet,"
as Dene prefers to put it, scoffed and marvelled at such
weathercocks of the Church, and received even with scant
respect the peace-offering of fifty tuns of wine.

Reynolds abandoned the king.

The Chancellor Baldock, who had accompanied Edward
in his flight and been arrested with him, when the benefit of
clergy was claimed on his behalf, was handed over
to the care of Bishop Orleton.   Years afterwards it
was charged against the bishop that he had brought
his old enemy to London, where he was seized by the citizens
and lodged in Newgate, on the plea that the bishop had no
safe prison of his own in London.   There, after fruitless
attempts to convict him of treasonable practices, he was
so vilely treated that he perished miserably before the
following Easter.   The hated Ministers fell easy victims to
the popular fury ; it only remained to take measures with
their master.   Here again Orleton played a prominent and
odious part, "the architect of all this evil," as one writer
calls him.   It was decided at the Parliament of London that
Edward must resign, four of the prelates only refusing to
concur.   Stratford and Orleton went to Kenilworth together
to bring him to consent, and the latter with vindictive rhetoric

Sinister action of Orleton.

forced upon the ears of the poor fainting king the necessities
of speedy resignation, that so at least his son might mount
the throne.   But this was not enough.   While the king lived,
his enemies could not feel secure, harsher measures and more
fatal steps were urged upon his guards.   It was believed that
the same bishop took a leading part again in this, sending
an ambiguous missive, that might be so read as either to
sanction his murder or forbid it (*Edvardum occidere nolite timere
bonum est*).   The story illustrates at any rate the popular
belief of what might be expected from such a crafty and
unscrupulous politician.

After the revolutionary crisis which closed this ignominious
period, social order could be soon restored in the name of
Unpopularity a new monarch, but the bishops could not easily
of the regain the moral influence which they had forfeited
bishops. by their disloyal and self-seeking conduct.   Respect
for their religious character was not likely to be strengthened
when it was seen that some of them were rewarded without
delay for their treachery and intrigues in the last reign.
The temporalities which had been withheld, as it was
thought, by the jealous influence of the Chancellor Baldock,
were restored at once to Orleton of Hereford and Ayermin
of Norwich.   Orleton was honoured with a special mission
to the pope, and used his opportunities at Avignon, at the
moment when the See of Worcester became vacant, to get
the preferment for himself (1327).   The Crown had not been
consulted in the matter, but the resentment of the new
government was short-lived, and three months afterwards he
was put in full possession of the episcopal estates.   But the
people had longer memories, or judged in a less indulgent
spirit.   Bishop Grandisson of Exeter would not hear of any
summons to a council to be held in London.   It was not safe for
him, he said, to venture into such a hornet's nest.   The cautious
Hethe of Rochester refused also to be present at the council.
He had shown, indeed, no lack of courage in the Parliament
by which the late king was deposed, and stoutly braved the
threats which followed his refusal to concur in what was
done.   But now he mistrusted the wisdom of his brethren,
and knew how much their moral influence was weakened
During the year of revolution a riotous mob had forced its

way at night into his own cathedral and talked of pillaging
the convent, where for a week he had to lurk in shelter. He
had since fortified his manor-houses, where like scenes had
been repeated, and such outbreaks of turbulent defiance
were threatening signs of social troubles which were yet to
follow.

We have now to trace the growth of a spirit of opposition
to ecclesiastical pretensions, which had different rallying cries
as time went on, and often charged its objects and
methods of attack. At first it was a question   Anti-clerical
movements.
mainly of privileges and material rights; there was
no talk of doctrine or church practice. The movement may
be called anti-clerical at times, as it questioned the status
and privileges of ecclesiastics, but the objections urged related
chiefly to the dignitaries of the Church or to the great
religious houses, whose exclusive claims were held to be
opposed to equity or general well-being. Later on it was
not so much anti-clerical as anti-papal, for it was felt more
and more keenly on all sides that the aggressions of the
Court of Avignon disorganised the national Church, robbed
responsible patrons of their rights, drained off vast sums to
be spent on alien objects, and paralysed the administrative
powers of the bishops.

The monastic houses were the first to be attacked. The
days of their spiritual ascendancy had passed away. No one
thought of founding a new order, scarcely even of   Attack on
endowing a new convent. But the old abbeys,   Bury St.
Edmund's.
entrenched in their feudal and manorial rights,
stirred civic and rural jealousies alike, and seemed to bar
the path of progress. The revolutionary spirit, excited by
a time of turbulent misrule, found here a natural object
of attack. In September 1326 Queen Isabella, with her
foreign soldiery and English nobles, rested for a while at
Bury St. Edmund's on her way from Harwich, and borrowed 800 marks which had been left by the justiciary in
the convent's charge. The rebellion, which swept away
resistance, was a very striking object lesson to the discontented townsmen and the villeins who lived upon the abbey
lands. The monks had an easy time, it seemed, in their
stately home or on their manors, where thirty-two of them

were enjoying their ease in the country air soon afterwards. Why, they asked, should villeins and burghers submit so tamely to hard landlords when great nobles and bishops had gained all they wanted by a timely show of force? So on January 15, 1327, 3000 rioters broke into the convent, seized the prior and carried off the charters on which the monks relied as evidence for their claims. A block and axe were set up as a warning in the market-place, and the abbot, under pain of death, signed a charter of civic privileges and a deed of pardon. The troubles lasted on for many months; scenes of violence were followed by the strife of words ; but in the autumn the rioters broke out afresh, burning and pillaging not only in the convent precincts, but in twenty-two of the manors of the abbey. The outbreak was quelled at last by the strong hand of the law ; the town was fined 2000 marks ; some citizens were hanged, and more than thirty of the secular clergy were convicted of taking part in the disorder, while it was well known that the active sympathies of the friars had been in favour of the town against the convent.

There were grave disturbances of a like kind at St. Alban's. When it was heard that the noisy crowd at the Guildhall had
St. Alban's. seen nobles and bishops take the oath to confirm the charters of their civil rights, the example was a tempting one to follow. The lower orders of the town began to agitate and band themselves together, and then, emboldened by their growing numbers, they forced the notables to join them in the demands which they put forth. These were that the town should be a privileged borough, with rights of free election of burgesses for Parliament, of jury for pleas before the justices, of assize of bread and beer, and rights of common and hand mills—all of which they claimed to have enjoyed in olden times. The convent would not hear of such concessions. The townsmen flew to arms ; tried to storm the abbey walls, and, failing in their efforts, would have starved out the defenders by slow siege. The sheriff was bidden to levy the *posse comitatus* to relieve the abbey ; and after fruitless attempts to come to terms and further resort to violence, the matter in dispute was referred to arbitration and decided in the main against the monks, who agreed,

only after urgent pressure from the king, to abide by the award.

The grievance took another form at Canterbury. There in 1327 came a demand upon the city to provide a contingent of men-at-arms required by the king for service in the war in Scotland. The citizens agreed to send twelve soldiers to Newcastle-upon-Tyne, and called upon the monastery of Christ Church to take part in the expenses. The prior, supported by a letter from the archbishop, declined upon the ground that all the possessions of their house had been held always in free alms, subject to no contribution of the kind. He begged the citizens therefore to excuse them, "having regard to the Church of Canterbury, which is the most august and freest in subjection to the Church of Rome, and to the glorious martyr St. Thomas, and to the other good and holy bodies which therein lie." Little moved by this appeal the bailiff and the townsmen met in the graveyard of the Preaching Friars, and resolved that no one, under penalty of being driven from the town, should tenant any of the convent's houses, or sell food to the monks or buy from them; that a deep ditch should be dug outside the convent gates, and that none of the inmates should go in or out; and above all that no pilgrim should be allowed to enter the Cathedral unless he swore to make no offering at the shrine. The prior, however, would not yield even to these threats, and a royal writ was sent down for their protection, and duly copied in their letter book.

The spiritual character of the monastic houses was dropping out of sight, and their discontented neighbours resented their refusal to share as landowners the common burdens and waive the feudal privileges that were growing out of date.

It was natural also that the bishops should be thought of not so much as fathers in God and spiritual guides, but as lawyers and statesmen, keen and business-like in secular concerns, but with no great care for the vital interests of the Church. As younger sons of noble houses, or as successful servants of the Crown, they had thrown themselves with eagerness into party struggles,

[marginal notes:] Christ Church, Canterbury.

Defiance of Episcopal authority.

and their political intrigues had fatally discredited their sacred calling. As their characters inspired often scant respect, their official acts were roughly questioned, and scenes of violence and disorder even in the churches proved how much ecclesiastical authority was weakened. The solemn visitations of metropolitan or bishop were interrupted, not as before with formal protest or appeal to Rome, but with naked show of force from men-at-arms or riotous mobs. The episcopal registers of the period refer from time to time to the "lewd sons of Belial," who are warned as wanton disturbers of the peace in holy places. The elements of disorder were at hand ; it needed only a strong personal or party motive—the fear of fines or penalties likely to be imposed ; resentment at inquisitorial procedure ; claims of local independence—to stir the smouldering discontent into a flame and cause it to break out in scenes of passionate confusion. Petty disturbances recur in the same spirit ; here a savage assault on an archdeacon's official ; there a collector of the bishop's dues beaten in the market-place ; or a rural dean seized by the throat and forced by an angry knight to swallow a letter of warning from the bishop, together with its seal and silken thread. The disregard for ecclesiastical authority was not found only among laymen. The clerical order set a dangerous example when bishop defied his metropolitan, and parish priest publicly insulted his diocesan. When the haughty Grandisson of Exeter closed the doors of his cathedral, and barred the archbishop's way with armed retainers, the king had to interpose in the interests of peace. A rector of Bromley, deprived for breach of order, sent a chaplain in full canonicals with bell and lighted candles to excommunicate the Bishop of Rochester in his own cathedral church. But the monks were the worst offenders, and did most to show contempt for all authority except that of the pope. They grievously resented insubordination on the part of the burgesses or villeins who lived under the shadow of their walls or in their manors, but they strained every nerve themselves to shake off all control from the leaders of the National Church.

The Abbey of St. Augustine's, Canterbury, was beyond most others contumacious in its independence. Its rivalry

with its great neighbour of Christ Church accounts perhaps
for the early refusal of its abbots to make profession of obedience to the archbishop.   These scruples were over-   St.
ruled, however, and the papal Bulls on which they Augustine's,
relied as evidence were proved to be impudent Canterbury.
forgeries and burnt in the king's presence by the Bishop of
Evreux, whose certificate thereof was handed over to the
chapter of Christ Church.   In the time of Winchelsey the
struggle was renewed.   The abbey not only claimed to be
exempt itself from episcopal control, but tried to extend its
immunities to all the churches of which it owned the
patronage.   By fraudulent misrepresentation of their status
in the past, so the archbishop complained, they induced
Pope Boniface to grant the privileges which they desired,
but the question was reopened three years later, and the
spiritual jurisdiction in the disputed parishes restored to the
archbishop.   "He left the monastery at peace," says the
chronicler of the house, but he had gained his cause.

The dispute was revived in 1329 when Simon Meopham
ruled the See.   Reynolds had passed away in 1327, soon after
his ignominious desertion of his royal patron.   Meo-   Disputes with
pham was a prelate of a different stamp.   "Poor in Archbishop
earthly goods, but rich in virtues," as it is phrased Meopham.
in the royal letter of commendation, he was no time-server
or worldly politician, but sincerely desirous of reforms.   So
anxious was he that his clerks and household servants
should be honest and clean-handed that his kinsmen instructed to select them were said to be "inquiring after
angels rather than for men."   He lost no time in beginning the visitation of the province, and that in no lenient
temper, if we may trust the lively description of the
notary Dene.   At Canterbury he required the monks of St.
Augustine's to produce the evidences needed to make good
their claims to the advowsons or the revenues of many
churches in the diocese.   This they persistently refused to
do, remembering possibly the exposure of their charters in
an earlier age.   The archbishop pronounced them contumacious, and after their appeal, objected to the arbitrator
sent to decide the cause.   In 1330 the proctor of the
abbey went to a manor-house in Surrey where the archbishop

was residing to cite him to appear before the court, but the servants who were waiting in the hall, resenting the fussy self-importance of the proctor, roughly handled him and his attendants and chased them with indignities away. The archbishop solemnly protested that he knew nothing of the outrage till it was too late to check it; friendly bishops testified that they had known him long as "modest and gentle and well mannered," but he neglected probably to use the recognised means of influence in the papal Court, and he was brought in guilty, while in the original suit, in which he would not appear, heavy damages were given against him, and he was excommunicated in default of payment. He seems to have looked upon it as a form, galling to his pride, but purely technical and out of date, and took no steps to gain relief. Three years later he owned to the Bishop of Rochester, who went to visit him, that he cared little for absolution, harassed as he was by disappointed hopes and failing strength. When he died the sentence had not been withdrawn, and Christian burial was denied him in his own cathedral, till five months later a new Abbot of St. Augustine's thought good to absolve him that his remains might be laid at last with due honour in the tomb which was prepared.

Meopham had done his best—it was not much—to keep the dignity of English churchmanship free from the taint of worldly interests and ambitions. With his successor Archbishop Stratford. the threads were intertwined once more. The Chapter of Canterbury, knowing the wishes of the king, elected Stratford to the primacy, and the pope anticipated or confirmed their choice. He was lawyer, man of business, statesman; ecclesiastic last and least of all. Promoted to Winchester in 1323, with entire disregard of the wishes of the Crown, he had suffered for his boldness, being for a year refused possession of the temporalities of the See, till Archbishop Reynolds intervened in his behalf. In the troubled times which followed, his attitude was ambiguous if not disloyal, and he took a leading part in the proceedings which finally displaced the king in favour of his son. But he was soon out of sympathy with the new government in its unconstitutional courses, and by supporting the Lancastrian party incurred the jealous enmity of Mortimer—the queen's paramour—from whose murderous designs he escaped only by hurrying from one hiding-place to another, till the usurper's death relieved him of his fears. He stepped at once into the place of chief-adviser of the young king, and was the foremost figure in the Council. For ten years he and his brother Robert (Bishop of Chichester, 1337) held the great seal alternately, and did good service as honest and laborious if not brilliant statesmen. His chief rivals and opponents were Bishop Burghersh of Lincoln, who was chancellor during Mortimer's few years of power, and who had been suggested to the pope for primate, and Bishop Orleton, who since the beginning of the reign had made good use of interest and intrigue to gain preferment. Orleton first pushed himself into the See of Worcester in 1327 by papal favour, and then again in 1333 the influence of the King of France at Avignon procured him the valued prize of Winchester. Edward, indignant at the intervention of a foreign ruler, lodged a protest at the appointment before the papal Court on the ground that Orleton had called the late king tyrant in his sermon before the University of Oxford, and had been guilty of the death of Baldock by purposely exposing him to the violence of an angry mob. Orleton defended himself successfully, but he kept aloof thenceforth from offices of State, though he regained some influence at court, which he was not slow to use against his rival Stratford when the opportunity was given.

It came ere long during the troubles of the war with France. Embittered by the backwardness of his allies, and the sense of his inadequate resources, the king listened to malevolent advisers who laid the blame of failure on the neglect or disloyalty of his ministers, among whom Stratford was the guiding spirit. The influence of the Court was anti-clerical, and the archbishop's efforts to curb extravagance were especially resented.

In 1340 the king returned suddenly to England, to find the Tower of London undefended. Bishop Stratford of Chichester, who held the great seal, and Bishop Northburgh of Lichfield, the treasurer, were removed from office and two laymen appointed in their room. The archbishop, hearing of the disgrace of the

Edward's quarrel with Stratford.

chancellor his brother, and of the arrest of high officials, retired at once to Canterbury, to be safer from the storm. He was summoned thence to London to prepare to cross the sea to answer to the suit of merchants of Louvain to whom he had bound himself for the payment of a debt contracted by the king. He sent letters of excuse and warning, of which Edward took no heed. Then followed a striking scene. On the anniversary of the martyrdom of S. Thomas of Canterbury he preached to the assembled citizens on the text, Ecclus. xlviii. 12: "He was not moved at the presence of any prince," which was applied of course to the surpassing merits of the saint. He went on to speak of his own life that had been devoted to the service of the State, and to deplore the time that had been spent in secular concerns to the neglect of his religious work. He hoped henceforth to give himself to the higher duties of his office, and to the defence of the rights of Church and State. Then, while the clergy stood around in full canonicals and with candles in their hands, he pronounced a series of excommunications against all who violated the Great Charter, or tried by slanderous imputations to turn the hearts of the people from their spiritual fathers. Letters to the same effect were written to each of his suffragans, to be published by them through the province. He wrote also to the king to protest against unconstitutional arrests, and appealed to the judgment of his peers. Edward replied in a long letter of violent invective, which was also published to the world. In the *libellus famosus*, as it is called, he spoke of Stratford as a broken reed, who had caused the inglorious failure of the campaign which had begun so well, by the neglect to send the promised funds from the grant made by the Commons. Councillors and soldiers, one and all, cried out against the traitor whose sloth or fraud had brought on them disasters, and had urged the king to return in haste to England to have a thorough scrutiny of the accounts. To that end he had arrested the clerks who were suspected, and to get at the truth desired the presence of the moving spirit of the administration that had proved unworthy. But in his idle fears, in spite of the safe-conduct offered, Stratford had refused to leave his sanctuary, and would only answer in Parliament the charges made

against him. This is the real answer, stripped only of its
wordy and abusive rhetoric, but the letter goes on in still
more discreditable terms to lay the blame on Stratford of
all the extravagances of the king's earlier years, of the aliena-
tion of Crown property, and the prodigal gifts by which the
treasury was drained.

Stratford replied at once at even greater length, meeting
the charges point by point, and his language was temperate
but firm. The king's embarrassments were in no way due to
him, for he had laboured honestly and loyally in his service.
The grant which the king waited for so anxiously was pledged
to his creditors beforehand ; during the whole period of the
war Stratford had drawn for himself only £300, and he was
ready to answer fully every charge before his peers.

A weak rejoinder followed, with much abuse but no
attempt at proof. Meantime Parliament had been summoned
for the 23rd of April, and the archbishop came to London to
be present. At Westminster Hall he was met by the king's
chamberlain and the steward of the household, and was told
to present himself at the Court of the Exchequer to answer
the charges brought against him. He went thither after
some demur, but said that he needed time to meet the
charges, and retired to the painted chamber, where he sat
awhile with other bishops and waited for the king. But
Edward would not meet him, and the business was adjourned
from day to day. Orleton was sent with the chancellor to
urge him to submit, and took the opportunity to deny that
the *libellus famosus* came from his hand, as was supposed.
Another time the chamberlain and knights tried to bar his
way to the king's presence, but after much railing and many
curses from them he forced his way into the chamber, and
the king retired as he went in. He offered to clear himself in
Parliament ; a committee of the Lords reported that no peer
should be judged except before his peers, and the archbishop
was at length allowed to see the king, and a formal reconciliation followed. No attempt was made to push the charges
further, and no evidence was taken on the subject.

The archbishop had posed repeatedly as another Becket,
but the king's servants were readier with their tongues than
with their swords. He served once more on the Council

Board, but neither he nor his brother undertook again the highest offices of State. The lay ministry was not long-lived, however, and a few years later both the great
Stratford's
retirement. seal and the treasury were entrusted to ecclesiastics as before. For many years afterwards — almost till the close of Edward's life—the government was mainly in their hands, while the king was busy with his wars abroad. But it was lay in spirit if clerical in name. It sympathised with the country in its discontent at the burdensome exactions of the pope, and passed the Statutes which repelled aggression.

Yet as Parliament grew stronger, and the Commons realised their power, it was natural that more impatience
Discontent
at clerical
privileges. should be felt at the disproportionate share of influence and wealth possessed by a single order in the State. Complaints were made that since the passing of the Statute of Mortmain lands had been acquired which did not pay their proper quota of taxation; that unwonted demands were being made for tithes on the woodlands; that the spiritual authorities allowed serfs and women to make their wills, which was contrary to reason, as was urged, and that "outrageous" fees were charged as probate duties by the officials of the bishops' Courts. The Commons begged, in 1344, that no petition of the clergy should be granted to the prejudice of Lords or Commons till it had been examined by the king with all his council. In the Parliament of 1352 the ecclesiastical estate represented its own grievances in regard to the treatment of members of their body brought before the justices on criminal charges, when the "privilege of clergy" was not properly allowed. Simon Islip (Archbishop of Canterbury, 1349-1366), writing to the bishops on the subject, told them that counter complaints were made by the laity in Parliament of the laxity with which clerical delinquents had been treated, let loose upon the world after a while, as if licensed to commit murder with impunity. He made stringent regulations for the watch and ward and prison fare of such offenders.

The sense of rival interests which found peaceable expression in Parliamentary petitions showed itself meantime in turbulent riots and broken heads at Oxford. The old-standing jealousies between the scholars and the townsmen broke out with violence in 1355.   The fray began with the insolence of unruly scholars who were drinking at the Swyndlestock tavern, near to Carfax, and broke the host's head with one of his own tankards.   It ended in their entire discomfiture, for the townsfolk, aided by the countrymen who flocked in at their summons, overpowered the resistance of the clerks with much pillage and bloodshed, and showed no mercy in their hour of triumph. "The crowns of some chaplains," we read in Wood, "that is, all the skin as far as the tonsure went, these diabolical imps flayed off in scorn of their clergy. . . . Divers others, whom they mortally wounded, they haled off to prison, carrying their entrails in their hands in a most lamentable manner."

Town and gown at Oxford.

Lecturers and scholars withdrew in resentment from the city, and threatened a permanent secession.   It needed the intervention of the king to secure the good-will of the university, which, indeed, was bought at the price of the surrender by the city of much of its powers of self-rule. St. Scholastica's day (Feb. 10) was a time to be observed henceforth with penance and humiliation.

It may be fanciful to refer to the same cause the many cases of which Knighton tells us at this time of churches broken into, and shrines and reliquaries despoiled by sacrilegious hands.   They showed, at any rate, that the fear of ecclesiastical penalties was weak, and the plunder of Church property a tempting resource in time of need.

Sacrilege.

AUTHORITIES.—Besides the *Flores Historiarum* and Hemingburgh and Walsingham, referred to in Chap. I., the special authorities for the reign of Edward II. are the *Annales Londonienses* the *Annales Paulini*, the *Gesta Edvardi de Carnarvon, Vita Edvardi secundi auctore Malmesburiensi*, and *Vita et Mors Edvardi secundi*, contained in *Chronicles of the Reign of Edward I. and II.*, ed. W. Stubbs, 1882-83 (Rolls ser.) ; *Johannis de Trokelowe et Henrici de Blaneforde Chronica et Annales*, in *Chronica Monasterii S. Albani*, ed. H. T. Riley, 1863 (Rolls ser.).   For the troubles at the convents the *Literæ Cantuarienses* and the *Chronicles of St. Alban's and Bury St. Edmund's* may be consulted, and for the condition of the North of England *Historical Papers from the Northern Registers*, ed. J. Raine, 1873 (Rolls ser.).   For the early part of the reign of Edward III. see references in Chap. V.

CHAPTER IV

THE BLACK DEATH

A.D. 1348–1349

THERE had been natural signs of general exultation at the
brilliant successes won by English arms at ,Crecy,
Neville's Cross, and Calais, and the rich spoils
brought back by the victors to their homes. A new
sun, says Walsingham, seemed to have arisen on the people
in the plenty of all things, and the glory of such victories.

The rapid spread of the plague.

Tournaments, else discouraged by the ruling powers, and
public spectacles of all kinds had been held with great magnificence ; extravagance in dress, not confined to a single sex
or even to the laity, was a matter of doleful comment in the
chronicles. But the feeling of triumph was short-lived, and the
festivities were soon changed to scenes of general mourning.
A dreadful visitant stalked through the land, spreading alarm
and desolation where it passed, and stamping on the face of
social life the traces of an influence that was to last for many
a year to come. To the Church, as well as to the State, its
consequences were momentous, and contemporary writers in
all lands spoke of it with a cry of horror, and marked its
rapid course as that of an angel of destruction.

The plague, now known by its modern name of the Black
Death, from the dark blotches which it marked upon the
skin, appeared in England in 1348, first, as it was said, in
Melcombe Regis in Dorsetshire, but before that it had been
known to be already near at hand. Bishop Ralph of Shrewsbury issued letters in August recommending through his
diocese of Bath and Wells processions and stations in the

churches to avert "the pestilence which had come into a neighbouring kingdom from the East." The pestilence, first heard of in the south-western coasts, passed rapidly from place to place during the autumn and the winter months, and struck down its victims everywhere without distinction.

On the 1st of January the bishops were told that Parliament, which should have met on the 19th, was to be prorogued till the 27th of April, in consequence of the sudden visitation of a deadly plague which was spreading around Westminster. In March, however, it was needful to postpone it indefinitely, for the ravages of the pestilence increased there and elsewhere, and the outlook was very dark. The plague-stricken lived commonly two or three days only, sometimes but a few hours after they were first attacked. It was said to spare the rich and noble for the most part, and to spend its force most among the poor. This was not wholly so, of course, for besides one of the king's daughters, John Ufford, an old servant of the Crown, died of it before his consecration as Archbishop of Canterbury, and, Thomas Bradwardine followed him a few months later in 1349, leaving only memories of piety and learning, and a gentle influence for good at court, where he was known as the king's chaplain and confessor. But doubtless it was true that the plague, terribly contagious as it was, spread with most intensity among the narrow streets, where the townsmen were most closely packed together, or in the dark and dirty hovels of the peasantry, where the conditions of air and food and clothing were such as to propagate most surely and swiftly the germs of the disease. A pope at Avignon could find safety in his spacious palace where great fires were kept always burning, and few were admitted to his presence, and for like reasons the nobles and the ruling classes suffered less than others who could do nothing to screen themselves from the infection.

The pestilence raged with unabated force till May 1349; it lingered on for some months more, and renewed its attacks at varying intervals for thirty years. What was the real loss of life it is impossible to state exactly, for in that age no national statistics were available. Contemporary writers speak for the most part in vague and

Details as to losses of clergy.

general terms, and no stress can be laid upon the estimates, which vary from one-fifth to nine-tenths of the population. For the most part the only precise data to be found concern the clergy. The diocesan registers show in what great numbers the beneficed clergy died at their post during this time. Week after week we see that others were always ready to step into their places and come for institution to the bishops who were living on unscathed for the most part among their people. " In East Anglia in a single year," we are told, " upwards of 800 parishes lost their parsons, 83 of them twice, and 10 of them three times in a few months," to say nothing of the chaplains and stipendiary priests, of whom no definite account is given. The Bishop of Rochester lost so many of his household that scarcely any one was left to serve in any office. Of other bishops we know only that they remained steadily at their post and did their duty manfully.

Of many religious houses again we have precise details. Their heads came also for institution to the bishops, and the tale of vacancies can be made out. Light is thrown too by the monastic chronicles on the losses in the rank and file, for "the pestilence raged," as Archbishop Parker put it spitefully, "among the impure crowd of monks." Some convents were entirely desolated. " In the house of Augustinian Canons at Heveringland prior and canons died to a man. At Hickling only one survived." At Meaux only ten were left out of fifty monks and the lay-brothers. At St. Alban's forty-seven of the inmates, besides many scattered in the cells, sickened and died, together with the abbot, "and this," says the chronicler, "we believe to have taken place, that the angelic man might not have to appear alone and unattended in the presence of his judge." Most of the convents suffered grievously ; many never recovered from the shock ; some were absorbed in consequence in other houses. One, however, Christ Church of Canterbury, suffered but little, thanks, as it is thought, to the purer sanitary state due to its plentiful supply of water, and to the great drainage works provided by an enlightened abbot of old time.

Church usages and customary arrangements were inadequate to meet the strain of this terrible catastrophe. The space in the churchyards was often speedily exhausted, and

new ground had to be hastily provided. The funeral rites
were hurried over, or in default of mourners the unrecog-
nised dead were huddled indiscriminately into one
common grave. Priests were too few to shrive ^{Church rules}
the dying, or caught the plague themselves in ^{relaxed.}
their deathbed ministrations, or from the pestilential air of
the graveyards by which they dwelt, for it has been held to
have been largely due to cadaveric poison. The Church,
therefore, relaxed her rules of discipline, and through the
pastorals of the bishops encouraged the faithful in the hour
of urgent peril to confess their sins to one another in the
full assurance, as one says, that "such confession would be
profitable to them for the remission of their sins according to
the teaching of the Church," and all who heard confessions
of the kind were pledged to absolute secrecy in every case.
The Sacrament of the Eucharist might be given by a deacon
when no priests could be found, and the people might rest
satisfied that faith would supply the place of extreme unction,
when time or means were lacking.

The ranks of the clergy were being thinned so rapidly
that extraordinary measures were required to fill the gaps.
Ordinations were multiplied with papal sanction. The Bishop
of Norwich, to take a single case was authorised to ordain
sixty young men below the age fixed by the canons, and other
restrictions were relaxed. A lower standard of acquirements
was accepted, laymen of more zeal than learning, whose wives
had lately died or were old enough to live without scandal
elsewhere than in a nunnery, were admitted to Holy Orders ;
in many cases incumbents just appointed were passed rapidly
through the lower stages to the priesthood. Yet notwithstanding these concessions many churches, we are told, were
left without any one to minister within them.

The accounts of our own chroniclers, curt and jejune as
they mostly are, enable us to realise the immensity of the
disaster, and the universal gloom, but for literary ^{Extremes of}
descriptions of the immediate effects of the plague ^{recklessness}
upon the mind and temper of society we must ^{and remorse.}
turn to foreign writers such as Boccaccio, who lived through
like experiences in their own homes. There we may see in
more detail and in more highly-coloured pictures the same

extremes of what we hear in England, of the outburst of
callous selfishness and luxurious self-indulgence on the part
of many who tried to live wholly in the pleasures of the
present, shutting their eyes alike to the uncertainties of
the future and the miseries of social life around them.
To others it seemed that the mysterious scourge was but
the instrument of God's displeasure at the sins of a guilty
people, and they tried to win exemption for themselves and
others by fervour of remorse and far-fetched forms of self-
abasement. "We exhort you in the Lord," said Bishop
Edyndon writing to the monks of his Cathedral, "to come
before the face of God, with contrition and confession of all
your sins, together with the due satisfaction through the effica-
cious works of salutary penance. We order further that every
Sunday and Wednesday all of you, assembled together in
the choir of your monastery, say the seven penitential psalms,
and the fifteen gradual psalms, on your knees humbly and
devoutly. Also on every Friday, together with these psalms,
we direct that you chant the long litany, instituted against
pestilences of this kind by the holy Fathers, through the
market-place of our city of Winchester, walking in procession,
together with the clergy and people of the said city. We
desire that all should be summoned to these solemn processions and urged to follow them in such a way that during
their course they walk with heads bent down, with feet bare
and fasting ; whilst with pious hearts they repeat their
prayers, and putting away vain conversation, say as often as
possible the Lord's Prayer and Hail Mary." At Hereford
it was hoped that the dread visitant would be kept at bay
by the shrine of the sainted Cantilupe, which was carried
from the Cathedral in procession through the town. But of
these penitential exercises none were so striking as the processions of the Flagellants or the Brethren of the Cross, who
came to England only at this time, but had been known before
in Germany and Holland. They slowly paced the streets in
pairs with bared shoulders and back, chanting their solemn
litanies the while, and scourging themselves with knotted
cords weighted with iron spikes. From time to time they lay
upon the ground, with hands outstretched as in remembrance
of their Saviour on the Cross, but in different attitudes

according to the nature of their special sins, while their
leader scourged them as they lay around him.

If we pass from the immediate effects to later issues we
shall find some grave and unlooked-for social changes
resulting from the pestilence, and these were felt
in the Church as in the State. Though at first   Economic
the scourge fell most heavily on the labouring   effects.
classes, it soon produced a marked improvement in their
social status, and in the long-run a general enfranchisement
of servile labour. In numberless manors so many of the
peasants had been swept away that there were no arms to
till the land, which was lying fallow and neglected. Labour
was everywhere in such request that it naturally raised its
terms, and was not content to remain in its old home and
work for the customary pittance. In the towns the artisans
found it easier still to raise their terms and insist upon a
higher payment. Landowners and employers looked upon
the sudden rise almost as a violation of the laws of nature ;
the government, which sympathised with their distress, tried
but ineffectually to repress the claims of labour by the strong
arm of the law ; statutes of labourers were passed ; rates of
wages fixed which it was not lawful to exceed ; when these
were disregarded on all sides fines were levied on the employers who broke the law, and stiff-necked labourers were
lodged in gaol. Many fled to hiding-places in woods and
forests for a time, and those who were caught were subjected
to heavy fines. But all to little purpose.

This object-lesson was studied with care in other quarters.
There is ample proof that a large part of the clergy had
perished from the plague, and though volunteers
pushed in to take their places, there were not nearly   Increase of
enough to meet the needs. The survivors seem to   stipends.
have often sympathised with the labouring thousands in their
desire for higher wages, and probably they were among the
" counsellors, maintainers, and abettors " of the villeins
referred to in an Act of Richard II. Many not only
sympathised but followed the example set. With the sudden
rebound of energy and hope every department of social life
competed for the services of the educated few ; there were
gaps to be filled in every profession, and rewards often larger

than the Church could offer. The unbeneficed clergy were too few at first to do all the work expected of them as private chaplains, chantry priests, or ministers in charge of the churches of non-resident rectors. They had been scantily paid before, receiving often less than the pay even of a common soldier. Many of the necessaries of life were rising rapidly in cost; they could not live on the old stipends; like the peasants and the artisans they wanted higher pay, which the pluralists who bid against each other for their services were obliged reluctantly to give.

As the government took the side of the employers in the agricultural movement, so the bishops seem to have sympathised entirely with what they thought the grievance of the beneficed clergy. We cannot read without a thrill of wondering indignation the hard and pitiless invectives hurled by wealthy prelates at their poorer brethren who would not be content to "officiate in parish churches, with the cure of souls thereunto belonging, with six marks for their annual stipends." "The unbridled covetousness of men," says Archbishop Islip, "would grow to such a height as to banish charity out of the world, if it were not repressed by justice. The priests that now are, not considering that they have escaped the danger of the pestilence by divine providence, not for their own merits, but that they might exercise the ministry committed to them for the sake of God's people and the public good, nor ashamed that lay-workmen make their covetousness an example to themselves, have no regard to the cure of souls though fitting salaries are offered to them, and leaving that betake themselves to the celebration of annals for the quick and dead, and so parish churches and chapels remain destitute of parochial chaplains, and the said priests, pampered with excessive salaries, discharge their intemperance in vomit and lust, grow wild and drown themselves in the abyss of vice, to the great scandal of ecclesiastics and the evil example of laymen." . . . "If any priest of our province, under any colour whatsoever, receive more by the year than five marks without cure of souls, or six marks with such cure, let him *ipso facto* incur the sentence of suspension from his office, unless within a month he pay what he received over and above

[marginal note: Bishops scolding and threatening.*]*

that sum to the fabric fund of the church in which he celebrated."

Ralph of Shrewsbury, Bishop of Bath and Wells, writes in his pastoral to condemn the " insatiable avarice " and the " contemptible thirst for unjust gains " that was becoming a marked feature of the times.   It is true that the complaint referred to the vagrant habits that were formed by so many of the clergy, who would not tie themselves to settled cures because they found it more profitable to be free for work more highly paid.   So Langland wrote :—

> Persones and parisch prestes pleyned hem to the bischop
> That here parisshes were pore sith the pestilence tyme,
> To have a lycence and a leve at London to dwelle,
> And syngen there for symonye, for silver is swete.

> Some serven the kyng and his silver tellen,
> In cheker and in chancerye chalengen his dettes
> Of wardes and wardmotes weyves and streyves,
> And some serven as servants lordes and ladyes,
> And in stede of stuwardes sytten and demen.

In the face of hard facts, however, censures and expostulations were of little use, and Knighton tells us that no chaplain could be found to serve a parish for less than £10 or ten marks at the least, and few cared to accept a vicarage that was not worth twenty marks or £20. It could not well be otherwise.   The economic changes which resulted from the plague affected before long every social class.   While the prices of agricultural produce in its raw state were not materially raised, the cost of rural labour in its simplest form increased by at least 50 per cent, and the wages of the artisan still more.   Everything, therefore, to which labour adds its main value was enhanced in price. The spending power of the peasants became larger, with no great increase of their expenses, and as one result of their easier conditions, their wives and daughters ceased to work much in the fields for hire.

The rise maintained.

On the other hand, for all employers of labour, and all who lived upon fixed incomes harder times set in.   The vicar of Selborne, for example, found it needful to press the prior and the convent of Austin Canons as impropriators of the parish church to increase his insufficient income, and "to avoid a lawsuit," an agree-

Hard times for employers.

ment was effected. "On account of the present pestilence and the scarcity of the times " he was to receive annually for the term of his life a pension of 2s. 6d., together with sundry tithes of fruit and wool and hay from certain lands in the parish, "in augmentation of his vicarial portion for his life."

It has been said that one class emerged from that dreadful year much richer than before. "The lords of the manors, the representatives of what we now call the country gentry, were great gainers." No doubt the estates passed into fewer hands and became larger, and many of the tenants' holdings escheated to their lords. But they, too, seem to have suffered financial embarrassment meantime, and greater estates did not mean more wealth. Heriots and fines, of course, fell in, as many of the feudal tenants died ; but this was but a temporary gain, and the rise of wages was a permanent loss. The manor rolls of Manydown, which belonged to the wealthy convent of St. Swithun's, Winchester, illustrate the changes in this respect. In 1354 the vicar of Wootton was unable to pay as usual for the acres which he rented, and which he had not means to cultivate. A list is given of the holdings thrown on the lord's hands by the tenants' deaths, for there were none to take their places. "There is allowed to Hugh—the receiver of the convent—fifty-nine shillings and fivepence halfpenny of rent in arrears for divers lands and holdings now in the lord's hands for lack of tenants by reason of the pestilence, which money he cannot levy." "Six years later the land had not recovered, those tenants who survived being unable to pay their rents, so that the holdings lapsed to the lord." From the figures given it is clear that the convent could not cultivate its lands to such profit as formerly : it raised out of the holdings which had lapsed only half the amount of the moderate rents which the tenants had paid before. Four years later another roll gives somewhat similar details.

The pastorals of the bishops failed, therefore, in their intended objects, but the unfeeling language may well have rankled in men's minds, and from this time we may note the growing sense of jarring interests and divided sympathies between the higher and the lower clergy, as in the country at large between the landowners and the peasants.

Another result of the great plague was a general falling off in the number of the inmates and the means of the religious houses.   Many of them had been in dire financial straits before.   They had overbuilt themselves, or Effects on convents. mismanaged their affairs, or fallen into the hands of money-lenders, when the liberal gifts of pious founders ceased to flow.   The pestilence thinned their numbers and so lessened their expenses, but it greatly crippled them in other ways.   They had lived upon the produce of their lands, but now labour became scarce and dear, and the profits of their half-cultivated manors disappeared   In their estates, there-fore, as indeed generally throughout the country, another system soon began to be adopted.   Instead of the old capitalist cultivation, with a bailiff on each large estate, tenant farming before long was introduced, such as had been only exceptional before, where estates were too far away for easy access to them.   At first farms were let on stock and land leases for a term of years or lives, the owners provid-ing the farm stock, to be replaced at a fixed rate at the expiration of the lease.   This was a convenience on both sides, as it employed the stock-in-trade of the landowner, who might hope to take the land into his own hands again with little cost, while it gave the tenant time to acquire the capital which he would want to work the farm on any other system. The religious houses, like the rest, dealt in this way with their estates, keeping, however, often in their own hands a home farm to supply the community with its produce.

The change was a gradual one, of course ; some tried to struggle on, but the profits which had been once made under the old system—which have been calculated as nearly 20 per cent on the capital invested—had almost disap-peared, and at last the bailiff was replaced by the tenant-farmer, who could drive a harder bargain for the labour needed, or be content with smaller profits.   For the character and the reputation of the monks themselves it was unfortunate that they should be thus wholly divorced from the active cares of agricultural life.   They had long ago forsaken the manual labour prescribed in their own interest by the old Benedictine rule ; the improved methods of their model farms, the new experiments and importations, the successful sheep-breeding

G

of the Cistercian houses were mainly matters of the past, but at least while they held the estates in their own hands the management and supervision provided varied work for the energetic members of their body. When that was given up too many of them were left with little but their time upon their hands, and as their spiritual zeal visibly declined there was more likelihood that their neighbours would regard them as a mere encumbrance on the land. The rents, however, cannot for a long time have replaced in value the profits made under the old system, and the period of transition was a hard one for many of the religious houses. Some never recovered from the blow, though churches were appropriated to them to meet the exhaustion of their diminished incomes; the shrunken numbers did not increase; fresh recruits came in but slowly, as so many interests in the active world competed for their choice. To fill the empty places left by the monks who had been lost, or to eke out their scanty means, boarders were often taken in the convents, and their example may have had a disturbing influence on the order of the homes. But of this more will be said presently.

There was grave danger that a high standard of learning in the clergy could not be maintained, for the monastic Decline in learning and character. schools trained fewer candidates for Holy Orders, and the halls and lecture-rooms of the universities had been almost deserted while the pestilence was raging. So threatening was the prospect that the king addressed a letter to the bishops on the subject, and Gascoigne treats the time as an epoch in the history of Oxford from which he dates the beginning of a decline in morality and learning. The foundation of new colleges was for a while arrested, though when it was taken up again the results of the plague were referred to as a leading cause, as in the endowments of Canterbury and New College, by which the benefactors wished to replenish the ranks of the learned clergy, which had been dangerously thinned. The social disasters may have also caused a sudden check to many a scheme of church enlargement. Later in the century indeed, when prosperity revived, new fabrics rose on every side, though with a marked change of architectural features; for, whatever was the cause, the history of the art reveals after this epoch a gradual decline in some of the higher elements of beauty.

Of the losses of the friars by the plague we have much less in the way of definite statistics, for there was nothing to bring their names into the bishops' registers or the manorial rolls ; but Luke Wadding, the historian of the Franciscan Order, accounts for the decline in the character and reputation of the Mendicants after this time by the changes which resulted from the great disaster when the rules of salutary discipline were relaxed and unfit candidates received.

On the other hand, it has been thought that the deeper earnestness of devotional feeling which may be noticed in some writers in the period which follows, as also the spread of Guilds of a more definitely religious type, point to a movement in a different direction and a more reflective cast of thought than had prevailed before. It seems hazardous, however, to assume in such cases any causal connection with the plague on such precarious and slender evidence as is forthcoming.

AUTHORITIES.—Notices of the ravages of the plague occur in several of the chronicles of the period, especially in those of Knighton and the Eulogium, but definite facts must be sought chiefly in the Episcopal Registers or Manorial Court Rolls. The economic effects were examined by Thorold Rogers (*Six Centuries of Work and Wages*, pp. 215-242), and Professor Cunningham in *Growth of English Industry*. Its influence in East Anglia has been vividly illustrated from local sources by Mr. Jessopp (*The Coming of the Friars*, etc., pp. 166-261). A monograph of Dr. Gasquet (*The Great Pestilence*, 1893) traces the course and results of the plague in other parts of England in much detail. The scientific side is dealt with in Dr. C. Creighton's *History of Epidemics in England*, Camb. 1891.

CHAPTER V

ANTI-PAPAL AND ANTI-CLERICAL MOVEMENTS

King Edward III., 1327–1377. Abp. Bradwardine, 1349. Islip, 1349.
Langham, 1366. Wittlesey, 1368. Sudbury, 1375–1381

THE great plague materially affected the administration of
the English Church and the temper of its clergy. The long
Jealousy of war with France had no less important influence
alien influence on the legislative changes which affected its rela-
in the Church, tions to the Papacy, and determined its status as a
National Church. The rumours of wide-reaching contro-
versies had been heard long before; papal Bulls published in
our churches launched their spiritual thunders against the
"sons of perdition and nurslings of malediction," who denied
the primacy of Peter and called in question the authority of
popes. Marsiglio of Padua and William of Ockham, the
pride of English schoolmen, were thus solemnly denounced.

But abstract questions did not interest men greatly. Vener-
ation for the Papacy was deep and earnest; spiritual claims
found willing ears, if they were not pushed too far into the
sphere of material concerns. Papal aggression had gone on
so long without substantial check that there seemed little risk
in carrying it farther. Protests were sometimes made with
spirit, when the prerogative of the Crown had been ignored,
as when Orleton was promoted to Worcester. From time to
time governors at Dover or the Cinque Ports were bidden to
seize obnoxious bulls, and sheriffs instructed to disallow their
evidence in any pleas. But the force of all this was sadly
weakened when the king stooped to ask the pope to annul
a formal election by the chapter and to promote a favoured

servant.   The Papacy and the Crown had often conspired together in the past to force their will upon the English Church, and replenish their funds at her expense.   The old story was repeated when in 1330 the king and pope agreed to share between them the tenths which for four years were to be levied by the authority of the latter on the revenues of ecclesiastics.

The war with France, to which England was deeply pledged by the pretensions of its king, strengthened the old feeling of repugnance against the influence of aliens in the Church.   Before this the jealousy _{especially French,} had been chiefly felt at the Italians and Savoyards promoted here by papal influence or court favour; but now the intruders were odious as enemies as well as aliens. The Court of Avignon was French in natural sympathies; the cardinals were mostly French by race; it was hard to believe that the pope himself was neutral.   Benedict XII. sent his two cardinals to plead for peace in England (1338), but their language seemed so favourable to France that Archbishop Stratford answered them publicly, and the greediness with which they tried to extort unwonted procurations made their cause more odious still.   The pope might describe in weighty terms how the Emperor Lewis was under the Church's ban for his heresies and schisms, but he was the ally of England, and the spiritual censures launched against him, if they had any force at all, were used on the French side as armaments of war.   The letters which passed between Edward and Benedict betrayed the growing irritation.   It had seemed enough before to issue an occasional State Paper, to make formal inquiry or to raise a protest.   Bishops-elect had again to renounce phrases prejudicial to the Crown, which as before were stealthily intruded in the papal Bull.   In 1334 came a despatch in the king's name to the bishops to ascertain what foreign clergy held benefices within each diocese.

Benedict was at least chary of his favours and had grievously discouraged the greedy expectants at his court who hoped and waited for vacant benefices in other lands.   The reckless prodigality, however, of his _{and of heavier Papal} successor, Clement VI. (1342-1352), was a startling _{demands,} contrast to such caution.   He welcomed with open hands the poor clergy who flocked at his invitation to Avignon to share his bounty, to the number of 100,000, it was said. When his lavish grants had exhausted the resources of his patronage, he laid his hands on the ecclesiastical dignities that fell in on every side, and reserved future vacancies for his own disposal in the most wide-sweeping terms. In itself there was nothing new in this, but the arrogance of the language used offended all classes in England, and the Crown was now more ready to take up the challenge.

The papal attack on patronage had begun in 1226 when two prebends in each cathedral church were demanded by the pope. An attempt was made, but unsuccessfully, in 1239 to extend the claim to benefices in private patronage. In spite, however, of frequent protests and remonstrances the rights of chapters and bishops were constantly invaded. At Salisbury, for example, in 1326, the dean, the precentor, the treasurer, two archdeacons, and twenty-three prebendaries were Papal nominees, and no less than eight were waiting with the right of succession to prebends as they became void.

The system of interference with episcopal appointments had been of gradual growth. It had been exercised often in disputed cases, when reference was made to the appellate jurisdiction of the pope, and when a bishop was translated from one See to another, or raised to be a cardinal, the pope had dealt directly with the vacancy thus caused. But from the beginning of the fourteenth century the right of direct patronage was claimed, and the system of reservation and provision was extended from the lower preferments to the episcopate itself. Sometimes a technical flaw in the process of election was discovered, or a bishop-elect wearied out by long delays, when he applied for confirmation, was induced to resign and then reappointed by the pope's free grace. But the language became more arrogant in time. It was not enough to mention the papal provision following on the canonical election; the Bull which appointed Simon Islip to the See of Canterbury referred indeed to the fact of the election, but only to imply that it was contemptuously swept aside (*spreta electione facta de eo*). Throughout the whole reign of Edward I. the pope pressed with success his claims to patronage, though the Parliament

of Carlisle in 1307 forced the grievance on the attention of
the king.   In spite of a temporary check a bolder attitude
even was assumed, and Bull after Bull professed to confer
the temporalities of the See on each new bishop.   During
the next reign episcopal appointments were constantly reserved; the chapters were rarely allowed to have a voice,
while the Crown often stooped to have its favourites
promoted by the pope.   Edward III. so far had ventured
only on occasional protests, and the force of these was nulli-
fied by his requests for the preferment of some trusted friend
or servant.   Clement VI. might tell his cardinals in 1345
that if the King of England were to beg for an ass to be made
bishop, he must not be denied.   But the real temper of the
Court of Avignon and the haughty insolence of its pretensions
can be measured by a scene which followed the appointment
to the primacy of the learned and pious Bradwardine (1349),
when an ass came into the presence of the assembled pope
and cardinals with the petition hanging to his neck that he
too might have a bishopric.

Meantime the laity of England had grown more impatient
of abuses which their ruler bore so calmly.   Stung by the
attempt of Clement to enrich his cardinals with
dignities in the English Church, the Commons
presented in Parliament a petition on the subject
Remonstrance of the Commons.
in terms so strong that the clergy did not venture to take
part in it (1343).   A grave remonstrance was drawn up by
the Lords and Commons on the 13th of May, to be carried
to the pope by Sir John of Shoreditch, a baron of the Exchequer.   Ecclesiastical endowments had been given in old
time by their forefathers, as they urged, for the service of
God and man, that priests might in each church pray for
the founders' souls and edify the people, but aliens, who
knew nothing of the people's tongue or mode of life, had
been intruded by the indulgence of popes past and present,
to the chilling of devotion, and the peril of men's souls, and
the discouragement of charity and wholesome discipline.
They beg him therefore to take fresh order and withdraw his
system of provision.   The letter, if we may trust the account
which comes from Adam Murimuth, was received in a very
bitter spirit by the pope and much consternation by the

cardinals, and the bearer had to listen to many harsh remarks upon his message. The pope denied that he had often put aliens into posts in England. "Holy Father," said Sir John, "you gave the Deanery of York to Cardinal Talleyrand of Perigord, whom all our nobles think a deadly enemy of our king and of his realm." That said he departed in hot haste from Avignon, where he had spoken with such dangerous frankness. The chronicler himself, a dignified ecclesiastic, recounts the expedients by which the popes had filled their coffers, and taunts his countrymen as long-suffering asses on whom any burden might be laid. The popular feeling on the subject was shown in a tournament at Smithfield, where the pope and twelve cardinals were represented by mummers playing in the lists.

On the 23rd of July the sheriffs were ordered to proclaim the prohibition, issued in compliance with the petition of the Commons, against the agents and receivers of all such papal grants. Instructions were given to search for and seize at the ports all papal Bulls. From fear or negligence the orders were often disregarded, and a long proclamation was issued therefore in January 30, 1344, restating the grievances in question, and insisting that the prohibition of the last year should be enforced. Clement seems to have thought that Archbishop Stratford was the real author of the resistance to the authority which he had claimed, for the king wrote a special letter to disabuse the pope's mind of this impression (August 30, 1343), as he had done before for Archbishop Meopham (January 6, 1332), who had been suspected of attempts to check the activity of the papal agents. Clement, alarmed at these restrictions, pressed the king for their withdrawal, and irritated by his failure used his influence more strongly on the side of France in the long debate which ended in the renewal of the war. The Commons, on the other hand, petitioned in the next Parliament that the ordinances in question should be made permanently binding as a statute of the realm. Again in 1346 they urged that alien priories should be seized into the king's hands, together with the benefices of other foreigners, and the pensions granted to certain cardinals by the pope. The following year the Commons returned once more to the subject; urging that in spite of ordinances and petitions the abuses were not checked, and praying that penalties against provisors might be enacted in a permanent statute.

Again a like petition was presented in 1351, and at last was passed the memorable Statute of Provisors, which enacted that for all ecclesiastical dignities and benefices the lawful rights of the electors and patrons should be secured, and that preferments Statute of Provisors. to which the pope had nominated should be forfeited for that turn to the Crown; further, that any holders of papal provisions who disturbed or impeached the rightful occupants, duly collated by the lawful patrons should be arrested and brought before the Courts of Law for the offence. The urgent remonstrances, so strongly worded and so frequently repeated, show that the abuses were widely and deeply felt. It was not that the English gentry were defending their private rights of patronage, for the advowsons of lay patrons had been scarcely called in question since the failure of Gregory IX. in 1239. From the days of Henry II. the king's courts had constantly maintained that they alone had cognisance of the rights of patronage, which were not to be questioned by Church courts or Canon Law. Any interference with them was a breach of English law, and lay patrons had their remedies against provisors, and might be trusted to assert their rights. The spiritual patrons dared not do so in defiance of the pope, and the statute was passed to protect them against themselves, or rather to defend the interests of the Church of which they were trustees against their natural timidity and scruples. The forfeiture to the Crown of the preferment to which the pope laid claim with their consent was in effect a penalty imposed because bishops, chapters, and other spiritual patrons would not do what the State regarded as their duty. The executive, however, was often indifferent or half-hearted, or played into the pope's hands for personal objects. Edward III. has little claim to credit in this matter. The legislative work was taken in hand only at the urgent entreaty of his subjects, though the long struggle with France, and the French sympathies of the papal Court, made him readier doubtless as a man of war to assume the posture of defiance.

It is clear that what chiefly rankled in men's minds was

the thought that their bitter rivals profited so largely by the resources of the English Church. They talked of aliens in their petitions, but they meant French cardinals, abbeys, and ecclesiastics. Had the popes at Avignon shown any moderation, or dispensed their favours with a more impartial hand, it would have seemed natural enough that the pope, like the king, should be able to reward his servants, and that the English Church should do its part to maintain the costly machinery of the papal system. National churches had their own endowments, but the central power had to live upon the contributions of the faithful. The drain of gold to France, however, was a real evil in an age when the volume of foreign trade was very scanty, and it would take long to replace the coin exported, while England's loss was a gain to her great rival. Serious minds too were revolted by the stories heard of the unblushing simony which went on under the shadow of the papal palace in the city, the immoralities of which Petrarch was painting at this time in the darkest colours, and the English Parliament branded afterwards *la peccherouse cité d'Avenon*, where the brokers of benefices procured "by simony that a caitiff who knows nothing and is worth nothing shall be promoted to churches and prebends of the value of a thousand marks."

As regards episcopal appointments the results of the statute were perhaps a questionable gain. Free elections were a matter of the past. The Crown secured

The Crown gained what the pope lost. such influence as could be wrested from the pope. In the interest of the State indeed it was important that the prelates, who formed so large a proportion of the House of Lords, should not be directly nominated by a foreign power, and a system was adopted which disguised to some extent the actual changes. The forms of election and provision lasted on : but the chapter commonly elected and the pope provided the person nominated by the king in the· letter sent with or after the license to elect. The road to a bishopric lay through political service or court favour, to the neglect often of the unobtrusive worth and piety which a conscientious pope might have discovered and rewarded.

While these measures against "provisors" were being

taken, the king's lawyers had been trying to use a Papal Bull for the advantage of their master. Attempts were made to increase his patronage, which was already large, covering as it did the rights of infants who were in ward to him, and vacant bishoprics, as well as all churches that belonged to the Crown estates.

The Crown's use of Execrabilis.

In the case of pluralists, some of whose benefices were *de jure* void by the Bull *Execrabilis* of 1317, though not actually vacated, the Crown claimed the right to deal with them as vacant, and to present to them when it laid hands on the temporalities of a See after the death of the prelate to whom the patronage belonged. It proposed, that is, for its own benefit to enforce one-half of a papal constitution, while it ignored the other half which had "reserved" for the pope's own use the benefices which pluralists resigned. It would do this, moreover, without the certificate of any spiritual court that the Canon Law had been actually enforced. This led to a petition from the clergy presented to the king in the Parliament of 1351, which asked that no civil court should take cognisance of any voidance *de jure* of a benefice before a mandate had been sent to the Ordinary to hold inquiry in the matter. The answer given was ambiguous, as was also the statute founded on it, which left the question at issue between the justices and bishops undecided. But it was held afterwards in the Courts of Common Law that on the acceptance of a second benefice with cure of souls the first became void *ipso jure*, and the patron might present to it if he would. The secular courts enforced directly the rule prescribed by Canon Law.

There were, however, grievances which had long been felt at the encroachments of the papal Court on the civil tribunals of the land. Suits about the temporal possessions of the Church were decided in the Civil Courts, but unsuccessful suitors, especially provisors, appealed to the papal Court in order to reverse the judgments given at home against them. Already in 1344 and 1347 the Commons had complained of this abuse, and petitioned for penalties in the case of such delinquents. In 1353 a Statute was passed at their request—the first of those called *Præmunire* from the opening words of the writ by which the

Statute of Præmunire.

sheriff was bidden to summon the offender. Its language was very general: it did not name the pope, or Rome, or Church, but enacted simply that whoever should draw any out of the realm in respect of pleas the cognisance of which belonged to the king's court, should in default of his appearance to stand his trial forfeit lands and goods, and be outlawed and imprisoned. The assent of the prelates is not mentioned in the Act, and they certainly protested in 1365 when suitors in the papal Courts were distinctly brought within the scope of the Statute of *Præmunire*, and the protest was repeated in 1393. This, however, was in itself only a saving clause in favour of the canonical authority of the pope and the interests of their order, and had no effect upon the permanent influence of the legislation which was to rank henceforth as the great bulwark of the independence of the National Church.

Clement VI. had passed away while these statutes were in progress (1352). His irritation at the restrictions imposed or threatened was increased by the refusal to allow pilgrims to leave England during the Great Plague to take advantage of his offers of a general indulgence in the Jubilee at Rome. It did not seem a fitting time to gather great multitudes together for the contagious pestilence to spread the faster, and English gold could be better spent for national purposes at home. One of his last acts as pope showed clearly how little love he had for Edward or his kingdom. He had been asked to appoint an English cardinal, and at his request two bishops were singled out as worthy of the honour. A liberal creation of cardinals soon followed. Twelve Frenchmen gained the prize, but not one Englishman was named.

Irritation of Clement.

His successor, Innocent VI., was a pope of a different stamp. As a strict reformer he was opposed to the ecclesiastical abuses of non-residence. But his sympathies were thought to be strongly on the side of France, as was implied in the taunting epigram which was posted up in many places after the victory of Poitiers,—

Disputes with Innocent

Ore est le Pape devenu Franceys e Jesu devenu Engleys.
Ore sera veou qe fra plus, ly Pape ou Jesu.

He would abate nothing of the old pretensions of his See,

and they soon brought him into conflict with the recent legislation. Thomas de Lisle, Bishop of Ely, had been involved in
a dispute with Blanche, Lady Wake, a cousin of the king, and
failing in his lawsuit complained, much to Edward's indignation, that he could not get justice done him because royal
influence was used against him in the courts.   Soon afterwards a servant of Lady Wake was murdered by the bishop's
chamberlain.   The case came on for trial before the Justices
of the King's Bench ; the bishop was found guilty of shelter-
ing the criminal in his house after the deed, and the temporalities of the See were forfeited (November 1357).   The bishop
fled to Avignon, and appealed to Innocent, who cited the
parties to appear before him and excommunicated them
when in default.   One of them died meantime, but by the
pope's orders his grave was opened and his remains were flung
into a dirty pond.   The king, to vindicate the authority of
his Courts of Justice, had proceedings taken against those
who had without his sanction published the Bull in England.
Two messengers who were carrying the pope's injunctions to
the English bishops were thrown into Newgate, where they
died.

The following year there was another matter of dispute.
The See of Lichfield and Coventry was vacant, and Robert
Stretton, a chaplain of the Prince of Wales and sometime
official at the papal Court, was nominated by the king and
elected by the chapter.   The pope questioned his fitness
for the office, and sent for him to come to Avignon and be
examined, where he was rejected as of insufficient learning.   In this case Innocent did not venture to provide.
Edward maintained his nomination, and after a vacancy of
two years, and further examination by two English prelates, in
which the candidate was " plucked " a second time, the pope
suddenly gave way, and Stretton was consecrated at last
(September 1360), though the archbishop refused to assent
to the proceedings.

Difficulties were raised in the same way in the case of
William of Wykeham, who was now rising into note as
Edward's trusted servant and adviser.   He had been surveyor
of the works at Windsor Castle, and became (1359) chief
warden of that and other great castles of the south of

England, where his duties included powers of control over
the materials and workmen required for the fabrics, though
there is no actual evidence of the architectural skill
assigned to him by the respect of later ages. Preferments
had been heaped upon him, before he was in Holy Orders,
to an extent astonishing even in that age, and among
others the Rectory of Pulham, which the king claimed to
dispose of while the temporalities of Ely were in his hands,
and as to which Wykeham was prosecuted in the papal
Court by Bishop de Lisle. His attitude in this case made
him a marked man, and when he was presented to a prebend
in the church of Bishop Auckland in 1361, the pope sent
directions to a bishop to examine him to see if he had
scholarship enough to take the prebend. He refused, however, to submit to this, and chose rather to resign the gift.

The conflict was renewed under Innocent's successor,
Urban V. In 1365 a new Statute was passed, not merely
re-enacting the measures against the encroachments
on the rights of patronage which had long been
complained of, including in this case "the lay
patrons of the realm," but also definitely barring the jurisdiction of the papal Court in causes the cognisance of
which belonged to the king's courts. Urban V. took up
the challenge, and demanded the arrears of the tribute
of 1000 marks, promised by King John, the payment of
which had been suspended for three-and-thirty years.
The answer to this in full Parliament was deliberate and
final. All orders joined in repudiating the claim, and it
was decided that the whole force of the realm would combine, if need were, to resist it. The prelates who had only
agreed to the stringent clauses of the preceding year with
the reserve that they assented to nothing which might
prove to the prejudice of their estate, were now heartily
at one with the laity of England in their refusal to admit
the pope's antiquated claims, and it was a clerical ministry
whose action had provoked the challenge.

There was one dissentient, however, and to his passionate
pleading in favour of the pope's pretension we owe the
first appearance in political debate of John Wyclif, to
whom the gauntlet was thrown down. The pamphlet which

[marginal note:] and his successor.

he wrote in answer took the form of a summary of speeches made upon the subject by the lords temporal in Parliament, which he may indeed have heard himself as a commissioner or possibly as servant of the Crown (*peculiaris regis clericus* he calls himself), but more probably adopted as a convenient dramatic form for the expression of his thoughts. The arguments seem too fine drawn in their logic for the speakers, and read as if they were coined in Wyclif's mint.

William Edyndon, Bishop of Winchester, died in October 1366, and by the king's desire the chapter readily elected Wykeham, who as secretary to the king and keeper of the privy seal had gained a paramount influence at the council board. As Froissart says, " there reigned a priest in England called Sir William de Wiccan . . . so much in favour with the king, that by him everything was done, and without him they did nothing." Pope Urban did not venture to defy, though at least he might ignore the statutes lately passed. In a Bull addressed to Wykeham he said that he had reserved the appointment during the lifetime of the late bishop, and that he was seeking to provide a fit successor. Meantime he constituted him administrator of the Church of Winchester in spirituals and temporals alike. He insisted, that is, on the right which Parliament denied, and inserted the obnoxious clause which papal nominees had been forced always to renounce At length, however, after nine months' delay and special entreaty of the king, he condescended to issue his Bull of provision by way of reservation to William, whom he styled now Bishop-elect of Winchester (July 1367).

There was nothing in the conduct of the primates of the period to cause friction between the powers of Church and State. Simon Islip (1349-1366) a lawyer rather than divine, applied his familiarity with Canon Law to questions of Church discipline more than to ecclesiastical pretensions. He disallowed the antiquated claims of the Bishop of Lincoln to limit the free choice of the chancellor at Oxford ; he settled finally the old dispute of precedence with his brother of York ; he would take no part in the protest of the hot-headed Bishop de Lisle of Ely at the action of the king's courts, or the papal censures

The Archbishops of Canterbury —Islip,

of the officers concerned; but he wrote in the letter called *speculum regis* in terms of bold remonstrance to King Edward upon the abuses of the royal household and the oppressions of its agents. He gave freely for the education of the clergy, and would have no needless outlay for his funeral rites.

Simon Langham (1366-1368), who was transferred from Ely to Canterbury on Islip's death, had only time to show his sympathy with Regulars by putting a monk in Wyclif's place at Canterbury College before his acceptance of a cardinal's hat and Edward's wrath drove him hastily from England. The king, when he heard that Urban without consulting him had made the archbishop a cardinal, broke out into an unreasoning fit of passion and confiscated the temporalities without delay (1368). Yet to have one friend whom he could trust in the papal Court was an advantage, and so perhaps he felt after a time, for he allowed ecclesiastical dignities in England to be heaped upon him contrary to the spirit of the recent laws. Langham, on his side, could not forget the past, and when he came back on a special mission (1372) as mediator for peace, he showed a deference to Edward which provoked the jealous censure of the court of Avignon, and he had to explain on his return that he had only doffed his hood half-way in the presence of the king.

Langham,

William Wittlesey (1368-1374), in the weakness of his failing health, had no decided policy or nerve to further or thwart the papal demands or national claims, and left no mark on the Church which he feebly steered through troubled waters.

Wittlesey.

The brilliant period of English chivalry had been succeeded by inglorious and disastrous times. Pestilence, war, and taxation pressed heavily on an impoverished people; clerical ministries were discredited by failures; clerical wealth was eyed more jealously; and against both the growing discontent was soon to find a voice. As thirty years before the ministry of Stratford had been displaced by laymen, so again in 1371 the Parliament petitioned for a like change, that "sufficient and able laymen" should be appointed then and ever afterwards to the chief offices of State, seeing that the *gentz de seinte eglise*

A lay ministry.

could not be called to account (*justiciables*) like other men.
The vote of censure was a grave one, as it implied moral
rather than intellectual defects.   Though haughtily received
by Edward, it was acted on at once, and William of Wykeham
and the other ministers gave place to laymen.

The Earl of Pembroke was prominent in the anti-clerical
opposition, whose sentiments found expression in the apologue
on the possessions of the clergy, which is reported
for us by Wyclif as coming from "a lord more
skilful than the rest."   It was spoken in reply The apologue on disendowment.
to a claim put forth that monastic lands should be ex-
empted from subsidies to the Crown.   The birds once held
a meeting, and to it came an owl that had no feathers
and seemed to suffer much from cold.   She begged the
other birds to give her some of theirs.   They pitied her and
gave her each a feather, till she was covered over with a
plumage not at all becoming.   But soon a hawk appeared in
quest of prey, and to defend themselves or fly away the birds
wanted their feathers back again ; and when she would not
give them, each of them snatched back her own, and she
had to hurry off in pitiable plight and barer than at first.
The obvious moral was that in time of need Church property
might be resumed in the interest of those who gave it.
Convocation took warning at the threat, and voted a large
grant in aid, to which even the smaller benefices and the
stipends of the unbeneficed clergy were assessed.   The disaster
of the Earl of Pembroke, captured soon after by the Spanish
fleet, seemed to the chronicler a fitting judgment on his
hostility to Holy Church.

A grant of £50,000 was made by Parliament, to be
levied on a new principle, taking each parish as the unit of
taxation ; but with a strange ignorance of the facts it was
assumed that there were 40,000 parishes, while there were
but 8600.   But though it started ill and fell more and more
into contempt, the lay ministry lasted on in office till the last
year of Edward's reign.

During this period a curious scene, which reflected the
temper of the times, is described by a monastic chronicler.
Pope Gregory XI., hard pressed for funds to carry on the
war against the Florentines, asked for a subsidy on the ground

of his feudal claims as lord paramount of England, and a great council of the Black Prince and the lords spiritual and temporal was held at Westminster to con-

Council at Westminster. sider his demands (1374). The prelates were to debate the subject first, and the lords temporal on the morrow. At first Archbishop Wittlesey contents himself with saying, "the pope is lord, we cannot deny that," and all the other prelates say the same. The provincial of the preaching friars begs to be excused from giving a vote upon so serious a question, and advises that the hymn *Veni creator* or the mass *De spiritu sancto* shall be sung for the Holy Spirit's guidance. A monk of Durham discoursed upon the text, "Here are two swords," and tried to prove from it that St. Peter had both the temporal and spiritual power. A friar minor urged in answer that the command, "Put thy sword into its sheath," implied that Christ did not claim for Himself or His apostles any temporal dominion, but taught them to relinquish it. An Austin friar reminded them that the Church distinguished Peter by the keys, Paul by the sword. "You, my lord prince, were wont to be Paul carrying the sword. Only take it up again, and Peter will recognise Paul once more." So ended the debate on the first day. The archbishop remarked after it that there used to be good counsel in England without the friars; to which the prince retorted, "It was your folly that obliged us to summon them. Your counsel would have made us lose the kingdom." On the morrow the archbishop said that he knew not what to say. The prince burst out in passion, "Answer, ass, it is your duty to instruct us all." Thereupon the archbishop said, "I am of opinion that the pope is not lord here," and so in consequence said the prelates one and all. Even the monk of Durham said the same, and when the prince asked, "Where are the two swords, then," he answered, "My Lord, I am better informed now than I was yesterday." The temporal lords, of course, took the same view, and the pope's demands were disallowed.

Another illustration may be given from the same source of the same temper of resistance. In 1376 the pope, whose delegates in Italy had by their misgovernment roused a general league against them, excommunicated the Florentines, who took a leading part among the states. William Courtenay, Bishop of London, published the Bull without any sanction of the Crown, and therefore in defiance of the law. The Florentines in London, endangered by this Act, which exposed them to pillage by the populace, appealed to the government for its protection, and entered the king's service as his bondmen. The bishop, who had preached publicly in favour of the Bull, was bidden by the chancellor to withdraw what he had said, and warned that if he braved the law he might forfeit bishopric and all besides. He obtained leave with difficulty to revoke by proxy. The deputy, with marked effrontery, denied that the bishop had said anything upon the subject, and even rebuked the people for believing that he had. "Strange," he went on to say, "that when you hear so many sermons here, you have not learned to understand them rightly."

Meantime, however, in spite of ordinances and occasional resistance the old abuses lasted on. The executive ignored the illegalities of the papal agents, though the Commons brought forward their grievances year *Old abuses lasted on.* after year. In 1372 they petitioned that non-resident clergy, whether denizens or aliens, should not have the incomes of their benefices sent abroad. In 1373 they complained of illegal provisions and disturbance of the freedom of elections, and alleged that alien nuns exported treasure and betrayed State secrets. In 1374 the Crown issued a writ of inquiry to the bishops to ascertain the extent to which aliens held English benefices, and sent envoys to Bruges, of whom Wyclif was one, to deal among other matters with the ecclesiastical questions in dispute. The conference came to nothing, for some of the commissioners were thought to be incapable or faithless.

Next year (1375) Pope Gregory gave his decision on the subject, but his Bulls, though they seemed to make large concessions, left the substance of his claims un-touched, and in 1376 the Commons, whose *Petition of the Commons.* patience clearly was exhausted, reviewed the whole history of the subject in a weighty and elaborate petition, which showed that the executive had largely failed to enforce the existing laws. It was styled in the margin of the rolls "a bill against the pope and the cardinals," and certainly the indictment was unsparing as it was pathetic.

Clergy and chivalry, which should go hand in hand for the furthering of a people's welfare, have given place, it says, to simony and greed, and hence the shame and misery of the present evil days with their scourges of famine, pestilence, and war. The court of Rome should be a source of sanctity to all the nations, but the traffickers in holy things ply their evil trade in the sinful city of Avignon, and the pope shears his flock but does not feed it. No king in Christendom has one-fourth part of the treasure that goes from England to the pope. His cardinals, who are our enemies almost to a man and are more numerous than ever, have English deaneries and prebends, and are sent time after time here on various affairs of state, and the English church always has to pay their procurations, while they buy up the rich benefices likely to be vacant. Subsidies are levied on the clergy by the pope to pay for the charges of his wars, and they dare not deny him. His collector lives in state like a duke or prince in his great house in London, with an army of clerks and spies to gather up the first-fruits and the subsidies, while the bishops, translated from See to See at the pope's pleasure, have to cut the timber on their manors or borrow from their friends to meet the heavy charges levied on them. It is the jubilee of the king's long reign, the year of grace and joy, the petition adds almost in irony, and what could possibly cause greater gladness than timely deliverance from evils so fatal to the well-being of Church and State. It was indeed a sorry jubilee for king and people; disasters abroad, mis-government at home disgraced the closing years of Edward's life.

The Parliament of 1376 was fondly called "the good," because of its impeachment of the men who were thought to

Wykeham prosecuted.

have enriched themselves and sacrificed the public interests by scandalous abuse of their influence at court. Wykeham took a leading part in the proceedings and pressed for the refusal to allow postponement of the trial of Lord Latimer for misconduct in the war —a refusal not forgotten when his own turn came to be attacked soon after A sudden change came with the death

of the Black Prince (June 1376), who had supported the
movement of reform.   John of Gaunt, Duke of Lancaster,
was left in power uncontrolled   Parliament was dissolved ;
its work undone ; Latimer and others whom it had condemned were released from prison, and as a counterblast
Wykeham was singled out for prosecution before a great
council at Westminster, in which the chief officers of State
and of the Household sat with judges, bishops, and other
barons.   The Commons had urged that ecclesiastics could
not like other men be brought to justice.   We may see in
Wykeham's case how far the immunity extended.   He was
charged with "sundry grievous articles . . . and defaults to
the prejudice hurt and reproach of the king and of his
realm."   "He craved counsel and day because he could not
so speedily answer," but was at first denied what he had
himself refused to Latimer.

The first charge discussed was that he had long before as
chancellor remitted at his own discretion to Sir John Grey
of Rotherfield part of the fine due to the Crown for a license
to take possession of certain lands and tenements.   His plea
was that the fine had been put too high at first.   There was
no evidence of any personal interest on his part, but he was
sentenced to pay 100 marks for every penny which the
crown had lost by the transaction, making in the whole
960,000 marks.   Other charges followed, very wide and
general in their terms, but dealing with actual losses in the
war with France, which may have been caused in part by
the want of forethought and energy of Wykeham and his
colleagues.   Lancaster pressed the council to condemn him
without delay, but the bishops present stated to the lords
that "as concerning his parson and his spiritualties they had
not to do nor to judge."   With the king's assent, however,
they seized upon his temporalities, "and they hunted the
said bishop from place to place both by letters and by
writtes, so that no man could succour him throughout his
diocese, neither could he, neither durst he, rest in any place ;
and therefore he then brake up household and scattered his
men and dismissed them, for he could no lenger governe
and meinteyn them ; sending also to Oxford, whear upon
almose (alms) and for God's sake he found (maintained)

sixty scollers, that they should depart and remove every one
to their frendes, for he could no lenger help or finde them ;
and so they all departed in great sorow and discomfort
weeping and with simple cheer." Funds, however, were
urgently required for the service of the State. Parliament
was summoned (1377) but would vote no taxes till their grievances had been discussed. Convocation (moved by William
Courtenay, Bishop of London) refused to act unless the
Bishop of Winchester was present in his place, and the duke
had to give way, and in effect to withdraw the proclamation
by which the bishop had been forbidden to appear within
twenty miles of the king's person.

Meantime the Duke of Lancaster was preparing to take
part in another public trial, in which he intervened
in the interest of the accused, but again, as it
seemed, in a spirit hostile to the Church.

Wyclif and John of Gaunt.

John Wyclif had been long the foremost figure in the
schools of Oxford, where his speculative subtleties and bold
theories had been matter of debate in academic circles. In
the great world he was best known by the startling boldness
of his repudiation of the claims of Rome and his language
about Church endowments. In this connection he has
already been before us as present possibly in the Good
Parliament and certainly at the Conference of Bruges. These
utterances attracted the attention of the Duke of Lancaster
who, with little sympathy for his high-minded character and
earnest aims as a reformer, was ready to accept the aid of a
political ally whose high repute gave weight and dignity to
the cause for which he acted. Wyclif had already pointed
with some scorn at the clerical servants of the Crown, like
Wykeham, who were climbing nimbly by court favour to
promotion while scholars could not rise. "Lords will not
present a clerk of learning and of good life, but a kitchen
clerk or a penny clerk (clerk of accounts), or wise in building castles . . . though he cannot well read his psalter."
The scholar was duped by the scheming politician, who
wished indeed to humble the proud Churchmen, but
had no thought to reform the Church itself. To the eyes
of the chronicler of St. Alban's the duke's malice against
the Church is proved by this unholy compact between

the noble profligate and the dangerous heresiarch, the latter
of whom he styles the "pseudo-theologian or real theomachist."
It may, perhaps, have led to the proceedings which immediately followed.

Convocation met on February 3, 1377, and Courtenay
and other bishops, alarmed by the vigour which Wyclif had
shown of late in the pulpits of London churches,
put pressure on the reluctant primate to summon Wyclif's trial
at St. Paul's.
him for trial before them.

Simon Sudbury was now Archbishop of Canterbury (1375-
1381), and his attitude might seem suspicious. Had he
not long ago (1370) roused the anger of the pilgrims to
the shrine of Becket by scornful words which sounded like
an insult to the memory of the martyr? As Bishop of London
he had attached himself to the interests of John of Gaunt,
the protector of Wyclif, with whom he had been associated
as commissioner at the Conference of Bruges. By the
influence of Lancaster the archbishop received the Great
Seal in 1380.

On the 19th of February 1377 Wyclif appeared before
the tribunal at St. Paul's, but not without support, for the
Duke of Lancaster and Henry Lord Percy, Grand Marshal
of England, were at his side, with four friars learned in
theology and opposed by the principles of their orders to
all clerical endowments, who had been specially retained
by the duke for his defence. The Londoners were already
crowded in the church, for Wyclif was popular among them,
but the marshal had a way roughly cleared among them by
his armed retainers, and this led to an unseemly altercation
between him and Courtenay, Bishop of London, who protested
at such masterful behaviour in the church. After much
hustling and confusion they made their way into the Lady
Chapel, where the trial was to be held, and there Lord Percy
ordered Wyclif to be seated, as he would have to answer
many questions and have need of rest. The bishop urged
that it was but seemly that the accused should stand before
his judges. The marshal, supported by the duke, replied
with angry taunts, and the bishop answered in like fashion.
Lancaster swore that he would humble the pride, not of
Courtenay alone, but of all the bishops of England, and

that his high birth should not avail him, for his parents—the Earl and Countess of Devonshire, that is—should have enough to do to help themselves. The bishop answered calmly that he put his trust in no man, but in God alone; and the duke, still more enraged, was heard to mutter that he would drag him from the church by the hairs of his head rather than put up with such affronts. The Londoners, incensed already at the duke, because of a proposal made in Parliament on the same day to abridge their privileges and lower the dignity of their mayor by vesting the government of the city in the king's marshal, could not restrain themselves when they heard this insult to their bishop, and the meeting broke up in confusion, without a single word from the accused, who is said to have behaved with indescribable insolence but never refers to the subject in his writings. The chronicler discerns in the whole scene a device of Satan to protect his favoured servant.

On the morrow there was a riot in the city, where the news spread that the marshal had a prisoner in his house contrary to law. The duke and marshal, taken unawares, while the threatening crowds were gathered at the Savoy, fled from the dinner-table for their lives, and took refuge at Kennington with the Princess of Wales. When she intervened in the interests of peace, the citizens demanded among other things a fair trial by his peers for the Bishop of Winchester, who had been condemned unheard, as well as for Peter De la Mare, the late Speaker of the Commons. But, notwithstanding this, Wykeham's name was specially excepted from the articles of general pardon granted on occasion of the jubilee and rehearsed in the king's presence before certain of the Lords and Commons. The temporalities of the See were further settled on the young Prince of Wales, but three months afterwards, and only three days before the old king's death, June 21, 1377, they were restored to Wykeham on condition that he would fit out three ships at his own expense for the king's service.

The reversal of the sentence was so sudden, and the court influence had been so strongly used against him that popular fancy found it hard to understand the change. According to the gossip of the day, reported in the chronicle

of St. Alban's, the bishop, making himself "friends of the
mammon of unrighteousness," begged the help of Alice
Perrers, the king's mistress, who on her own terms,
as it was thought, won over the king and overruled   Sentence re-
                                                         versed.
the malice of the duke.   The story is a most unlikely
one, inconsistent as it is with all that we know of Wykeham's
character.   Even dropping out of sight all higher motives,
we can see that with a change of rulers evidently near at
hand, and with the support of clergy and Londoners secured,
Wykeham might well have been content to wait awhile
without stooping to use so vile a tool.   A few weeks later
(July 31) the young king Richard II. granted Wykeham
by formal writ a general pardon, absolving him "for
ever of the aforesaid articles, and of all other crimes and
offences whatsoever . . . willing that all men should know
that . . . we do not think the said bishop to be in any
wise blameworthy in God's sight of any of the matters thus
by us pardoned, remitted, or released to him ; but do
hold him, as to all and every of them, wholly innocent and
guiltless."

The evil days of persecution were not long for Wykeham,
but the clouds were not rolled away so speedily over Wyclif's
head.   He did not put himself forward in political
debate, but his public utterances had already   Wyclif
                                                     accused.
offended too many interests, and shocked too many
deep-rooted convictions for him to be left long undisturbed.
Critical eyes had been busy with his writings, and nine-
teen propositions gathered from them had been sent to
the pope the year before, that he might take action if he
pleased about them.   Among them were the following : that
temporal rulers had the right to take away Church property
in case of grave error or abuse ; that Church discipline or
the power of the keys should be strictly limited to spiritual
offences, that even the Roman pontiff might lawfully be
corrected and accused by laymen.   Accordingly on May 22,
1377, Gregory XI. issued five Bulls to the king,
the Archbishop of Canterbury, the Bishop of London,   Bulls against
                                                          him.
and also to the University of Oxford, directing them
to take or sanction proceedings against Wyclif.   Nothing
was done however till 18th December, when the prelates

forwarded the commission to the Oxford chancellor and directed that Wyclif should be cited to appear before them once more in February at St. Paul's. The papal Bull itself was not received with much respect at Oxford, for it sharply censured the careless indifference to Wyclif's errors, and bade the authorities hand him over as a prisoner for trial, though they had no power to do so in obedience merely to a papal mandate, while the archbishop only asked that he should be cited to appear before him. With this request they probably complied. Wyclif is said to have been charged by the vice-chancellor not to leave his rooms, and reminded of his oath of obedience as a graduate to his control, a stretch of authority for which the vice-chancellor was himself afterwards imprisoned. According to the same writer the conclusions referred to in the Bull were handed over for examination to certain regent masters in theology, who reported to the chancellor that in the schools they would be recognised as true, though they had a startling sound to those who heard them. Walsingham indeed laments in melancholy terms the degeneracy of the University, that had so deeply fallen from its former height of wisdom as not to be ashamed to let truths be called in question which even a Christian layman could not doubt.

Wyclif for his part put forth written statements addressed respectively to Parliament and the general public, defending the theses which had been condemned by showing the point of view from which they had been stated.

Wyclif's defence.

A warning message sent from the king's mother, probably at Lancaster's suggestion, and carried by Sir Lewis Clifford, of whose sympathy with Wyclif we hear more, seems to have caused an adjournment of the court ; this sat however some time afterwards at Lambeth, but the Londoners again pushed into the chapel with clamorous interruptions, and the prelates, overawed by so many signs of sympathy with the accused, did no more than bid him have good care not to offend the laity by publishing any more the questionable theses. The chronicler of St. Alban's, who had before complained bitterly of the culpable neglect of Archbishop Sudbury to take earlier proceedings against Wyclif, now rails at the bishops for the cowardice with which they bowed

before the storm in spite of the brave words which they had
used. "As reeds shaken by the wind," he says, "their speech
became as soft as oil, to the public loss of their own dignity
and the damage of the Church. They were struck with such
a terror that you would fancy them to be as a man that
heareth not, in whose mouth there is no reproof."

But it is clear that the conditions of the time soon after
the Bulls arrived in England were all in Wyclif's favour.
The king passed away in June, and the Bull   Political
addressed to him could have no effect. The   conditions in
thoughts of men were fully occupied with the details   his favour.
of the Coronation and the French attacks upon the coast.
The new Parliament was strongly anti-papal in its temper,
and moved to keep by force in England all the gold that was
being sent out of it to the papal Court or foreign ecclesiastics who held preferment here. Wyclif, we are told, had
been directed to draw up an opinion for the young king and
his council on the question of the State's right to restrain
the exportation of such funds in spite of the pope's demands
for them and the threats of spiritual censures. Wyclif's
paper affirmed the right in unhesitating terms on the ground
alike of the law of nature and the authority of Scripture, as
well as of the interest of the State at large. With the court
and the Parliament his testimony had undoubted weight.
Archbishop Sudbury was thought to sympathise with him;
in the University of Oxford his influence was very strong;
the Londoners were clamorous in his behalf; the bishops
could not safely venture to lodge him in prison, as the pope
directed, and could not even then take further steps against
him.

With this the personal attack on Wyclif ended. His
language became more aggressive, it is true, as touching the
doctrines of the faith and the authority of the Church, but
popular favour and the support of powerful protectors,
together with the death of Gregory XI. and the confusion
caused by the Great Schism (*v.* p. 163), enabled him to live
undisturbed at Lutterworth and end his days in peace.
Meantime, however, the University of Oxford and afterwards
the Church at large, were distracted by the efforts made to
extend or arrest the movement which he started. But his

influence on religious thought and his attitude as a reformer require fuller treatment, and must be reserved for separate discussion.

AUTHORITIES.—Various chronicles in the collection entitled *Anglia Sacra*, vol. i., are useful for this period as for that of Chap. III., especially the *Historia Roffensis* of W. de Dene. For the disturbances at Bury St. Edmund's, St. Alban's and Canterbury, reference may be made to the authorities mentioned at the end of Chap. XIV. Many bitter comments on the ecclesiastical conditions of the times are to be found in the *Chronicle of Adam Murimuth*, ed. E. M. Thompson, 1889 (Rolls ser.). For the general history of the reign Robert de Avesbury, *Historia* (Th. Hearne, 1720), may be consulted, and *Roman Canon Law in the Church of England*, by F. W. Maitland, 1898, for questions relating to Papal provisions and the Bull *Execrabilis*. The *Continuatio Eulogii* in *Eulogium Hist.*, vol. iii., ed. F. S. Haydon (Rolls ser.), is of special interest for the later part of the period. The official documents referred to are found in the Rolls of Parliament and Rymer and Wilkins. The proceedings against Wykeham and Wyclif are described with special fulness in the *Chronicon Angliæ*, ed. E. M. Thompson, 1874 (Rolls ser.), and the theses attributed to Wyclif may be found in the *Fasciculi Zizaniorum*, ed. W. W. Shirley, 1858 (Rolls ser.).

CHAPTER VI

JOHN WYCLIF

THE contemporary writers, monks or church lawyers as they were, speak of Wyclif in the very darkest terms, but they admit that he was a commanding personality at Oxford, exerting a potent influence on religious thought both in the university and in the greater world. Little is known, however, of his early life, and there has been much question as to some recorded facts. The very name of his birthplace, as given by Leland, Ypreswell, now Hipswell, close to Richmond in Yorkshire, was misread by Hearne, to the great embarrassment of later writers, who could find no Spreswell on their maps. Confusion with a namesake, as it would seem, has also made it difficult to trace with precision his career at Oxford, where three of the existing colleges and a hall that has disappeared have claimed him as an inmate. All the evidence, however, points to the conclusion that he began his university career at Balliol, where he became first fellow and then master, leaving it to reside in the country benefice of Fillingham, in Lincolnshire (1363), and thence passing from one preferment to another till he accepted finally from the Crown the rectory of Lutterworth (1374), in which he died (December 31, 1384). These benefices, it should be noted, were held only in succession, not together after the custom of his time, and in this he was entirely true to his own principles. Much of his time, however, in the intervening period was spent at Oxford, for he had rooms at Queen's College at various times between 1363 and 1380. He had two years' leave of absence from his

Wyclif's career at Oxford.

parish in 1368 that he might devote his time to study. Possibly he was warden between 1365 and 1367 of Canterbury Hall, which was founded by Archbishop Islip to foster the interests of learning in the clergy. Either he or a namesake at Merton College held that office for a while by the appointment of Islip himself, who shortly before his death displaced for the purpose a Benedictine monk, whom he had allowed as the nominee of Christ Church, Canterbury, to be the first head of the house. The foundation deed gave power to succeeding primates to draw up fresh statutes, and Archbishop Langham—whose sympathies as ex-abbot of Westminster were with the Regulars — immediately gave the headship to a monk, and excluded the secular clergy from the house. Wyclif and others appealed to the pope against the proceedings, which appear to have been hurried through informally, but the question was decided in favour of the monks, and the seculars were finally shut out. A contemporary chronicler not only identifies the reformer with the warden who was thus deposed, but also assumes that a feeling of natural resentment embittered his mind henceforth against both monks and pope. The reference to the dispute in Wyclif's treatise *De Ecclesia* deals with it only as a well-known incident, but does not imply strong personal interest in the writer, and we may set aside entirely the discreditable motive imagined by a rancorous partisan.

There can be no doubt, however, that Wyclif was the leading figure in the academic circles of his day : one of the last of the great schoolmen before he became known as the earliest of the reformers. Writers who loathed his later influence regarded him as the " flower of Oxford scholarship," "incomparable" in learning, "transcending all in the subtlety of his thought." He had an intimate acquaintance with the Aristotelian as well as the scholastic literature, though in his complete ignorance of Greek he could deal only with the Latin versions of the former. He was well read in the Fathers, especially Augustine, with whom his sympathy is shown in his predestinarian language, and with Chrysostom, of whose homilies he made at times large use. But above all other books the Bible was the main object of his study ; he never

A leading figure there.

wearied of referring to it as the absolute standard of appeal, and he showed constantly the most intimate acquaintance with its text. In one volume of a single work some 700 quotations from it may be counted, and contemporaries recognised his reverence for it when they styled him the *Doctor Evangelicus.*

They were the old questions of logic and philosophy on which he exercised for many years his speculative powers, dealing as a Realist with scholastic problems. The titles of his earlier works have no aggressive sound, and though some of his conclusions might be start- *Questions with which he dealt.*
ling, the treatment is professedly ideal, and as such not to be applied at once to the world of stirring action. But his strong convictions concerning the endowments of the Church and the need of resistance to the papal claims, made him known ere long in the outer world, where, as we have seen already, he appeared as the ally of John of Gaunt and the trusted adviser of the Crown. From the material interests of the Church he passed on to deal with the more vital questions of its constitution and its creed. In regard to these we may trace a gradual change of attitude, but only in the last few years of his life did he exhibit a thorough-going opposition to the distinctive tenets and usages of the Mediæval Church, and pour out with astonishing rapidity—but with countless repetitions—in rugged Latin and in homely English the controversial pamphlets by which men knew him best.

There was one guiding principle throughout, urged ever with increasing earnestness, that Holy Scripture is the final standard to which reference must be made ; tradi- *The Bible the sole standard.*
tion and authority have no independent claims. He explained, indeed, as late as 1376 that to understand the Scriptures rightly he would trust not only to reason trained in philosophic methods, but to the approved interpretations of the doctors of the Church, but not much later he insisted that " the Holy Spirit teaches us the meaning of Scripture, as Christ disclosed its sense to the Apostles." The " pure theologian," to his mind, adopts this view, while the " motley " divines (*mixtim theologi*) lay stress on tradition besides Scripture. This is, indeed, not only the highest, but to him the sole source of religious truth. " No custom in the

Church, confirmed by popes or observed by saints, is to be praised save in so far as Jesus Christ confirms it."

This sweeping thesis, which he affirms without hesitation with regard to doctrine, was pushed to far lengths in later days. Consistently maintained, it implied the present duty to return without delay to the bare simplicity of the Apostolic Church, with its undeveloped dogmas, its rudimentary system of Church government, together with the scanty ritual and homely forms which alone were possible in the "upper room" where St. Paul could preach, or in the hiding-places of the Catacombs. Let us see to what extent it was applied by Wyclif, and how far it led him beyond the natural desire to correct the obvious abuses of the times, which numbers of earnest men deplored with him.

In his conception of the Church no stress was laid on any visible signs of admission or membership. It included, besides the blessed in heaven and the saints in The Church purgatory, the true men who lived a Christian life, "that should be afterwards saved in heaven." He protests often against the vulgar error that understands only the clergy by the Church, and insists again and again that it contains "all that shall be saved" and no more. The language is predestinarian, but he guards against the Pharisaic pride that might boast of its assurance of the privileges of the elect, for his conception is ideal and applies only to a church invisible, since in the church militant on earth "we know not whether we shall be saved, we know not whether we be members of Holy Church." Some are foreordained to salvation in the eternal purposes of God; of others it is foreknown that they will sin and fall away. These last he seldom calls reprobates, but foreknown only (*præsciti*), and with regard to them he tries hard but ineffectually to reconcile with logical precision the mysteries of God's absolute power and foreknowledge with the responsibility of man's free will. It is God's grace that draws the elect immediately to Himself, without the need of earthly forms or priestly mediation; no test can help us certainly to distinguish the true and the false members of the Church, but we may apply cautiously the moral standard, and trust that where we see the natural fruits of grace the membership is actual and not apparent only.

The Bride of Christ, however, has been sadly materialised and degraded by the coarser influences of the world. She lived in unsullied purity through early days of poverty and persecution. The temptations of wealth have been more fatal, for " the fend had envie therto, and bi Silvestre preest of Rome he broughte in a new gile, and moved the emperour of Rome to dowe (endow) the Churche in this preest." It is the old fable of the donation of Constantine to which Wyclif here refers, the first symptom of decline, the actual source of unnumbered evils in the life of Christendom. His convictions on this point had been slowly matured ; guardedly expressed in earlier writings, they become passionately vehement at last.

He had long before clothed his theories of property in feudal forms, developing the strangely worded thesis, " Dominion is founded in grace," which he had borrowed from Fitz - Ralph, the Archbishop of Armagh. All men hold what they have of God directly, and on the same tenure of service. All who stand in grace have not only the right to, but the actual possession of, the gifts of God. " All things are yours," the apostle says to the believer, " whether things present or things to come." But the wicked who do not render the due service to the lord in chief of whom they hold may be rightfully deprived of all lordship whatsoever, while, as there are many righteous and each is lord of all, charity that seeketh not her own, seeketh to have all things common. The theory of course is transcendental ; its communism is not meant to be applied immediately to the concrete facts of common life. God allows, and man must therefore be content to see, the present order of things with all its evils and abuses, limit and modify for a time the influence of the ideal good. " God should obey the devil," as he puts it in the startling paradox quoted with horror by his critics. The civil order, the temporal authority, has its own proper sphere with which the Church may not lightly meddle. Temporal rule belongs to earthly lordship, not to pope or priest; the spiritualty must be strictly confined to its own spiritual work, and if it strive to pass these bounds the State should interpose to claim its own. The theory,

I

purely speculative as it might be, was ominous enough. It condemned, even while it tolerated, much of the existing order; it seemed to encourage communistic dreams; it emphatically protested against papal sovereignty and the feudal lordship of the prelates. Here surely was enough to justify alarm and call for papal Bulls.

But Wyclif went much further and attacked not the lordship only but the endowments of the Church. The practice of Christ must have been meant, he urged, to be an example for all times; apostolic poverty should be the Church's rule for all her teachers. Passages of Scripture, relevant or not, were pressed into the service. The sons of Aaron were to have no portion in the land of promise, for God was "part and heritage of all his priests." "Ye shall give them no possession in Israel, I am their possession" (Ezek. xliv. 28). Why should a Christian priest want more, and not "having food and clothing therewith be content." They should not be "lords over God's heritage, but ensamples to the flock" (1 Peter v. 3), like Jesus Christ, who "for our sakes became poor, that we through his poverty might be rich" (2 Cor. viii. 9). "The disciple is not above his Master," are the Master's words, and Christ, who lived in poverty, Himself bade His true ones give up all to follow Him. Wyclif is never weary of insisting on the evils caused by the possessions of a wealthy clergy, the covetousness and simony to which they lead, the heavier burdens of taxation on the Commons, the scantier charity towards the poor, the fear of loss and hope of gain which pervert the preacher's message to the world. He would have the clergy subsist entirely on the free-will offerings of the people, and would disallow all legal claims on their part to tithes or settled property; "it belongeth not to Christ's vicar nor to priests of holy church to have rents here on earth." Of the higher orders of the hierarchy he speaks with vehemence on this account in all his later writings; they have what by right belongs to the temporal power, they should no longer be allowed to rob the State. To the objection that for order's sake gradations of rank must be maintained, he replies that that which Christ ordained is alone sufficient for His Church.

Endowments fatal.

It was long indeed before he reached this stage of thought. Almost to the last the spiritual pretensions of the Papacy, the imposing symbol of the union of Christendom, of moral force enthroned in the consciences of men, powerfully appealed even to his bold self-confident judgment.   He stood forward from the first indeed to denounce the exactions of the papal agents, the exorbitant demands, the manifold abuses which he deplored as moralist, and as patriot resisted ; but of the Papacy itself he long spoke in reverent terms, even while asserting his right to criticise its action and sweep aside its claim to be infallible. Even as late as 1378 the election of Urban VI. stirred in him fond hopes of happy changes soon to follow.   " Praised be the Lord, who has given to our Church in these days of her pilgrimage a catholic head, an evangelical man who in reforming the Church that it may live in accordance with the law of Christ, begins in due order with himself and his own household.   So from his works should we believe that he is our Church's head."   Even after the Schism he still speaks of Urban as " our pope," though with the careful reservation that if he should swerve from the straight way it would be better to do without him as without his rival.   The events that followed seemed to justify the warning words ; the clash of arms came close upon the war of words ; Urban called for a crusade against the anti-pope, and the selfish cruelties of the war changed Wyclif's tone at once.   The Papacy became to him thenceforth an accursed thing ; the Schism, much to be deplored at first, seemed now a blessing in disguise, for the power of antichrist was weakened, as it was divided against itself.   " Christ has begun to help us graciously in that He has cloven the head of antichrist and made the one part fight against the other."   Pamphlet after pamphlet deals in uncompromising style with the spiritual powers which the popes had claimed, tests them by the Scriptural standard, rejects them as immoral and absurd. Christ is the sole head of the Church ; the primacy of Peter is not to be proved ; the infallibility of his successors is a dream, their claim to canonise the saints a mere presumption; their title to excommunicate usurped.   The system of in-dulgences again, or the pope's claim to dispense the treasure

The Papacy attacked,

of the accumulated merits of the saints, is but a "founed (fond) blasphemie blabred withouten grounde," "the lewedste heresie that ever was found of freres." The moral abuses of the Papacy are as constantly attacked: its pride and world-liness, the open simony encouraged in its exercise of patron-age, its oppressive misgovernment, its arrogant pretensions, which set at naught the counsels of Christian humility, the falsehood, hypocrisy, and strife so often fostered by it.

But Wyclif's attacks went far beyond the pope. The whole ecclesiastical system was at fault. If the root of all blasphemy was to be found in the action of the court of Rome, "the twelve daughters of the dia-bolical leech" might be recognised in the various grades of the hierarchy, from the cardinals to the door-keepers themselves. The college of cardinals was the hinge (*cardo*) of the door of the "broad way that leadeth to destruction"; they blasphemously compare themselves with the apostles, but there is no Scriptural warrant for their rank. The imperial clergy (*clerus cæsareus*), as he fancifully called the higher orders, were demoralised by the lordship and wealth which followed on the fatal gift of Constantine; they, too, had usurped the temporal power and wealth which the State should, in the interest of both, wrest from their un-worthy hands, setting them to do their proper work in the lowly spirit of their Master, no longer led astray by the "lust of the eyes and the pride of life."

and the whole ecclesiastical system.

They had no right even to their official rank, for prelates were unknown in early days, are needless in later times. Simple priests had spiritual power to ordain and confirm as well as they. "Why may not a poor priest bless a young child with a rag and oil?" The formal acts of consecration and the rest, in which the bishops take so prominent a part, are not of the essence of the faith, and they would do much better service if they preached the Word instead of claiming such exclusive powers and excessive fees, for as "popes will have the first-fruits for benefices they give, so bishops take a hundred shillings for hallowing one church," and "for writing and sealing of a little scroll twelvepence or two shillings, as at ordination." Many of them indeed, bishops *in partibus*, forget entirely their promises to convert

Bishops.

the heathen, never think of visiting the countries from which
they take their titles, and spend their time in ceremonial work,
"become rich bishops' suffragans, pillage and rob our people
for consecrating churches, churchyards, altars, and ornaments
of the Church."

Wyclif would make short work with the vested interests
of archdeacons and their officials, and the fines for which
offences were commuted.   Two cords, he says,
by which the devil drags down souls to hell, are   Archdeacons
the groundless terror of excommunication and the   rural deans.
hope of fictitious absolution : abuses both on which officials
thrive.   Rural deans in their diabolical malice make money
out of the sins of lust, and are to be shunned more than
the harlots whose vices they encourage.   The non-residence
and secular employments of the clergy should be strictly disallowed.   Christ's service was neglected while they served the
world ; it was dangerous even to allow them to go to the
universities to study, and to attend lectures there on law and
science.   Scholastic studies indeed breed heresies, and have
done more harm than good.   Simple priests may be better
teachers than the learned universities, for the apostles took
no degrees.

If the secular clerks of high rank found little favour in the
eyes of Wyclif, he did not love the regulars the more.   The
monks and Austin canons—possessioners as he calls
them—were the second and third sects who had   Monks and
fallen away grievously, like the first sect of the   canons.
prelates, from the pure ideal of the Church of the first days.
"These irreligious that have possessions, they have commonly
red and fat cheeks and great bellies."   Idle and self-indulgent,
they squander national wealth, and do no service to the State
or to the poor.   By flattery or hypocritic arts they have
acquired numberless advowsons to the sad loss of the parishes,
whose interests they ignore.   "The appropriation is got by
false suggestions made to antichrist, by falsehood to the nobles,
and covetousness and simony, and wasting of poor men's
goods.   And yet they do not the office of curates, neither in
teaching nor preaching, nor giving of sacraments, nor receiving
of poor men in the parish, but set an idiot for vicar or parish
priest that cannot do the office of a good curate, and yet the

poor parish maintains him.   And no tongue may tell in this world what sin and wrong cometh thereby."

The friars were the worst offenders in his eyes: perhaps because their standard seemed to him in theory the highest, and its total failure the most grievous.   They professed Friars above all, a life of poverty and usefulness, and he long spoke of them with sympathy, for their aim seemed to come nearest to the rule of Christ, and he hoped even to the last to attract the earnest-minded of them to his side.   But he formed at last a very different judgment of their practice, and scarcely a single one of all his later pamphlets ends without some bitter words against them.   If the Council of London could discover twenty-four erroneous conclusions in his works, he or a follower found twice as many heresies or errors in the friars, and in this he avowedly takes up the mantle of the Archbishop of Armagh, who thirty years before had pleaded vigorously against them before the papal Court at Avignon.   "In his days indeed the bishops hated the pseudo-friars, for they helped to pay his costs, but now Herod and Pilate have become friends."   The different orders, Carmelites, Augustinians, Jacobites (Dominicans), and Minorites (Franciscans) each furnished an initial letter to make up the name of Caim or Cain, by which Wyclif often brands them.   It may be well to reserve for another chapter the inquiry into the characteristics of the friars in the days of their decline, noting here only that Wyclif pours his scorn upon them as the most zealous advocates of papal claims, worldly and covetous and superstitious in spite of their saintly and ascetic airs, hunting down the poor priests whom he had trained for mission work, and stoutly defending the sacramental theory that seemed meaningless to him.

For in the later stage of his career the controversy chiefly turned on the language in which the Eucharistic mystery and tran- substantia- tion. should be explained.   The Real Presence he was ready to affirm in simple faith, but the change of sub- stance following on the words of consecration, the current theory that is of transubstantiation, which assumed that the substance of Christ's body replaced the invisible substance of the elements of bread and wine, whose qualities remained unaltered to the senses;—this was, he said, a logical absurdity, quite inconceivable to sober thought; it was even "the abomination of desolation" of the prophetic vision. "It was not trowid before the fend was loosid (*i.e.* 1000 A.D., Rev. xx. 7) that this worthi sacrament was accident withouten suget (substance)." This seemed the crowning heresy of the bold thinker; it was for this his poor followers languished in prison or perished at the stake; when this was recanted life was spared. Yet it did not touch the central doctrine of the faith, but only the philosophic terms in which it was explained: a matter of the technical language of the schools, in itself unthinkable to minds untrained, fatal alike, he says, to grammar, logic, natural science.

He had long endeavoured to reconcile the accepted dogma with the language of Scripture and the rules of logic; he had not till late in his career ventured to attack it, and to the last he says that he is willing to be His chief ob-
ject of attack. taught if the bishops will only show him any proof. There were indeed various theories of rival schools to explain how the apparent qualities of the sacramental elements could remain after the mysterious change of substance, to one of which he seems to have inclined himself in earlier days.

There was the theory of absolute accidents. Some held with the Scotists that qualities had a reality of their own and could exist without the support of the substances to which they naturally belonged. The qualities of bread and wine might still be there when the Real Presence had replaced their natural substance. This was accepted generally, he says, in the mountainous parts of Wales and Scotland. Others thought with Thomas Aquinas that quantity might give permanence and support to the form, colour, and taste which could be seen and felt in the apparent elements. This counted most partisans through the wide diocese of Lincoln. Nearly the whole province of Canterbury, again, singled out the quality of weight as giving the reality and absoluteness which was needed.

In dealing with these various theories his arguments abound in hair-splitting subtleties of scholastic logic, and therefore perhaps it has been said that his own position was as metaphysically abstruse as those which he so violently attacked. But to say this is not to represent the matter fairly. It is

possible indeed to connect his language on the Eucharist with
his earlier attitude as a Realist towards the controversial
questions of the schools.   But this does not promi-
His own position.   nently appear in his elaborate treatises upon the subject, the *De Eucharistia* and *De Apostasia* of his latest
years.   In them he was chiefly concerned to prove that the
sacramental elements remained unchanged in substance after
consecration : the order of nature was not set aside by special
miracle, but Christ's body was also there by supernatural
grace ; the term transubstantiation might be used indeed, but
in the sense that "there is a change from the exclusion of
any entity but bread to sacramental coexistence."   His theory,
that is, comes nearest to what has been known as consubstan-
tiation, as opposed to rival doctrines of "identity" or "im-
panation" : but commonly he seems to shrink from formal
definition, using his keen logic mainly for negations, and he
quotes approvingly the words of John Damascenus, "we must
believe that 'this is my body,' not inquiring how."

The vehemence of his constantly repeated protests against
the pretension to "annihilate the substance of the bread" by
the priest's words of consecration would be hard to understand if it were a question only of the philosophical terms to
be employed.   But to his mind the adoration of the Host
was pushed to idolatrous extremes, and strengthened the
hold of superstition on credulous and ignorant fancy.   It was
clearly connected in his thought with the extravagance of
sacerdotal claims, with the impostures and the mercenary
temper which he denounced so strongly in the ecclesiastical
system of his times, and in the widely extended practices of
the masses for the dead.

It has been asserted by his critics that he made the
efficacy of the Sacrament wholly dependent on the spiritual
Other sacramental questions.   conditions of the ministrant.   This is true certainly
of later Lollards, and the language of a contem-
porary bishop, Thomas Brunton of Rochester,
points to it as the actual teaching either of Wyclif or the
preachers whom he sent abroad.   We read, however, that
"a cursed man doth fully the Sacraments, though it be to
his 'dampnynge.'"   The holy influence which comes of
Christ's real presence does not change ; yet he did insist in

his final treatment of the subject that the value of the mass varied with the character of the priest, in so far as a good man's prayers were more acceptable to God, and his commemorative rite acted with a higher potency on the spiritual condition of the worshippers around him. The withholding of the cup from lay communicants is not brought prominently forward, as by his Hussite followers, for it had not yet been authoritatively ruled. Nor does he directly controvert the usage which distinguished seven sacraments, though he speaks slightingly of some of them, and insists that in the wider sense of the term there might conceivably be more. But he had little sympathy for most of the symbolic and ceremonial practice of the Church.

The whole theory of penance seemed to him to need revision ; the forms of absolution to be mechanical and unreal, hindering the natural and direct relations between the conscience and its God. Confession Confession
and penance.
should be public, free, and unconstrained : the law of secrecy regarding it was "a sacrament of the devil." "Christ made His servants free, but antichrist hath made them bond again "—the system of the confessional, that is, had subjected the consciences of men to priestly bondage. The traffic in indulgences was odious and degrading ; the practice of pilgrimage should be discouraged, for people would do better to stay at home and keep God's laws than to make offerings at the thresholds of the saints.

On some points indeed his tones were wavering and undecided, as on the belief in purgatory and practices of fasting. He has language of high reverence for the Virgin Mother, but of prayers for her intercession, as for Wavering on
some points,
that of the saints generally, he speaks somewhat slightingly, as often pushed to harmful lengths, and good only in so far as the feelings of devotion to the Saviour may be quickened by them. There is no fierce invective against images and relics, as with his followers in after times : they may even be adored, if the mind be chiefly fixed on the Creator, but he called attention to the danger of superstitious usages connected with their worship. In some respects the associations of the past were potent with him still.

But a national reformation, carried out under his guid-

ance, would have meant very sweeping changes, and would
he would have broken completely the visible continuity of
have carried church life.   For prelates, as we have seen, he
reforms far. found no warrant in Holy Scripture: " By ordinance of Christ priests and bishops were all one.   Endowments he condemned.   Priests should live by free-will offerings, and might marry if they pleased.   They should not be
endowed and wifeless against God's authority.   "God ordained
priests in the old law to have wives, and never forbade it in
the new law."   Forms and ceremonies should be disallowed
which could not be shown to have had Christ's sanction.
Freedom of growth, elasticity of organic systems in the Church's
outward life would be arrested by this rule ; no license could
be granted to variety of symbolism to suit the different stages
of religious thought or feeling.   Art as the handmaid of the
Church would have little room to breathe, for "gay windows
and painted houses" are spoken of with disfavour like
church music.   "God forbede that ony christene man
understonde that this here synsynge (incensing) and cryinge
(intoning) that men usen now be the beste servyce of a
preest, for Jesus Crist and his apostlis useden it not."   To
what he calls the "joly chauntynge that stireth men and
women to daunsynge" he applies the words, "this people
honoureth me with their lips but their heart is far from me."
Preaching is the one thing needful.   "Public prayer is good,
but not so good as preaching, for no priest that dwells with
us knows whether his prayer be better than prayer of the
people."   "If our bishops preach not in their persons, but
hinder true priests from preaching to their sheep, they are in
the sin of the bishops that killed Jesus."

There is no reason to suppose that Henry VIII. had any
intimate knowledge of the works of Wyclif, which had long
disappeared from sight in England, or was deter-
The king as mined in his policy by any arguments which might
supreme head.
be read in them, but he might have found in the
treatise *De officio regis*, written soon after 1378, a formal
defence of his own position as supreme head of the Church.
The right of the king to redistribute ecclesiastical possessions,
to devote them even to civil objects in the interest of the
State, is stated there without reserve.   The clergy should be

entirely subject to his jurisdiction, and be deprived by him
of temporal lordship; it is his duty to insist, through the
action of the bishops, on the residence in their parishes of a
learned and zealous clergy, for which purpose the disciplinary powers of provincial councils should be strengthened.
Foreign courts of justice should have no authority, and
Canon Law itself carry no weight except so far as it can be
proved to be in agreement with the law of Christ.

One editor of some of Wyclif's treatises speaks of "his
essential moderation," "paradoxical as it may seem"; another bids us mark that he only "cautiously and
conditionally" calls the pope antichrist; a third
tells us that "his experience taught him that deep-
rooted prejudices and old customs must be treated with a
gentle hand." As regards doctrine the estimate of his
moderation will vary with the ground on which the critic
takes his stand. He held firmly and fervently such essential
principles of the faith as most Christian communities accept;
he spoke reverently of one sacrament at least; but he would
certainly, if he had had the power, have made a clean sweep
of most of the ministerial forms and ancient usages of the
Church. Judged by his own standard his own position was
a false one, alike in his old days of Oxford life and in his
latest years of parochial retirement. To found colleges was a
mistake; endowments were baneful to religion; employment
of beneficed clergy in the service of the Crown was not to be
justified; the usual duties of a parish priest at Easter might
be irksome to one who had spoken with contempt of
"rowning (whispering) in a priest's ear" and "singing in a
painted church." We cannot find indeed in any of his
works a definite scheme of an organised church order to
replace the hierarchical system which he vehemently attacked.
A presbyterian clergy, ministering in homely guise in
buildings unadorned, receiving the necessaries of food and
clothing from the free-will offerings of their flock, bearing
their frequent protest at the worldliness and pride and faulty
Gospel of the old church, laying little stress on any forms but
very much on preaching,—such seems the ideal of his
homilies, and this, with such sweetness and light as it could
carry with it, might be possible in days to come.

Wyclif's
"modera-
tion."

If it be a question of language rather than of doctrine, his sermons like his controversial pamphlets show that the "gentle hand" could be very forcible at times; he owns himself to some harshness of tones and vindictiveness of temper. His parishioners at Lutterworth may have been a little startled when they heard of the prelates who "with stinking words and law made God's law unsavoury," and were but "horned fiends to be damned in hell"; and of the "stinking orders" of the friars, whose letters of fraternity might be "good to cover mustard pots," but not "to win men bliss." Had he not written about the pope as "the head vicar of the fiend," and a "sinful idiot who might be a damned devil in hell," as "glowing with satanic pride and simoniacal greed"; of the cardinals as "incarnate devils"; of the monks as "gluttonous idolaters committing whoredom with the devil," and of confessors who were "idolatrous, leprous, and simoniacal heretics?"

But let us not forget that the abuses which stirred his wrath were very scandalous and widespread, and that earnest feeling cannot always stay to pick its words, while language which offends us with its coarse invective seems in an earlier age to have caused no shock to less fastidious ears. His critics certainly flung back the mud with equal zest, as may be seen in what Fuller calls the epitaph written for him at St. Alban's. "The devil's instrument, church's enemy, people's confusion, heretics' idol, hypocrites' mirror, schism's broacher, hatred's sower, lies' forger, flatteries' sink, who at his death despaired like Cain, and stricken by the horrible judgment of God, breathed forth his wicked soul to the dark mansion of the black devil." Others, punning on his name, turned it into "weak-belief" or "wicked-life," and Adam of Usk spoke of him as Mahomet, who preached "incontinence to the young and confiscation to the rich." Our verbal currency, like the coin of the realm, finds its value changing, though Wyclif himself perhaps did much to fix it in his more enduring work.

For his name has always been associated with the earliest versions of the Scriptures in our English tongue. Up to his time the Latin Vulgate only was in use, though consider- able portions had been translated into Anglo-Saxon long

before, and also into Norman French, while the Psalter had
been put forth in early English half a century before. Contemporary evidence connects him with an entirely   The new
new version. A well-known passage of the chronicler version of
of Leicester conveys not only the statement of   Scripture.
the fact, but also the conservative jealousy which it excited.
"Wyclif translated the Gospel from Latin into the Anglican,
not the Angelic tongue . . . and thus the Gospel pearl is
scattered and trampled upon by swine. What was wont to
be precious to clergy and laity alike is now become a vulgar
laughing-stock to both, and the jewel of the clergy is exposed
to the mockery of the laity, so that becomes for all time a
common thing which had been before a talent entrusted from
above to the clergy and doctors of the Church." John
Hus, the Bohemian reformer, a few years later refers to
the accredited report that "Wyclif translated the whole Bible
into English." Archbishop Arundel, writing to the pope in
1412, says that Wyclif, "the child of the old serpent" and
"fostling of antichrist," had "filled up the cup of his malice
against Holy Church by the device of a new translation of
the Scriptures into his mother tongue." A Provincial Council
at Oxford had indeed already in 1409 proscribed any such
version of Scripture texts by questionable hands without
authoritative sanction. Among the many anonymous pamphlets and homilies in English of this period those which
are with most reason ascribed to Wyclif refer in various
passages to such a work as being actually carried out, to the
urgent need of it for the instruction of the simple, and to
the antipathy with which it was regarded in high quarters.
    "One great bishop of England, as men say, is not well
pleased that God's law is written in English to laymen;
and he pursueth a priest, and summons and troubles him,
because he writes for men this English." . . . "But one
comfort is of knights, that they savour much the Gospel,
and have will to read in English the Gospel of Christ's
life; and "as Lords in England have the Bible in French
so it were not against reason that they had the same
sentence in English." So again, as the high priest and
Pharisees of old had the stone made fast upon the sepulchre
of Christ, "so do our high priests, . . . they dread that

God's law shall quicken after this, and therefore they make statutes stable as a stone . . . and this they mark well, with witness of lords, lest that truth of God's law, hid in the sepulchre, break out to the knowledge of the common people. O Christ, thy law is hid yet, when wilt thou send thy angel to remove the stone, and show thy truth to thy folk." No names, however, are given in this connection.

Our public libraries contain a large number of English MSS. of the whole or portions of the Scriptures, and 170 of these have been described in the great work of Forshall and Madden on the subject. These have always been regarded as the work of Wyclif and his fellow-labourers, though with two exceptions they contain no name or certain mark of authorship. One MS., however, with many marginal corrections, which ends at Baruch iii. 20, is called by the contemporary scribe the translation of Nicholas of Hereford, a well-known follower of Wyclif. A second bears the mark of Purvey, his intimate associate in his latest years. This may, indeed, be meant only as a sign of ownership, but it is now accompanied in the volume by a distinct MS., which there is good reason to believe was actually written by him to serve as a general preface to the books of the Old Testament. The copies fall into two classes, which seem to represent respectively an earlier and a corrected version. The book of Purvey contains portions of both versions, and the pages which are supposed to have been written by him as a sort of prologue to the whole, are also found, in whole or part, in other of the MSS. Another interesting volume preserved in the Bodleian Library, written by five different penmen, with marginal erasures and corrections, looks like the original manuscript of the translation of the Old Testament.

Many copies exist.

On such evidence, combined with the study of the language of the versions, it is supposed that Wyclif, with the assistance of his friends, carried out a complete translation from the Latin Vulgate. Hereford's labours must have been suddenly arrested by his prosecution in 1382, and confinement in Rome after his appeal. Some years later corrections were thought needful, and a revised version was taken in hand by Purvey and others who sympathised with the reforming

movement, but this, it is believed, was not actually completed
until after Wyclif's death.

Further efforts have been made to trace the earlier stages
of the undertaking.   In MSS. of the same period may be
seen commentaries on the several Gospels, and
the book of the Revelation, and passages of the Supposed
authorship.
Epistles, consisting largely of extracts from the
works of earlier divines, but the Scriptural text embodied in
them mainly agrees with the earlier of the two versions just
described.   They are accompanied by prologues which are
unmistakably Wyclifite in tone.   These, it has been thought,
were preparatory studies, leading up to the great work.   This
is, however, a purely conjectural account, with no evidence to
support it beyond the language of the prefaces, in which the
author speaks of himself as a "synful caytif," or as a "pore
caitif lettid fro prechyng for a tyme for causes knowun of
God," or as a "symple creature of God."   Notwithstanding
the general similarity of tone, there is little to remind us in
them of the method and special style of Wyclif.

On the whole then it appears that contemporary evidence
connects him with the new translation of the Bible and points
to no other source, and the many copies of it which exist
have always been regarded as the work of Wyclif or of his
fellow-labourers, and are closely connected with other literary
work which is certainly Wyclifite in tone, though not perhaps
actually written by himself.   But though the plan of the
work may have been suggested and the undertaking organised
by Wyclif, it is impossible to ascertain how much of the
translation was actually written by himself, as he and his
chief critic Thomas Netter of Walden are completely silent
on the subject ; it may be noted, however, that in the Lollard
trials "Wyclif's gospels" are referred to as in the hands of
the accused.

The language of the translation betrays indeed no doctrinal
bias.   It is hard to see why any should be looked for.   The
special objects of attack were the various orders
of the clergy, and the forms and organisation No doctrinal
bias.
of the Church.   It was quite easy to quote passages
about antichrist and the great beast, and Scribes and
Pharisees and false prophets.   With sweeping generalisations

and audacious logic lengthy passages of St. Paul's epistles could be applied to the systems of the day without much straining of the actual words. In a later age, when new translations were proscribed, it was rather the prefaces and notes that betrayed the bias and provoked the censure than the language of the text itself.

In the absence of such questionable features there was no reason why the new versions should be permanently regarded with mistrust. It was an age of translations, and

How far for-bidden. they spread rapidly in neighbouring lands. The primate in his funeral sermon on Queen Anne—so runs the record—said that it was more joy of her than of any other women that he knew, for "she had in English all the four gospels with the doctors upon them. And she sent them unto him, and he said that they were good." If the rulers of the Church would not provide translations, and no contemporary witness says they did so, or that the episcopal sanction which Archbishop Arundel required in 1409 was ever given formally, men would naturally take those which they found ready to their hand, and which contained apparently nothing to excite suspicious fears. The copies which remain are of very varied kinds ; some small and rudely penned, such as humble sectaries might use ; others richly bound and sumptuously prepared for princely homes. Some found a place in the libraries of religious houses, some passed formally through courts of probate in which ecclesiastical authority was supreme : it does not therefore seem that their circulation could have been generally forbidden, though in the trials of heretics of low degree the study of "Wyclif's gospels" was regarded as suspicious, while nuns and others might "have license" to read the psalms in English.

A bishop here or there may possibly have sanctioned in his diocese the use of some translation, whether by Wyclif's friends or other hands, but contemporary writers have said nothing and apparently knew nothing of any encouragement to men engaged upon an authorised version. No existing copy claims certainly any such sanction, as was commonly the case in later days when "imprimaturs" were obtained from the officials of the Church of Rome. When John Stafford, Bishop of Bath and Wells, in 1431 threatened with excommunication any who translated the Scriptures or copied such translations, he made no reserve in favour of any accepted version.

Two points, however, should be noted. In the English homilies which, though anonymous, have been ascribed on the best evidence to Wyclif's latest years, lengthy passages of the Gospels are inserted, and the text Objections. of these is quite distinct from either of the two forms of the version now in question. The author of the Sermons apparently had the Vulgate before his eyes, and rendered it in such a way as he found convenient at the time, in singular neglect, it must be owned—if he was really Wyclif—of what is thought to have been the favourite work of his old age.

Again, Sir Thomas More expressly stated that he had himself seen "Bibles fair and old in English which had been known and seen by the Bishop of the Diocese, and left in laymen's hands," and which were distinct from those of Wyclif. The testimony stands alone; it is not likely that it was a vague remembrance of the Anglo-Saxon Gospels, but it is possible that he may have noticed the variations in the text of the two versions of the period, and have explained them wrongly. In any case his evidence is unsupported, and it is not enough to serve as a foundation on which may be safely built up a new theory—such as has been lately put before us—which would make over both the versions known as Wyclifite to the orthodox labours of entirely unknown hands. Nor is the theory strengthened by the questionable statement that the bishops showed no marked disfavour of translations. We may remember, also, that the devout Caxton, whose ideal of the parish priest reminds us of Chaucer's well-known picture, was busy later on with his printing press in the Almonry of Westminster. If there was an Authorised Version, which the bishops were willing to have freely read, would he not have been attracted to it, or to some part of it at least, even as a trading venture if from no higher motive, and have given some copies of it to pious uses at his death, instead of the Golden Legend which he bequeathed to his parish church in 1491?

But it was not enough to Wyclif's mind to have the Bible in the people's tongue without some further agency to publish it abroad. More teaching was the one thing needful;

K

for lack of that the ploughman in the well-known poem had
had hard work to learn his Creed; preaching was
to him the priest's first and greatest work, far more
precious than the administration even of the Sacraments, for the sermon infinitely excels every other

earthly work. But then it must be Gospel preaching : not
a set of fables or droll stories strung together, as was the
habit of many in his day : not showy rhetoric to dazzle or
amuse, but solid and instructive, setting forth, first, the literal
and then the mystical meaning of the text, delivered not in
the "fat places" only, but in country hamlets, where the
need was mostly felt.

Doubtless there has been exaggeration on this subject.
Preaching in the Middle Ages was not a lost art or a
forgotten practice; there were models and handbooks written
for the pulpit, if men only cared to use them. But we learn
from other sources that the neglect was often very real, and
that the friars, who took up the work at first with such
success, had long since fallen into looser ways. Dante,
indeed, had spoken fiercely of the sorry jests and witticisms
with which the sermons of the day were spiced :—

> Ora si va con motti e con iscede
> A predicare, e pur che ben si rida
> Gonfia il cappuccio, e più non si richiede.
> (*Parad.* xxix. 115.)

So Wyclif tried to train men for the work. While at
Oxford he had lectured to them, not as holding a special
professorship, as has been fancied, but by right of
his degree as Doctor of Divinity. He composed
for them his treatises on the Pastoral Office and the

like, and when his mouth was closed in the old schools of
learning he went on to write his homilies in Latin and in
English, which might serve as models for the use of his
"poor priests." He was in some sense "the founder of a
new order, anticipating in the combination of the regular
with the secular element something of the views of Ignatius
Loyola, but in its practical aspect bearing a nearer re-
semblance to the lay preachers of John Wesley, such as they
were while his strong hand was yet upon them. To be

poor without mendicancy, to combine the flexible unity, the swift obedience of an order with free and constant mingling among the poor, such was the ideal of Wyclif's simple priests." They were to be poor, for so alone it seemed could they follow the example of Christ and His disciples. Like the Mendicants, they were to move among the people freely, and outshine them in what had been thought to be the friars' special work, and, it may be added, if only they followed the example of their teacher in his homilies, they would stir among their rivals a very natural resentment by their indiscriminate invectives.

AUTHORITIES.—The Wyclifite literature is of considerable bulk. In addition to those mentioned above, especially the *Fasciculi Zizaniorum*, with its introduction by Dr. Shirley, we have as original authorities the Latin treatises published by the Wyclif Society in many volumes (London, 1883), of which several are referred to in the text. There are also the *Trialogus*, ed. G. Lechler, Oxon. 1869 ; *Select English Works of Wyclif*, ed. T. Arnold, Oxford, 1871 ; *English Works of Wyclif hitherto Unpublished*, ed. F. D. Matthew, 1880 [E. E. T. S.]. The best modern work upon the subject is *Johann von Wiclif von G. Lechler*, 1873. The early English versions of the Bible are described in *The Holy Bible in the Earliest English Version*, ed. R. T. Forshall and Sir F. Madden, Oxf. 1850. *The Old English Bible and Other Essays*, by F. A. Gasquet, D.D., 8vo, Lond., 1897, present the novel theory referred to in the text. In opposition to this theory see article in *Historical Review*, Jan. 1895, by G. F. D. Matthew. In the quotations from the English works the spelling has commonly been modernised for the convenience of the reader, as it was simply phonetic and varied often. A few only are given as specimens of the old style.

CHAPTER VII

THE SPREAD OF WYCLIFITE SENTIMENT

King Richard II., 1377–1399. Abp. Courtenay, 1381. Arundel, 1396.

THE spread of Wyclifite sentiments went on apace in all classes of society during the closing years of the four-teenth century, but much of this was due to the spirit of the times, and personal influences can-not always be assumed, nor is it possible to measure their extent.

Impatience at the wealth of the clergy.

The vast possessions of the Church were often eyed with natural jealousy, and the laws of Mortmain expressed the misgivings even of her friends. No hostile feeling there-fore was betrayed by the Statute of 1391, which checked the attempts that had been made to evade those laws by special trusts created for the purpose. The ideal of apostolic poverty for the whole order of the clergy was an article of Wyclif's creed ; this discredited in his followers' eyes the system of legalised endowments and spiritual lords, and strengthened the resentment felt at bishops neglecting their proper work to serve as Ministers of State, or swell the crowd of noble hangers-on at court. A century earlier friars like Kilwardby and Peckham had mounted the primate's chair, and personal simplicities were blended with official pomp ; Sudbury himself was not of noble birth ; but now the younger sons of noble families were being pushed up rapidly to high places ; the chief dignities fell to a Courtenay or an Arundel, not as theologians, or even as laborious statesmen, but as the bearers of illustrious names, who rose and fell with party influence and court intrigues. These changes probably intensified the bitterness of the reforming spirit, and made the protests of Christian democracy sound all the louder ; but at the same time they strengthened the powers of resistance, and forged new links of union between the temporal and spiritual lords.

First action was taken in another matter in which ecclesiastical privileges were at stake. The abuses of the rights of sanctuary had long been an offence to the instincts of order and to common sense. Some, *Privilege of sanctuary.* we are told, who had ample means to pay their debts, took refuge in the precincts of Westminster, and living there at ease laughed at their creditors, for the immunities extended not to their persons only but their goods. A scene of bloodshed at this time forced the whole question on the public mind. Two squires, escaping from the Tower, where they had been lodged because they would not give up a Spanish prisoner to the court, took sanctuary at Westminster. One was dragged away, and the other murdered in the choir, in the interest, as it was thought, if not by the orders, of the Duke of Lancaster. The bishops excommunicated the guilty authors and agents of the outrage, excepting indeed the duke by name with others of the royal family, but not escaping his resentment. The whole question of sanctuary was brought up therefore in the Parliaments of Gloucester (1378) and of London (1379). Archbishop Sudbury and the other prelates solemnly protested at the profanation of the sacred building by the recent acts of bloodshed, and asked for due amends to Holy Church for such " horrible wrongdoing." In reply it was averred that certain doctors of theology and of Canon and Civil Law had been examined on the subject, and their opinion was that " neither God nor pope nor king could wish to grant such privileges of immunity " now abused by fraudulent debtors. The prelates on this unlooked-for change of issue had no answer ready, and the matter was adjourned, but finally it was decided to curtail the rights of sanctuary that had been so abused.

The startling events which filled much of the history of this period had a profound effect on public thought and feeling. The great Schism which began in 1378 shattered

for many years the unity of Christendom, and fatally discredited the papal dignity and spiritual claims.   In
England it strengthened immensely the reforming
movement, and made entire mistrust, defiance even,
of a pope seem not merely a patriotic but a religious duty.
On the other hand, a social earthquake shortly afterwards
caused a panic which worked on the conservative instincts
and led cautious spirits to shrink from teachers who seemed
to speak in revolutionary tones.

Effects of
the Schism.

The popular uprising associated with Wat Tyler's name is
one of the most familiar chapters of Mediæval story, but it
concerns us here only in so far as it is related to
the history of the Church and illustrates the moral
conditions of the times.   We need not dwell therefore on the dramatic features of the march to London, the
havoc wrought at the Temple, at the Hospital of St. John at
Clerkenwell, and at the Savoy, where the splendid mansion of
John of Gaunt was ruined, or the entry into the Tower, where
the guards made no defence.   The murder of the chancellor,
Archbishop Sudbury, deserves more special mention.   The
rioters hunted for him as the guilty cause of past misrule.
They found him in the chapel, where he had passed the
night in prayer, and rushed upon him shouting, "Where is
the traitor, the spoiler of the realm ? "   They would not heed
his quiet words of warning, but dragged him out, an unresist-
ing victim, and hacked at his throat with bungling butchery
till he died.   It was the insurrection of the labouring thousands, but it was not the work of starving or despairing men.
The poll-tax may have been an odious impost and the occasion
of a local outbreak, but it was not the cause of the whole
rising.   This was a widespread and concerted movement,
though not entirely simultaneous, with one common feature
in all parts,—the wish to burn old deeds and court rolls and
replace them with new charters..

The
peasants'
insurrection.

Besides the notable incidents which were acted out with
such tragic effect before the eyes of king and court and
citizens of London, there were many scenes here and
there which illustrate better in detail the efforts to
be quit of villenage, with its burdens and restrictions.
The claims in this respect of the great religious houses were

Convents
attacked.

odious above all others both to the rural tenants on their
manors and to the townsmen who lived close to the Abbey
walls.   Discontent was always smouldering.   It had, as we
have seen already, blazed up in red-hot heat some fifty years
before.   Now it burst out again at the same places.   With
encouragement and promises of help from the insurgent
leaders, riotous crowds gathered about St. Alban's, opened
by violence the abbots' prison, rifled the preserves and
fishponds, broke up the pavement of the abbots' parlour,
and carried off the stones of the handmills laid there in
penance by delinquents of an earlier generation.   They extorted also franchises and charters in the forms dictated
by them to ensure surrender of the feudal rights enjoyed
for ages.   The tenants of twenty manors of the abbey were
not slow in following the example set them at the centre.
It was a reign of terror for the poor monks, till the king
himself arrived upon the scene, and the royal justiciar sat in
judgment on the ringleaders of the riot, who found scant
mercy at his hands.   Discouraged, but not penitent, the
townsmen cowered before the storm, and waited for better
days.   The manorial serfs shrunk also into quiet, showing
only by incendiary fires that they did not love the monks
the better for their failure.   At Dunstable like riots followed.

The great Abbey of St. Edmund's suffered even worse
treatment from the insurgents in their neighbourhood.   John
Wrawe, chaplain of Sudbury in Suffolk, a moving spirit among
the peasants, had organised a local rising in concert with
Wat Tyler, the Kentish leader, and many of the secular clergy
were concerned in it.   The Chief Justice, Sir John Cavendish,
was murdered, probably for the part which he had taken in
enforcing the Statute of Labourers in the county.   The
Abbey felt itself at once in special danger.   Within its walls
there had been troublous scenes of late, in which both
townsmen and factious monks had been involved.   The prior
therefore, hearing of the rising, and knowing the temper of
the townsfolk, fled away in haste, but was betrayed and
murdered on the road.   Some others of the Abbey shared
his fate.   The rioters carried off the deeds and charters
which concerned them ; promises of further concessions were
extorted, and precious jewels and relics had to be made over

to the town in pledge. The riot was suppressed in time to save the monks from more humiliations; the town was fined heavily, and the ringleaders—parsons some of them—were hung and quartered.

At Peterborough there was danger of like violence against the monks, but Henry Despenser, the fighting bishop (*pugil ecclesiæ*), who had scattered the rioters with great slaughter at Norwich, arrived opportunely on the scene, and routed the townsmen and the tenants of the Abbey lands, showing no mercy to the poor fugitives, who were pursued even to the Church, and cut down pitilessly beside the altar. "The Bishop deigned to give them absolution with the sword (says the chronicler of Leicester), that so the words of Holy Writ might be fulfilled, 'thou shalt break them in pieces like a potter's vessel.'"

At Cambridge the rioters vented their spite on such old documents as could be found. At St. Mary's the university chest was broken and the muniments destroyed. There was a bonfire in the market-place and "an ancient beldame scattered the ashes in the air, exclaiming, 'Thus perish the skill of clerks.'" It was dangerous, says Walsingham, for any one to be taken for a clerk, and still more if he had an ink-bottle at his side. Schoolmasters too were roughly used and made to take an oath not to teach children grammar any more. Lawyers were in danger of their lives.

The enemies of Wyclif were not slow to discern, or to imagine, a connection between his teaching and the troubles of the recent insurrection. Some saw in them the chastisement of heaven on the heresies which he had spread among a credulous people. Others were sure that Wyclif's teaching must have had a revolutionary influence in social questions as well as in matters of the faith. It was his "poor priests" who must have done the mischief, travelling as they did among the people, sowing the seeds of discontent, and organising a general uprising through the eastern counties.

Wyclif's treatise *De dominio* indeed was but academic and ideal, and he had ceased to call in question the rights and property of the temporal lords, confining his attacks to the possessions of the clergy. He specially defends his

preachers from such charges. "Some men that are out
of charity slander 'poor priests' with this error that
servants or tenants may lawfully withhold rents or services
from their lords, when lords are openly wicked in their
living." Yet it does appear in one of his Latin homilies
that the "unjust steward" was no knave, but tender-hearted
for the tenants whom he would relieve from their excessive
rents. He reprobates in another work the cruelties of the
insurgents and the murder of the primate, but it must be
owned that his censure is somewhat mild. They were guided
by an instinct of justice, as it seems, but did not act quite
legally. The clergy deserved yet heavier punishment; they
stirred up the French war, he said, the cost of which led to
the exactions and to the riot which they caused. They
should have devoted their superfluous wealth to lighten the
burdens on the needy. The secular employments of the
prelates were a scandal to the people: the chancellor-primate
was the most notable offender in that way; when he convoked
the wealthy clergy "it was like an arch-devil calling to
his imps." It was pointed out by Wyclif's apologists that
the insurgents showed special hatred of the Duke of Lancaster, who had been his protector a few years before,
and special favour to the friars, to whom at the time he
was bitterly opposed. But this argument does not prove
much. Wyclif had many sympathisers among the citizens of
London when they rioted against his patron in the streets
and put him in danger of his life, while the chronicler of
Leicester, who hated Wyclif, had a notable tenderness for
John of Gaunt. The alliance between them was short-lived,
and the peasants may have never heard of it at all, and had
good reason to mistrust the selfish schemer. The favour
shown to the friars is not conclusive, for the country folk
were not thinking of their controversial attitude as to the
mysteries of the faith, but of their simple life as wandering
preachers.

There can be no doubt that there were many of the clergy
at this time who must have deeply sympathised with the
peasants' longing for more freedom. Born in a state of villenage
themselves, they found the gate of liberty in Holy Orders. The
claims of the lord upon their labour ceased when they were

enrolled in the service of a higher Master, and his consent had therefore to be asked and often paid for when the studies began which were to be followed by the tonsure. The Commons complained indeed in 1391 of this promotion by means of learning (*par clergie*) as too frequent for their liking. Those who had escaped themselves could not but have a lively fellow-feeling for their kinsmen and their neighbours on whom the old restrictions were still binding. And they were drawn nearer to the class from which they sprang, and farther from the privileged orders by the repressive legislation of the recent past. A Statute of 5 Rich. II. mentions those who go " from county to county and from town to town in certain habits under pretence of great holiness, preaching not only in churches and graveyards, but in markets, fairs, and other public places where people mostly assemble . . . which persons do also preach divers matters of slander to cause discord and dissension betwixt divers estates of the said realm both temporal and spiritual, to the great peril of all the realm."

Sympathy of the clergy.

One of these, John Ball, had been well known for years, and the burden of his harangues is described for us in like terms by the chroniclers of St. Alban's and by Froissart. The latter speaks of him as taking his stand in the churchyard when the congregation left the church, and saying to the assembled crowd, " Good people, things never will go well in England till goods are all in common, and there are neither villeins here nor gentlefolks." And they would remind each other in the fields, or as they walked from one village to another, " This is what John Ball says, and he says truly." According to the chronicler of St. Alban's he took for the text of his sermon to the insurgents at Blackheath the words of the old song—

John Ball.

> When Adam dalf and Eve span
> Who was thanne a gentilman ?

The chronicler of Leicester speaks of Ball, indeed, as the forerunner of Wyclif, for he had been many years before the world as travelling preacher, and had been lodged in the archbishop's prison at Maidstone as a pestilent

agitator.   The rioters are said to have broken open the
prison doors and freed him, as they certainly did in other
cases.   But the "poor priests," whom Wyclif had been
sending out for some time past into the country hamlets,
came from the same class, had the same sympathies, and
may well have shared the sentiments of Ball.   Without any
social programme dictated by their master, they had heard, no
doubt, his theories of dominion founded upon grace, of the
corruptions of a wealthy clergy, of apostolic poverty, of the
right to take away the gifts abused.   The theory was
socialistic, if the conclusions were not practically drawn.
What wonder if they did so apply it and make it part of the
gospel which they preached.   Only by some such agency,
familiar with the rural life, speaking to the people in the
people's tongue, can we explain the widespread combination
organised, prepared, stirred suddenly to action on so large
a scale in so many centres far apart

The phrases that have come down to us in old English as
passing between the leaders of the movement under their
feigned names of Jack Straw, Jack Milner, Jack *The temper*
Carter, and Jack Trewman, are such as may have *of Piers*
been used often by the rustic preachers : complaints *Plowman.*
of the evil days when "falseness and guile have reigned too
long" and "true love is away"; hopes that now "skill may
go before will" and "right before might"; prayers that "they
may stand manly together in truth in the name of the Trinity
and by their Lady's help."   They may seem but poor dog-
gerel mainly, but the spirit is that of the "Vision of Piers the
Plowman," which in its earliest form had been already for
twenty years before the world, and gained a popularity that
made its names and phrases familiar to thousands of the
people.   With nothing revolutionary in its tones, with no
word of dissent from the Church's ancient creed and practice,
its author, William Langland, had expressed in homely language
much of the strong feeling that was burning in the hearts of
thousands, the passionate impatience at the evils that were
widespread in the social life around them.   A poor cleric
himself in minor orders, earning a scanty pittance probably
in church choirs or scrivener's office, with little reverence for
lords and ladies, or the proud emblems of official pomp, he

had the most earnest sympathy for the hardships and the trials of industrious poverty in rustic garb, which he had known intimately before he became familiar with the life of cities.   He speaks with bitter irony of pope and cardinals, bishops and clergy, such as they were too often, not as they might be in a reorganised society.   He abounds in varied illustrations of the degraded ideals and the demoralising influence of monk and friar ; he fiercely exposes the shortcomings of ecclesiastical lawyers and officials ; but the true royalty and priesthood are to his eyes divinely sanctioned ; they should rest on the loyal support and affections of the people.   Reason and conscience are vouchsafed to man to be his guide, with Scripture for the ultimate standard of appeal ; moral tests, not ceremonial observances, are all-important.   The poorest labourer can have light and leisure enough to find his way along the path of duty, and excel in holiness and charity the would-be teachers and rulers of the world.

In the letters which passed between the insurgent leaders, if we can judge fairly from the scanty fragments that have been preserved, there were no angry threats like those in the later stages of the movement, when the ranks of countrymen were swollen on the march by outlaws or disbanded soldiers.   The men who wrote as Jack Carter, "Ye have great need to take God with you in all your deeds," had no thought of the acts of savagery that Wyclif of course condemned.   But like him they from the first complained that "clerks for wealth work woe," and like him they sympathised with the townsmen of St. Alban's or St. Edmund's, who smarted under the burden of old privileges and feudal claims. Whatever we may think of the influence of Wyclif's teaching and that of his poor priests upon the earlier stages of the peasants' rising, there can be no doubt that many at the time confidently assumed that the two sets of facts stood in intimate relation to each other.   The confession made by John Ball before his execution, or invented for him afterwards, states this without disguise, and the excesses of the rioters in London threw a lurid light on what might else have passed unnoticed as the social vagaries of a theorist.

Wyclif had gone on to attack without disguise the

time-honoured dogmas of transubstantiation. It was quite
safe to call him to account for this however men   Wyclif's
might be divided as to Church property or papal   tenets
claims.   The high-born Courtenay, who followed condemned.
Sudbury as primate, was a man of resolute temper, embittered
probably by the memory of his failure to proceed with
Wyclif's trial at St. Paul's, determined now to act warily but
firmly. The first step was to judge the thought without explicit
reference to the thinker.   In May 1382 an assembly of
divines was summoned to the Church of the Blackfriars to
consider certain questionable teaching of the times.   The
" Earthquake " Council, as it was called from the startling
disturbance which was variously interpreted as a warning on
either side, condemned twenty-four articles which had been
publicly set forth in the University of Oxford and spread by
wandering teachers through the country.   Ten were branded
as heretical, as impugning the true doctrine of the Eucharist,
of auricular confession and the authority of the pope.   Fourteen articles were censured as erroneously dealing with
Church property, the religious orders, and the right to
preach and teach.   That some of these theses, like the
startling paradox that " God ought to obey the devil," should
be condemned was a foregone conclusion ; it remained only
to apply the sentence.   A mandate was issued by the archbishop to the bishops and to the University of Oxford stating
that the theses had been examined by men of ripe learning
and experience with whom he had taken counsel, and that
no one should be allowed to lecture or teach to that effect.

Something more than spiritual censures was desired,
and for this the concurrence of the State was needful.
Parliament was held in May 1382, and the archbishop, after
deploring the heresies and licence of itinerant preachers,
moved that instructions should be given to the king's officers
to seize any whom a prelate should desire to have arrested.
An ordinance to that effect was agreed to by the Lords, but
the Commons in their next sitting in October complained
that it had been enrolled as a Statute without their consent,
and begged that it should be withdrawn, and this accordingly
was done.   The king, however, had also, on July 12th of the
same year, by royal patents given powers to the bishops to

seize and detain in their own prisons, till further action of
the king or council, any who should publish or defend the
obnoxious theses.   With their hands thus strengthened,
the authorities of the Church proceeded without loss of
time to vigorous action.

Coercion was first to be applied at Oxford.   The university
was the centre where the obnoxious articles were first put
forth, and the wandering preachers trained.   Its
highest officials, supported by a large body of
opinion in academic circles, were now in favour
of the speculative novelties, and still more of the intellectual
freedom which made their discussion possible despite the
protests of bishops or of pope.   Dr. Berton, the chancellor,
and an assembly of doctors had indeed already condemned
as heretical the sacramental theory of Wyclif.   He had
appealed against the sentence.   Lancaster, who came expressly down to Oxford, tried in vain to silence him, and he
put forth a further statement of his creed.   Soon afterwards new officials were appointed who were in Wyclif's
favour.

The archbishop's mandate was treated with contempt, his
commissary silenced, and encouragement given to sermons
before the university·of the most defiant type, and notably by
Philip Repyngdon, of whom we shall hear more.   But on
the 12th of June Dr. Rugge, the chancellor, was cited to
appear at Blackfriars before the archbishop and his council
of divines, and forced to declare heretical the theses lately
censured.   He was solemnly warned, threatened with excommunication if he persisted in his contumacy, and ordered to
publish in the university the mandate which had been
suppressed, as also to withhold from Wyclif and his leading
partisans all right of public speech or scholastic exercise
within the university.   As he complied with a bad grace,
and showed that he was of the same mind still, he was
censured by the Privy Council, which sent instructions to
Oxford that the teachers of heresy must be silenced.   One
of the royal household had been insulted there a few
years before, and lampoons on the king were sung under
his window.   The royal chancellor had sharply censured the
independent tones of the university authorities, and talked

Coercion at Oxford.

even of degrading them.   They were now to be effectually
humbled.   Meanwhile Nicholas of Hereford, Philip Repyngdon, and John Aston, the most prominent advocates of the
new doctrines, had been summoned for examination by the
archbishop and appeared before his council.   They put in
written confessions of their faith, but these were judged to be
unsatisfactory and evasive.   Aston was condemned as a teacher
of heresy on the 20th ; the other two not appearing for final
judgment on July 1st were excommunicated for contempt
of court.   The ban pronounced on them was solemnly proclaimed at Oxford and throughout the province of Canterbury,
and this was followed by royal patent to the university (July
13), directing diligent inquiry for all the teachers or the
books which helped to spread the heresies.   Accordingly a
few years later we read of the expulsion from Queen's College
by the Archbishop of York, as visitor, of several Fellows
whose sympathies with Wyclif were too marked.   Vigorous
search was made throughout the country, especially in the
dioceses of London and Lincoln, where the novel opinions
were most widely spread ; the " poor priests " were hunted
down, the friars helping freely in the chase, and in October
Repyngdon and Aston were tracked out, and making at last
a full submission, were absolved by the archbishop from the
ban, and restored to all the privileges of their degree.
Nicholas of Hereford escaped to Rome, where he was
imprisoned by the pope, to whom he had appealed, and
remained there till 1385, when rioters in the city broke
open the papal prison and set him free.

   The strange thing is that the prime mover in all the
trouble was left to close his eyes in peace at Lutterworth,
while his poor followers were hunted down on every
side.   It is true that, if we believe the chronicler of   *Wyclif left in peace.*
Leicester, Wyclif was summoned by the archbishop
to appear before him at Oxford in a full court, when he entirely
recanted the articles condemned.   But there is no evidence to
support this statement, which is quite alien to Wyclif's character.   In the confession in old English which is there ascribed
to him, not a single tenet is withdrawn, and the language on
the Eucharist is quite consistent with his general teaching.
The official summary of the Provincal Council, which met,

November 8th, at St. Frideswide's, Oxford, is quite silent on the subject, though the formal submission of Repyngdon and Aston was received there, and it cannot be believed that Wyclif obtained rest by disguising his convictions. Far from that, a memorial was laid before Parliament by "the heresiarch of execrable memory," which reaffirmed in the plainest terms his favourite theses of independence of Rome, apostolic poverty, the unscriptural status of the friars, and the errors of transubstantiation, with other conclusions which "would make the ears of a faithful hearer tingle." The attitude of this Parliament, which complained of the pretended Statute that had never had its sanction, probably arrested further action against the bold thinker, in whose case it was not safe to push matters to extremes.

The Commons declared that they would not bind over themselves or their descendants to the prelates more than their ancestors had been bound of old, and Wyclif had powerful protectors. There were members of the council even who at heart were at one with him in his views about the Church, and their influence may have shielded him, for he cannot have been thought less dangerous—though he was charged with heresy—than the humbler men who were hunted down around him. Possibly a stroke of palsy may have also saved him from attack. For in 1384 in his last days he was cited to the papal court, but excused himself from going with the words, "God has constrained me to the contrary."

There was one event at this time which cannot have been without its influence in strengthening the reforming movement. Henry Despenser had been promoted to the See of Norwich by the pope as a reward for military service, with slight regard for spiritual fitness. The old combative instinct showed itself at once in him during the insurrection of the peasants. Next year he received a commission from Pope Urban to head a crusade against the adherents of the antipope, and into this he threw himself with all the ardour of a man of war. Indulgences were promised far and wide on the most liberal scale; noble women in their mistaken piety poured their treasures into his military chest; and as the antipope had secured the obedience of

The crusade of Despenser, 1383.

France, Englishmen eagerly took up the enterprise as a sort
of national duel. But Wyclif's soul was stirred with indignation at the news. He passionately denounced the expedition
as a scandalous abuse of sacred names and high professions,
with its lying impostures to deceive the credulous, and deeds
of horror sanctioned by would-be vicegerents of Christ. The
crusade was an utter failure ; a few gleams of success at first at
the expense of the poor Flemings, who were no parties to the
quarrel, nor even on Clement's side ; and then after a fruitless
siege of Ypres an ignominious retirement from the field,
to be soon followed by the bishop's impeachment and
disgrace.

The chief centres of Wyclifite influence at this time seem
to have been Oxford, London, Leicester, and Bristol. In
London the people had showed their sympathies with
the new doctrines by their attitude at the trial of
John Aston, as they had done before in the case
Wyclif's
influence in
London.
of Wyclif himself, who had "hurried from church to church
to spread his opinions there." The irreverent crowd
presumed to break open the doors of the council hall where
the archbishop was seated with his theologians and doctors,
and to disturb the course of justice (1382). Moreover, with
the sanction of the mayor, the citizens ignored at the
same time the episcopal jurisdiction in cases of sexual
immorality, and dealt themselves with the offenders on the
plea that the spiritual courts were grossly lax, and from
sordid interests accepted money fines for grave offences. A
few years later (1387), when Peter Pateshul, an Austin friar,
became a Wyclifite, and was disturbed in his preaching as
an apostate by members of his order, the Londoners not
only thrust them out of the church, but following them in
angry crowds, would have set fire to their house, if one of the
sheriffs had not quieted the storm with gentle words. And
so the Londoners are spoken of as "not right believers in
God nor in the traditions of the forefathers, as withholders of
tithes and abettors of the Lollards."

At Leicester, where one of our informants lived, a few
miles away from Lutterworth, the movement spread rapidly,
and ardent preachers found enthusiastic hearers. Among
them William de Swinderby was the most famous. He had

sometime as a hermit declaimed against feminine extravagances and the deceitfulness of riches, then joining the reformers he changed the subject of his preaching and
At Leicester, bitterly attacked the character and claims of the
clergy of the day.   Dressed like a hermit still, he came as
"in sheep's clothing," we are told, "but inwardly he was a
ravening wolf."   Suspended from preaching in any church
or holy ground, he would not be silent, and the people
flocked to the old mill-stones which he used as a pulpit on
the high-road.   At length the Bishop of Lincoln called him
to account.   Three friars of different orders came forward to
accuse him and produced a muster-roll of his "pestilent
seductions," but the Duke of Lancaster stepped in to save
him on condition that he recanted his errors publicly where
he was known.   That done, his popularity around soon died
away, and he retired to Coventry, whence too he was
hunted out.   It was at Leicester also that John Aston
preached in the hearing of our informant, who describes
him as among the most indefatigable of the poor priests,
who, staff in hand and careless of all personal comforts,
sped on foot restlessly from place to place, denouncing
ecclesiastical abuses, and calling with outstretched hands
upon the people to relieve the bishops of the burden of
their wealth.

John Purvey laboured specially at Bristol, to which he
retired from Lutterworth after his master's death.   A man
of simple garb, saintly aspect, and unwearied
and Bristol, energy as preacher, he shared above all the spirit
of his master Wyclif.   His friends alone were "the true
preachers"; all the rest, friars especially, were to his mind
false.   To the eyes of the monk of Leicester he and others
of his type were all alike in what seemed their scandalous
abuse of their opponents, in the domestic and party strife
they stirred, "followers of Mahomet rather than the gentle
Jesus."

In the diocese of Salisbury, so the bishop was informed,
there were irregular forms of ordination, on the strength
of which wandering preachers assumed priestly functions
with the sanction only of their peers.

The fervour of new convictions violently shook at times

the habits of reverence for old associations. Men heard
with horror that the statues of the saints were roughly
handled and sacramental elements profaned by and
being put to common uses. One woman in London Salisbury.
set up an altar in her chamber and taught her daughter
to burlesque the action of the priest in the solemn function
of the mass, with dress and tonsure all complete,
continuing the practice till it reached the bishop's Irreverence.
ears, and the offenders were made to do penance for their sin.
Such indecencies account for the fierce intolerance with which
the chroniclers of Leicester and St. Alban's inveigh against
those who were striving "to rend asunder mother Church in
whose bosom they were reared." "That the ark of the Church's
faith might not be hopelessly shattered by these rude shocks,"
the Lords and Commons in the Parliament of 1388 appealed
to the king against such teaching, and he issued letters
patent to the bishops enjoining them to take vigorous
action, and providing that commissioners in each county
should hunt out dangerous writings and bring up for trial
any who might have issued or helped to publish them
abroad.

But during this period at any rate persecution appeared
only in its milder forms. Writs of arrest might indeed have
been demanded against the stiff-necked and scornful if they ignored the spiritual censures launched Little
persecution.
at them, but in these earlier days they commonly
explained away obnoxious phrases, or put in some form of confession which was accepted by the court, or submitted themselves
without reserve to the judgment of their "Father in God."
Thus in the archbishop's visitation of the diocese of Lincoln
some inhabitants of Leicester, and among them a chaplain
and a female recluse, were cited to appear before him, and
after some delay they "abjured their profane dogmas" and
did penance in public. One walked through the streets
barefoot and bareheaded, stripped to his shirt and drawers,
holding in one hand a lighted candle and in the other an
image of St. Katharine, to which he did obeisance three times
in the market-place to make amends for his insult to the
saint, whose statue he had broken up with contumely to boil
his cabbage.

Walter Brute, a learned layman, graduate of Merton College, Oxford, was denounced to the Bishop of Hereford as a "child of Belial," who had been many times accused of the "cursedness of heresy." He appeared before the bishop at his manor of Whitbourne, and to the charges brought against him he made answer by "divers scrolls of paper," in which he rehearsed his creed, saying that if the pope made any laws contrary to Christ's Gospel of charity, he was an "idol of desolation" and a "pestiferous mountain infecting the whole earth." After abounding in many Apocalyptic figures he begged to be excused in that he was "not plentiful in pleasant words." The bishop probably agreed with him in that, but he merely told him that his writing was "too short and obscure," and desired him to answer "more plainly and more at large." Brute readily took up the challenge, and drew up a declaration which certainly was not too short this time, for it fills fifty closely printed pages of Foxe's *Acts.* It exhibits an intimate familiarity with Scripture, and vehement invective, combined with acute reasoning, against some of the authorised doctrines and practices of the Mediæval Church, with much, of course, about Antichrist and the Number of the Beast. After an inquiry which lasted through three days, Brute gave way and made a public recantation at the cross in the churchyard. But the sentiments which he retracted, under urgent pressure, were not stamped out so soon, and the sympathy of the people's poet found expression in the lines of "Pierce the Ploughman's Crede":—

Walter Brute recanted.

> Byhold opon Wat Brut whou bisiliche thei pursueden,
> For he seyde hem the sothe.

There is one feature of interest that may be noticed in the trial. Among the names of those who sat on the Commission we may read that of Nicholas of Hereford, once a prominent Wyclifite, who was in 1382 excommunicated for contempt of court (*v.* p. 143). After his return from Rome he had submitted like the rest and received a special protection from the king, in case the past should be brought up against him. He became chancellor and afterwards treasurer of Hereford cathedral, and the duty was im-

Nic. Hereford.

posed upon him of helping to condemn solemnly what in earlier days he had stoutly maintained to be the truth.   The feeling of his former friends found natural expression in a bitter letter which has been preserved, accusing him of putting his hand to the plough and looking back, and becoming therefore a master of the Nicolaitans, blind and unskilful to expound the Scripture.

The prelates of the period happily had little of the fanatic zeal of the inquisitor.   The writers of the time indeed complained in piteous terms of the culpable indifference of the bishops, who saw the evil plainly and heard the call to action, but "made light of it, and went their way, one to his farm, another to his merchandise."   In the earlier stages of the movement Archbishop Sudbury no doubt held back, either from partial sympathy with the new doctrines or from tolerant and cautious temper.   Courtenay, his successor, was more resolute ; Wakefield of Worcester denounced the novelties in his pastoral of 1387 ; Despenser of Norwich would allow no Wyclifites undisturbed within his reach.   But they had little interest in nice questions of theology, though they could not brook open defiance of the dogmas of the Church.   There were men of rank and influence, however—whose names are recorded for us—who deeply sympathised with the "poor preachers."   If those loud voices could be only silenced, it was hoped that the dangerous novelties might be forgotten, and the whole movement die away.

It did not pass so speedily, but gave very soon a startling proof that it was still a living force, and must be reckoned with by the rulers both of Church and State.

In 1395 two prominent adherents of the new doctrines in the House of Commons, Sir Thomas Latimer and Sir Richard Stury, laid before Parliament a memorial which summarised the special tenets of their party, and petitioned for the State's help to enforce them.   The leading principle in this appears to be that moral verities, faith, hope, and charity, must be the rule by which all spiritual dogmas and practices should be tried and measured.   Judged by this test, the temporal possessions of the Church, with the pride and pomp to which they ministered, and the secular

Attitude of bishops.

Petition in Parliament.

employments of the clergy, which distracted them from their own religious work, were alike radically faulty. Priestly celibacy, auricular confession, the vows of nuns and pilgrims, were on the same account condemned. The sacerdotal system as enforced by Rome—"stepmother of the English Church"—was far other than the "holy priesthood" recognised by Christ's apostles. The memorial was posted up on the doors of Westminster Abbey and St. Paul's, where it appealed to a wider audience and was discussed more freely than in Parliament, where it seems to have been still-born. But Convocation was alarmed, and called upon the archbishop to take prompt measures to defend the faith from such aggressions. The bishops, startled themselves at the memorial, sent in haste a deputation to the king, who returned without delay from Ireland to suppress the revolutionary programme, and silence by dire threats its leading promoters in the Commons. He forced even the suspected partisans of heresy to take an oath to renounce their schemes.

Archbishop Courtenay died in 1396, but his successor, Thomas of Arundel, showed at once that he desired resolute action against all innovators in religious matters. In his first year a Provincial Council was held in St. Paul's Cathedral, in which Wyclif's characteristic tenets were of course condemned ; but Arundel saw that it was needful to do something more to arrest the spreading movement. He first encouraged a learned controversialist, Thomas Netter of Walden, to write an elaborate book called the *Doctrinale* to refute the dangerous tenets. He was minded also to go on to more repressive measures. But his immediate action was suspended by his own personal troubles connected with grave political affairs.

Thomas Arundel, Archbishop of Canterbury, 1396-1414.

In the Parliament of 1397 a bold attack was made upon the government in a Bill which was laid before the Commons and accepted by them, and the condition of the royal household was also severely handled. There were too many bishops always in attendance, it was said, maintained with their retainers at the king's expense. It was prayed that they might dwell on their estates and not at court, both for the relief of the king and also for the help and salvation of their subjects. The king

Complaint of the king's household.

took grievous offence at these bold words, but accepted the humble excuses of the Commons.   The member, however, who had proposed the article obnoxious to the court, Sir Thomas Haxey, canon of several cathedrals, was adjudged in Parliament to deserve a traitor's death.   But he was claimed by Archbishop Arundel, and saved by privilege of clergy.

The primate himself had soon cause to fear the worst for his own life or fortunes.   His brother, the Earl of Arundel, fell suddenly a victim to the resentment or the fears of Richard ; the archbishop became first a prisoner, then an exile, and soon afterwards he was translated by Boniface IX. to St. Andrews at the king's request, the treasurer Roger Walden being nominated in his stead to Canterbury, 1398.   Little minded to submit to this disgrace, he threw himself unreservedly into the intrigues and plots which finally dethroned Richard and gave Henry of Lancaster the throne.   Thanks to these political convulsions, there was a breathing-space during which the religious malcontents had peace, but they had reason in the long-run to rue the change.

Fall of Archbishop Arundel.

Richard's own sympathies had been strongly marked at times in favour of repressive measures, and as his epitaph at Westminster records, he " overthrew the heretics " when revolutionary tones were heard, or archbishop or pope were urgent in the matter.   He had acted promptly, though fitfully, in his writ to the bishops in July 1382, and in his support of the primate's authority at Oxford.   He had written in strong terms against Swinderby and Brute, and passionately resented popular movements in the Commons in favour of reform.   But the gentle influence of Queen Anne, till her death in 1394, if not directly used in the interest of the reformers, gave encouragement to what they had at heart,—the spread of truth by the use of an open Bible.   Bohemian scholars who had come in the train of their princess, or were attracted afterwards to her new home, carried back with them to their native land the books of Wyclif which they had read at Oxford or elsewhere, and began the religious propaganda which issued after a few years in the tragedy at Constance (*v.* p. 167), followed by

Attitude towards reform of king and court.

the terrible convulsions of the Hussite wars. Whatever may have been the sentiments of Richard or the leanings of his Bohemian wife, Wyclifite influence had been strong among his courtiers. With the altered policy of a new dynasty came a marked change of temper in dealing with free thought.

A description of public sentiment upon this subject would be incomplete without some mention of the satiric poems of the times. Formal history reflects chiefly the opinions of great men in Church and State; its materials were compiled by monastic chroniclers or secular clergy, and among them, in literature at least, scarce a voice was raised in favour of the followers of Wyclif. It was quite otherwise with the homely poems that passed from mouth to mouth among the people. Severely moral in their tones, passionately impatient with vices and follies in high places, they appealed to the same popular tastes as the "Vision of Piers Plowman," and took a more decided part than Langland in the great controversy of the age. In place of his satire, with its lights and shadows, we find unqualified invective, as in a song against the friars in which the writer says of them :—

Popular poetry Wyclifite.

> All wickedness that men can tell
> Reigneth them among ;
> There shall no soul have room in hell,
> Of friars there is such throng.

Another poem called the "Complaint of the Ploughman" is completely Wyclifite in tone. The prelates are described as luxurious and proud, turning holy Church into a prostitute. Priests oppress their flocks, spend nothing on the poor, lead guilty lives and sell the Sacraments ; their place in the other world shall be that of Dives. Poor preachers are hunted down and put in prison. The officials of the Church courts are greedy and extortionate. For an incontinent act a man must pay twenty shillings, and then have licence to do the like for a whole year. This curious poem takes the form of a dialogue between a pelican and a griffin, as advocates respectively of the reformers and the old order of the Church. Worsted in argument the griffin flew away in a rage, but returned with a motley flock of ravens, magpies, kites and others as allies.   The pelican took to flight thereon ; but he too returned after a while, bringing with him the phœnix, who made havoc of the party of the griffin, slaughtering many of them and driving the rest away into their hiding-places, which they left no more.   This prophecy, written probably before the fourteenth century was closed, implies a curious insight into the fact that the hold of the Wyclifites upon the mind of the country was too partial and precarious to endure, and that a long time must elapse before the phœnix would appear and the old order pass away for ever.

The people's jingling ballads, written in the vulgar tongue, were mainly on the same side, before the panic caused by the people's rising in 1381 had died out of men's minds ; but a poem was written in Latin by one who sincerely thought that the revolutionary excesses connected with the names of Wat Tyler and Jack Straw had been largely brought about by the bold sectaries, who had unsettled the foundations both of Church and State.   Christ's garden had been beautiful and fruitful here, he sang, till the old enemy of mankind had sown the tares, but now the Lord's vineyard was laid waste ; " O now plague-stricken land, that didst teem with all sound learning free from the taint of heresy, stranger to all error, exempt from all deception : now thou rankest as the chief in all schism, discord, madness."   The new preachers of strange doctrines were the authors of division among the laity and clergy, guilty of incendiary ravages and servile war.   " John Balle taught us this, when for his villany he paid the penalty of death : that there was a nest which harboured a vicious brood and reared them to the shame of the whole realm : pointing to the sect of Wyclif, the primary cause of the strife which caused panic in our land, giving proof manifest how grave the folly was which it spread like poison through the people."

The poet Gower wrote for a more cultivated public, choosing classical metre for his Latin verses.   Clear-sighted and outspoken as he was in his attacks upon the general corruption and misgovernment John Gower, died 1408. at the end of Richard's reign, he could see no good in the religious novelties brought into the world, he thinks, by Satan, and spread by hypocrites for their own nefarious ends.

AUTHORITIES.—The fifth book of the *Chronicle of H. Knighton* (Rolls ser.), which has many details of the Wyclifite movement, is not apparently by Knighton himself. Walsingham and the *Chronicon Angliæ;* Foxe, *Acts and Monuments of the Christian Martyrs*, ed. G. Townsend, 1841 ; *Political Poems and Songs relating to English History*, ed. F. Wright, 1859-61 (Rolls ser.), must be referred to, as also the *Vision of Piers Plowman*, ed. W. W. Skeat, 1867 ; *Pierce the Ploughman's Crede*, ed. W. W. Skeat ; *L'épopée mystique de William Langland*, J. J. Jusserand, 1893.

CHAPTER VIII

A NEW DYNASTY

King Henry IV., 1399. Henry V., 141?. Henry VI., 1422. Abp.
Arundel, 1396. Chichele, 1414.

RICHARD THE REDELESS—the ill-advised—as he was called in
Langland's poem, had shown no lack of affection for the Church.
Many of the bishops were his personal friends or _{Scenes of law-}
trusted servants, several were spoken of as his _{less violence}
_{under Richard.}
boon-companions ; they owed their places often to
court favour ; there were still offices of State to be conferred,
and good things to be picked up by nimble hands.

The example was a tempting one to follow ; one poor
benefice was not enough for any who had family interest or
winning ways. The pluralist, absent from his cure, cared little,
the poet Thomas Hoccleve tells us, if it rained or snowed upon
the altar of his dilapidated chancel ; his flock might pine in
vain for " holy sermonynge," " He recketh never how rusty ben
his schepe." The laity on their side were not always mindful of
regard for the ministerial office or for sacred places. They
carried their feuds into their churches and assaulted the priest
as he went about his work. The bishop meantime was far
away, and unable to protect his clergy. The parson of Hilgay
was pursued for a distance of two leagues by turbulent
neighbours with naked swords and clubs, and dared not go
near his church or parsonage to hear the confessions of his
parishioners even in the time of Lent. The ringleaders were
so strong in local influence, or " of such horrible maintenance,"
that it was idle to look for help to common law or sheriff,
and the suppliant appealed directly to the chancellor and

Royal Council. Another parson sought redress in the same quarter. He had had to take steps to get his customary dues from the executors of a deceased parishioner. Excommunicated for default of payment, and backed up by a powerful patron, they occupied the church in force, so that no mass could be sung on Christmas morning, or on the festival of Epiphany, and they tried even to force the parson to take to flight through the windows of the chancel. A third petitioner complained that when he was already robed for service in his church at Whitsuntide another priest with a body of armed men rushed in, and threatened to cut off his head unless he ransomed himself at once to save his life. He had to take his vestments off, and leave the church to enter into a bond for £20, and let them seize meantime all the stock upon his glebe. His enemy's local influence was so great that his only hope lay in the chancellor's sense of duty.

Such incidents may serve to illustrate Hoccleve's statements, that it was a time of lawless violence when the strong took the law into their own hands, and the courts were often Weak bishops. powerless to do justice. They also show that the Church had urgent need of resolute rulers, who would use their large powers of administrative control, and the sanctions of their spiritual courts, to make the parochial clergy do their duty, and screen them from outrage in their work. Such men were rarely to be found, it seems, among bishops tied to business of State, or pliant courtiers chosen to amuse their master in his lighter moods, or as the Chancellor Robert Braybrooke, Bishop of London, not overweighted with nice scruples, when the Greal Seal had to be used in questionable ways. They did not make others suffer much for conscience' sake, nor did loyalty to their royal master cost many of them dear. Poor friars were found to cherish his memory and spend their lives in his behalf, but the bishops for the most part were content to accept the new regime.

Roger Walden, indeed, had to give way at once before Arundel, whom he had displaced at Canterbury, and his jewels were seized as he was trying to remove them ; but he was not harshly treated, and after a few years of obscurity he gained the See of London by the generous support of the archbishop. Thomas Merke, Bishop of Carlisle, was one of the few

who were faithful to Richard to the last, but though present at
the Parliament in which Richard was deposed, there is no
evidence that he raised his voice in his behalf, or uttered
anywhere in public the fine sentiments which Shakespeare put
into his mouth. He took part in the plot to set Richard
again upon the throne, and was found guilty, but was soon
again at large, and though he lost Carlisle and was translated
by the pope to an obscure See of Samaston, *in partibus
infidelium*, as Arundel had been to St. Andrews, he was
allowed to take up occasional work for other bishops. One
or two more are said to have been imprisoned or banished
for a while. Richard Clifford, however, afterwards Bishop
of Worcester, one of the king's closest intimates, risked
nothing for his royal patron's sake, but lived to vote for
Martin V. at Constance, and possibly to determine his
election.

Archbishop Arundel was the leading spirit in the policy
which the new dynasty adopted; a capable and resolute
statesman, with no pretensions as a theologian or a
scholar, but determined to defend the recognised
creed and institutions of the Church, and to crush
all opposition with a strong hand and little mercy. He had large
claims upon the gratitude of King Henry, whom he had helped
to seat upon the throne, and as chancellor as well as primate
he could do more than any man to shape the policy of the
Crown while he influenced the temper of the clergy. Henry
had from the first relied upon the bishops for support, and
pledged himself to respect the interests of the Church. His
father, John of Gaunt, indeed, in bygone days had threatened
its temporal possessions; he himself in earlier life was heard to
say, in jest or earnest, that "princes had too little and the religious had too much," but as king he kept his promise faithfully.
The support of the Church, which he looked for in return, was
not given so fully as he might have hoped. In the plots and
insurrections which disturbed his peace for years, ecclesiastics
of high rank freely joined; the friars were mutinous and
disaffected; Convocation was often niggardly and backward
in its grants; but the king was not provoked by all this to
change his attitude, and he resisted Parliamentary attacks
upon the possessions of the clergy, to whom he looked for

Henry IV. supported the Church.

loyalty to the established order, while he posed also as defender of the Faith against heretical assaults.

In his first Parliament the "benefit of clergy" was specially confirmed, but this privilege was speedily withdrawn when Walden and Merke and others were put upon their trial for their part in the conspiracy to restore Richard to the throne. All were found guilty, and two priests died a felon's death at Tyburn, but the ecclesiastics of high degree were soon released. Their attitude, as they were personal friends of the deposed monarch, was natural enough, and they met with signal clemency.

Benefit of clergy disregarded.

The early years of the new dynasty were full of varied troubles which combined to cause a general unrest and disaffection. Philip Repyngdon, sometime Wyclifite and Chancellor of Oxford, now abbot at Leicester and friend of Henry, painted in a letter written to him a gloomy picture of the disorganised society, but had no remedy to offer save the truism that the king should do his duty. Others had little hope from that, and would appeal rather to the passions of the people.

The begging friars were very busy. Full of sympathy for the popular misery and discontent, they caught up greedily the rumours that Richard was not really dead, passed on jingling scraps of prophecies that might mean anything or nothing, which the sainted John, Prior of Bridlington had written, as they fancied, for their comfort, and fanned the flame of discontent in every little gathering in the streets or village tavern. Many were arrested, especially Grey friars, and found short shrift and little mercy. A chronicler gives us some details about the trials in which the king himself took part. In one of these a friar of Aylesbury admitted that he had expressed joy when he heard the rumour that Richard was alive, for he and his were much indebted to that monarch. "If he and I were fighting on the field of battle," asked the king, "whom would you side with?" "Certainly with him, with staff or whatever weapon came to hand; and if we won the day I would make you Duke of Lancaster again." Then, said the king, "you are no friend to me, and by my head, you forfeit yours." The friar was tried and condemned, dragged on a hurdle through

Friars disloyal,

the streets, and hung at Tyburn, and his head was stuck on London Bridge.

Next came the turn of the older religious houses to show their disaffection.   In Essex there had been turbulence and local feuds for some time past among them; restless spirits were excited by false rumours; designing knaves went to and fro with lying tales, and in 1404 treasonous conspiracies were being hatched, in which the abbots of St. John, Colchester, St. Osythe, and Byleigh, with many of the monks, took part.   Being less resolute, however, than the poor friars, the more prominent of them tried finally to save their heads by giving evidence against the other malcontents and plotters, and the whole movement ignominiously collapsed.   A rogue indeed, by trade a sawyer, relying on these tales of disaffection, gave evidence of a treasonable plot in which fifty-seven abbots and priors, and other dignitaries, had conspired with Owen Glendower against the king, but he was hanged himself as a false witness.

and monks.

Meantime the clergy, secular and regular alike, were growing indignant at the repeated demands for further grants to meet the expenses of the Crown.   The king had promised at the outset of his reign that no tax or tallage should be laid upon them, except under necessity.   They were told that his financial straits were very urgent, and from causes beyond his own control; but like the Commons they felt that the expenses of the royal household were too large, and the grants to his favourites too lavish. Hard times made themselves felt in their own homes, and they sorely resented the burdens laid upon them.   It needed all the influence of the primate, and the muttered threats of jealous laymen, and the proposals of confiscation actually made in the "unlearned Parliament" at Coventry in 1404, to force them to consent to subsidies with which the king on his side was ill content.   Wealthy bishops were ready with their loans, which enabled him to meet the pressing calls, and it was not wise to estrange his best supporters.

Burdens laid on the clergy.

Yet Henry risked a further strain upon their loyalty when he doomed Archbishop Scrope to a traitor's death.   That prelate had shared the discontent which was widespread among the clergy of the North, and had been in sympathy

with the insurrection of the Percies. He took part in an
ill-concerted rising with other disaffected spirits, and put out
in a lengthy proclamation an appeal to the public
conscience against Henry as having connived at
the murder of the king whom he dethroned.
Among other charges bearing on the political
conduct of affairs, it was stated that in spite of his pledges

Richard Scrope, Archp. of York, executed 1405.

he had burdened the clergy with inordinate taxation, and
brought before secular courts and put to death friars, monks,
priors, and abbots, without regard to the " benefit of clergy "
which he had promised to observe. It was urged also,
besides, that he had maintained the " nefarious " statutes
which, to the grave discredit of religion, took from the pope
all power to dispose of the offices of the English Church.
Deluded by the colour of negotiations, the insurgent forces
left the archbishop to his fate. He was arrested, and
the king, urged on by rash advisers, decided on his death.
Despite the protest of Sir William Gascoigne, the Chief
Justice, who insisted that by the laws of England a bishop
could not be condemned to death, despite the urgent
remonstrances of Arundel, who had ridden in hot haste to
Bishopsthorpe, an irregular form of trial was hurried through,
and without delay the archbishop was ignominiously beheaded. This impolitic act of vengeance made Scrope a
martyr in the people's eyes ; pilgrimages at first were frequent
to his shrine.. The pope, Innocent VII., was moved to excommunicate all who took part in his execution, but the king
with caustic wit replied to his inquiries by sending him
the prelate's armour, and asking him to see " if this be
thy son's coat or no," only to meet with the rejoinder, " an
evil beast hath dèvoured him."

It had been one of Henry's first acts after his accession
to declare that he would see that the Church should have
worthy rulers. It remains to ascertain what was
his attitude in the many questions of ecclesiastical
preferment. Scrope's manifesto painted the exist-

Abuses of patronage.

ing abuses of patronage in the darkest colours. Scarce a
prelate could be found, it stated, who had not made an
unholy compact to retain a half or a third of the value of
the benefices which he had to give ; young illiterates were

promoted who could bear witness to the sins of spiritual
patrons; the universities were being ruined, for no regard
was paid to worth or learning—a complaint which Hoccleve
earnestly repeats: these abuses were explained to be consequences of the Statutes of Provisors when they were
enforced.   Extravagant as the statements sound, they come
also from less questionable sources.

In episcopal appointments Henry asserted his will strongly.
He repeatedly refused to accept the papal nominees; thus
Richard Clifford was kept out of Bath and Wells;
Adam of Usk was disappointed of his hopes of Episcopal
Hereford; and Robert Hallam was not allowed to appointments.
go to York.   For some years, indeed, Sees were kept vacant,
as neither pope nor king was willing to give way, but
Henry's resolution proved the stronger.   It was the principle
that he withstood; the men whom he set aside were of varying character and antecedents.   Clifford had been regarded
as King Richard's boon-companion, faithful to him to the
last, but was now Keeper of the Privy Seal.   Adam of Usk
had been once a gay roysterer at Oxford, prominent in
"Gown and Town"—"chief champion of the Welshmen"
is his own phrase; then he settled down quietly to legal
work and was employed as Commissioner in high affairs of
State; but in 1400 "the old Adam" in him broke out afresh,
and he sallied forth as a highwayman and robbed a traveller
at Westminster of horse and purse.   As this made the neighbourhood too hot for him, he betook himself to Rome to sue
for the pope's favour, and the bishopric that was long in coming.
Robert Hallam was perhaps the most distinguished man of his
time for dignity and learning; Chancellor of Oxford; prominent as councillor both at Pisa and at Constance; one of the
few men of his time who opposed religious persecution on
the ground that "God willeth not the death of a sinner."

The king was not more yielding to the chapters than to
the pope.   Prior Tottington, chosen by the monks of Norwich, was put in prison by him for a year, before he was
allowed to take possession of the See, for when the *congé
d'élire* was given they had not waited for the nomination of
the Crown.   His own choice naturally fell on his own
ministers and agents—on Henry Bowet, his trusted confidant

and treasurer (Archbishop of York); on Thomas Langley, keeper of the Privy Seal (Bishop of Durham); on Nicholas Bubwith, who was treasurer (Bishop of Sarum). The servants of the Crown were worthier men than those of the last reign, and filled the episcopal office with more dignity if not with much distinction. The statesman Arundel, the learned Hallam, Chichele the future primate, were not selected by himself; and his half-brother Beaufort, whom he seated at Winchester on Wykeham's death, though a great figure in the world of politics, was more at home in the council-chamber than his diocese, and was little credited with high ideals or even with consistency of blameless life.

The king readily accepted, if he did not himself originate, the decree of the great council (February 1408), which put at his disposal for the expenses of his household the possessions of the alien priories which had repeatedly been seized by the Crown in time of war, as well as the income of any bishopric which might be vacant. We read of no protest at these precedents for secularising the property of the Church, and the bishops themselves were complaisant enough. It might seem little as compared with the sweeping schemes of confiscation lately issued, but it was a difference not of principle, but of degree. On the other hand, the king's gifts to the Church were not excessive. He was indeed the "pious founder" of a chantry of St. Mary Magdalene on the battlefield near Shrewsbury, but he did little more for it than rob four parish churches of their tithes for its endowment, and grant it the privilege of a yearly fair, which cost him nothing, though the neighbouring town perhaps had reason to complain.

In estimating the attitude of Henry towards the rulers of the Church it must not be forgotten that he lived during the shameful period of the papal Schism, which had wide-reaching influence in every Christian land. The ostensible causes of the scandal may be found in the overbearing violence of Pope Urban VI., whose want of tact and self-restraint disgusted the cardinals, who had reluctantly elected him under pressure, as they urged afterwards, from the populace of Rome when it clamoured for a Roman or at least an Italian pope (1378). But for the real causes we must look back to the long-continued residence of the papal Court at Avignon—the so-called Babylonian captivity of the Church. For seventy years and more French influence had been dominant at that court; the cardinals were mainly Frenchmen, who had no mind to leave the ease and refinement of their palaces at Avignon for the rude turbulence of Rome and the strife of Italian factions. The electors of Urban had fondly hoped to return home from their banishment, but they soon found, to their dismay, that there was no hope of that from their new master, who outraged their self-respect by his want of courtesy and tact. Then they bethought them speedily of the constraint at Rome which marred their choice, declared it null and void, and elected Robert of Geneva, with whom as Clement VII. they presently went back to France.

Dynastic interests or national feuds determined the allegiance of the different States of Europe to one or other of the rival popes. National quarrels, bitter enough already, were still more envenomed by the religious sentiments invoked; ecclesiastical thunders rolled over the combatants, as pope and antipope excommunicated the supporters of their rivals, and the parodies of a crusade began, till they were hissed off the stage as an ignominious failure. Urbanists and Clementists passed away, with the popes from whom they took their names, and still the scandal to the patience and faith of Christendom continued. *Influence of national feuds.*

The world, indeed, soon wearied of the spectacle; pious souls mourned to see the Papacy, the symbol of Church union, degraded by this sordid strife; the religious orders were distracted by the jarring claims on their allegiance, and the disputes by which they were rent sometimes in twain. The abuses and anomalies of the schism were tempting themes in England alike for earnest Lollards and irreverent wits, but from the remoteness of both papal centres the political intrigues and complicated questions in dispute were realised less clearly. England was protected in large measure by her Statutes of Provisors and Præmunire from the burdens which pressed with increasing weight on other countries from the exactions of the two papal Courts. The two strong popes—Benedict and Boniface *The world wearied of it.*

—whose names were so much in men's mouths elsewhere, were comparatively little heard of here.

Gregory XII., deserted by his cardinals in 1408, and threatened with a General Council, made a bid for the support of England by making Bishop Repyngdon, the king's confessor, one of his new cardinals, but the Englishmen of note who were in Italy at the time had sided with the deserters, and Henry, pressed by Arundel, promised to support them at all risks (*etiam si conscindi debeamus in frusta*).

The archbishop had already summoned a special Convocation to debate at St. Paul's upon the crisis. In his letter the

The Convocation at St. Paul's. Church was likened to Rachel weeping for her children—the champions of the faith—and refusing to be comforted, because she could not find them. The ground was parched and dry, though the health-giving waters—the pope and cardinals that is—were at Lucca; but the mouth of the well was closed by the great stone of vainglory, and there was no Jacob there to roll it off. The pope had ignored all his fair words and earlier pledges, had created new cardinals, and worn out the patience of the others till they appealed from the Vicar of Christ on earth to the Church's Head in heaven, and to a general council which could sit in judgment on the doings even of ruling pontiffs. They now sent from Pisa to implore the active sympathy of English churchmen. The king, "most Christian champion of the Church," was ready to sanction and promote their efforts in the cause. This reference to Henry's action in the matter probably weighed more with the archbishop's readers than his frigid rhetoric and inappropriate figures. At the meeting, which was largely attended by all orders of the clergy, while the king himself was present (July 1408), it was agreed that payment of papal dues should be suspended till the Church had one undisputed head.

Finally, in 1409, it was decided to send representatives to Pisa, and Bishops Hallam and Chichele, and Thomas

English delegates at the Council of Pisa. Chillenden, the experienced prior of Christ Church, Canterbury, with other delegates who accompanied or followed them, at their own charges, or at the cost of their religious orders, arrived on April 24, with a guard of two hundred mounted men, a month after the

opening of the Council.   Bishop Hallam was treated there with
marked respect, and had the first seat on the Bishops'
Bench, on the left hand of the cardinals, on the ground
that England was evangelised by Joseph of Arimathea before
the other nations.   He at once addressed the assembly at
great length, and his resolute advice is said to have decided
his wavering colleagues to reject the overtures of Gregory, to
pronounce both popes schismatics, and to proceed to a fresh
election.   Peter Philargi, once a beggar boy of Crete, now Archbishop of Milan, was elected on June 26.   The decision of
the Council was recognised without much delay in England,
after complimentary letters had passed between Pope Alexander
V. and King Henry, in which reference was made to a meeting
between the two in Lombardy in 1393, and to the pope's early
studies and distinctions won in the University of Oxford.

But after a few months Alexander sickened and died, and
the masterful Baldassare Cossa stepped into his place.   Yet
the electors fully knew that his character and
antecedents were in striking contrast to the spiritual John XXIII.,
May 1410.
ideal of his great office.   Indeed, in the course
of the same year Archbishop Arundel denounced a certain
" fox " who, with " damnable presumption," ascribed " enor-
mities " to our " modern " pope.   The bloodshed and rapine
of camp life, the sensual excesses publicly reported of him
in the recent past, made his election to St. Peter's chair,
if but a tithe was true of what was rumoured, a monstrous
outrage on the moral sense of Christendom.   It seemed,
indeed, that the strong hand had lost its cunning when
he rose from being legate to be pope ; and difficulties
thickened round him, till he was forced to bid for the support
of Sigismund, king of the Romans and future emperor, and
submit reluctantly to his hard conditions of summoning a
General Council to be held at Constance, an imperial city
where Sigismund's authority was paramount.

The prospect of the promised Council deeply moved the
heart of Europe.   There was a general desire on all sides for
some wide-reaching changes.   Earnest spirits in
every land were denouncing the deep-seated abuses Desire for
reforms.
in the Church ; the complaints were being formulated not by hot enthusiasts or Hussites only, but by monks

and theologians whose orthodoxy was undoubted. It may be enough, however, for our purpose to describe the moderate programme of reform which was drawn up by the University of Oxford at the request of Henry V. As an official document it is expressed in guarded language, with none of the vivid colouring and passionate invective to be found in the contemporary pamphlets. It briefly specifies under forty-six articles the more notorious evils in the Church's corporate life which called for prompt and effective treatment in the coming Council. It recognises the claims of John XXIII. to obedience as rightful pope, but hopes he may have grace to retire freely from his office in the interests of union and order. Indulgences should not be hawked abroad for sale, nor excessive fees demanded by the papal Curia, nor benefices granted "in commendam"; simony, and nepotism, pluralities and non-residence, appropriations of churches or intrusion of alien incumbents, monastic exemptions, clerical worldliness and immoralities—these were the sore places in the Church's life which were laid bare with an unsparing hand. The Crown decided that the bishops of Bath and Wells, Salisbury, and St. David's, and others lay and clerical, should appear at Constance, with full powers to act as the representatives of the English Church.

The Council opened formally in November 1414, but some months passed before the princes, bishops, theologians, and sightseers mustered in full force. The Italian prelates on the scene far outnumbered those from other lands, and fifty new bishops had been made by Pope John for the purpose. But when the English delegates arrived on January 21, Bishop Hallam suggested that the Council should be organised by nations as in the universities, and that an equal number from each nation should finally decide on every question. This was accepted by the French and Germans, and their consent was fatal to the Italian opposition and the pope's hopes of leading the Council as he pleased. On all sides it was agreed that the one thing needful was the concurrent abdication of the three claimants to the Papacy, and to discourage John yet more papers were circulated which laid bare without disguise the scandals of his earlier life. At last he promised to resign

Council of Constance, 1414.

if his rivals did the same, but he shuffled and procrastinated, and then escaped to Schaffhausen in disguise. He was cited to appear before the Council to answer to the charges based on a terrible record of the scandals of his life, and finally was ignominiously brought back and solemnly deposed (May 29).

Before this steps had been already taken to defend the faith, and these were to lead ere long to the disastrous strife of the revolutionary movement in Bohemia. Hus, in whose writings there is little more than the thoughts of Wyclif in Bohemian dress, had been long promi- *Death of Hus, 1416.* nent as a teacher in the University of Prague. As preacher in the chapel of Bethlehem he appealed to the national instinct, which had been deeply stirred by the pretensions of the German students, as well as to the desire for ecclesiastical reforms which were sorely needed through the land. Formally condemned by the Archbishop of Prague in obedience to a papal Bull, he had been urged to appear before the Council, and plead his cause as the champion of reform. The safe conduct given him by the emperor was set at nought and he was put upon his trial. His judges heard him patiently and with such fairness as was possible at that day, but there could be but one issue with an accused who would retract nothing unless he could be proved to be in error. He was solemnly degraded from his priestly office and handed over to the civil power to be burnt, and a year later his friend Jerome of Prague followed him also to the stake. Both met their doom with calm composure, but the flames which were kindled for them set their native land ablaze.

The Council now proceeded to consider schemes of ecclesiastical reforms. But mutual antipathies and feuds of jarring factions asserted themselves strongly and embittered the debates. In March 1417 the French *Reforms and feuds.* delegates formally protested that England should not rank as a separate nation in the Council, as it was not on a par with France, Italy, Germany, or Spain, which included several states in each. Either it should be included in the German nation or the whole system of voting should be changed. The protest indeed found little favour, but the English answered it with much parade of argument, and some questionable facts and figures. They urged that the lands subject to the English king had a far greater extent than those of France, including 110 dioceses, while his adversary of France had only sixty. It was 800 miles long and had 52,000 parish churches, and was converted by Joseph of Arimathea, while France had but 6000, and owed its Christian faith to Dionysius the Areopagite.

The cardinals and the curial party now began steadily to urge the election of a new pope to close the schism. All else could wait for that. Many were weary of the long delays, and feared the Council might disperse before a pope was chosen. So long as the resolute Hallam was alive, his great influence secured steady support to the reforming policy. But he died in September 1417, and his colleagues were then ready to discuss with the cardinals the forms of a new election. Henry V. may have thought the time had come to yield, and his uncle Henry Beaufort, probably with his consent, found himself conveniently near the scene of action. It was suggested that he should be asked to mediate between contending policies, and with his help it was arranged that a pope should be elected. On November 11 the choice was made, and Oddo Colonna was announced as the new pope, to be known henceforth as Martin V. According to Walsingham the election was decided by the sudden announcement of Bishop Clifford of London that he would vote for "my lord the Cardinal Colonna," which was followed by general agreement. If we believe Gascoigne he owed his rise to Beaufort, whose intrigues displaced a better man. It was soon found that the Council had a master, and the sanguine dreams of the reformers faded speedily away. The cardinals, who were morally guilty of the schism, had saved their privileges and high position, and the status of the Papacy itself.

One of Martin's first acts as pope was to repay his debt of gratitude to Beaufort by offering him a cardinal's hat. It was rumoured also that it was intended to appoint him for life the special representative (*legatus a latere*) of the Roman See in England, and to obtain a licence for him to keep as cardinal his bishopric of Winchester. The first of these would have been an unprecedented change; legates had been sent before on

Election of Martin V.

Henry Beaufort, Bishop of Winchester, 1405.

special missions and with temporary powers; a life appointment of that kind would seem to supersede the Archbishop of Canterbury as standing legate (*legatus natus*), degrade the highest official of the English Church, and be a visible sign and instrument of constant interference with the free action of its constitutional life.

The primate Chichele, unlike the high-born Arundel and Courtenay who preceded him, had nothing but his talents, and the influence gained by his steady industry in the service of the Crown as lawyer and diplomatist, to strengthen his ecclesiastical position. He was naturally alarmed and wrote to Henry V. in urgent terms to deprecate the innovation, and the danger was averted by the king's refusal to allow Beaufort to accept the proffered honours.

Henry Chichele, Abp. of Cant., 1414-1443.

For the king's policy as regards the National Church was like his father's, and his serious conviction in religious questions was much stronger, "all his intente being," as a contemporary document expresses it, "to lyff vertuously in mayntenynge of holy church." He listened favourably to Hoccleve's plea to write to the pope to confirm the chapters' choice, rather than ask for his own nominee to be preferred. He sympathised with the grievances alleged at the high fees of the courts Christian, and with the petitions of the Commons as to non-residence and pluralities. He warned the leading monks that each must set his house in order, but he gave no signs of large reforming schemes, or of any jealousy of the possessions of the Church, which he heartily supported. His benefactions to the Church took the old form, which was becoming rapidly a matter of the past, of founding religious houses. Besides a convent in the manor of Sheen, established for Carthusian monks, he endowed a more important one at Isleworth, of the order of St. Bridget of Sweden. Syon convent, like the Gilbertine houses of early date, was intended for inmates of both sexes. For a century and more its high repute did honour to the memory of its royal founder, and though dissolved in evil days its members clung together, and came back after a long exile to an English home.

Religious attitude of Henry V.

Martin V. had soon perceived that the old position

of the Papacy could not be restored in England unless the antipapal legislation of the past could be repealed. The Statute of Provisors barred the way when he would reward his ministers, and fill the highest posts with trusted agents. The Statute of Præmunire sadly limited the rich harvests reaped before from Roman Bulls and appeals to Roman courts. It was of vital moment to sweep them both aside, and he spared no efforts to effect this end. In 1421 he begged Henry V. to take the task in hand. Next year, at the opening of a new reign, he wrote in urgent terms to the regent to the same effect. As nothing came from these appeals to statesmen, he vented his anger on the leading churchmen, who seemed lukewarm in his cause. He would humble their pride of local independence and show them that he was their master. When Chichele gave notice in 1423 of indulgences that would be granted to pilgrims to the shrine at Canterbury, he was sharply rebuked by Martin, who spoke of his presumption in setting up his tabernacle of salvation in the face of the apostolic seat as being like that of the fallen angels who desired "to set up on earth their seat against the Creator." In 1426 Beaufort was nominated cardinal once more to protect the interests of Rome in England, and there was now no strong ruler on the throne to forbid him to accept the honour. He was urged to bear in mind the splendid devotion of St. Thomas of Canterbury to the interests of the Church, and to use his influence with all classes to secure the repeal of the detested statutes. The clergy were to preach on the subject to the people, and the University of Oxford was specially required to exert its energies in the same good cause.

Martin V. attacks the statutes,

It was on Chichele, however, that the storm fell at last with fury. In a letter to the two archbishops, in which as an affront to the Primate of all England the See of York was given the first place, the pope rebuked them in the haughtiest tones for their criminal indifference to duty in presuming to meddle with the patronage to which he had himself the exclusive right, as defined by the constitutions of the earlier popes. He bade them take note themselves, and warn formally all others whom it might concern in England, that all the claims

and Chichele.

of the Holy See which had been thus reserved were guarded
by ecclesiastical sanctions of the weightiest kind, notwithstanding any papal concessions that might be pleaded,
or any customs or statutes even of the realm.   Chichele
could not meet the storm with any show of dignity or
spirit.   He thought or wrote mainly of the personal aspect
of the question.   Malevolent detractors had poisoned the
pope's mind against the Duke of Gloucester, the Protector,
as if he were hostile to the Church, an allusion probably to the
supposed influence of Beaufort, the duke's constant rival.
They had spoken bitterly against himself to shorten his days,
or drive him to resign his office, though he was but the loyal
creature of the pope, too old and feeble to defend himself
in person.

Martin's reply was peremptory and stern.   The reference
to the Protector was irrelevant talk ; let the archbishop answer
for himself, not with fair words but prompt and loyal action ; it
was not, as he was credibly reported to have said, mere sordid
interests of lucre, but the honour and dignity of the Holy
See that were at stake.   The archbishop must warn urgently
the councillors of the king to repeal the execrable Statute of
Provisors, which impugned those rights to the peril of their
souls and the ignominy of the State.   No pleas could be
accepted in default of prompt performance of that duty.

It was soon rumoured that the pope, mistrusting the
sincerity of Chichele and impatient of delay, had decided to
supersede the archbishop as legate by the appointment of
Cardinal Beaufort in his room.   Chichele refers to this
possible insult in a letter of protest to the pope, but in
indefinite language, as an attack on the holy see of Canterbury, never made since the days of St. Augustine.   The
Bull which suspended Chichele from his office of legate and
from all jurisdiction over cathedral dignities during a vacancy
was presented duly to the archbishop by the papal nuncio
on March 29, 1427, but was demanded at once in the
king's name to be sent unopened to the Protector, as derogatory to the Crown and contrary to the statutes of the realm.
In anticipation, however, of the papal missive, the contents
of which were noised abroad, the archbishop had been busy
with a protest.   It affirmed that he was an obedient son of

the Apostolic See, but that in the possible event of any attempt of Pope Martin V. or any other to impair his rights and the prerogatives of his See and his privileges as legate, he appealed to a General Council representing the Universal Church, before which, when next convened, he was entitled to submit formally his claim of right. This mention of a Council was most distasteful to the pope, and may have made him hesitate before pushing matters further.

Meantime the attack upon the aged prelate was met on all sides with expressions of sympathy and national feeling. The bishops joined in a collective protest; the University of Oxford set its seal to a long and weighty testimonial; the lords temporal combined to sound his praises; the ready pen of Abbot Whethamstede of St. Alban's with its stock of inapposite Scriptural allusions was enlisted in the cause to defend the chaste Susanna, attacked by the malignity of wicked men, and to appeal from the calumnies of Babylon to the judgment of a Daniel, to be found haply on the papal throne.

Remonstrances in favour of Chichele.

The pope was little moved by this outflow of laudatory rhetoric, and wrote only in curt phrase to Chichele to tell him that it was clear that the will might be wanting in him, but not the power, to serve the Church. Later in the year, after direct appeals both to the king and Parliament, he poured out on Chichele a stream of vehement invective against what he called the shameful neglect of duty and the sordid self-seeking of the prelate who stood by, like a dumb dog, while the wolf was injuring the sheep. The execrable statutes had made the king supreme over the Church of England, as if he were Christ's vicar upon earth.

Further indignities.

Chichele submitted to the indignities thus heaped upon him and stooped to be the advocate of papal claims. When the next Parliament had met, the two archbishops, with five of their suffragans, but unaccompanied by any of the lords temporal, appeared at Westminster before the Commons (January 30, 1428). The primate discoursed at length upon the text, "Render to Cæsar the things that are Cæsar's, and to God the things that are God's," pleading for the repeal of the statute against

Plea to repeal the statutes.

Provisors, and dwelling tearfully upon the peril to their souls' health and the welfare of the realm if they braved the spiritual thunders that were threatened. The Commons did not share his fears, nor feel inclined to modify the statutes of the realm at the command of Rome. They presented, however, a petition to the Crown to the effect that false charges had been laid against the archbishop of acting with disregard to the privileges of the Court of Rome. Ambassadors should be sent, therefore, to beg the pope to give no credence to such slanders, and to suspend all such proceedings. The king assented, and in July 1428 instructions were given for the payment of the envoys to be sent to Rome.

Martin's attempt to intimidate the English Government had failed; the hateful statutes were not withdrawn, but he had humbled the primate, and shown him to the world as holding a merely delegated power. *Martin's policy.* Constitutional usage required the king's sanction for the admission of an extraordinary legate into England; the withdrawal from the archbishop of the ordinary legatine authority, as threatened by Martin, would only have left Chichele independent of control so long as he was supported by the Crown. But Chichele was old and feeble and cowered before the storm. Martin had succeeded in asserting by a vivid object- lesson the old theory of the Papacy—now furbished up anew—that all the bishops were but papal delegates, whose authority was in all points derived from the supreme pontiff.

Another feature of his policy was a startling innovation on the earlier practice. Cardinal Beaufort's rivalry with the Protector Gloucester had long distracted the councils of the State and disturbed the peace of London; his *Cardinal Beaufort.* wealth and energies and royal birth had gathered powerful adherents round him. When their head became a Roman prince, his followers tended to be papal partisans. From that source came the "underhand intrigues," the backbitings of "jealous rivals," the "scandalous imputations" to which reference is made so often in the letters of Chichele and his supporters. In the crisis of the struggle Beaufort indeed was far away, taking part in an ill-starred crusade against the Hussites, but he returned in 1428 to raise money for the pope, who asked for a grant from the clergy for the Bohemian war. The Duke of Gloucester declined to recognise his legatine authority. As cardinal he had retained his bishopric, and this was called in question by the duke in April 1429, when the bishop claimed as Prelate of the Order of the Garter to officiate at the festival of St. George. The matter was debated before a Great Council specially assembled for the purpose, and the Lords agreed that there was no precedent for his retention of the bishopric as cardinal, and begged him to waive his claim to take part in the ceremony, for they were unwilling to prejudice the rights of the king while still a minor in such a questionable matter.

He had vacated his place in council, but in December 1429 the Lords in Parliament requested that he would resume his seat, only abstaining from attendance when any matters were in question which concerned the relations of the king or his realm to the Holy See.

The cardinal's mission gave occasion for further friction between the Roman Court and Chichele, who wrote to the

Refusal of a subsidy to the pope.

pope in 1429 to complain that he was charged with conspiring with his brother of York and other prelates to reverse a decision of the clergy to grant a notable subsidy for the campaign against the Bohemian heretics. It was easy for him to state that no such grant had been intended or withdrawn, for the cardinal had chosen to have men rather than money, but the archbishop appears not to have been quite so hearty in the cause as he would have it thought. The grant, indeed, was not of much avail; for news came of disasters to the English arms in France, and the forces levied for the papal expedition were detained by the cardinal to serve in the French war, much to the indignation of the pope, who in consequence withdrew from him his legatine commission.

The direct advantage gained by the Court of Rome from the services of Beaufort was not great, for while in England

Beaufort retains his bishopric

he was absorbed in his rivalry with Gloucester, and his influence at home was prejudiced by the papal livery which he had donned. Indeed the question of his right to retain the bishopric of Winchester was raised again on November 6, 1431, before the

Great Council, when the precedents were brought forward of the retirements of Kilwardby and Langham. It was agreed only that the records should be searched, and the judges should be asked for their opinions. But the Commons sent up a petition that he should be secured from pains or penalties for any offence under the Statute of Provisors, or for acceptance of any papal Bulls. To this the king assented, and the cardinal's status was not questioned any more.

His claims to precedence over the archbishop might be readily conceded, for they could be made to rest on his royal blood, not on his papal honours; but when Archbishop Kemp of York became a cardinal, and was allowed *and precedence.* also to retain his dignities in England. Chichele was less disposed to let him take the foremost place. In the House of Lords the higher claim of the Primate of all England could not be disputed for no foreign prince sat there by right. As to precedence elsewhere the question was referred to Pope Eugenius IV., and his decision was a foregone conclusion in Kemp's favour on the ground that cardinals were set by the pope over the Universal Church.

We may note, however, that, in his later years, Chichele took a different tone in the long-standing controversy between council and pope from that of earlier days. At Constance his influence with the king had been *The Council of Basel, 1431.* thrown decisively into the scale against the pope; at Basel the instructions given to the English envoys laid stress on moderation and respect for the authority of the ruling pontiff. It may be that the resolute self-assertion of a strong central power in the Church had had some influence on the old man's mind, and so when he begged to be allowed to lay down the burden of an office too weighty for his feebleness to bear, and suggested the choice of a successor, it was John Stafford whom he named, a friend of Beaufort, and like him a papal partisan.

Though he was not of commanding genius, nor resolute enough to confront the haughty arrogance of Martin V., his name stands high above those of *Chichele as ruler* the other primates of the fifteenth century. His aim throughout was to be the constitutional ruler of a

National Church ; Convocation was to be regularly convened, not merely to grant subsidies and present petitions
to the Crown, but to advise on matters of administration, and
to guard the faith by its judicial action.　Trusted adviser
as he was of Henry V., he would not enforce his will by
royal mandate, nor use authority delegated by the pope.
Though lawyer and statesman in his prime of manhood,
he made the ecclesiastical duties of his high office his
foremost care.　As Bishop of St. David's he had wished to
devote himself entirely to spiritual work.　When the primacy
was forced upon him the friendship of the king and the
obligations of his rank in the Privy Council involved frequent
labours of diplomacy and statecraft which could not be
neglected.

We may sweep aside as unattested fiction the malicious
charge mentioned by Hall the chronicler, and passed as
current coin by the poet Shakespeare, that the
war with France was urged on by his fiery rhetoric,
inspired by the desire to divert the interest and
energy of Englishmen from the threatened spoliation of
the Church.　In the next reign he confined himself mainly
to religious duties, and took little part in the struggles of
the rival factions.　While sympathising with the popular
policy of Gloucester, and dreading the papal influence of
Beaufort, he came forward at times for the sake of peace to
mediate between them.

*not the
cause of war.*

He had deeply at heart the interests of learning.　It was
not without good reason that the University of Oxford, in the
letter which it wrote to deprecate the wrath of
Martin, laid such stress on the loving care of the
archbishop which had brought so many pious and
learned clergy "into the vineyard of the Lord of Sabaoth."　As
early as 1417 he had taken note of the discouragement and
loud complaints in academic circles that halls and lecture-
rooms were being fast deserted, because preferment went by
favour only, and modest worth found no rewards.　He
passed through Convocation an appeal to patrons to present
only members of a university, and ruled that no one but
a graduate should be a dignitary of the Church.　It was less
easy to secure enforcement of such rules, and again in 1421

*His care for
learning.*

and 1438 he encouraged in Convocation the public utterance of the complaints that were renewed in the ancient seats of learning.

He gave far more than fair words and kindly condescension. Trained himself in Wykeham's noble foundations of Winchester and New College, he followed in later life in the steps of that great man. He purchased Founded
All Souls. many of the estates of the alien priories which were being confiscated for Crown uses, that they might serve as an endowment for the stately and enduring monument to which his name has been linked in later ages,—the College of All Souls at Oxford, the first stone of which he laid in 1438. As a secular college this was happily spared the fate which befell at the Reformation another college called St. Bernard, built for the Cistercian monks, with which his name was also linked as founder, though neither the buildings nor the statutes of the college dated from his time. The haughty pope, who had treated him with such insolence, made another use of the funds which the subservient piety of Christendom poured into his coffers. The Roman noble spent largely, indeed, and liberally in repairing the ancient basilicas of Rome; but much of his wealth was left by him in his kinsmen's hands for the aggrandisement of the Colonnas, one of whom he had made a cardinal, while still an ignorant boy.

AUTHORITIES. —The authorities for the subject of this chapter are, in addition to Wilkins and the Rolls of Parliament and others already mentioned, Raynaldus, *Annales Ecclesiastici ; Chronica Mon. S. Alb. Annales Henrici quarti*, ed. H. T. Riley, 1866 (Rolls ser.) ; *Memorials of Henry the Fifth*, ed. C. A. Cole, 1858 (Rolls ser.) ; Clement Maydeston in *Anglia Sacra*, i. 369 ; J. L'Enfant, *Histoire du Concile de Pise*, 1731 ; Von der Hardt, *Magnum Concilium Constantinense*, 1697-1700 ; *Preceedings of the Privy Council*, ed. Sir H. Nicholas, 1834 ; Bishop Creighton s *History of the Papacy*, vols. i. and ii. ; J. Loserth, *Wyclif u. Hus* 1883. See also *History of England under Henry IV.*, by J. H. Wylie.

CHAPTER IX

THE PERSECUTION OF THE LOLLARDS

DURING the last twenty years of the fourteenth century, as we have seen, novel convictions spread rapidly through the social life of England. Oxford was the source and foster-mother of the new ideas; the citizens of London and other of the larger towns had given a ready hearing; humble enthusiasts had carried them widely through the Midland Counties and the west of England; voices had been raised to plead for them in Parliament, and noble men were known to favour them at court. So far there had been apostles many, but few martyrs. The bishops had been slow to move at first, and when they perceived the danger, the procedure and the sanctions of their courts were ineffectual to arrest the movement; the obnoxious tenets were commonly withdrawn after tedious inquiry and debate; the teachers were silenced for a while, but often to resume their work with fresh spirit on another scene. The accession of the House of Lancaster was fatal to their hopes, for Church and State combined at once to use their powers of coercion. Henry IV., perhaps from conviction and policy alike, showed them no favour. One of his first official acts was to issue instructions to the sheriffs, warning them against the preachers whose " nefarious opinions were repugnant to the canonical decisions of Holy Mother Church." A few days afterwards the newly-elected Speaker of the Commons, Sir John Cheyne, was at his own request excused by the king from the further

The Lollards rapidly increased.

duties of his office, having been denounced by the archbishop
at St. Paul's before the clergy as a renegade who had renounced his deacon's orders without licence, and become
hostile to the faith.

The term "Lollard," which was constantly applied at this
time to the religious malcontents, had been used before in
German towns to designate the men who chanted or
mumbled hymns and sacred music, and so corre- *Statute De hæretico.*
sponds alike in origin and meaning to the epithet
of "canting" in our own tongue.   But those who were
masters of a little Latin saw in the word a fanciful resem-
blance to the *lolia* or tares that spring up among the
fields of wheat, as heresies and fast-growing errors check
the spread of truth.   The Lollards were soon to feel the
weight of the powers that were leagued for their destruction.
Convocation immediately drew up articles against them.
Early in 1401 the clergy, urged on by the archbishop,
presented in Parliament a strong petition against the new
sectaries, whose "illicit conventicles" and treasonous books
excited the people to sedition and tended to discredit
the rights and liberties of the Church.   Ecclesiastical
discipline failed to check the evil, as the "heretics" evaded
it by passing from one diocese to another.   All who preached
without licence should be silenced, and the civil power
should step in to strengthen the bishops' hands.   This was
followed by a brief petition of the Commons to the same
effect, and this with the consent of the Lords was embodied
in the famous statute *De hæretico*.   By this an offender
convicted before a spiritual court, if still impenitent, was to
be handed over to the secular power and burnt in public
"as a warning to the rest."   Meantime, even before Parliament broke up (March 10), or the statute was actually in
force, the bishops in Convocation had been busy with the
Lollards.

On February 12, William Sawtre or Chatrys, chaplain of
St. Osyth, Walbrook, was with others brought up for trial
before them.   He had already been convicted of
heresy by the Bishop of Norwich, and had recanted *Sawtre executed.*
publicly at Lynn in 1399.   But his convictions
were too strong to be thus silenced, and he preached

again in London as he had before at Lynn, and found himself ere long before the court of the archbishop. Various articles were urged against him, but the question really turned upon the theory of transubstantiation, and this he persistently declined to hold, though they reasoned with him for three hours ; he was sure only that the Body of Christ was in the Sacrament, the Bread of Life. He was sentenced as a relapsed heretic to be degraded from the privilege of clergy. They stripped him of his vestments, took the paten and the chalice from him, the symbols of Holy Orders, and handed him over to the civil power, for the limits of spiritual discipline were reached. That very day the king signed the order for his execution (February 26), though the statute was not yet passed, nor the sanction of the Commons asked for, and the poor prisoner was hurried to the stake as if in fear lest some rising of the Lollards might rescue the victim from the flames, March 2, 1401. It is possible indeed that the execution was pushed on to assert the authority of the Canon Law, to which indeed the king's writ referred, as requiring such a doom. The king and lords had agreed already that heresy must be stamped out, and the statute was very useful for the purpose. It might seem safe therefore to anticipate the promised sanction for poor Sawtre's doom, and assert that it was the Church's right, as by a decretal of Boniface VIII., to have heretics punished, independently of statute law.

It was an evil precedent indeed, ominous of many horrors yet to come. English life had been singularly free before from charges of heresy and the horrors of such deaths. "The roasting men to orthodoxy and enlightening them with fire and faggot was a discipline not understood in the early days," says Collier, though we do read of a deacon of Oxford burnt for turning Jew from love of a fair Jewess, and of one or two who suffered for unbelief at Dublin, while Wyclif himself had said that in certain cases he might well be burnt to death. There was nothing in it, it is true, to shock the feelings of that age, which could calmly bear the most revolting forms of execution, as in the case of traitors and coin-clippers, but we cannot look back without a thrill of shame at the first of a

long line of judicial cruelties in which the authorities of
Church and State concurred.

Others were brought up soon afterwards for trial, but not
with the same fatal issue. John Purvey, the inseparable
friend of Wyclif (*comes individuus*), translator of the
Bible, after being "grievously tormented" in the Some
recanted.
prison of Saltwood, recanted at Paul's Cross, but
relapsed, as it seems, for he was once more imprisoned under
Chichele. Many more did the like ere long. Sir Lewis
Clifford, once a man of influence at court and prominent
among the Lollards, now saw the error of his ways, and
penitently laid an information against his former friends.
He was not alone in this. Did not Repyngdon, the ardent
friend of Wyclif, see the light of truth at last, and follow it
till it led him to the abbot's chair at Leicester, and thence
to the See of Lincoln (1408), and to the honour even of a
cardinal's hat? Was not Aston, once the heretic of Oxford,
now severely orthodox, said to be loud in denouncing what
he formerly maintained, though Foxe speaks of him as
faithful to the death?

Others were of more unyielding temper. John Badby,
a poor tailor of Evesham, was not to be daunted by the
bishops and noble lords who sat in judgment while
he refused to retract the confession of his faith. Badby
burnt, 1410.
The archbishop, who had long reasoned with him
earnestly, seeing at length that "the poison of asps was
under his lips and no grace of the Holy Spirit in him,"
handed him over to the secular power, with the prayer that
he might be spared the pains of death. The Prince of
Wales, in pity at his cry of anguish when the flames rolled
round him at the stake, counselled him earnestly to withdraw
from those "dangerous labyrinths of doctrine," and promised
to save his life if he would but say one word. But that word
he never spoke. The poet Hoccleve, the repentant prodigal,
has much to say about the prince's tender heart and "piteous
lamentacioun" over Badby's "stynkyng errour," but for
himself he wishes that all Christ's foes were served as he was,
"brent into ashen drye," and indeed there is little evidence
of sympathy elsewhere.

Another, William Thorpe, showed no lack of steadfastness

when the archbishop and his clerks reasoned with him for
long hours, trying to bewilder him with captious
W. Thorpe. logic.   Thorpe, nothing daunted, told the story
of his early life, how his friends desired to have him made
a priest, but he had no mind to it, till at last, when he saw
that they would not be comforted, he asked for leave to
seek the counsel of those priests whom he heard to be of
best repute for wise and holy living.   When asked, "Who
are those holy men and wise of whom thou hast taken thine
information?" his answer was, "Sir, Master John Wyclif was
holden of full many men the greatest clerk that they knew
then living, and therefore he was named a passing ruly man
and an innocent in his living, and herefore great men
communed oft with him, and they loved so his learning, that
they writ it, and busily inforced them to rule themselves
thereafter.   Others there were also, with whom he had
communed long and oft, Aston, Repyngdon, Hereford, and
Purvey, and more, and though some of those men be
contrary to the learning that they taught before, I know well
that their learning was true that they taught, and therefore
with the help of God I purpose to hold and use the learning
which I heard of them.   But after the works that they now
do, I will not do, with God's help."   After long inquiry he
was led forth into "a foul unhonest prison," where he
sickened perhaps and died, for nothing more is known about
his fate.

In the history of Parliament it is possible to trace the ebb
and flow of two conflicting currents of opinion.   Part of the
programme of the Lollards was well known to be
Threats in what is now called liberationist; they wished to
Parliament. relieve the Church from her endowments, to set her
free to do her spiritual work without the degrading influence
of sordid motives.   Many were ready to take part in this,
though they had little sympathy with further projects of
reform, and we may overrate the strength of the Lollard
party if we measure it by the importance of the attacks,
threatened or real, upon the possessions of the clergy and the
monks.   At a council held at Worcester in 1403 the plea of
poverty was urged on behalf of the reluctant clergy, but men
pointed to the bishops' pomp and train, and threatened to

strip them of their plumes, and make them feel what poverty really was.   In the meeting of Parliament at Coventry (1404), called "unlearned" because the lawyers were excluded, it was deliberately proposed to confiscate the temporalities of the Church.   The archbishop urged that the clergy bore their full share of all the national burdens, reminded the king of the pledges of the Great Charter and his oath that the rights of the Church should be upheld, and taunted the knights of the Shire with the failure of their promises that the Crown would largely benefit by the seizure of the alien priories. The project was not countenanced by king or lords, and was not even enrolled as a petition of the Commons. Again in 1405 like threats were heard at Worcester, but in both cases Archbishop Arundel came forward to defend his order with angry words and show of force.   Any one who ventured on such violence, he said, "schal for his spoyling have as good knokkis as ever had Englishman," as we read in Capgrave.   Once more at Westminster in 1410 we find that an elaborate estimate was laid by the knights of the Shire, before the king and lords, of the wealth wasted in the maintenance of monks and prelates, which might be better used for the support of the Crown, the army, and the poor, while ample sums would still remain for the real work of the Church.   Rough estimates of this kind had been already made by Wyclif, and in more detail by his confidant John Purvey, and there is no reason to doubt that in this Parliament the Lollard influence was really strong.   It was proposed indeed to modify the statute *De hæretico* that the clerks convicted might not be imprisoned in the bishops' prisons ; but later in the session the Commons prayed that the petition already presented in their name might be withdrawn, and this was granted.

It was only on the question of endowments that the reforming movement could point to any signs of Parliamentary support.   In 1406 the Speaker of the Commons presented a petition in which Lollardy was described as a grave danger to the whole social system, threatening as it did with communistic schemes the possessions both of the temporal and spiritual lords, and exciting the people with disloyal rumours that Richard

Petitions against Lollards.

was still alive to claim the throne. They begged that the sheriffs and magistrates should take immediate action, without waiting for a sentence of the spiritual courts. The petition was agreed to, and the statute to be founded on it was to hold good until the next Parliament; but nothing more is known of it, though it is possible that some commissions issued afterwards by the king's authority for the suppression of heresy may have been taken in compliance with the wish expressed.

But if Parliament shifted its attitude, and blew thus hot and cold, the primate never wavered in his course. He would face the evil at its source and crush it there. From Oxford the malign influence had spread, so Oxford must be purged. The memories of Wyclif were still living there, and his spirit had not wholly passed away. For a document appeared in his behalf which professed to have the signature and seal of the chancellor and masters of the university, gathered in St. Mary's Church on October 5, 1406. They vouched for him as having been blameless in life, peerless in learning and orthodox in faith. A copy passed into Bohemian hands, but the document was disputed as a forgery at Constance when brought forward in the interests of Hus. We may believe that it expressed the academic mind, even if it had not the official stamp, and though he knew nothing of the document as yet, the archbishop summoned a Provincial Council to meet at Oxford in November 1407. In this Council constitutions were put forth in his name, and were approved in a Convocation held in London at St. Paul's (1409), which subjected all sermons, pamphlets and translations of passages of Scripture to the strictest censorship, and provided for a monthly inquiry to be held by the heads of colleges and halls into the behaviour in this respect of all the inmates, whatsoever their degree. After much debate the censors were appointed, and these with deliberate care proceeded to condemn 267 passages culled from Wyclif's writings. They were not all agreed themselves, and the petulant young masters defied and pasquinaded even censors, constitutions, and the stormy threats of Arundel himself, when he compared Richard Fleming and others to beardless boys, who

Arundel at Oxford.

"tried to read before they could spell, and deserved to be well birched."

Matters dragged awhile, till the archbishop determined to enforce discipline at Oxford by a solemn visitation. The chancellor, Richard Courtenay, with the proctors, relying on a papal Bull of dispensation given in 1395, repudiated the jurisdiction of the primate, Resistance overborne. and barred the doors of St. Mary's when he came to hold inquiry. Two days were spent in interdicts and threats of excommunication, and riotous outbreaks of the scholars ; and then it was agreed to refer the dispute to the judgment of the king, and before him appeared in September 1411 archbishop, chancellor, and proctors. The decision was not long delayed. It confirmed the primate's right of jurisdiction, degraded the chancellor, lodged the proctors in the tower, and flogged some of the scholars. The graduates, now fairly frightened, grovelled in the dust, and sent a piteous address to the archbishop. The obnoxious books were burnt at Carfax, and a copy of the 267 passages condemned was kept in the library of St. Mary's to be a warning to the students of the future. It is of interest to note in this connection that the Richard Fleming to whom Arundel referred in such contemptuous language, though a Canon of York and proctor lately, did not allow his fancy for religious novelties to hamper him long in his career. He rose to be Bishop of Lincoln, and it was by his order, following the bidding of the pope, that all that was left of Wyclif's body was dug up and flung away.

Up to this time there is little evidence that the Lollards had been other than inoffensive men with religious interests at heart. They had been stigmatised indeed as Communists and disloyal agitators, in the petition Sir John Oldcastle. of the Commons, but we know of nothing to justify the charge save the idealism of Wyclif, and occasional vagaries such as that of Robert Hoke, who held that " the lords temporal were bound by the law of God to have all things common." But in the reign of Henry V. persecution turned the dreams of reform into schemes of revolution. Arundel saw that it was not enough to burn a poor tailor or a humble chaplain, but he must strike at higher game if he would arrest the spreading movement. The chief Lollard of the time was Sir John Oldcastle, known also as Lord Cobham, since his marriage with the heiress of that barony, a soldier of repute and the king's personal friend—a scholar too, who could write a Latin letter and quote St. Chrysostom and St. Augustine— who had openly encouraged the sectarian preachers on his estates and in his castle.

Under pressure of the archbishop, Convocation moved against him, but he treated with contempt repeated summons to appear before the spiritual courts, and after the king had vainly reasoned with him, he was arrested and committed to the Tower. Before he was brought up for trial, he wrote out a confession of his faith in a simple summary of articles of Scripture. Not content with this, his judges insisted on precise answers to their questions on the Eucharist, auricular confession, pilgrimages and relics. As to the first he replied that the Sacrament was Christ's very body in the form of bread, but he would not allow that it ceased to be material bread after the words of consecration. He would not satisfy them on the other points, and growing more vehement as they tried his patience, said that " churches were mere abominations "; and burst out at last when asked about the pope: " He and you together make whole the great antichrist, of whom he is the great head; you bishops, priests, and monks are the body, and the begging friars are the tail, for they cover the filthiness of you both with their subtle sophistry." The archbishop then read the sentence of the court which condemned him as a heretic, and committed him to the secular power, " to do him thereupon to death." Hoccleve wrote a poem on the subject, but as in the case of Badby, in no gentle mood. He complains that Oldcastle had been a manly knight, but only cursed caitiffs could now agree with him, for he is God's foe, and has sold his soul to the devil. He should not dispute about Holy Writ, but learn romances of chivalry instead of cackling of Scripture like the women of the time. If he will not submit to Holy Church, let him be burnt. Hoccleve gave expression, doubtless, to a very general feeling, that to swear big oaths in the teeth of Lollard protests became a brave soldier

Condemned as heretic, 1413.

more than pious talk. As a ballad put it, playing on his
name—

> Hit is unkyndly for a kni ht
> That shuld a kynges castle kepe,
> To babble the Bible day and night
> In resting tyme when he should slepe.

Oldcastle escaped shortly after from the Tower, and
remained at large four years, during which time the country
was disturbed with rumours of conspiracies and
seditious movements in which he was thought to be
concerned.   The most notable of these was the
scheme of the malcontents to meet in arms in St. Giles'
Fields in January 1414, which was baffled only by the
prompt resolution of the king, who closed the city gates, and
encamped with a strong military force upon the ground.
Arrests and executions followed, "many of thaym were
take and drawe and hanged and brent on the galowes."
Parliament met soon afterwards at Leicester, and the chancellor stated in his opening speech that they were summoned
partly to give advice and aid against the Lollards.   A
new statute was passed, in which the civil power was to
take the initiative itself against the heretics ; the Justices
were now empowered to inquire after them directly, and the
sheriffs were bound to execute the writ of *capias* issued.
The persons so arrested were to be delivered to the ordinaries,
and tried by the spiritual courts, and in case of conviction
were to forfeit lands and chattels to the Crown, in addition
to the dreadful doom which followed when they were handed
over to the secular arm.   Meantime the real or supposed
relations of Oldcastle with the Welsh rebels and the Scots,
and the seditious temper of the Lollards, gave the king much
trouble during the French war, but at length the fugitive
was taken in the Welsh marches, and brought to London,
where he was hung as a traitor without delay in St. Giles'
Fields, and his body was burnt as that of a heretic upon
the gallows (1417).

A century later a biographer of Henry V., Robert
Redmayne, wrote in high terms of praise of Oldcastle, while
disapproving all the Lollard schemes of confiscation ; but the
bitterness of contemporary feeling is preserved for us in the

Oldcastle's escape and death.

pages of the earlier chronicler, Thomas Elmham, who regarded him as the great Apocalyptic dragon, and represented
him as declaring himself to be Elijah, and as by way
of fitting punishment passing away from earth by
fire, after declaring that he would rise again the third
day. The sturdy sufferer for conscience' sake was travestied
by playwrights as a tipsy braggart, though afterwards regard
was had to the wishes of Lord Cobham, who claimed descent
from him, or possibly to the scruples of an age of Puritan
reaction, and the name of Sir John Fastolf was perhaps with
slight change of spelling taken in his place, and Shakespeare
wrote, " Oldcastle died a martyr, and this is not the man."

Popular estimation of him.

There is little trace afterwards of Lollard conspiracies or
disloyal plots until the year 1431, when "a certain rogue
tainted with Lollardy, best known as John Scharpe
of Wygmoreland, created a certain commotion
among the people by throwing about and dispersing written
papers in London, Coventry, Oxford, and other towns, against
the religious who held possessions. The insurgent by the
aid of God was taken at Oxford . . . and beheaded; whose
head placed upon a stake at London Bridge afforded a
lamentable warning to all his followers." A copy of one of
the papers thus dispersed has been preserved. It prays
the king to resume the temporalities of the prelates, as in the
scheme of 1410, but proposes to leave untouched the lands
of cathedrals and colleges, of Carthusians and Crouched
Friars.

John Scharpe.

After this the Lollard sectaries counted no more on rank
and title and the arms of worldly force, but shrunk as far as
might be out of sight, meeting only in obscure
conventicles, or passing from hand to hand the
" Wicket," attributed to Wyclif, or their " Lanterne
of light," or "the Regimen of the Church," or "the Pore
Caitiff," or "the Book of the new law." For a time we read
of many parish priests among their number, who busied themselves with quiet ministrations, while they discouraged ceremonial forms and held aloof from festive gatherings and the
processions even of their brother clergy, as at Lincoln, where
the " irreverence of their wilful absence " was complained of.
But bishops were on the watch, and their prison discipline

Obscure sectaries.

was stringent, and Oxford purged by Arundel was no more
a nursing mother.   One after another passed away—some
in the dark cell, others at the stake—or kept their convictions to themselves, for the trial of Hus at Constance
recalled official thought to the Wyclifites at home, and the
disastrous failure of Bohemian crusades made pope and
prelates bitter and vigilant to crush all signs of sympathy in
England.   Thus in the year 1428 we read of a Council at
St. Paul's in which proposals were made, but not warmly
welcomed by the heads of the religious houses, that the
convents should be used as prisons for the Lollards sent
to them by the bishops.   A number of persons—five of
them priests—were formally examined, and stress was laid
on the bold words used by one Ralph Mungyn against the
unchristian warfare encouraged by the pope against the
Hussites.   The accused, who had been in bad repute for
twenty years at Oxford and elsewhere, confessed to an intimate
acquaintance with Peter Clerk (or Payne), a prominent
Wyclifite of Oxford, who took afterwards a leading part in the
Bohemian troubles.   He had also for twelve years the gospels
of Wyclif in his keeping.   The rest of the accused abjured
their errors, but Ralph Mungyn, being obstinate, was sentenced
to imprisonment for life.

The Bishop of Norwich had been present at the Council
at St. Paul's, and on his return to Norwich a diocesan synod
met in his palace to take action against what seemed   William
a pressing danger.   Among some parishes on the   White.
borders of the two counties of the diocese a movement had
been going on, with the active sympathy of some of the clergy
who were in charge.   William White, who had been cited
before a Convocation at St. Paul's in 1422, and there
under urgent pressure had renounced obnoxious tenets,
could not rest quietly in Kent, but took refuge in Gillingham,
where he gave up clerical attire and tonsure, took a wife,
and helped to encourage the novel doctrines that were
spreading round about.   He was now tracked out, and after
failing to appear at St. Paul's when he was cited, was brought
up for judgment as a relapsed heretic at Norwich.   The
terrible doom of the poor sufferer at the stake caused such
general horror that his friends and supporters shrunk into

silence, speedily disavowed their tenets when examined, and submitted to such forms of penance as were imposed.   More than 120 of the Lollards of the diocese are said to have been thus by public pressure reconciled to orthodox profession.

A sturdier courage was exhibited by others.   In the next year, says a chronicler of St. Alban's, "two priests, Lollards and sheer heretics," were burnt in the city of Norwich, "to the confusion of the infidels and exultation of those who believe in the Catholic faith."   In 1430 "a ribald tiler of Essex," as the same writer calls him, "who despised the seven Sacraments," was burnt alive.   So malignant was his heresy, that the miscreant's bones were infected with the venom, and a neighbour who took up a bone afterwards where the stake was fixed, sickened and lost his arm by blood-poisoning.   "A sign of great vindictiveness," says our informant, as if the untoward incident had been the result of special malice.   He gives another proof of his vehement prejudice against the Lollards.   In the same year Richard Hoveden, a wool-winder, was also burnt on Tower Hill, who "believed in no Sacrament of the Church save matrimony only."   In his agony he cried out, "O God the Father, have mercy upon me," and showed thereby his heresy, thinks the chronicler, seeing that he despised the invocation of saints.   In 1440 Richard Wyche, an Essex vicar, was also burnt on Tower Hill.   People went on pilgrimage to kiss the ground where he died and carry off his ashes as relics, and this went on for a week, till the mayor and aldermen put a stop to it by force.   The Vicar of Barking mixed sweet spices with the ashes and so deceived the people, who thought that "the sweet flavour had come of the ashes of the dead heretic."

Persecution, thus applied in earnest, arrested in many places the spread of novel doctrines, but the force of the movement was not spent, only driven underground. The fires of enthusiasm were even rekindled in some breasts by the memories of suffering martyrs, and the "Bible-men," as they were called, who were now laymen nearly all, drew themselves apart, and shrunk from contact with the sacerdotal influence which they detested.   Learning had deserted them, rank and influence wholly shunned them,

Other sufferers.

Lollards lived on.

but many an honest artisan and quiet burgher hoarded
jealously some pages of the English Scriptures and some
confessions of the martyrs, spoke darkly of the wiles of
antichrist, and fondly hoped that they and theirs were
numbered in the Church of the Elect. It has been said,
indeed, that the Lollards must not be regarded as a sect with
a distinct creed to propagate, and it is true that they were
not an organised party, pledged to a definite set of doctrines.
But in every case which was tried before the courts, when
we read the specific charges that were brought against the
accused, or hear details from other sources, we find that the
essential principles were always those of Wyclif, just as it has
been lately shown that the chief writings of the Bohemian
Hus were drawn almost verbally from the same source. The
central thesis that the Bible is the only standard of authority
was the leading principle of Wyclif, and this was
fatal in their eyes to much of the ceremonial
system and institutions of the Mediæval Church.
Wyclif in his last few years advanced rapidly in his antipathies and negations, and his followers pushed on to some
conclusions which he did not formulate, but might soon have
reached. He did not appeal, as many did, from a pope to a
General Council, or to a "consensus" of the doctors of the
Church, but relied on his own reason as the interpreter of Scripture. The Lollards did the like, but they were not learned men
or subtle logicians as he was, and they naturally fell at times
into extravagances of Biblical exegesis, in which each was a
pope unto himself. Priest or divine was not needed to
instruct them ; any humble Christian might hope to be
inspired to get the right meaning of the words he read ; for
"to whom shall I behold," said a favourite text of Scripture
in their version, "but to a little poor man, broken in heart
and trembling at my words" (Isaiah lxvi. 2). If a man
would keep God's law, they said, he should have the true
knowledge of the sense of Scripture and then he should
reject all arguments against his judgment. To make them
independent of all human teachers, they needed only the new
translation of the Bible, and the elements of school learning
to enable them to read it ; give them but a widespread system
of popular education, and England might become a "holy

Wyclif and the later Lollards.

nation and peculiar people." Bishop Pecock, of whom more must be said presently, tried to show them that the Bible could not cover all practices permissible to Christian men, "for how shall we dare to wear breeches which the Bible does not mention ; how justify the use of clocks to know the hour." He warned them that if the clergy be not learned, or if laymen will not listen to them, but trust each to his own judgment, so many divers opinions should rise in men's wits that all the world should be cumbered therewith. They would then agree only in such wise as dogs do in a market when each of them teareth another's coat. Divisions had already shown themselves among them here at home ; some were called "doctor - mongers," others "opinion-holders," others "neutrals," and though the sense of the terms may be obscure, they point to the disintegrating tendencies of such beliefs. But some of the consequences were as yet remote, or only shadowed out in rudimentary forms.

Meanwhile it was natural enough that where there was little guidance or control, some carried their principles to extremes or pushed familiar texts too far. Some believed capital punishment and war unlawful, and would have no taking of oaths at all allowed. Some would prohibit trade in luxuries or articles of fashion. Swinderby thought it wrong to imprison any one for debt. Another held that the Jewish Sabbath should be observed, and that pork should not be eaten. One would have it that "the devils which fell from heaven with Lucifer entered into the images which stand in the churches, and have long lurked and dwelt there, so that the people, worshipping these images, commit idolatry." Purvey wished that all the books of Canon Law could be burnt because of their many heresies. Another thought that Holy Scripture does not warrant much singing in church, and many held that a child was not baptized if priest or sponsors were in deadly sin. They quoted strangely inappropriate texts to justify their practices or censures, as when by mistaking the meaning of the Latin of the Vulgate they found in 1 Peter iv. 12 a warning against pilgrimages, or when they found reason in 1 Cor. xiv. 38 for their own title for themselves as the

Fanciful and extreme doctrines.

"known" men or the saved. In their version the passage
stood, "if any man unknoweth, he shall be unknown," or as
Sir John Fastolf quotes it in his will, "Saynt Poule the
appostyl saithe, he that is ignorant . . . God Almighty shall
hym not knowyn to his salvacion."

Some again combined the new doctrines with superstitious
practices which had no natural connection with them.
Thus John Boreham, parish priest of Salehurst,
was accused of having taught "pestiferous errors," Superstitious
practices.
and of having tracts of accursed reading in the
vulgar tongue. He fled away to London, but was seized
there and brought up for trial at Chichester in the cathedral
before Bishop Praty. He owned to the possession of books
by Wyclif and the Gospels in English, and also some books
of incantations, and confessed that he had used exorcism
to expel demons. He believed that by charms and ad-
jurations made over willow wands he could cure fever as long
as the ends of such rods were hung round the sufferer's
necks. Probably the records of such trials in the country
districts, if preserved, would give many cases of similar
vagaries.

Thus, though there were no authorised leaders and no
definite programme, there seemed to be two sides to the
Lollard movement, and both threatened the dominant
practice and institutions of the age. It was hostile to some,
if not to all, the endowments of the Church. It seemed in
many ways to be heretical as well, and that in times when
champions of the faith, gentle and benevolent like Chichele,
had no misgivings as to their duty to crush out false
teaching with the strong hand of force.

The monks were most in earnest in this matter. It was
not only that their endowments had been often called in
question by the Lollards, and themselves attacked
in trenchant style; but all the experience of their Bitterness
of monks.
cloistered lives made their judgments narrow and
intense in questions of the faith. And so the monastic
chroniclers breathed fire and slaughter when they made
mention of these revolutionary tenets. The mitred abbots,
who had large powers of jurisdiction over their manors and
impropriate churches, hunted out all who were suspected,

and dealt with them severely in their courts. Bishop
Alnwick of Norwich, who was so hard upon them in 1428,
had been himself a monk of St. Alban's, and in the
chronicles of that great house the abbot appears sitting in
judgment on his tenants and imposing ignominious penances,
which could not have made them love him more.

As late as the year 1489 we find in Alnwick's Register the
formal recantation of a heretic, who sought for reconciliation
in the following terms: "I Stephen Swallow,
layman . . . confess that . . . by the space of
thirty years and more . . . I have holden . . .
that in the Sacrament of the Altar remaneth the substance
of material bread . . . and that Christ is not in the same
Sacrament really in his own bodily presence. . . . Also
that baptism, confirmation, orders, penance, matrimony, and
all Sacraments of the Church be void and of none effect.
Also if a man be contrite in his heart, and make his confession secretly and inwardly to God, that then all outward
confession by mouth is superflue and unprofitable. Also
that the pope is an old whore, sitting upon many waters
having a cup of poison in his hand. . . . Wherefore I
Stephen aforesaid . . . all the abovesaid heresies . . . and
all other damned opinions . . . solemnly abjure." The
Episcopal Registers of Lincoln show that in that wide diocese
there were many malcontents, and here and there a "lettered
weaver" who had the Gospels in English and other forbidden
books. Under urgent pressure and in fear of death they
commonly recanted, but others took their place. In 1491
Bishop Russell, being "fatigued and vexed at Oxford by
many heretics," began to make extracts from the work of
Thomas Netter of Walden, the controversialist already mentioned, "especially from the part on the Sacramentals against
which the Lollards most inveigh." Despite his efforts, administrative and literary both, Lollardy was spreading in the
time of his successor. At the end of the century the movement had not died away in London. It was a Sunday
spectacle, which the citizens enjoyed, to see the Lollards
stand before the preachers at Paul's Cross with the appropriate
symbols of their shame. Thus on January 17, 1497, "two
men bare fagots before the procession at Paul's Cross, and

Many recanted.

upon the Sunday following stood other two men at Paul's
Cross all the sermon time, the one garnished with painted
and written papers, the other having a fagot on his neck,
. . . many of their books were burnt before them at the
Cross." At Oxford again, Wood lets us know that "any
scholars who had anything extraordinary in them were tinged
with Wiclivism."

It might well have been thought indeed by some that it
would prove but a passing eccentricity of religious sentiment
soon to be forgotten. There was little mention of
it in high places; formal history ignored it; its
revolutionary accents had been silenced; it had
long ceased to have in any sense an organised party, or be a
visible power in the land. Poets and chroniclers had defamed
it; statesmen and ecclesiastics had used their weapons of
coercion; but still the spirit was not dead. Sour and censori-
ous the Lollards might well be, for they had little cause to
love the rulers of the Church; uncritical they were and narrow
in their Bible readings, for they had little chance of sounder
learning; but the leaven of their earnest influence was working silently among the people. It gave support to many a
protest against ecclesiastical abuses, some of which found
voice among the Commons. It could welcome a true man
even in a dignitary of the Church, if his voice had only the
ring of protest at the corruptions of the times, though the
influences that had shaped his thoughts might be quite
unknown to them. Thus one suspect of heresy referred in
his defence to the Gamaliel of Scripture who "had a good
repute among the people": "much like he was as it seemed to
me to Dr. Colet, Dean of St. Paul's, while he lived." Another
took a friend "divers Sundays to go to London to hear Dr.
Colet."

We read that there was prophecy current in Lollard circles
that their sect "shall be in a manner destroyed, notwithstanding at length they shall prevail and have the victory against
all their enemies." There was more truth in it than seemed
likely at the time. The reformation of the sixteenth century
came indeed in very different guise. The decisive steps were
taken by the Crown; its leading personalities knew little of
those humble sectaries, and looked to other lands for guidance.

The movement went on.

But yet the ground had been prepared at home by many an unknown hand ; the old fabric of ceremonial formalism and superstition had been undermined ; disruptive influences had grown more intense because so forcibly repressed ; and in the later stages of the long movement of reform the underground forces which had been working silently showed themselves at last without disguise, and the Church had cause to rue in bitter earnest the stern intolerance of her summary treatment of dissent in earlier days.

AUTHORITIES.—The sources of our knowledge are much the same as in preceding chapters, but we must add Pecock, Reg., *The Repressor of over-much Blaming of the Clergy*, ed. C. Babington, 2 vols. 1860, Rolls ser.

CHAPTER X

CHURCH GOVERNMENT IN EVIL TIMES

King Henry VI. to Henry VII., 1422–1485. Abps. Arundel, 1396 ;
Chichele, 1414 ; Stafford, 1443 ; Kemp, 1452 ; Bourchier, 1454 ;
Morton, 1486.

IT has been seen that the Papal authority was so firmly rooted
that the resolute statesmanship of Martin V. had easily regained the influence which had been grievously
endangered by the scandals of misgovernment and
schism. But the narrow obstinacy of Eugenius IV.
Delegates sent to Basel.
brought it once more to the brink of ruin. With much reluctance after urgent pressure Martin had agreed to the
meeting of a Council at Basel, but he died before it
actually met. His successor, Eugenius, mistrusting the ominous tones of independence heard there, decided to dissolve
it, and summon another in its place in some Italian town
(November 1431). The Council would not give way, and
plunged at once into a long conference with the Hussites, in
which no terms of lasting peace could be secured.

Meantime Chichele had issued the summons to the
Council, and in July 1432 general leave was given in the
king's name to all who desired to attend it ; Convocation,
aware of the order to dissolve it, voted twopence in the £
of Church property for the expenses of its representatives.
The University of Paris was eager in the cause, and
wrote to her sister of Oxford to urge her to take part in
the good work. Oxford, oppressed by poverty, begged Convocation to lend a helping hand, and provide the needful
funds that English scholars might take part in the reformation of the Church. In a long series of formal documents the

Crown provided payment for its delegates, sanctioned the export of their valuables, gave them special powers to act in its behalf, and assumed throughout the right of control over the ecclesiastical proceedings.

A year later the enthusiasm was cooling down in England. The language used at Basel had been too bold and threatening; there was talk of deposing Eugenius *Sympathies* if he would not own that a General Council ranked *estranged.* above a pope; the Council was organised too much upon a democratic basis, and had swept aside the principle of division into nations, and with it much of the power of State control. King Henry VI. wrote (July 17, 1433) in warning terms to protest against the violent language used about the pope, and to complain of the irregularity of the proceedings and the treatment of his envoys. In November the Convocation of Canterbury decided that the pope had power to dissolve the Council, and that their obedience was due to him, whatever the Council might do to depose him. Soon afterwards, however, Eugenius, who was a fugitive from Rome, hard pressed on all sides by the enemies whom his rashness had provoked, gave way perforce and formally recognised the Council (January 1434), and sent delegates to preside. It was a signal triumph won, but it was less easy to make a wise use of the powers thus asserted. There was much cry for reforms, but the different interests in the Council could agree only in attacking the privileges and pretensions of the pope. The growing rivalry, coupled with disputes about the transference of the Council to Avignon or Italy, led to a complete rupture, after which Eugenius dissolved the Council (September 1437), and the Council retorted by suspending him (January 1438). The English government made no secret of its sympathies. Henry wrote to the pope to accept his choice of Ferrara for a council and promised to withdraw his subjects from Basel if they ventured to refuse. To the Council he urged that princes had a right to be consulted before such extreme measures were adopted, and regretted that all his hopes were blasted by their action. In May 1438 Archbishop Chichele laid before Convocation the pope's Bull which transferred the Council to Ferrara; Lords of the Privy Council spoke in the

king's name of the high importance of the business to be
transacted there for which men of mark and dignity were
needed, and a rate of fourpence in the £ was reluctantly
agreed to by the prelates and proctors of the convents, while
the other orders persisted in refusing to contribute.

The reunion of Christendom, for which the pious Henry
cared so much, seemed for a while to be secured and to give
lustre to the pope's fading credit. Greek and
Latin theologians at Ferrara and at Florence vied
with each other for a time in the fence of subtle   Reunion of Christendom.
words, but the Greek empire was in the agonies of its death-
throes, and the Emperor of Constantinople was ready to pay
any price for speedy support, such as the pope offered.   Pressure was put on the keen logicians in his train ; delusive terms
of union were agreed on ; articles were propounded which
slurred over the questions in dispute, and a sort of subjection
to the Papacy accepted, which was soon to be indignantly
repudiated at home by Church and people.   After such
encouragement like attempts were made to reconcile the
Armenian and the Ethiopic churches.   The good tidings
were received with enthusiasm by the devout Henry.   In
1439 he expresses in a letter to the pope his fervent gratitude
for the reunion with the Greeks, which he hopes will be the
earnest of future blessings.   In 1440 he is beside himself
with joy because he hears that the Armenians have come
into the fold.   In all history there was nothing, as he thought,
comparable with this double triumph ; it should have con-
ciliated even the stony hearts of the men of Basel, but at
least he and his kingdom will be firm in their allegiance to
Eugenius.   Accordingly little interest was shown in England
in the further action of the Council, and in the short-lived
schism which it rashly caused by the election of an antipope.

During the reign of Henry VI. the gentle piety of the
sovereign and the distractions caused by rival ministers
offered a fair field for the assertion of papal claims.
Bishops were provided, Bulls despatched, collectors   Papal claims checked at times.
nominated, tenths demanded as before.   If we look
only at the language used at Rome, we see the plenitude of
papal power reasserted, and even unprecedented claims
advanced.   It is true, indeed, that there were statutes of the

realm which Martin V. had clearly seen to be a fatal barrier in his path, and the Commons would not hear of any tampering with these defences of the patronage and property of the Church. If attempts were made at times to reassert to the full the earlier license of provision, there might follow a sharp and summary reminder of the need of caution. Thus, to take only a single case, in 1424 the pope promoted Bishop Fleming of Lincoln to the vacant archbishopric of York, although the king had already sanctioned the proposed translation of the Bishop of Worcester. But Fleming was at once compelled by the Privy Council to relinquish his pretensions, and proceedings against him by the forms of law were only stayed on his promise to exert his influence at Rome in favour of the rival candidate. The temporalities of Lincoln were restored to him, after a petition from him to that effect, in which he urged that he was grievously distressed by debt meantime. The pope, to save appearances, translated him as " Richard of York " back to Lincoln, but Kemp of London was allowed, after papal provision, to have York. Nor were the bishops always more ready to give up their patronage at the pope's bidding. Eugenius IV. wrote to Bishop Gray of Lincoln to complain that he had presumed to fill up the archdeaconry of Northampton without awaiting his good pleasure, though the office had been vacated by a cardinal, and was therefore claimed by Rome. The bishop persisted, and the protest was in vain. Bulls were often sent to England, but not always published with impunity, for in May 1427 the papal collector was imprisoned by the Privy Council for the delivery of such unauthorised despatches. Subsidies, again, might be demanded by the agents sent from Rome, as for crusades against the Hussites by Martin V., or against the Turks by Pius II., but Convocation could ward off the claim in the first case by pleading the prohibition of the Crown, and in the second instructions were sent by government to the archbishop to the effect that he and his suffragans might not tax themselves or the clergy in Convocation, but that money might be collected for the good work, with the king's sanction, in each diocese.

An important concession had been made when Beaufort

was allowed to retain his See of Winchester while cardinal
and legate. The privilege which the Council had
with hesitation declined to disallow, because of his
royal blood and services of State, was first asked
for as a personal favour by King Henry of the pope, and
then taken as a matter of course.   One after another of the
Primates of all England became princes of the Roman
Court, members of the papal Council, pledged by their
office to support and carry out the policy of Rome.   John
Kemp was legate *a latere* as well as cardinal bishop.   When
archbishops became papal delegates the National Church
visibly surrendered much of its independent status, and it was
part of the same change that the forms of self-government
through provincial synods were in this age commonly
neglected.

Cardinals keep their Sees.

The exemptions from episcopal authority which the
religious houses prized so much, both for themselves and
for the parishes dependent on them, had been
carefully defended by the earlier popes as a
counterpoise to the local influence of the bishops,
but now such privileges were readily withdrawn.   Per-
missions were given freely to dissolve monasteries which
had fallen into hopeless weakness, large visitatorial powers
were granted to deal with flagrant scandals that called
loudly for reforms.   With many inconsistencies and frequent show of weakness the Crown maintained the rights
which the great statutes of the last century had enforced ;
it protected Church property and patronage, reserving for
itself the practical monopoly of episcopal preferment.   But
the ecclesiastical machinery was centralised as it had never
been before, and the National Church had feebler powers
to take in hand any of the wide-reaching reforms which
the Great Councils had aired impressively but failed to
carry out.   Little could be hoped for from the primates,
they were scheming politicians, busy with the cares of State
and strife of parties, with scant leisure or interest in higher
work.

Exemptions withdrawn.

Stafford was a successful lawyer of noble birth, for
eighteen years Chancellor of England, but he scarcely
fulfilled the prophecy of Chichele, in the letter to the pope

which recommended his successsor, that as a spiritual father his appointment would in every way be advantageous to

John Stafford, Abp. of Cant., 1443-1452.

the Church. As a statesman of experience and weight he did good service to the cause of peace in a time of crisis by issuing with Waynflete in the king's name the unauthorised proclamation of immunity which dispersed to their homes the riotous followers of Cade, but as metropolitan he made no mark, and of his administration there is nothing to record.

His successor, Kemp, played a very prominent part in the diplomacy and statecraft of his times. King Henry, who knew

John Kemp, Abp. of Cant., 1452-1454.

well the value of his services, spoke of him with regret after his death as " one of the wisest lords in all this land," unpopular as was his policy of peace with France. Yet he was scarcely ever seen at York during his long tenure of the northern primacy, from which he was translated to the southern province two years before his death. Able as he was, and assiduous at the Council board, the ecclesiastical duties of his high offices seem to have been utterly neglected.

Bourchier lived in the stormy times of civil strife, and steered his course warily through the troubled waters. As

Thomas Bourchier, Abp. of Cant., 1454-1486.

parties rose and parties fell he was all things to all men, though not otherwise much like the great apostle ; for his elastic principles could adapt themselves to changing fortunes, where rigid consistency would have been an inconvenient virtue. He had therefore his reward from Yorkists and Lancastrians alike. He owed his cardinal's hat to Edward's favour, but persuaded, probably in good faith, his master's widow to entrust her second son, Richard, Duke of York, to the cold mercies of the usurper Richard, at whose coronation he took part, as afterwards at that of Henry of Richmond, who dethroned him. He was not always irresolute and yielding, for he showed no mercy to poor Reginald Pecock, a brother-bishop who had no friend at court, and who had wished to convert the Lollards rather than to burn them. Bourchier had been Bishop of Ely for ten years, and is said to have officiated once only in his cathedral, on the day when he was installed there. As primate he was often heard of in the ceremonials of State, and published a pastoral on the lack of morals and decorum in the clergy, without proposing by precept or example a transcendental standard, and the net gain to the Church of his influence with the Crown is to be found in the concessions that tithes should be taken on big trees, and that the "alibi" of the Statute "Præmunire" should not be strained unduly to include ecclesiastical courts within the realm.

Morton, promoted from the bishopric of Ely to be archbishop and cardinal, was the personal friend of Edward IV. and the trusted minister of Henry VII., and most of his strength was thrown into the councils of State and the intrigues of party. As primate he carried to its farthest limit the principle of ruling the Church as papal delegate, armed on occasion with special powers granted by the State. He summoned Convocation only to procure the needful subsidies for the Crown and sometimes for himself, and for pastorals substituted papal Bulls. As minister of Henry VII. he bore the odium which attached to an administration regarded as grasping and vexatious. In the outward life of the Church he was careful to provide securities for decency and order, would drive dissolute clergy from the taverns where they loitered, but stop the mouths of fervent preachers at Paul's Cross who railed at the shortcomings of their brethren ; he curbed the excesses of the monasteries by papal leave, and curtailed the rights of sanctuary. But he dealt with the symptoms rather than the causes of the evils of a demoralised church, provided for discipline rather than for freedom, for decorum more than for the enthusiasm of spiritual life. The friends of learning and culture might feel sympathy for the patron of Sir Thomas More, and the University of Oxford could point to the solid benefactions of its chancellor, but as a father in God he dealt mainly with the conventional aspects of the ecclesiastical problems of his times, and therefore he left some corners of the establishment a little better swept and garnished, but did little to protect it from the worst foes of its own household.

John Morton, Abp. of Cant., 1486-1501.

As might be expected in the face of such examples, the general standard of Episcopal duty was not high ; too many were engaged in secular business or in attendance at the Court, and commonly absent from their Sees.

The bishops.

It is true that if we look only at the letters written by or for King Henry to the pope we may think that there was no lack of worthy Churchmen. "He wished to have only virtuous men around him," was the answer to the protest of the Commons at the favourites at court, and so the bishops whom he nominates have signal merits in his eyes. Of Lyndewode, the official of the Court of Arches, whose *provinciale* embodied all that was local and distinctive in the English Canon Law, he writes that he was "a man so chaste, honest, and inflexibly just that wherever he goes he purifies all things by the integrity of his life." His influence in that case might have been of use, for the king wished to send him to Hereford, among what he calls a "ferocious and uncivilised people."

Lyndewode.

But in the troubled times when Cade's followers marched on London there was much complaint about the bishops; the rioters at Salisbury laid violent hands on their own prelate, William Ayscough, with the cries, "he has always stayed at court and never lived among us or kept open house, so let him die."

Ayscough. 1438-1450.

Adam Moleyns of Chichester, who was killed by a turbulent mob at Portsmouth, was a far-sighted statesman with a true sense of England's foreign policy and the value to her of sea power, but his ecclesiastical character did not screen him from attack, for he was treated as an unpopular minister of State and not a bishop.

Moleyns, 1450.

William Booth of Lichfield was perhaps the most unpopular prelate of the times, bitterly attacked in political lampoons, and included by the Commons of 1450 in the list of persons whom they desired the king to banish from his palace. The next year, to the general disgust, Booth was promoted to the See of York. Gascoigne calls him "the unworthy bishop whose memory will be accursed for ever," describes him as illiterate and immoral, a common lawyer who had never taken a degree, intruded in a See by provision obtained through influence at court. He is said to have disliked men of learning and good repute, shamelessly promoting his young kinsmen to good places in the Church.

Booth, Abp. of York, 1452-1464.

Of the promotion of another a strange account is given by

the same writer. John De la Bere procured the Deanery of
Wells by papal provision and by royal license, but
the chapter refused to accept the nomination, and De la Bere.
barred with armed force the access to his stall. Further
Bulls were issued to excommunicate the obstinate canons, but
with no effect, and at last, after liberal expenditure on friends
at court, to prevent further scandal he was made Bishop of
St. David's by agreement between pope and king (1447-1460).
Some years after there was a movement among the married
clergy in his diocese to conform to the canons and put away
their wives, and a deputation came from them to beg the
bishop to strengthen their resolution by some special order.
But the bishop "of detestable memory," as Gascoigne calls
him, refused to give his sanction to the change, not from any
pity for their wives, but confessedly from unwillingness to lose
the heavy fines which they regularly paid him to connive at
the violation of the canons.

George Neville, brother of the great Earl of Warwick, was
perhaps the most signal example of the abuse of Church
patronage which then prevailed in favour of men of
court influence or noble birth. As a boy of fourteen Neville.
he held by papal dispensation a canonry at Salisbury as well as
a stall at York. At the age of twenty-three he enjoyed the
income of the See of Exeter until he was of canonical age for
consecration. He became Archbishop of York in 1464, and
was prominent in the party struggles of the times, but there
is little evidence of active interest in the higher interests of
his province.

There were indeed good men among the bishops, able
administrators, liberal friends of art and learning, lavish in
their benefactions to universities and schools.

William Alnwick, bishop first of Norwich then of Lincoln,
was the tutor and adviser of King Henry, and forwarded
his favourite scheme of founding a "solemn school
and an honest college of sad priests" at Eton. He Alnwick,
was a strong ruler, prompt to repress either stiff- 1426-1449.
necked heretics or Deans (v. p. 246), and the west front of
Norwich Cathedral and the tower of his Palace at Lincoln,
justified the funeral inscription which speaks of him as an
"erector of costly buildings."

Thomas Bekynton was raised by royal favour to the See of Bath and Wells (1443) as a reward for long and varied ser-

Bekynton. vices in diplomacy and law, and his correspondence shows him busy and capable in administrative work, and an intimate friend of men of letters, while the architecture of Wells still shows the traces of his liberality and taste.

Walter Lyart of Norwich was a friend of scholarship and

Lyart, 1446-1472. learned men, and left a monument of his munificence in the vaulted roof of his cathedral.

William Waynflete of Winchester and Eton was fitted by piety and learning for the highest office in the Church, but he

Waynflete, Winchester, 1447-1486. was of humble birth, and he was passed over for the primacy in favour of the high-born Bourchier, son of the Earl of Essex. · Waynflete followed in the steps of Wykeham, in whose noble foundation at Winchester he had been scholar and headmaster; like him he was a munificent benefactor to the cause of learning, securing for the endowment of his college of St. Mary Magdalene the lands of decayed religious houses; like him he had to face the jealousy of faction, which called him even "the devil's shepherd " in a bitter ballad, where it said of him—

> He wolle not suffre the clerkes preche,
> Trowthe in no wise he wille not teche.

Not only was the primacy bestowed upon another, whose chief merit was what the Commons called "his great blood," but he had reason to fear worse evils, for in 1451, in the presence of some bishops and of a notary public, he signed a formal document to the effect that he had peaceable possession of his See, which he had obtained canonically, but he feared disturbance in his rights, and appealed to the pope and claimed protection of the Court of Canterbury. The threatening storm passed over, and in later years his loyalty to the Lancastrian cause was not resented in the hour of Yorkist triumph.

Men had often little love for the statesmen-bishops, kept far from their Sees for many years by business of State, but Thomas Rotherham of Lincoln and of York (1472-1500), and Chancellor in 1474, was a man of high character and

beneficence, though there is no trace of any visit to his See
of Lincoln for eight years, and after times had cause to thank
William Smith, Lord President of the Welsh Marches, and non-
resident Bishop of Lichfield and Lincoln (1493-
1514), the founder of Brasenose College, Oxford. Statesmen bishops.
Commonly, however, while noble factions strove in
those evil days for place and power, the highest posts in Church
as well as State were the prizes for which they fought and
scrambled; bishops owed their places to the favour of a Duke of
Suffolk or of York, and were often violent partisans themselves.
Not indeed that they were always Englishmen of high birth or
influence.   Lewis of Luxembourg, Archbishop of Rouen, to
reward his services in France, was administrator of the diocese
of Ely, and four Italians followed each other towards and after
the close of the century in the See of Worcester.

There was one, of a distinct type from all the rest, whose
singular idiosyncrasy and ill-starred fate deserve a more detailed account.   Reginald Pecock, Bishop of St.   Pecock, Chichester, 1450-1457.
Asaph and afterwards of Chichester, was a learned
Welshman, who owed his promotion probably at first
to the favour of Humphrey, Duke of Gloucester, the rival of
Beaufort, and head of the antipapal party.   But Pecock
startled the world in 1447 by a sermon at Paul's Cross, in
which he deeply offended earnest laymen, while he seemed to
be deserting the interests of the English clergy and the
principles of his noble patron.   The general complaint
against the bishops of the age, pushed home by the Lollards,
and amply justified by facts, was that they were careless
of their primary duties, did not live among their people, and
discouraged preaching by their influence and example.   Pecock
set himself to prove that a bishop might do more for the
furtherance of the kingdom of God by attending to the
special duties of his office than by preaching formal sermons
or public delivery of the Gospel message.   Parish priests had
been entrusted with the care of souls, the bishop's function
was to administer a whole diocese, to confirm and to ordain,
and to do all this worthily required much learning and a
holy life.   He seems to have expressed his thought un-
guardedly, for he afterwards explained that bishops were not
bound to usual forms of oratory, like the "babblers in

the pulpit," but should explain and develop scriptural truth; his words, however, were taken in their natural sense. To plain men he seemed to be defending what they felt to be among the worst abuses of the time, the distraction of the bishops' energies from their proper work by the glittering prizes of court favour. "Men of every class are crying shame upon the bishops," as we read, "who heap up riches and wish to be called lords, and be served on bended knees, and ride in stately cavalcades, yet will do nothing to save men's souls by preaching; either they do not know how to preach, or they cannot spare the time to do so because they are too much absorbed in business and pleasure." Not content with this questionable thesis, Pecock went on to defend his order from the charge of simony, so often brought against it. The large sums demanded in the pope's name before their election was confirmed, were not the price paid for the sacred office, as coarse tongues wantonly affirmed. The pope was the supreme ruler of the Universal Church, its revenues were in theory at his disposal: they did but give him of his own, or such part as he might need for the administration of the whole. This argument might be pushed too far, and the clergy must have felt that such a defender was not to be welcomed in the interests of their Church, making so light as Pecock seemed to do of the protection of the statutes of the realm. An apology was called for, but it took the form of an attack upon the authority of the early Fathers, whose writings did not countenance such thorough-going assertion of the papal claims.

The matter was not carried further at the moment, for the authority of Rome was then in the ascendant, but there were sharp-sighted critics on the watch, eager to take advantage of unguarded words. They found their opportunity at last. In meeting the objections of the Lollards that sundry practices and tenets of the Church were not grounded in Scripture, he had argued that revelation was intended to supplement and not displace reason, which was an original and independent source of truth and morals, and by his method of dealing with these dissidents, he had laid himself open to attack. It was discovered that he had spoken slightingly of General Councils, that he had implied

Tried for heresy.

that the Universal Church could err like the great Fathers, that he had used questionable language of this or that Article of Faith. He was a voluminous writer, hasty and self-confident, fond of irony and paradox, and it was easy to find ambiguous phrases whose natural meaning sounded like heresy to those who wished to find it. These were certainly not the real motives for attack. He had made enemies already by his trenchant style and his unpopular theses. There was probably some special under-current of party fear or hatred; an incautious letter was written by him to Canning, the Mayor of London, and in 1457, when the Yorkists were in power, there was a concerted movement of the Lords of the Council, loudly encouraged by the London pulpits, which issued in a formal trial for heresy before the archbishop and his assessors in the Chapel of Lambeth. Found guilty of contradicting the doctors of the Church and impugning the authority of the Councils, Pecock preferred to abjure his errors rather than be handed over to the power of the secular arm, to be fuel for the fire. He publicly recanted heresies of which he does not seem to have been guilty; his books were burnt at Paul's Cross before a great crowd of spectators, amid passionate outcries from all sides against him, while he muttered, "my pride and presumption have brought on me these reproaches." The bishops of the province had copies of his recantation sent to them to publish in their dioceses; the Chancellor of Oxford and the doctors went in state to Carfax, where all Pecock's writings that could be found were given to the flames, and Abbot Whethamstede of St. Alban's raised a pæan of triumph at the fall of the "impious intoxi-cator who had imbibed the poison of perfidiousness, that he might . . . infectiously inform the simple people in the faith." But when his enemies were not content with this, and sent him as a prisoner to Canterbury, declaring his See vacant, he appealed to Rome as his only hope of succour. Three Bulls were sent in his behalf, but to receive them was to contravene the law. Commissioners reported to the king that the "damnable doctrine and pestiferous sect of Reynold Pecock exceedeth in malice all other heresies to us known by hearsay or by writing." Bourchier had his victim immured for his remaining years in a "secret closed chamber" in the Abbey of

Thorney, with "one sad person to make his fire and bed," and nothing but prayer-books and the Bible to occupy his thoughts.

It is a piteous story. Whatever may have been his faults of temper or his indiscretions, he was perhaps orthodox in all His book essentials, and certainly the ablest defendant of against the Church order which that age had seen. In his Lollards. *Repressor of overmuch Blaming of the Clergy* he has left us a closely-reasoned temperate reply to some of the chief objections of the Lollards to the principles and practice of the Church, such as he had gathered in social intercourse with the citizens of London, and not from controversial writings. He does not call them by harsh names, nor deal with them from the high ground of authority, but calmly appeals to sober reason in defence of ancient usages, in the spirit of Hooker's weighty argument against the Puritan position that "Scripture is the only rule of all things which in this life may be done by men." There is nothing sophistical or captious in his method; his learned work, the first English treatise of polemical theology, if we except the pamphlets of the Lollards, is already modern in its arguments and tone, tolerant in an intolerant age. So little, however, was his position understood in his own and later times, that the acute disputant in favour of the old order has been regarded as infected with the heresies of Wyclif. Foxe even inserts in his roll of Protestant martyrs the extreme champion of papal claims, and the *Index expurgatorius* of Madrid called him a Lutheran professor at Oxford.

While nobles and lawyers were nimbly climbing to high posts of ecclesiastical preferment, and Pecock suffering for his love of paradox and ill-judged apologies for his Gascoigne at Oxford. order, a quiet scholar passed a life of studious retirement in his rooms at Oxford, honoured indeed as chancellor in academic circles, but wholly unknown to the great world. He looked out, however, from his study windows watching social changes with eager eyes and an open ear for all that might be learned of ecclesiastical conditions. He filled his notebooks of theology with illustrations drawn from the men and manners of his time, and recurred again and again in the most mournful terms to the many grave abuses

which seemed to clamour loudly but vainly for reform.
Pessimist and querulous as Thomas Gascoigne was, and over-
coloured as his pictures may be, we cannot disregard the
light his lamentations throw on the conditions of the Church.
He was no disappointed place-hunter, envious of more
successful rivals, but a scholar of sufficient means, happy in
his books and university routine, who resigned a valuable
rectory within a year of his induction because his health
was too weak for the work which he would not do by deputy,
content to live on till his death in 1458 in his hired rooms at
Oriel, and preach from time to time before the University at
St. Mary's.   The theological dictionary, or *Liber Veritatum*,
which contains his estimates of contemporary life, was lodged
after his death in the Library of Lincoln College, where it
remained but little known till passages selected from it were
published a few years ago.

Of the bishops he could commonly find little good to
say; it was in his eyes an unpardonable sin that they
resided so seldom in their Sees, and did so little to
edify their flocks, or encourage the preaching of   Criticised
the Word.   It was to this neglect that he ascribed   bishops,
in part the murder of the two bishops in 1450 (*v.* p. 204),
and the danger of many of the clergy, and yet some of them
were bold enough to say that all the violence of the rioters
was due to the excitement caused by passionate sermons.

This dread of pulpit oratory, or the desire to control
its utterances, had been shown often in high places, both
on social and religious grounds.   Gascoigne often   deplored
dwells on a constitution of Archbishop Arundel,   discourage-
sanctioned afterwards by Statute (1401), by which   ment of
preaching was inhibited when the license of the   preachers.
diocesan was not given.   Soon afterwards, says our author,
the archbishop's throat was choked, so that he could not
speak or swallow, and men thought his death the judgment
of God upon the man who, to silence a few heretics, had
stopped the tongues of nearly all the preachers.   Succeeding
rulers had acted in like spirit.   Nor were bishops alone
guilty; court officials were afraid lest good King Henry
might be told too freely of abuses by which they profited
themselves.   Lord Say, as Chamberlain, and others made a

peremptory rule that no sermon should be preached at court of which they had not seen a copy, unless the preacher promised that he would not speak against the king's ministers or household, nor attack the measures of his Privy, or, as the writer calls it, his depraved Council. Shortly after Gascoigne's death we hear of a sturdy Wykamist who came up to Coventry to preach before the king, and disregarding the instructions given, told his audience with uncourtly frankness that "the men that preached there had but simple sermons, for their purpose was all turned upside down." He was sent away at once in dire disgrace and empty-handed, "had for his labour to ride one hundred and sixty miles in and out, and all his friends full sorry for him."

The haughty demeanour of the noble prelates of his day was sorely distasteful to the simple-minded scholar. The high-born Stafford was a great offender in this way. "Lately," we read, "a poor man came to the servant of an archbishop, the son of a great lord, and said, "I wonder that the archbishop does not give audience to his subjects in his own person as his predecessor (*i.e.* Chichele) used to do." The servant answered, "My lord was not brought up in the same style as his predecessor," meaning by this that his master was of noble birth, while the other was a poor man's son. Gascoigne had much besides to say about the shortcomings of the bishops, their indifference to Christian disgraces in the East when Constantinople fell before the Turks; of the scandals of pluralities; the non-residence which they allowed to chaplains, some of whom lived neither with their bishop nor at their cure, but spent their time in sport and self-indulgence. He had an anecdote to tell about himself which illustrates his estimate of the prelates of his day. Henry VI. asked him one day at Windsor why he was not a bishop; and he answered, "Sir, if I wished to make my fortune honestly I would rather be a skilful cobbler than the most learned doctor of divinity while things are in their present state in England."

He believed sincerely in the parochial system of the English Church, and the burden of his complaints was mainly this, that it could not be fairly worked unless patrons

Pride and faults of bishops.

and bishops chose good men to be parish priests, with
needful encouragement by precept and example to discharge consistently the duties of the office. He
never wearied of insisting on the primary source of   Abuses of
evil, the scandalous abuse of patronage, as to which   patronage.
ecclesiastical personages were the worst offenders. He tells
many times over the story of a poor simpleton who, by some
strange freak of fortune, had been preferred with license
of the pope to several prebends, rectories, and the archdeaconry of Oxford, but who was quite illiterate, and not in
holy orders. His income was collected by his agents, who
boarded him out in a family at Oxford with an allowance on
which he got drunk every day and talked profane nonsense
in his cups. "I, Professor of Holy Writ, heard this archdeacon saying in the year of our Lord 1440, 'I care not for
your clergihood; I have more money than great doctors,
and know my Creed as well as they do; I believe there
are three Gods in one Person, and I believe what God
believes.' This nonsense I, Chancellor of Oxford, heard
with my own ears from his mouth."

Like all others who really cared for the strength and
vitality of parochial life, Gascoigne was no friend to the
monks or the appropriations of churches for their
benefit. "I know," he says, "a rector who from   Appropriation
the endowment of a single church kept twenty   of churches.
youths at school and at the university, and trained them for
the priesthood. The monks do nothing for the poor parishioners whose tithes they get, though they say they pray for
them and provide an ill-paid vicar. Not content with the
tithes, they try to get the fees and offerings in the churches,
refuse even to allow parish churches to have fonts, that
they may force parents to bring their children to be baptized
within the abbey walls."

With the now scantier number of good priests Gascoigne
connects the growing spirit of litigiousness, illustrated in the
Paston Letters, which abound in references to the
courts and legal phrases. "Disputes used to be   Litigiousness.
settled by the good handling and counsel of the beneficed
clergy without being brought before the courts. Now for
want of such worthy rectors, suits are multiplied and lawyers

on the increase, pleaders who defend the bad from partiality or fear."

Besides the prominent evils which have been illustrated above he dwells upon the abuses of dispensations and indulgences and absolution. "Sinners say nowa-days, 'I do not care how many sins I may have committed in God's sight, for I can easily get at the very shortest notice a plenary remission of any fault and penance by indulgence granted by the pope, whose deed in writing to that effect I can have for a fourpence or a sixpence or a game at bowls.' People, he goes on, travelled with baskets full of letters of indulgence, which they hawked about the country to all who cared to buy; some cried, 'Now Rome comes to our doors; she sells her favours to all who offer money.'"

Indulgences.

The general impression left by Gascoigne's notes on the condition of the Church is most depressing; we may think his pictures over-coloured and his temper too desponding, but we have no reason to doubt his honesty and powers of observation, and we have no brighter and more favourable estimates of the same period with which we can contrast it. We cannot doubt indeed that there were lights as well as shadows to be painted. There were good men busy with their unobtrusive work in many a humble parsonage, as well as in the bishop's palace. There was keen parochial zeal, and splendid charity, and reviving taste for letters, of which more must be said in later pages. On all sides, however, the fifteenth century appears one of the darkest periods of the Church's history; anarchy and confusion in the social system are accompanied by disorder and misrule in the ecclesiastical conditions; if we take up one after another the different forms of the order and the institutions of the Church, we find the symptoms on all sides of disorganisation and decline. While the *Paston Letters* show us how the country magnates made light of the restraints of law and justice, we find a Bishop of Bath and Wells writing in 1447 to complain that the tenants of the Earl of Somerset at Langport had driven their priest away by force, and beaten the bishop's officers, and buried their dead without resort to the rites or ministers

General dis-organisation of the Church.

of the church.   In the following chapters we shall see that
many of the religious houses were bankrupt in funds or
reputation, the cathedrals badly served by dissolute choirs ;
the universities bewailing with scant dignity their shrunken
numbers.   The lawlessness and feuds of the nobility reacted
with fatal force upon the discipline of the Church ; its
members scrambled and intrigued for ecclesiastical preferments, monastic offices, and university degrees ; high-born
prelates nimbly deserted falling thrones, if they had not
even schemed to undermine them.   Richard III. could
readily find preachers like Dr. Shaw and friar Pynkney to
declaim with such shameful eagerness on his behalf as
"to lose credit and conscience and voice altogether."   It
was not enough for Bishop Stillington of Bath and Wells
to support the claims of Richard with the story of his
brother's secret marriage, which would bastardise his children,
but he must carry on his intrigues in the next reign with
"horrible and heinous offences imagined and done by him
against the king," and cause grievous trouble when he
sought a sanctuary at Oxford, and die finally a prisoner in
Windsor Castle.

The Crown meantime treated the Church with due respect,
and chose its chief ministers from among the bishops.   But
the influence of Edward IV., gay and licentious as
he was, did not make for righteousness, and Richard   The ruling
vainly tried "to plausibleize" himself, as Fuller puts   powers still
it, by gifts to religious houses, as to Middleham   showed it
due respect,
and All-hallows, Barking, by moving the bishops to correct
the immoralities of the inferior clergy, and by fair sounding
phrases, which called out the praise of Convocation on his
"most noble and blessed disposition."   Henry VII. especially
favoured the Observants, the strictest order of the Grey Friars,
and founded three new convents for them, but during his
reign there was more thought for outward decorum than for
real reforms.   Neither Parliament nor Convocation had much
to say about the fortunes of the Church.   It was no longer true
indeed, as had been said of Edward's reign, that "the sound
of all the bells in the steeples was drowned by the noise of
drums and trumpets."   But the primate, armed by the pope
with legatine authority, and acting as minister of the Crown,

had a free hand in such regulative measures as he cared to take. Exempt monasteries could be visited, where his injunctions would have caused a great storm in earlier years. Old endowments were diverted to foundations of another kind. For devotion and discipline, which were two sides of the old conventual ideal, had now been provided for in separate forms in the chantries and colleges of the newer type. The former indeed, though they came to the birth so rapidly during the last half of the fifteenth century, were soon to disappear, but the latter, as will be seen presently, had a long history of usefulness before them.

Though the character of many of the prelates could inspire no great respect, and the whole ceremonial system had been weakened by the criticisms of the Lollards, the *and the people rever- ence and affection.* Church was still strong in her hold on the sympathies of English men and women. Still, as before, the wills of the middle classes contained a multitude of bequests for the enrichment of the parish churches and for local charities connected with them, though there is evidence in visitation records of grievous waste and fraud, trusts misapplied and endowments wholly lost. Great stress was laid on the ministrations of the Church for the souls of the deceased, though the interest may have been somewhat languid in the days of health and strength, for then as at other times there were complaints that people " were lothe to come in Holy Churches and lothe to here Goddis service. Late they come and soon they go away." An Italian traveller remarked, however, that the people were very regular at mass, and liberal in their almsgiving on Sundays.

Church building was carried on with vigour all through the fifteenth century. Rich merchants, who had prospered *Church building.* while nobles spent their lives and fortunes in the civil wars, gave freely of their substance, and numbers of fine churches in the town and trading districts—sometimes with merchants' tokens on their walls — bear witness to the wide diffusion of the national wealth, as also to the altered features of the national art. For the Decorated style had reached its full development, and had abruptly ceased after the middle of the

fourteenth century. To the earlier period belong the
lovely lines of tracery, the changing moods of subtle fancy,
the exquisitely sculptured foliage of the Chapter House at
Southwell, and the nave of Beverley, and the angel choir
of Lincoln, as also the varied beauty of the windows of Exeter,
and Carlisle, and York, and the Southern Rose of Lincoln. In
the Perpendicular that followed, the peculiarly English style,
of which pure and early types may be seen in the re
modelling of the Norman work at Winchester and Gloucester,
merits of quite a different order may be found. Its lines
were mainly vertical instead of curvilinear and flowing, and
it drew its name from the long, straight mullions of its
windows, often firmly braced by massive horizontal transoms.
Their structural strength made it possible to build upon a
different plan. The clustered pillars rose in unbroken lines
to statelier height; the upper lights of the clerestories were
enlarged at the expense of the galleries (triforium) below, and
lofty naves and spacious aisles were flooded with the light
that streamed from the great windows of uniform design with
which the whole length of solid wall was pierced, as notably
in the Chapel of Henry VII., Westminster, and St. George's
Chapel, Windsor. We may read this as a symbol of the
coming changes, when a glaring light was to be turned on the
traditional practices and doctrines of the Church laid bare
to a cold criticism, which was intent on intellectual conditions
to the discouragement of mystic rites and imaginative moods,
while the English versions of the Scriptures, multiplied apace
by the new printing presses, were to diffuse the spirit of
inquiry and enable multitudes else uninstructed to follow
with interest the progress of reform.

AUTHORITIES. — The chief authorities for this chapter are *Memorials
of Reign of Henry VI.; Official Correspondence of Thomas Bekynton*, ed.
G. Williams, 1872 (Rolls ser.); T. Gascoigne, *Loci e libro Veritatis*, T.
E. Thorold Rogers, Oxford, 1881; *The Repressor of overmuch Blaming of
the Clergy*, by Reg. Pecock, ed. C. Babington, 1860 (Rolls ser.); *Relation of the
Island of England*, C. A. Sneyd, 1847 (Camden Soc.); *The Paston Letters*,
ed. J. Gairdner, 1872; *Lives of the Archbishops of Canterbury*, vol. v., by
Dean Hook, 1867; *Dives and Pauper*, attributed to the Carmelite, Henry
Parker, 1536; *Church History of Britain*, Th. Fuller, 1868.

CHAPTER XI

THE MEDIÆVAL BISHOP AND HIS OFFICIALS

THE antecedents of a mediæval bishop, and the grounds of his promotion, were of a very varied character. He might be a friar, like Kilwardby or Peckham, noted in the

Antecedents of the bishops. universities as a master of all the learning of the schools, and raised directly to the primate's chair. He might be a monk, whom one of the monastic chapters wished to honour as an eminent member of their body, on one of the rare occasions when it had full liberty of choice. Sometimes, when the influence of Avignon or Rome was dominant, the trusted agents of the papal Court found their rewards in Sees where they were almost entirely unknown, and even foreigners like Rigaud of Assier at Winchester or John and Silvester de Giglis at Worcester.

When funds were scarce to pay the heavy debt of loyal service in the field, an able leader of the papal troops, like Despenser of Norwich, could doff the coat of mail and assume the tonsure and the mitre, holding himself ready to show, when the cry to arms was heard, that his hand had not forgot its cunning. At times the younger sons of noble families were pushed at an early age into the highest posts, as when the Commons petitioned in favour of a Bourchier because of his high birth, and when he rose to Canterbury the archbishopric of York was filled by one of the distinguished name of Neville.

Commonly the road to the higher and more valuable dignities of the Church lay through the service of the Crown.

Clerks in minor orders, often skilled in the theory and practice of the law, did good work in some humble post in the king's treasury or wardrobe or elsewhere, rose by supple tact or steady industry, became skilful *Servants of the Crown,* administrators like Langton and Wykeham, or trusted diplomatists on foreign missions like Chichele or Bekynton, and then received a bishopric as substantial payment for their loyal service. There are many royal letters written to the pope, in which much stress is laid on the energy and good-will of those who were to be thus honoured, but with scant reference to the religious interests involved in the appointment. The clergy, as the educated class, were useful for all forms of skilled labour in accounts or clerkly service ; their work could be cheaply bought in the lower posts, as they had no families to provide for, and as they rose the necessary payments could be largely made by means of ecclesiastical preferments. For by well-defined usage as well as papal sanctions the obligation of residence was not to be enforced on the king's clerks, and dignities and parochial cures were heaped upon them often to an astonishing extent.

The prelates trained in such a school were likely to prove able administrators, clear-headed men of business, valuable links of connection between Church and State. Theologians would be found in the universities ; *and statesmen.* the convents might rear divines of saintly and ascetic type, but shrewd men of the world would bring from their experience of politics and secular concerns a distaste for extremes and no special love of popes. To put it thus, however, is to describe them at their best. There were flatterers also, feeble as well as false, who used their opportunities to curry favour, and climb up by backstairs to posts of honour. A strong ruler like the first Edward could gather strong men round him, use the brain-power of a gifted Burnell, or call out by natural antagonism the resolute courage of a Winchelsey, but the second Edward lavished his favours on time-serving and disloyal men, deploring afterward his mistakes in pitiful letters to the pope, and raised to the primacy the cowardly Reynolds, who meanly deserted the master who had made his fortune.

In the process of election there were several stages, and

in each various influences might be brought into play, the effect of which it was not easy to forecast. The *congé d'élire*, or the king's sanction, was required before the chapters could proceed to the formalities of an election; the temporalities, the estates and possessions of the See, had passed during the vacancy into the king's hands, and were only restored at his good pleasure; it was for the primate of the province to ascertain that canonical rules had been observed, and then to arrange for the ceremony of consecration.

Procedure in elections.

In earlier ages the pope did not directly interpose unless his authority was invoked to decide disputed cases. But these were many, and their numbers tended to increase. Disappointed candidates or their friends were on the watch to discover a technical flaw in the procedure; appeals were frequent, especially when, as in the case of Bath and Wells, or Coventry and Lichfield, the joint action was required of two sets of electors with jarring interests and rivalries of ancient dates. The pope had filled up vacant posts when the election was declared to be informal; it was a further step to sweep aside the action of the chapters, by reserving to the Holy See the absolute power of appointment (*v.* p. 86). From that time forth the choice was commonly a matter of arrangement between Papacy and Crown, the former being the ruling factor in the fourteenth century, but before its close, thanks to the Statutes of Provisors, the balance of power shifted, and the king gained all that the pope had lost (*v.* p. 90).

Sometimes, however, the forbearance of the Crown, or a vacancy or passing weakness in the Papacy emboldened a chapter to assume a momentary independence, and to put forward its own prior or some other for the post. Thus in 1310 there was a vacancy at Ely, and the Earl of Arundel and other magnates flocked thither to use such influence as they could. When the needful sanction had been procured for an election the monks decided that a committee should be chosen to act in the name of the whole chapter. As the seven nominated (*compromissarii*) could not agree, after a whole day spent in the discussion, the committee was discharged. A fresh body was selected in its place, and

Different methods.

decided in favour of John de Ketere, a brother monk. The
"Te Deum" was then chanted, and notice given that any
should come forward who desired to challenge the election.
A notary was on the watch to spy out any flaw, but he left the
Chapter-house muttering curses on the caution which had
guided them so safely through the necessary forms. In the
next century (1406) the monks of Norwich were assembled
in their Chapter-house to fill up the vacant bishopric.
A sermon was preached and the legal form was read which
ruled the methods of procedure, when suddenly the sub-prior
started up, and walking to the side of Alexander Tottington,
the prior, exclaimed, "In my own name and that of the whole
convent I give my vote for Dom. Tottington to be the pastor
and bishop of the Church of Norwich." The monks sat still
without sign of protest or assent, till one Stukle began to
chant the "Te Deum" aloud, and thereupon the others led
the prior at once to the high altar and announced that he
was duly elected by the form of *inspiration* as the bishop.
In other cases the whole chapter voted formally and the
election was decided by the majority of votes (*per scrutinium*).
But it was not without risk from the displeasure of the
ruling powers that the monks took their own course
without listening to dictation. Ayermin of Norwich, as
we have seen (*v.* p. 52), had to take sanctuary in his own
cathedral from the soldiers who were sent to seize him,
and Tottington, whose election was described above, was
imprisoned for a whole year at Windsor for venturing to
accept the office.

It was difficult and costly in such cases to obtain the
papal sanction. The bishop-elect must start within a month
on a journey to the Curia—as ruled by the Bull
"*Cupientes*"—to postulate for the dignity in   The Papal
question. Most frequently the candidate was set   sanction.
aside without much hesitation, in favour of some other with
more influence at Court or with a longer purse. Thus
the priors and convent of St. Swithun's, Winchester, proceeded to election in 1319, and presented one of their own
monks, Adam de Wyntone, to the king as the object of their
choice. The king gave his assent, though he probably had
heard of the Bull which had been signed in favour of Rigaud

of Assier a month before, in spite of his own repeated letters to cardinals and pope in the interest of another candidate. Poor Adam started for Avignon, in the vain hope of securing the pope's favour, and though disappointed stayed on at the Court to make interest for some promotion. Two years afterwards he was found there still by the new Bishop of Norwich, much in want of money to pay his way, for the convent could afford no more remittances, and only begged the bishop to do something for him. It was a stronger measure to reject a bishop-elect who had been already consecrated, but in 1333, though Robert of Greystanes, a monk of Durham, was duly chosen and consecrated by the Archbishop of York, the pope at the king's request had given the post to Richard of Bury, and the monk had to go back to his cloister and write out in his chronicle at leisure the story of his baffled hopes. It was a *Nominees of* yet bolder step to set aside the king's nominee *the Crown* when formally elected. The temporalities could *displaced.* always be withheld, and when this was persisted in, as under Henry IV. and Innocent VII., an inevitable deadlock ensued and Sees were left vacant for an interval of several years. It was still more dangerous after the statutes had been passed against provisors; the writ of Præmunire was a potent weapon to deter the most ambitious from accepting office by virtue only of a papal Bull, and few dared to face that danger.

The papal Court, however, had many ways of making its power felt, and asserting its own interests and claims. It *Long delays.* could keep a bishop-elect waiting wearily for long months at Avignon or Rome while the details of confirmation were delayed in spite of his entreaties, and of urgent letters even from the government at home to hasten matters forward. Some, sick at heart, were glad to resign the appointment altogether and throw themselves on the pope's grace (*v.* p. 86). Meantime, of course, large expenses were incurred, influential persons must be won over at heavy cost, and a variety of official fees had to be paid when the necessary deeds were signed.

Sometimes when the Crown insisted on its rights the pope, to cover his retreat, resorted to translations. He alone, according to the accepted theory, could loose the tie which bound a bishop to his See, and the power was exerted freely to increase the fees which were exacted for official deeds, as well as the first-fruits demanded in all cases. It was also used or abused in dealing *Translations.* with obnoxious prelates, at the suggestion of the civil power, as in the case of Neville of York, and Arundel of Canterbury, but we read of it more often as an expedient of finance, and as such grievously complained of.

Besides the grave difficulties to be faced in gaining the consent of king and pope, objections might be raised by the archbishop of the province, when applied to for the formal act of confirmation. The reformer *The Primate's confirmation.* Peckham refused repeatedly to admit bishops-elect on the ground of their offences against Canon Law in holding a plurality of benefices (*v.* p. 22). Winchelsey again rejected as incompetent Robert de Orford, Prior of Ely, when elected bishop (1302), but he appealed to be examined by the Papal Court, before which he rehearsed the subjects of inquiry put by Winchelsey and his own answers, the last of which he said that he had given not as a theologian but as a logician fencing with an awkward question. According to the chronicler, the pope smiled and praised his ready wit, but we read also that he came home £15,000 in debt.

At a bishop's death officials were appointed to have charge of the temporalities of the See during its vacancy, and a jury was impanelled in each manor to value the stock and appraise dilapidations. The Crown claimed *Straits of a new bishop.* as its own the corn found in the granges, and the incoming bishop had to pay also for the growing crops. Of Rigaud of Assier (1320-1323) a sum of £1475 was demanded on this account, and his successor paid as much as £2024 in the currency of the times. If to this are added the large sums paid to the cardinals and officials of the Roman Court and the grievous waste and damage to the episcopal estates caused during the interval by careless or dishonest hands, we shall understand the complaints so often made of pecuniary straits, and the frequent references to the money-lenders— Italians for the most part—whose dearly-bought help was needed during the first year or two of an episcopal career. We find indeed in the case of two bishops who ruled the See of Winchester for a few years only in succession (1316-1323) that they were unable to right themselves during their short tenure of office, and all the goods and chattels which belonged to the deceased bishops were seized on account of debts due to the Crown. The executors of Sandale—the trusted servant of the king—were remorselessly pursued. After more than twenty years the goods of the survivor were sold up, and at his death even his household furniture, which brought in about five pounds, in part payment of what was still due of the bishop's debt to the Exchequer.

This may serve therefore to explain what might else seem surprising, that lifeholders of rich manors should be reduced to beg for help from those below them. Thus at Exeter Bishop Grandisson (consecrated in 1327) wrote pressing letters to the cathedral chapter and the clergy, borrowed £40 of one vicar and as much from one of his archdeacons; peremptorily ordered those who had promised help to pay up their subscriptions, but did not succeed till March 1330 in getting his quittances from the papal curia, and that only with the aid of Italian bankers. His letters give a full description of his woes. While he was in this mood came a gentle reminder from the Archdeacon of Canterbury that there were certain complimentary presents which he looked for from the bishops who had been enthroned. But Grandisson was in no compliant temper. The canons, he said, in the rhetoric of his time, "distinctly forbid and condemn with terrible execrations any payment for the enthronement of a bishop." For himself, he would rather walk on foot and drink out of wood or glass than consent to such an imposition. The resources of his See were quite exhausted by the exactions of the papal Court, and his purse was empty. The Bishop of Worcester wrote somewhat offensively to support the claim of the archdeacon, but Grandisson was absolute in his refusal, which he seems to have made good.

The dilapidations valued by the juries in each manor were indeed of large amount. The demand on Bishop Edyndon's estate exceeded £2000, and that on Wykeham's was nearly £3000, but this might not be received from the executors for many months, and the

Dilapidations.

Crown meantime was an importunate claimant. The liberality of a preceding bishop had in some cases, as at Winchester and York and Exeter, provided a permanent live stock which was kept up at a normal figure, and handed over without charge after each voidance of the See. And by old custom, as a sort of feudal obligation, the tenants of the Episcopal estates paid what was called "Recognition Money," of fixed amount in each case, when the new bishop took possession of his lands. But this would barely yield a third of what the king claimed for the growing crops, and it must have been still harder to meet this and other burdens when the Parliament of 1408 enacted that the intermediate profits of a vacant diocese should be devoted to the maintenance of the royal household and no longer be reserved for a successor.

The temporalities, however, were very large. The Bishop of Winchester had at least fifty manors, some of them of wide extent and of great value. On the greater manors official residences were kept up with hall and chapel, ready at short notice to receive the bishop and his retinue. He journeyed from one to another of these manor-houses, transacting business as he went, checking the figures of his bailiffs, deciding judicially disputed questions, conferring the tonsure on this or that youth of promise or tenant's son, making inquiry into the troubles of unruly convents, whiling away a vacant hour by taking a run with the hounds or seeing the falcons fly, while the produce of the manor disappeared in the many mouths of men and horses. For as he travelled his train was numerous and his luggage bulky. In the household accounts of Bishop Swinefield of Hereford for 1289 we can trace his progress day by day as he travelled through his diocese, we can note the quantity and kind of the food consumed, the fish and fowl procured from his own farms, the casks of home-made wine tapped on the way, the supplies of venison for high days, the charges of the farrier for horse-shoes, and the doles bestowed daily on the poor. In many cases the hall and stables of an ordinary manor-house had been enlarged to suit a bishop's numerous train; some were old castles built as strongholds for days of civil strife; others of later date

The manors.

Q

had been enlarged with special license to "crenellate" and to "impark," when troublous times of anarchy made a cautious bishop seek the protection of strong walls, or more luxurious tastes were gratified by the inclosure of hundreds of acres of grass lands round their stately homes.

Seen on this side of his daily life the bishop appeared as a great landowner, whose relations to his tenants were some-
Feudal   what of the feudal type, softened doubtless by
rights.   the charities on which the Church insisted, and widened by familiar intercourse with the world of politics and law. But there were still some hard conditions of old feudal tenure, which were not made more lovely in the sufferers' eyes by the character or sacred calling of a bishop. Even the humane and liberal Waynflete was complained of on this score by his tenants at Eastmeon in a petition to Parliament, and though judgment was given by the judges in the bishop's favour, the grounds and bitterness of the discontent remained probably the same.

Still more serious was the conflict in cathedral towns. The history of civic progress records one long-continued
Civic   struggle against the disabilities of feudal tenure
impatience.   and the anomalies of local privileges and exemptions. Kings and nobles had bestowed charters, or surrendered for value given their ancient rights; organised union brought with it the confidence of corporate self-respect. But in the cathedral precincts and on church lands municipal authority had no power of control. By the fourteenth century the chapters had commonly obtained a license to draw a strong fence of walls and gates round what was to be called henceforth "the close," to prove sometimes, as at Lichfield, a source of danger in the days of civil strife. Unruly clerks might sally forth as disturbers of the peace and return to their own bounds again as a safe shelter; lawbreakers of all kinds found sanctuary where the city serjeants had no powers of arrest. As the Mayor of Exeter complained, "night walking, evil language, visaging, shouldering, and all riotous rule" went on unchecked, seeing that the mayor could no longer rule the king's people after his laws, nor do right as he is sworn to, for dread of my lord. At Norwich it was the same story, that the "citizens

rose up against their mother and tried to rob her of her rights," but the bishop "stood up as a tower of strength for the freedom of the house of God."

The occupiers of ecclesiastical tenements withheld their contributions to the general taxation ; they sought to throw on their less privileged neighbours the charges of keeping watch and ward ; they raised vexatious questions about rights of way and tolls and peculiar jurisdiction within the cathedral precincts. By special grant or ancient custom, as at Winchester and Hereford, great fairs were held under episcopal control, which closed inside the town all the traders' shops meantime, despite frequent discontent. Disputes on these points lasted on from one generation to another, debated with increasing vehemence as the townsmen realised their strength, with much appeal to ancient records and even prehistoric legends, wearying out the patience of chancellors and judges, before whom mayors and aldermen insisted with resolute pertinacity on the claims of equity and general well-being against the musty anachronisms of prescriptive rights.

Towns had grown up on Church lands under the shadow of Episcopal protection. The Bishop of Norwich was the lord of Lynn from early times ; he had obtained for it by charter from King John the privileges of a free borough, saving his own rights, but these were many, **Episcopal towns.** and stringently reasserted, as often as the town struggled to enlarge the borders of its independence. The mayor held office only at the good pleasure of the bishop, could not levy taxes or make distress without his sanction, had no command of the town gates, and could not force inhabitants to take up their franchise. Gradually the burghers gained new charters and wrested one right after another from their reluctant lord. The king's court, before which they carried their demands in 1352, might decide against them, but they would not submit in silence. If mayor and aldermen seemed inclined to waive their claims, there was grave danger from the common folk, who had less regard for ancient laws. The bishop in 1377, in spite of the warnings of the mayor, would have the town serjeant carry the wand before him, which was the special privilege of the mayor himself. None of the chief citizens would go with him in his train, and he rode forth with his followers alone; but as they went a turbulent rabble filled the streets, hurling staves and stones upon them, and broke the line of his retinue, which had to fly, carrying off their wounded from the fray. The town paid dearly for the insult to its lord, being heavily fined by the king's council; but seventy years later it renewed the struggle on the same question, and defied the bishop in its streets, till his serjeant-at-arms was forced to lay down his mace, the obnoxious symbol of the bishop's claims.

The interests of their broad lands in the country brought the bishops into conflict with their powerful neighbours. Thus Gilbert de Clare, the powerful Earl of Gloucester, Disputes with barons. laid claim to the chase of Colwall and Eastnor above Ledbury, from which the bishops of Hereford drew much of their supply of game. Cantilupe in the first year of his rule found the earl in possession of the district, and his foresters ranging through it at their pleasure. The bishop stood upon his rights, referred the matter to the law, and was ready with his champion, according to the old custom of judicial combat. But a jury composed equally of men of the two bordering counties met upon the spot and gave their verdict in favour of the bishop; and "the enormous trench of separation between the two possessions was thrown out by the disappointed earl along the ridge of the hill, where it remains a memorial of the contest to the present day." This illustrates what else might seem a curious entry in the household book of Bishop Swinefield. One of his retainers received, as his champion, an annual payment that he might fight in the name of his right reverend master on occasion of any lawsuit which had to be decided by wager of battle. One was actually arranged between the bishop and the Earl of Salisbury, and the bishop's fighting man was found to have sheets of prayers and incantations stitched in the linings of his clothes. It was a frequent matter of complaint that poachers trespassed in the bishops' parks or chases, and clerical offenders, neighbouring rectors even, are noted in the Registers as having been summoned to account for bold aggression. One paid a hundred marks for carrying off two hundred head of game.

We may pass on to review the various functions of the

episcopal office in itself, as distinct from those of a great landowner, or possible minister of State. The spiritualities of the See, which during its vacancy had been entrusted to the care of some official, Episcopal functions. were restored by the archbishop's mandate as soon as the election was confirmed, but the term denoted not so much the spiritual aspects of the office as the varied powers of local jurisdiction, and the emoluments connected with them.

Of confirmation rounds we find little or no mention in the Registers. The Synod of Winchester in 1308 ruled that the rite was to take place within three years of a child's birth, and parents who neglected it Confirmation. were to do penance for one day on bread and water. Children were brought wherever a bishop could be found, and sometimes more than once for the blessing that might follow, but as there was little rule or method, many were left altogether unconfirmed.

Of the ordinations at the Ember seasons the episcopal Registers give full details. The numbers are often very large, amounting repeatedly to hundreds in a Ordination. single diocese and at short intervals, once even in the first ordination of Bishop Stapeldon of Exeter reaching the astonishing figure of 1005. Nor is there any exaggeration or mistake in this, for the names are given in full. It is true that acolytes and sub-deacons are included in the lists—149 of the former at one time in the diocese of Durham—and that those who assumed the tonsure were engaged in many forms of skilled labour, as well as in specially religious work. But still the numbers of the ordained seem larger than might be expected out of a population that was not much more than a tenth of the present number, and in an age when the rudiments of book-learning are thought to have been rare. For those who had priest's orders the title was added as a matter of course, the benefice, or the religious house to which the candidate belonged, or, as in the case of seventeen at Winchester in 1317, the amount of patrimony, with the remark that they were content with that, five marks being the minimum. The grant of title carried with it awkward responsibilities at times. Bishop Northburgh of Lichfield (1322-1359) wrote to the Abbot of Haughmond that he must support one who had been ordained upon a title from that house, and had been stripped by robbers and left destitute. He insisted that the title gave a legal claim. Fraudulent compacts on the subject were complained of in provincial councils.

To inquire into the fitness of so many candidates can have been no easy task. Canons and councils had insisted on the need of definite examination, and Lynde-
Qualification
for orders. wode stated that it should go on for three days before the date of ordination. The *Pupilla Oculi*, a standard work, says that the tests should be applied not too stiffly but with moderation, for perfection was not to be looked for. Two prominent disabilities are noted. The first, that of illegitimate birth, could be dispensed with by a bishop in the case of minor orders, though the intervention of Rome was needed for the higher. The frequent reference to such exceptions is probably explained by the many unions among the clergy, which canonically at least were null and void. The second was the flaw of servile status. A villein's son was therefore often manumitted on the day when he became an acolyte. To receive the tonsure, while disqualified in this way, was a grave offence against Church law, requiring special forms of penance. Bishop Drokensford of Bath and Wells frequently conferred the lowest stage of minor orders on a festival at one of his own manors, probably on some tenant's son or a youth presented by a local patron.

In different Sees there was great variety of practice. One bishop, much engaged in business of State, rarely conferred himself the higher orders but issued letters dimissory,
Varying
usages. with which candidates could apply to other bishops, or he commissioned prelates with outlandish titles and ample leisure to undertake the duty in his stead. Another constantly varied the place of ordination, as he moved himself from one to another of his manors. Thus within a few years fifteen different centres were used by Bishop Langton of Lichfield for the rite. Candidates seem to have arrived sometimes with little previous notice. One came on an Ember day in 1323 to the Bishop of Bath and Wells, imploring him to give him the sub-

diaconate that very day, having failed to find elsewhere
an ordaining bishop. Another day a number of candidates
came from their far-off homes, footsore and weary, in pursuit
of their diocesan on the eve of an Ember season, and had to
be despatched in haste to another diocese that they might
not be disappointed of their hopes.

In admission to parochial charges the Registers of the
period show great laxity of practice. The Council of Lyons
in 1274 had ruled that no one under the age of
twenty-five should be instituted to a benefice. But *Licenses for study.*
Bonifice VIII. had in a decretal waived the limit of
age in favour of those who could only gain a chance of education through the funds of some preferment. Many, therefore,
were put in possession of a living long before they could discharge the duties of the office, and were allowed to spend
years at a university to qualify for their parochial work.
Noble patrons also and easy-going abbots put their relatives
and friends at an early age into such good berths as they could
find for them, induced the bishops to admit them, and to give
them leave to read at a university meantime. One family
named Pykelsleigh, in 1315, had three brothers who were
rectors in the diocese of Bath and Wells, all still in minor
orders, applying time after time for a renewal of their licenses
of non-residence for study. Sometimes a young applicant was
to come within a year to be examined, and was told how much
to prepare meantime. When like permission was given to
students of riper years, they might be required to return at
Eastertide to hear the parishioners' confessions, and give their
alms to their own poor. The fabric fund of the cathedral
often benefited by the fines levied for such a license. Leave
of absence was freely given for other causes besides the
prospect of academic study ; attendance on a noble family,
a visit to the threshold of the apostles, a pilgrimage to St.
James of Compostella, the duties of executorship to a
deceased prelate, and the ill-will of untoward parishioners
are among the many reasons given and accepted. Exchanges too were frequent, so much so at times as to imply
great facility of intercourse and diffusion of the knowledge
of local wants in distant countries.

When a clerk was presented to a benefice, the rural dean

was instructed to make inquiry in his chapter and ascertain the cause of vacancy, together with the antecedents and repute of the nominee. This procedure probably had scant results, when strangers came armed with their Bulls of provision from the pope. Bishops were stopped even on the road by the importunate claimants, handing in their papal warrants for a benefice of specified amount, haggling in unseemly wise over the offers made, protesting that the buildings were in bad repair, or the income not up to the figure stated in their brief. There was bitter complaint often of the embarrassment thus caused. Both king and queen expected a newly appointed bishop to find them some preferment for a favourite clerk; the archbishop by old custom made the same claim; influential people pressed for a pension for one of their dependents to be given as an instalment until some good benefice fell vacant.

Conditions of preferment.

When a vacancy occurred in the headship of a convent, the bishop had to ascertain that the election had been made in proper form, and his benediction qualified for the exercise of spiritual functions. The forms to be observed throughout were highly technical, and fill much space in the Registers, and they need not detain us now, but it may be of interest to note that hermitages even were dealt with in like fashion. The anchorite was shut up in his cell by a special act of inclusion, for which the bishop gave his sanction, and when a recluse wanted a confessor and petitioned for it, a door was made by the bishop's order, and the incumbent of the parish kept the key.

Abbots-elect and recluses.

It may be thought that more care was taken as to the sacred character of buildings than of persons. Not only was the Church consecrated solemnly, but the altars and bells, the oil and water used in its ceremonies were set apart by dedication. When the Church or its precincts were profaned by bloodshed, a special service of "reconciliation" was required to make them fit again for sacred uses. Burial in the churchyard was suspended; no mass or other service might go on within until a formal inquiry had been made by a commission as to the extent and causes of the desecration. If very slight, it was enough to sprinkle with holy water, specially prepared and sent.

Churches reconciled.

Winchelsey spoke slightingly of one reported by a fussy prior, as probably a mere bleeding of the nose. If serious, the diocesan or his deputy must be on the spot to go through the appointed rite. The official forms and procurations were expensive, and amounted to a heavy fine upon the parish. But the entry frequently recurs : a disputed title to the benefice ; a quarrel about tithes ; the arrest of a fugitive who fled for sanctuary ; a fray between a rector and a chantry priest ; a riot at a visitation ; violence used to a choleric parish clerk —any of these might end in bloodshed, and the regulations of the Church in this respect may have done good work in helping to discourage by its mulcts and penalties such disturbance of the peace. For these ceremonial acts the services of foreign bishops were often in request. Bishops *in partibus*, who took their titles from far-off Sees, Bishops *in partibus*. such as Chrysopolis, Sultania, Corbavia, and Nephtelim, or Irish or Scottish ecclesiastics driven from home by war or other causes, did much of the Church work, while chancellor or treasurer was detained at Court by business of State. There were adventurers also like Hugh, titular Archbishop of Damascus, who performed episcopal functions without license from Cambridge to Exeter.

While there has been comparatively little change in these aspects of the office, the personal activities of a bishop's daily life were very different from the experience of the present. The multiplicity of The daily round. engagements of all kinds, the public meetings in behalf of Church Extension, Home and Foreign Missions, Hospitals, Temperance, and Education, the long confirmation rounds, the sermons for a great variety of objects—of all such ministries as fill up the time and exhaust the energies of modern prelates, there are few traces in the career of a mediæval bishop. His interest showed itself in other forms : it did not find utterance so much in appeals to the feelings and the conscience, or move through the channels of societies "supported by voluntary contributions," as by the word of command and formal mandate, backed up by spiritual censures. Special pressure was brought to bear on behalf of a great minster, as at York, where at one time it was made a rule that absolution should be given to penitents only on the promise of a subscription to the fabric fund. Oratories were built and services provided with his sanction for the families and households of the gentry : 250 in the diocese of Exeter in the course of twenty years ; but the conditions commonly insisted on in the licenses conferred were that the parish church should lose nothing of the offerings due, and that the consent of the incumbent should be given, and no outsiders should come in. The bishop might be rarely in the pulpit, but he licensed preaching friars to stir up the devotions of the people. We seldom read of such invitations as that addressed by John of Drokensford to the clergy and leading laymen to come to him once a year to consult him on their spiritual health, but diocesan confessors were commissioned on a definite system to supplement the action of the parish priest. When works of public usefulness were set on foot, special contributions needed for the fabric fund of the cathedral or for parish churches in poor districts, bridges to be built instead of dangerous fords, or causeways over treacherous marshes, or when muddy roads were in great need of repair, it was a common practice for episcopal indulgence to be offered, remission of penances that might be presently imposed, to all who would take part in the good work.

Though a mediæval bishop exhibited less many-sided activity in religious and charitable work than we are now familiar with, the sphere of his coercive jurisdiction

Coercive jurisdiction. was much wider. He sent at stated times to demand that clerks arrested by the secular arm should be taken out of gaol and handed over to his keeping. If they pleaded innocence and could after public notice bring together an adequate number of acquaintances and friends to say that they believed them guiltless, while no conclusive counter-evidence was brought against them, they were held acquitted by this process of purgation and set free. If not, they did penance, or were fined, or were lodged in the bishop's prison for a varying term. A curious deed was executed by a gaoler at the end of the thirteenth century, who had suffered two prisoners to escape from such a prison-house at Ross. In it he bound himself under a penalty of £40 to be responsible in the bishop's stead for any loss or damages that might accrue from the results of his negligence and default. We read of a like deed executed by the porter of the Priory of Dunstable. Freedom sometimes came from the sympathy of friends and neighbours, for notices were put out that "sons of Belial" had broken with axes and hammers into the bishop's prison and let loose upon the world clerks charged with homicide or other heinous crimes. So large, however, was the number of the clerks, drawn often from the rudest and least cultured classes, that it is not matter of surprise if criminals were found among them, whose lives indeed were safe by "benefit of clergy," but who were too dangerous to be let loose again. A farthing a day, we read, was the outlay in one diocese on a prisoner's fare.

Clerical privileges were involved in another class of cases which caused much trouble to the bishops. Royal writs were frequently received demanding that proceedings should be taken to gather in what was due from clerical defaulters to the king's treasury or his courts of law. The payment of the tenths granted to the Crown were often in arrears. The bishops used as sub-collectors the chapters or abbeys, within whose walls the money could be safely kept, but the promptitude of these agents seldom kept pace with the necessities of the royal treasury, and scolding letters came, pressing for more speedy action. Claims also were sent in for debts to be recovered through the king's courts, for when the debtor was a clerk his goods could be touched only by the sequestration of the bishop. It was an unsatisfactory state of things throughout. The bishop was degraded by being made tax-gatherer for the Crown; his officials evidently had little heart in acting for the civil courts, and the facilities of evasion and delay encouraged dishonest clerks in most discreditable courses.

Royal writs.

The power of sequestration was a potent weapon which the bishop was not slow to use. If a rector was backward in paying his Peter's pence, or his procurations for the cardinals who came on the pope's behalf, or his farthing in the pound for a professorship at Oxford, when required; if he absented himself without a license, and left his sheep without a shepherd; if he had failed as executor to clear up his accounts, the mandate was issued, and his barns were locked up till payment was re-

Sequestration.

ceived. The administrative powers of the bishop over clerical conduct and discharge of official duty took other forms. The sanctions varied with the gravity of the offences, but in the last resort there was always the sentence of excommunication, with the possible appeal to the civil arm to enforce the bishop's censures.

The visitatorial power was a most important part of the disciplinary system of the Church, and if regularly carried out, threw light into the darkest corners. As such it Visitations, was frequently resisted, and papal exemptions raised effective barriers against its exercise, where it was most needed. If a bishop, like Grandisson of Exeter, could close the doors of his cathedral in an archbishop's face (*v.* p. 64), if the Bishop Palatine of Durham could warn off the northern Primate by the king's writ (*v.* p. 9), the bishops themselves found the cathedral chapters and the great convents as jealous of any interference with their practice. The latter often had their charters of immunity, which they had bought with a great price at Rome. The former pleaded ancient precedents, raised technical points of law, appealed when hard pressed to king or pope to protect their vested rights. There seem to have been at times good reasons for a chapter's fears. The Archbishop of York gave notice in 1381 that as diocesan he would hold a visitation in the Collegiate Church of Beverley, which a hundred years before had been laid under an interdict because it refused to allow its chief pastor to preach within the minster. Out of the thirty canons and choir priests three only answered to the call on the appointed day ; the rest had already lodged an appeal in London against the archbishop's action on the ground that he claimed to hold a canonry himself, and was so fierce that in his presence they were in terror of their lives. They were promptly excommunicated, and priests and choristers were sent from York to perform the wonted services. The archbishop, warned by royal writ to hold his hand, protested that it was a spiritual question, with which the lay courts could not deal. He had his way so long as his power lasted, and five years later some of the vicars choral were still on strike and in sore plight of destitution.

Beyond the cathedrals and the convents the system of

visitation was extended to the parochial churches through the whole diocese, which were inspected by the bishop or by commissioners acting under his ^{and parish} direction, after notice had been given that on a ^{churches.} fixed day the clergy of a certain district, and three or four parishioners of approved character from each church—not yet mentioned as churchwardens in the Registers—must present themselves for the inquiry. The cathedral chapters issued like commissions for their prebendal churches, conducted by members of their own body or officials. The solidity of the fabric, the condition of the furniture and service books were reported in much detail, and instructions were given in consequence to remedy defects, enlarge the churches and give more light and air. Bishop Stapeldon in the course of a few years issued many mandates to the parishes concerned to repair, here a roof, and there a chancel, to enlarge a church or add new aisles at a cost which ranged from twenty marks to £40. It was noted, however, that sometimes when parishes were scantily provided the needful furniture and ornaments were borrowed from a neighbouring church, to be returned of course next day. If the bishop went the round himself he expected to be treated with due honour and to have provision made for the wants of himself and his attendants. Woe to the parish which neglected the customary compliments when he arrived. Wymondham was put under an interdict by John Wakering of Norwich (1416) because it did not ring the bells at his approach, and Foxe quaintly says of Arundel that " he took great snuff and did suspend all such as did not receive him with noise of bells."

In dealing with the laity the bishop of old times had a wide sphere of jurisdiction, which might overlap that of the king's court and lead to conflict and prohibitions, but he dealt with offences in such cases as ^{Jurisdiction} immoralities and sins rather than as crimes or ^{over laymen.} wrongs. He took cognisance of the great variety of family interests connected with marriage and probate of wills, and of grave domestic scandals. In cases of adultery he struck sometimes at powerful offenders, made them do public penance, walking bare-head and bare-foot to the church or round the market-place, scourged by the archdeacon as they went, or even go on pilgrimage or to the crusades when a nun's chastity had been assailed. Open-handed violence to the person or the property of clerks, sacrilege, slander, and defamation, a broken oath in a case of arbitration, the use even of old weights which were no longer true; for these and more offences the weapon of excommunication was held always in reserve—and its threat soon brought men to submission—or if they proved obstinate and did not sue for pardon within forty days, the king's authority might be invoked and physical force replace mere moral suasion.

The bishop could exercise judicial power directly and in any place in his diocese, but the regular machinery was supplied by the Consistory Court through his Official, Consistory courts. who had his fixed law days and established methods of procedure, worked by advocates and proctors appointed with definite privileges and vested rights. There were often grave complaints of these courts, as indeed of all the departments of the "Court of Christianity," as it was called: vexatious citations or delays; unscrupulous agents and informers; excessive fees and other grievances are noted in the episcopal Registers and reports of Convocation, and doubtless were expressed with far more bitterness out of doors. In 1322 there was a formal visitation to which all who had any status in the ecclesiastical courts of Exeter were cited to appear, and searching inquiries made as to the general conduct of the court. Evidence was given that the advocates were quarrelsome in court, that some of the proctors were wine-merchants and innkeepers, and others much inside the taverns, to the discredit of their cloth. Examiners would not begin their work till they were paid beforehand, while others who were bound by rule to act publicly together did their business in their homes, and gave rise to grave suspicions.

Above the Consistory there was the archbishop's Court of Arches, and appeals to it were so frequent that each bishop retained standing counsel to protect his interests, The Court of Arches. when the judgment of his Official principal was challenged. There was often friction between the higher and the lower courts. In Peckham's days, as has

been stated (*v.* p. 8), the discontent was very general, and
Winchelsey and later primates found it needful, time after
time, to frame elaborate statutes for the methods of procedure,
and the conduct and fees of the officials.   From the Court
of Arches appeal lay to Rome.   At that supreme tribunal
the bishops had proctors always on the watch ; and cases
dragged on for months and years when powerful patrons
were engaged on either side, and no one was impatient of
delay but the pay-masters at home.

The coercive jurisdiction of the bishop was not only
limited by these rights of appeal to higher ecclesiastical
tribunals, but also by the checks which the civil
power could enforce.   The Crown could (1)
interpose its prohibition when there seemed to be
encroachment on the province of a secular court.   (2) It
could decline to grant the writ applied for after excommunication had been pronounced for forty days, and
in such cases the sentences had only spiritual sanctions.
The refusal indeed seems to have been rarely made except
when there was reason to suspect vindictive action on the
part of an official, or when the agents of the Crown had to
be protected, but prohibitions frequently recurred in the
early times of hot debate about the limits of ecclesiastical
and civil jurisdiction.   The industry of Prynne disinterred
numbers of these from the rubbish of the Tower, and gladly
copied them as evidence of the " intolerable usurpations "
of the papal Church.   We read of heavy fines in cases where
the writ was disregarded (*v.* p. 43).   But after a long struggle
definite boundaries were agreed upon between the two sets of
courts, though with occasional protests and attempts to cross
the line.

Inhibition from the king's courts.

The cognisance of immoralities was not seriously disputed
by the civil power, though it covered forms of conduct with
which the secular courts could also deal, but the corrective
machinery was limited to corporal punishments and penances,
to be commuted for fines only at the express request of the
delinquent.   Public opinion did not quarrel with the solemn
fustigations, or the doleful processions of offenders, but there
was much complaint of the informers who lived upon this
questionable trade ; vexatious procedure and unscrupulous

agents brought too often the ecclesiastical courts and canon law into grievous disrepute.

What has been said was much more true of the subordinate courts than of the Consistory itself. The archdeacon acted as the bishop's delegate in judicial duties within an area of varying but carefully defined extent. For such work a special training was required, and it had been the custom for archdeacons, already nominated to their posts, to be sent off at an early age to the Italian law schools. "Invariably they got into debt and wrote home for money; some of them fell in love and became the quasi-husbands of Italian ladies; some got a bad name for learning the Italian art of poisoning; some were killed in frays with the natives; all more or less illustrate the scholastic question which John of Salisbury proposes, 'is it possible for an archdeacon to be saved?'" The words describe indeed the experience of the twelfth century, but the spirit of those times had not wholly passed away. We still find, though more rarely, in the Registers the licenses to archdeacons for foreign study. Peckham in 1282 requests the Bishop of Exeter to take proceedings against the Archdeacon of Cornwall for his notorious malpractices. In Winchester (1308) the bishop heard that the citations were vexatious and unfounded, that his delegates exacted more than their proper dues, hurrying through their visits to the churches, but claiming procurations as if they gave a day to each, while every parish had to pay them a fixed charge of twelvepence, which went by the name of the "archdeacon's pig" or "lardar gift." In Exeter the four archdeacons were censured for their covetous exactions, and for defrauding the bishop of his recognised dues; they were forced to disgorge what they had grasped unfairly. One whose right to the office was disputed sent a band of armed men to force their way with violence and uproar into the church of Bishop's Tawton, another found his people "wonderfully headstrong and rebellious," but owned that he could not speak their language and was too old to visit them. Others in their courts of probate fraudulently connived at the neglect of the testators' wishes; another was so much disliked that a body of rioters broke

The archdeacons.

into the church where his commissary sat and sent judge, advocates, and registrar flying for their lives, and leaving writs and rolls at the mercy of the mob. All this and more, it should be noted, is stated in official language in a bishop's register in a single diocese in the course of a few years.

The rural deanery was then as now a subdivision of the archdeacon's sphere of jurisdiction : the chapters of the clergy met in it at intervals of a few weeks, and the arch- deacon or the rural dean presided. The constitu-   The rural tional rules passed in the synods were to be published   deanery. yearly in the chapters, and learnt by heart by parish priests. At the bidding of the bishop the chapters held inquiries as to benefices that had been vacated, and as to the characters of clerks presented to them ; they seem to have had some power at times of apportioning the taxes to be raised among them, and their machinery was used to publish official notices and mandates. In Chichester the clergy were bidden to attend the chapters regularly to report the misdeeds of their flocks. The dean had visitatorial and corrective func- tions over laity and clergy that were varying and ill-defined. He had to give notice in the churches and markets of the deanery when a clerk accused of crime offered himself for the ceremony of purgation at a fixed time and place, and to challenge any who knew of "just cause or impediment" to give evidence in public. He was also to inquire meantime into the antecedents and character of the accused. He issued citations, gave notice of suspension and sequestration, certified under his official seal the reports of commissions of inquiry, elections of proctors, letters of administration, and other official acts. He, too, was accused of grasping at more power, and using it for selfish ends. Peckham found it needful to guard against the abuse of trust and the "satanic craft" of false certificates of citation which rural deans were bribed to issue, and ruled that no such instrument should be granted under their seals till it had been read publicly in the parish church of the person cited. Grandisson com- plained that they appointed substitutes to do their work, giving them the use of the official seal : men of low character who falsified official registers and by their fraudulent acts brought the office into disrepute. Each deanery had its apparitor, who was not to take high airs, or ride on horseback on his errands to serve official notices except when the distances were great. Quivil of Exeter complained of the "damnable presumption" of these servants, who cited innocent people to the chapters to extort money from their fears. Later on Stratford denounced the "pestilent apparitors," who, with their ill-conditioned underlings on horseback, swooped like harpeýs on the clergy and lived at their expense, making a collection even for themselves four times a year, and harassing with their spiteful malice those who would not subscribe.

AUTHORITIES.—The fullest evidence for the matters treated in this chapter is to be found in the Episcopal Registers, of which the following have been published :—*Exeter Register*— Walter Bronescombe (1257 - 80) and Peter Quivil (1280-91), 1889; Walter de Stapeldon (1307-26), 1892 ; John de Grandisson (1327-69), 1894-97 ; Edmund Stafford (1395-1419), 1886, ed. F. C. Hingeston Randolph ; *Wykeham's Register*, 2 vols., ed. T. F. Kirkby, 1896-98 ; *Registers of John de Sandale and Rigaud de Asserio*, ed. F. J. Baigent, 1897 (Hampshire Record Society) ; *Calendar of the Register of John de Drokensford, Bp. of Bath and Wells*, ed. Bp. Hobhouse, 1887 ; *Calendar of the Register of Ralph of Shrewsbury*, ed. T. S. Holmes, 1896 (Somerset Record Society) ; *Bishop Norbury's Register*, summarised by Bp. Hobhouse in W. Salt, *Arch. S.* vol. i. Other unpublished Registers are quoted in the short Diocesan Histories published by the S.P.C.K. The letters of Peckham and Bekynton furnish illustrations, as do those of Grosseteste for an earlier period. See also *A Clerical Strike*, by A. F. Leach, in *Archæol.* vol. lv. 1. Economic details of interest are to be found in the *Roll of Household Expenditure of R. de Swinefield*, ed. J. Webb (1854-55) ; *Accounts of Executors of Richard, Bishop of London*, and *Thomas, Bishop of Exeter*, eds. W. H. Hall and H. T. Ellacombe, 1874 (Camden Society). The relations with the municipal authorities are described in *Shillingford (Mayor of Exeter) Letters*, ed. S. A. Moore, 1871 (Camden Society), and *Town Life in the Fifteenth Century*, Mrs. J. R. Green, 1894. vol. i. p. 333.

CHAPTER XII

THE CATHEDRAL CHAPTERS AND THEIR STAFFS

THE cathedrals fall under two different classes; they were either conventual churches ruled by some great religious house, or they were collegiate churches in which secular canons were installed. The details of conventual administration can be more conveniently treated in a separate chapter, and the former class will be here referred to only in their relations to the bishop and his See. The development of the cathedral chapter out of the rudimentary condition of a staff of assistant clergy gathered round the bishop belongs to a very early period of Church History. There it may be traced, first in its missionary aspect as working from the centre to minister in the bishop's widely extended parish, before the parochial system, as we know it, was begun; and, next, as an organised community still grouped round the bishop, engaged in part in the stately services of the mother church, and in the case of secular churches busy also in many forms of diocesan activity.

The early cathedral system.

But the state of things was very different in the fourteenth century, for some features of the original ideal had disappeared, and there were grave changes also since the days of a St. Osmund of Salisbury or a St. Hugh of Lincoln.

Later changes.

1. The chapter is then scarcely thought of as the bishop's council: the body of experienced advisers with whose help the administration of the diocese may be con-

ducted. When the canons meet, it is to manage their own business, with the dean and not the bishop to preside. As the lord of many manors the bishop makes his cathedral city one only out of numerous homes from which he issues his commissions of inquiry. The individual canons may act for him often as his delegates, but of collective council there is little trace.

2. The rule of common life has also vanished. From the first it was markedly distinct from the regular monastic discipline with its vows of enforced obedience and poverty, and it could not last long after the prebends were no longer given in cash or kind, but took the form of lands carved out of the chapter estates or assigned from other sources.

3. The prebendal system, with its separate estates and churches on them, implied to a large extent non-residence at the mother church. In early times, indeed, it was assumed that the canons were to be qualified for other forms of spiritual work besides the maintenance of the cathedral service. The appointment of the vicars choral was not an afterthought, consequent upon the neglect by the canons of their proper work, but an integral part of the cathedral system which was to be maintained in all its fulness, while the canons were away at their prebendal churches or else-where. The non-residence, which was at first intended to be occasional only, had now for most become the rule, as is amply illustrated by the reports of the episcopal visitations.

4. As the general obligation of residence was weakened, much more depended on the vigilance and care of the dignitaries who were left to represent the chapter: the dean, precentor, chancellor, and treasurer, or corresponding officers known sometimes by other names. Where the common fund left after the assignment of the prebends was small and with not much prospect of increase, there was little but a high sense of duty to keep the canons at their post; when there was more to be divided among the residents, it became the interest and practice of those already privileged to restrict the number of those who were to share the fund. But on all sides the complaint was that even the chief officials were often absent, and neglected in many ways their duties.

5. The general laxity spread downwards to the vicars

choral; for them a rule of common life had been provided, and their discipline had been made subject to the chapter as a whole, and not to the canon whom each represented. But the reports of the visitations abound in illustrations of the license and abuses that prevailed.

6. The increase of pluralities and dispensations materially affected the prebendal churches. The canons, often men of eminence in different careers of politics and law, held by favour of bishop, king, or pope a variety of good things in other places; their churches were, of course, left to the prebendal vicars, who were subject only to the jurisdiction of the dean and chapter or of a single canon. The supervision might be irregular and lax, and any disorganisation of the chapter must have reacted on the dependent churches.

After these general remarks we may proceed to review with more details some of the altered conditions of the times. All the secular cathedrals and large collegiate churches, *The dean in* with very few exceptions, had long had at their head *the bishop's* a dean, who was commonly chosen by the chapter. *place.* With a permanent chief and the free management of their separate estates, it was natural to aim at further independence. The monastic chapters had their prior, to enforce the ordinary discipline and administer the estates, and though the bishop had in theory been held to be their abbot, his authority could be exercised but rarely. The secular chapters had also drawn themselves apart in the absence of their head. For he was a great feudal lord, whose political duties engaged much of his attention, and whose manorial estates tempted him often to reside far from the mother church. Though the early statutes assigned to the bishop the leading part in all the services, when present in the cathedral, yet by making it the dean's office to rule the canons and their vicars " as regards the cure of souls and the correction of morals, and hear all causes relating to the chapter," they gave him an authority which soon tended to displace the ordinary jurisdiction of the bishop, who preferred to live elsewhere, while the palace in the city was left vacant. Attempts were often made to weaken and limit the visitatorial power, some of which have been described already (*v.* p. 10); a papal dispensation, the weakness or political distractions and embarrassments of a diocesan might for many years relieve an obstinate chapter of all fear of effective check upon its conduct or inaction.

As episcopal control became slight and rare, much more of course depended on the character of the dean who was the acting chief. We soon hear, therefore, of complaints of encroachments on the one side and laxity of discipline on the other. Thus Bishop Langton wrote in 1300 to the Dean of Lichfield, and in no gentle terms rebuked him for various infringements of the conditions of his office. He had apparently taken into his own hand some of the powers of the treasurer; he had ignored the rights of the canons in his visitation of the prebendal churches, and made too much of his state and dignity, while neglecting to discharge his appointed duties on high festivals in the cathedral. Grandisson some time after excommunicated the Dean of Exeter, and chastised him in strong language for his "theft and rapine" of parochial churches. When Bishop Alnwick had to interpose after long disputes at Lincoln, and to regulate the relations of the chapter (1439), he ascertained that the status of a dean was not clearly defined, and it had been left to local customs to determine it, but he remarked that "while the arch-enemy continually sits in ambuscade waiting for ecclesiastics," and while "there arise innumerable scandal-fraught contentions," the main cause of the cathedral mischiefs and evils of his day was to be found in the conduct of the deans. This strong language was justified perhaps, if it be true that Dean Macworth with a band of armed men dragged the chancellor from his stall.

His influence often lax.

On the other hand, a dean's continued absence or lax control might have a fatal influence on the spirit of the chapter. At York between 1342 and 1385 the deanery was held by three Roman cardinals in succession, who were of course never to be found there, and at Salisbury in 1374 dean, treasurer, and two archdeacons were all princes of the Roman court. Of the three other dignitaries on whom continuous residence was specially incumbent for the well-being of the cathedral system, complaints of absenteeism and neglect were frequent.

The precentor regulated the services of the cathedral and the instruction of the schools of song, and for the efficiency of the whole system continuous care and supervision were of course required. But when Adam Murimuth, a distinguished man of letters, was appointed to the post at Exeter, the Archbishop of Canterbury requested that residence might be dispensed with in his case as he was his Official in the Court of Arches. Neither the primate The precentor. nor the official seemed prepared for the attitude of Bishop Grandisson, who begged Murimuth to come at once as his services were needed on the spot. His letter passed from familiar banter to bitter irony as he reproached his old friend for being faithless to his earlier principles, tempted as he was by ambition, or, perhaps, by the desire to escape from the neighbourhood of an importunate bishop.

The chancellor again, according to the original conception of the office, was meant to exert a paramount influence on educational and theological interests at the centre of the diocese. He was responsible generally for The chancellor. the supervision of the grammar schools in the surrounding district, and often for the appointment of the masters. "He is the teacher," said Colet, "in erudition and doctrine, and is bound to lecture publicly in divinity, unto the knowledge of God and instruction in life and morals." The facts, however, seem to have fallen far short of the ideal. Bishop Grandisson complained in bitter terms of Meriet at Exeter, who slipped in and out of town irregularly, and let no one know when he was in residence; he "sucked" and "milked" freely the cathedral fund, but did nothing for it in return; he let his prebendal church and other buildings fall into ruins, and even pulled down some of them himself. Complaints of neglect of duty recur at other dates. Fitzjames, Bishop of Chichester, in 1506 noted that "of ancient date it was ordained that the chancellor should lecture continually or provide lectures in Divinity." But this was dropped "through the carelessness, fault, sloth, or negligence of certain chancellors." "The present chancellor has given it up on account of the word *continually*, such a duty being a natural impossibility."

The treasurer or sacrist was responsible for the due care of bells, vestments, ornaments, and treasure of the Church, and regulated the supply of tapers, wine, and bread. Sacrist. Much of the actual work involved was done by subordinate sacristans or sextons, and in the absence of their

head carelessness and neglect might easily result. Thus to take
a single case, we read of repeated complaints at Southwell in
the fifteenth century that the deputy sacrists supplied bad
wine and sour bread, and kept the vestments in disorder, and
failed to ring the bells at proper times, because the responsible
official was not at his post.

If the dignitaries were often irregular and lax in the
discharge of their official duties, not much could be looked
Absentees. for from the remaining members of the chapter.
They were, indeed, numerous enough to make the
necessary burdens very light ; among forty or fifty, as at Wells
and Lincoln, some few might be expected to be always in
attendance in the chapters.   But to the prebendaries generally
the discouragements to residence were many even from the
first.   There were the duties connected with the prebendal
churches ; there was the practice of pluralities which distributed the interest of many over different Sees ; there were the
glittering prizes to men of energy and influence at court ;
there were the duties of hospitality which could be escaped
by absence.   Thus at Lincoln any residentiary on his Sunday
turn entertained a large number of the cathedral staff at
dinner, and daily through the week some at luncheon and
some at breakfast, while the dean about thirty times a year
gave an " honorific` feast " to all the choir and all the
vicars, in order to make " life and work more pleasant to
them."   Like usages existed at Chichester and elsewhere.
The pecuniary advantages of residence were, however, in many
cases very slight.   The assignment of prebends had left the
common fund but poor and with little prospect sometimes of
increase, and such allowances as could be made from it were
not of much account.   Still early attempts were made to
encourage residence.   At Chichester, Exeter, Southwell, and
elsewhere we read of sums varying in amount from three to
twelvepence a day which were allowed to resident canons.
At Ripon in 1315 it was found that no single one of the
prebendaries was in residence, because there was no common
fund from which allowances could be made ; the absent
canons were therefore cited by the archbishop to appear and
to show cause why provision should not be made from the
estates of all the prebends for the special encouragement of

those who might reside.   Little seems to have followed from
this step, for in 1332 the report at a visitation was that the
church was "almost entirely desolate" and that no canon
was at his post.   At Exeter about the same time Grandisson
complained that the canons did not reside regularly, or keep
up the common table for their vicars, while they neglected also
their prebendal churches, and yet drew their share of the
common fund.

On the other hand, where that fund was large at first or
increased much in course of time, the few residentiaries grew
eager for restrictions, lest new-comers should diminish the
share which each received.   At Wells the canons, who at
first when coined money was scarce had received their daily
portion partly in money, partly in bread, like widows and
orphans in our system of outdoor relief, had in the fourteenth century, at the beginning of their residence, to give
a feast to all the officers of the Church at a cost which
reached at times the very large sum of 200 marks.   A papal
Bull in 1400 condemned the practice as a wanton waste, and
ruled that in lieu of it 100 marks should be paid by each to
the support of the fabric and other charges of the Church.
The chapter took the sum in question, but presently assigned
one-tenth to the fabric and another to the vicars, and
divided the rest among themselves.   The feasting went on,
however, as before at the cost of the new-comer, in addition
to the tax thus levied by authority.

At St. Paul's the state of things was much the same in the
time of Bishop Braybrooke (1382-1404).   There too the great
increase of the common fund made it pleasant for the canons
to reside.   Those who were already in possession limited
their numbers by the rule that the would-be residentiary should
spend 600 or 700 marks in providing good cheer for all the
rest.   Disputes arose, and the king, to whom the question
was referred, promptly disallowed the tax.

Few of the canons cared to face these great initial charges,
and most of them forbore to press their claims ; in process of
time the residentiaries became commonly a limited
and exclusive body, filling up their vacancies them-   Residentiary
selves, or by the action of the bishop or the dean.   canons.

The vicars choral formed, as has been said, an integral

part of the early staff of the cathedral, but they were for a long time closely related to the individual canons, whose deputies they were : lived in their houses, shared their board, were appointed and dismissed by them at their pleasure.   The indifference or slovenly behaviour of the superior officers reacted of course upon the conduct of all grades below them, and the reports of the visitations early in this period afford ample evidence of such demoralising influence.   At Exeter in 1328 Bishop Grandisson complained that some of the canons cared more for hawking and for hunting than for the worship of God ; some came late into the choir, and gossipped and behaved irreverently there. Some completely neglected the duties of hospitality and almsgiving.   Others received their portions at long intervals and carried them away, leaving nothing for the common table from which the vicars and choir - boys should be fed. Two years later he warned the vicars choral and singing-men of the chapter that he had heard—not this time in a formal visitation—that some of them threw the snuff of their candles on the heads of those who stood in the stalls below them so as to raise a laugh at their expense, and ridiculed or mimicked the mistakes which others made in reading or in singing, or impatient of delay loudly called to the officiating priest to get on faster.   He threatened them with the withdrawal of their stipends, and even severer measures if they proved rebellious.

There were various provisions made at different times to remedy these evils, by giving the vicars a more definite status and tightening the bonds of discipline.   They ceased to receive their stipends, each from a canon, and were paid from the chapter funds or estates specially assigned.   They were made to adopt in some churches a form of common life, and gained a corporate character with their own buildings and estates.   Thus in 1302 Archbishop Corbridge urged at Southwell the need of a change in favour of the vicars whose stipends were in arrears, " lest for want of them neglecting the divine service to which they are daily bound, and in which they ought to be assiduous, to your own and the Church's scandal they be compelled to rove about the country, as they used to do, and so provoke an outcry."

Vicars choral.

Corrective measures.

At Ripon at a later date it was found needful to rule that
the vicars should be brought directly under the archbishop's
control, and that the payment should not be left to the
discretion of the chapter.

At Wells a more extensive change was carried through by
Ralph of Shrewsbury in the middle of the fourteenth century,
and the story is thus told by Godwin. " This man is famous
for the first foundation of our Vicars' close in Wells. The
memory of which benefit is to be seene expressed in a picture
upon the wall at the foot of the hall staires. In it the Vicars
kneeling, seeme to request the Bishop in these words :—

> " Disperst about the towne, we humbly pray
> Together, through thy bounty, dwell we may.

He answereth them thus :

> " For your demand, deserts do plead, I will do that you crave,
> To this purpose established, here dwellings shall you have."

Yet the improvement of material conditions was not
always followed by a higher standard of decorum. At York
at the close of the fifteenth century grave disorders
were exposed at the visitations. Dignitaries on
whom residence was specially incumbent were absent from
their posts, and the neglect of duty spread downwards as of
natural course. The vicars came straggling into the choir
after the service had begun, and left before it was quite over.
The officials of lower grade paid little heed meantime to
what was going on, but chattered irreverently during the
celebration of the mass, and allowed noisy gatherings of boys
within the walls.

In the great collegiate church of Southwell triennial
visitations by the chapter of the inferior ministers appear to
have been regularly held, and the detailed reports
of some of them at the end of the fifteenth century
still exist. The chapter was commonly represented
by a single canon or even by the churchwardens only, and
the vicars choral, and chantry priests and deacons were questioned separately as to any complaints they had to make, or
as to their own defence if they had been accused of any
misdemeanour. The gravest and the pettiest charges are

jumbled together as if they were of like importance, together with the rare and mostly inadequate penalties inflicted. They were certainly no happy family ; they quarrelled and fell to fisticuffs or drew their daggers on each other ; irreverent and remiss in the discharge of their duties in the choir or at the altar, they disturbed each other by their loud tones while at service, walking about the church when they should be in their places, gabbling through their private prayers while the high mass was going on, or making their confessions while wandering about the nave.   Taverns and houses of ill-fame are often mentioned as their haunts. Many of the charges may have been the offspring of mere spite and slander on the part of their own colleagues, but many of the gravest were admitted to be true.   Often they were allowed to purge themselves by the evidence of friends who had been themselves before, or were to be soon after-wards, accused of the like faults.   Contumacy, however, which was by no means rare, was sharply dealt with : to reveal the secrets of the vicars' hall was mentioned as if it were a graver lapse than the coarse lusts of the flesh already named.   It is indeed a sorry picture.   The dignitaries were seldom there to set a higher standard of decorum, and to check the scandalous irregularities which were so frequent.   The canons themselves neglected their own duties, as appears from the same reports, curtailed their residence, gave each other dispensations, and let their prebendal houses go to' ruin, failing even to pay punctually the vicars' stipends.   At Beverley the sacrist, the chancellor, and two of the canons residentiary were charged with immoralities early in the fourteenth century, some of them repeatedly, and in most cases they confessed their faults.   In 1371 the Crown addressed to the Dean and Chapter of St. Paul's a letter of severe rebuke for the scandalous irregularities of the cathedral life : estates were mismanaged, revenues misapplied, holy vessels lost, and the conduct inside the walls was a disgrace to the ministrants and the officials.   At Chichester there were repeatedly sad stories of disorder.   The Chapter Acts of Ripon tell much the same story as at Southwell : the same scandals with loose women ; like charges of drunkenness and open violence, and easy methods of purgation, though trivial offences are not reported in such ludicrous detail. It is fair indeed to note that these subordinates and singing men, who were illiterate and of low degree, had nothing outside the church to occupy their minds. They had no parochial work; if they tried to do a little business it was an offence against church rule ; manly sports were thought unbecoming to their cloth ; games even like bowls and backgammon were forbidden ; at every visitation the use of dice and cards figures among the loose practices condemned. The formal scrutiny of the prebendal churches still went on ; the inventories of furniture and vestments were still compared and defects were noted down, with the complaints, if any, of the conduct of the vicars. We have nothing like the favourable testimony which, in the diocese of Exeter early in the fourteenth century, the parishioners bore to the characters of their parish priests (*v.* p. 257); many grave lapses are recorded ; the general impression left is that immorality and negligence were widely spread.

When we note the melancholy revelations of the daily life within the Close, or in districts subject to the jurisdiction of the Chapter, we can better understand the impatience which the townsmen of the period often showed at the privileges and immunities which those chapters claimed. The freedom from tolls and taxes which the canons asserted for themselves and for their tenants ; their civil and criminal jurisdiction ; their municipal powers of assize ; these became, of course, more odious in their neighbours' eyes, when there was so little in the character of the ministering clergy to inspire respect, so little apparent benefit to the community from these pretensions, beyond the perfunctory and slovenly performance of old ceremonial forms.

AUTHORITIES.—The condition of the cathedral staffs is illustrated by the *Chapter Acts of Ripon*, ed. J. T. Fowler, 1875 (Surtees Society) ; *Memorials of Beverley Minster, Chapter Acts Book* ed. A. F. Leach, 1898 (Surtees Society) ; *Visitations of Southwell Minster*, ed A. F. Leach, 1891 (Camden Society), together with the *Bishops' Registers* referred to in c. xvii. See also the *Statutes of Lincoln Cathedral*, ed. H. Bradshaw and E. Wordsworth, 1892 ; *The Cathedral Church of Wells*, by E. A. Freeman ; *The Cathedral*, by Abp. Benson.

CHAPTER XIII

THE CLERGY AND PARISH LIFE

WHILE the bishops and the canons were making history as statesmen, diplomatists, and lawyers, while the greater religious houses had their historiographers busily engaged in gathering up from visitors and correspondents the news of the great world which they chronicled together with the details of local interest, the parochial clergy lived their quiet lives, and went about the routine of daily work, and left few materials behind them to illustrate the story of their doings. The chroniclers passed them by in silence, and seldom spoke of parishes except when the monks succeeded in getting hold of the rectorial tithes, or protested against the visitations of the bishops in their exempt domain. Episcopal Registers tell us of clerical delinquents, of the non-resident and contumacious, but have no word to say of those who spent themselves in the unobtrusive round of common duty. Popular literature, which nowadays reflects so much of the varied conditions of all classes of society, was as yet in its infancy for English readers, and illustrated few scenes of clerical life save those which were adapted to the lively satire of the Canterbury Pilgrims or the melancholy diatribes of Gower. The fairer side is not often presented, though there is one marked exception in Chaucer's familiar portrait of the ideal parish priest, which, we may hope, was drawn mainly from the facts of actual life.

The clerical order was recruited from all classes of society, from the highest to the lowest.   The career of one of humble birth may thus be traced.   A villein brought his son, a lad of promise, before the Manor Court, and drawn from
all classes. paid the usual fine for permission to attend school in some convent or vicar's house hard by, his labour on the land being lost to the lord meantime.   He learnt his Catechism and a little Latin there, and by favour of the lord of the manor and others obtained his freedom and was made an acolyte when the bishop passed that way.   He could then carry the holy water to the houses of those who could not worship at the church, receiving for it some gratuity which was regarded as a poor scholar's privilege ; he could take care of the vestments and help the parish priest and look forward to the possibility of higher work.   Many of brighter parts or happier fortune attached themselves to the service of some magnate, acting as secretary or domestic chaplain, and were rewarded with a family living after years of attendance on their master's household.   Some passed into the convents, and if specially intelligent might be sent on to Oxford to qualify for higher work.   Many indeed rose in this way from the humblest ranks to the highest offices of Church and State. The Commons indeed eyed them with disfavour, and even men of their own class spoke of them as upstarts in the popular poems of the times.   We have seen that a definite title was required when the priesthood was conferred, and that in some cases it was noted that the family income was sufficient to maintain them, without any risk of burden to the bishop (*v.* p. 229).   These entries point to the.sons of the freeholders and merchants who were attracted to the service of the Church, or to the careers in the offices of State and Law through which ecclesiastics passed.   Stalls or canonries in cathedral and collegiate churches were largely filled by the younger sons of the nobility, and in the fifteenth century the prizes of the Church were monopolised by the great families of the land.   The clerical order, which drew its members from these different sources, was in touch with all the social classes, and though its exclusive privileges and vast estates seemed often odious and oppressive, the many sympathies and familiar intercourse thus brought about must have greatly strengthened its corporate powers of resistance to attack.

As regards the degree of culture and professional training of the clergy, exaggerated statements have been often made, and harsh criticisms have been generalised unduly. It has been said that they were deplorably ignorant, dumb pastors who did not and could not preach, but left their people to the chance instruction of some wandering friar. To exalt the merits of the Reformation it has been asserted that the Bible was before almost a closed book, of which even the priesthood had but little knowledge, and that it was a novel thought of Wyclif to bid his humble missionaries preach. It must be owned that there was no elaborate system of special training for the clergy, distinct from school or university, like the seminaries or theological colleges of recent date. But the greater convents had their schools; the chronicles that were compiled within their walls, written and read by monks, are for the most part full of biblical imagery and illustrations. Mediæval art in all its forms alike in secular and religious buildings appealed to the popular knowledge of the details of Bible history. At the universities, to which young rectors went by special dispensation for non-residence, the course of study lasted long; the works of the leading schoolmen which they read there were saturated with theology, much of the Canon Law with which they gained acquaintance bore directly on the experience of their life's work.

Education.

For ordination a real examination was prescribed, though not perhaps carried very far. The constitutions passed by the diocesan synods laid stress on a course of systematic exposition, to be repeated several times a year, of the essential doctrines of the Church. The subjects treated may seem rudimentary indeed, a sort of simple catechism for children rather than for teachers, but we may naturally take them as summaries of leading topics to be illustrated and developed with infinite variations in the pulpit. That there was early in the fourteenth century real and continuous instruction in the parish churches we may fairly assume from the answers which were given to the inquiries made by the Cathedral Chapter at the visitations of their churches in the diocese of Exeter. In each parish questions seem to have been asked about the parson's character and conduct, and the reply sent in by representative parishioners was commonly

that he preached well and thoroughly, or that he gave
adequate instruction to his people. The preaching was
simple and homely doubtless, consisting more in definite
teaching in the elements of Christian belief than in rhetorical
appeals. It could not always vie in interest with the racy
anecdotes and varied illustrations of the friars, who did not
stay long enough in any parish to exhaust their budget, or their
hearers' sense of novelty, but the home supply may not have
been less useful because it was often thrown into the shade
by its more showy rival.

Undoubtedly there is reason to believe that the terrible
ravages of the Great Plague thinned so rapidly the numbers
of the clergy that it was found needful to lower the
standard—not too high before—and to ordain many Effects of
the Plague.
who were slenderly equipped with learning (*v.* p. 75).
The evils of pluralities increased. Absenteeism appears
in Wykeham's Registers to be a very common evil ; clerical
exchanges were extraordinarily frequent, and a class of unscrupulous traffickers in Church preferment called forth a
vehement protest of Archbishop Courtenay against the
" choppe-churches " of his time. The stipendiary priests
who served meantime the else neglected parishes were drawn
in large numbers from a less educated class than the beneficed clergy of the past. In the fifteenth century learning
and piety declined ; war and anarchy distracted men's interest from higher things ; the bishops, though of higher
birth, were, with some notable exceptions, of far less
noble type than at the beginning of our period, and their
influence cannot have been good ; the universities complained that they were deserted and forlorn, and there
was ample reason for the strictures of a sad pessimist like
Gascoigne. But still it should not be forgotten that the
parish pulpits were never silenced by authority, though unlicensed preachers were, when the rulers of Church and State
took action to arrest the spread of Wyclif's tenets. Moreover
many manuals were written to guide the parish priests in the
composition of their sermons, and a large number of such
homilies were circulated, to be adapted or worked up in varied
forms for personal use.

When we speak of the moral character and reputation of

S

the mediæval clergy, we must be careful to remember some
of the distinct conditions which materially affect
the question. Their numbers bore a very different proportion to the whole population of the
country from that which now exists, and a large majority of
them proceeded from the humblest social strata. There
were 29,161 entered on the Poll-tax Records (1381), exclusive
of the very numerous friars. One in fifty-two Englishmen
above fourteen years of age, it has been reckoned, was nomin-
ally a cleric. They were not merely the educated and professional classes, but embraced besides nearly all forms of
skilled employment beyond those of trade and ordinary
manual labour. It cannot be supposed that religious motives
largely influenced the multitude of those who sought, and for
the most part never passed beyond, the inferior orders. They
had a livelihood in view, an easier career with better prospects
of promotion than the routine of country life afforded, just as
the children of our cottagers are glad to pass from the school
to the clerk's desk or the shop counter. It would not therefore be harsh to say, with Gower, that the "loaves and fishes"
and the desire to escape from manual drudgery tempted men
to take the tonsure, but he is speaking of the priests, and
his criticism is severe, because he drops out of sight all
higher motives in their case. The other inducement which
he mentions, the "benefit of clergy," was a real privilege, to
be valued even by the law-abiding in days of turbulent misrule,
when justice could not be relied on in the Civil Courts, but
afterwards an advantage chiefly for ecclesiastical delinquents
who were secured by it from penalties of death and mutilation,
and might hope to escape punishment by easy methods of
purgation. But clerical misconduct spread over such widely
different classes does not interest us greatly now.

Stress may be fairly laid upon the fact that in the parochial
returns of very early date, which have been above referred to,
the accounts are for the most part favourable.
"They see no reason to complain," though sometimes he is too old to do his work. Of course
there are exceptions, where they feel aggrieved because he
lets beasts of all kinds graze in the churchyards, much to the
befouling of the ground, or uses the church to brew his beer.

Marginal notes: Large and mixed body of clergy. Early returns of Exeter.

One parson is leprous, and yet to their grave risk will take part in the services in church. In other cases he absents himself too often from the parish, and at times we read, though rarely, that his morals are not beyond suspicion.

We should note again as we read some of the startling language of the synods and the earnest exhortations of the bishops, that however strict may have been the theory of the Church, the practice of a celibate Celibate in theory. clergy was not as yet firmly established in the fourteenth century. Many were actually married. Canon law might regard the union as concubinage, but it was not otherwise illegal, though steps could be taken to make it void. Bishops denounced it as an unholy thing ; the prohibitions of it were to be read in the ruridecanal chapters four times a year, that the threats of deprivation might be known to all concerned. It was ruled that a priest's son must not be allowed to succeed him in his cure, that suspected women must be put away, or refused the sacraments of the Church. Bishop Quivil of Exeter complained that the savings of the clergy were invested often by them for the benefit of their life-long partners, for the dying thought of them tenderly in their last moments, and he ruled all bequests made to them be null and void. The episcopal powers of sequestration and the regulation of the Courts made it easy to carry out the coercion thus enjoined, but it was a very questionable gain. Illicit marriages became perhaps less frequent, but when temporary connections took their place the scandal was far graver, and the effect upon the moral character much worse. The authorities, however, seemed less in earnest in such cases, and the penal discipline was not severe.

Of course fine things were always said in pastorals and constitutions about chastity and self-denial. Culprits with whom scandal was rife were duly cited and examined, but allowed to purge themselves on easy terms, or if they confessed their faults, the penances were slight, suspension rare, and deprivation scarcely heard of. Thus one vicar was required to pay six marks to the mother of his two children, and so provide a dowry for her, and to swear friendship with her friends and parents that the neighbours might live pleasantly together as before. An incontinent rector is fined 6s. 8d. and

sent back to his parish without scruple. The three incumbents of Itchenstoke, Bramdean, and East Tisted admit
concubinage, deplore their evasions and contempt of episcopal
authority, and offer to do penance as William of Wykeham
may prescribe, but the Registers say nothing more.

If grave lapses were regarded somewhat lightly, novelties
of dress and sumptuary extravagances called forth repeated
censures in the sternest language. A Synod of
Exeter (1287) entered into much detail as to the
prescribed form and size of the tonsure, and the
cut and colour of the clerical attire; another at London
(1342) denounced at great length the "abominable scandal"
of the "effeminate" practice of wearing the hair long, and the
"military" shape of the short capes and the wide sleeves and
flowing beards and costly girdles which the clerical dandies
of the time affected.

The exhortations which we read in the episcopal constitutions accepted by church councils were addressed to the
whole motley multitude of clerics, both of high and
low degree, and not to the priesthood only. We
might else be surprised at the warnings which recur
not to keep bad company, or haunt the taverns, or eat and
drink too much when asked out to dinner, or show excessive
fondness for play-acting and popular amusements. The
taste for field sports was a dangerous one, as bishops felt
when poaching rectors trespassed on their manors, and it
also brought the sportsmen into risk from the Forest Laws,
which were exceedingly severe. Even an archbishop was
called to account by the Justices of the New Forest, when
he indulged in a run with the hounds to vary the monotony
of a visitation round. At a manor court in Wiltshire in
1361 a whole band of clergy were convicted of night poaching, and there are many references in the Registers to like
offences.

We may fairly qualify and limit the conclusions to be
drawn from the statements found in episcopal Registers
and the Records of church councils, dealing as they do
exclusively with the darker aspects of parochial life, in the
frailties and shortcomings of the clergy.

But the evidence presented in the lamentations of the

poet Gower in his *Vox clamantis* cannot be ignored or treated
lightly. Page after page describes in woeful terms
the vices and the follies of the priests of different Evidence of Gower.
classes, rectors, vicars, stipendiaries and chaplains,
and there are no fairer features painted to relieve the
depressing picture. We may hope that it is overcoloured ;
satire at its best is incomplete ; but Gower was no cynic, full
of scorn at hypocrisy to be unmasked, with morbid insight
into the meaner side of human nature. He writes as a
moralist to whose eyes "the times are out of joint," and he is
deeply pained by the degradation of a high ideal. The
shortcomings of the clergy have in all ages furnished ample
materials for satire ; but such sweeping charges of coarse
vices as Gower recounts at length would be now simply
impossible for any satirist or critic and even after allowance
has been made for the ruder spirit of those times, it must
be owned that the level which they imply was very low.

We may pass on to consider next the forms and extent of
the provision made for the maintenance of the parochial
clergy. By the middle of the thirteenth century
their right to the tithes had become a recognised Disputes about tithes.
principle of the law courts, excepting when
documentary evidence could be adduced to show that any
had been assigned to a religious house. But how far the
right extended, and what persons could claim them in each
case, were questions not so easily decided. The constitutions
passed by the church councils, the rolls of Parliament, the
year-books of the law courts, and the registers of the bishops,
abound in details upon the subject. The titheable produce
of the land included not only the corn crops and the hay,
but fruit and honey, butter and cheese and wool, chickens
and doves, lambs and calves. The fish taken from the waters
and the venison from the forest, the gains of the miller and
the merchant, the professional man's earnings even were
subject to the claim, though probably as a counsel of perfection, without much legal sanction. The poet's gains are
even mentioned in the list, though they yielded probably an
inconsiderable addition to the rector's income. The big timber
in the woods was matter of debate, and Parliament and Convocation were often busy with the difficulties it involved. A

number of nice questions came up for discussion, and councils treated them at length. Sheep and cattle often moved from their winter to their summer quarters : how should the rival claims of different parishes be adjusted when the shearing-time came round, or when the cheeses were carried to the market ? When fishermen landed with their takings in a strange parish and sold their fish away from home, who was the tithe-owner in such case ? Tithe-payers were often out of temper. Millers tossed the handfuls of meal out of their sacks, but would allow no boxes to be kept at hand in which they might be gathered up in safety; dairymaids took their milk to church and left it by the altar; discontented landowners put pressure on their tenants to leave the tithe sheaves badly bound so as to fall to pieces on the way, or rot in the rains and be trampled on by the cattle before they could be gathered. Some insisted on a feast or a present to their servants before they settled for their tithes, or protested that as they had less than ten lambs or kids or other creatures they could not give a tithe in kind. These and other abuses were denounced in synods with much strong language in the present and threats of pains to follow.

The endowments of the past were not the only source of income; there were many customary payments, to which long usage gave almost the force of vested rights.

Customary dues. Taken singly they seem trifling, like the fines and dues of the manorial courts, which are entered carefully on the margin of the court rolls. But as these formed in the aggregate an appreciable part of the profits of the manor, so of the corresponding payments at the church. For the amounts in the thirteenth century we may take the entries in the Ripon chapter books, as there is no reason to believe that they differed much from what prevailed else-where. The marriage fee was fourpence in each case, to be multiplied of course largely to give the present value; for a following ceremony, called *benedictio thalami*, another penny. For each baptism the offering was a halfpenny, and the churching offering was the same. The plough money, or plough alms, was another penny. There were Easter dues of varying amount, payments for obits and special masses for the dead, and besides pieces of money put into the tapers used at

Candlemas, the candles at the bier in every funeral, the christening robes of infants were often left for the benefit of the church funds.   Usage as to these dues varied from place to place ; some of them were often taken for the maintenance of the fabric or for other charges, but mostly they were looked upon as the personal dues of the incumbent.   There was one more of considerable value, especially when the freeholders were many, that of the "mortuary" or "principal."   The wills of the period constantly contain the bequest of the "best animal" or my "best quick good," with the clause that ecclesiastical usage so required.   It was a custom that crystallised into law.   In theory it was regarded as a compensation to be made for tithes forgotten or withheld, and it was recognised by Edward I. that there was a claim with which ecclesiastical courts could deal.   But Archbishop Winchelsey told the clergy to have God before their eyes in taking it, and Langham in 1367 bade them be content with the second best beast, and not to claim any when only two were kept.   All this was often supplemented by the produce of the glebe.   It is difficult to speak with any certainty as to the aggregate result, when the sources of income were so many and so varied in amount, but the beneficed clergy do not seem to have had reason to complain that the provision for their maintenance was scanty, as compared with that of other classes.   When Gregory XI. appealed in 1375 for a subsidy for the defence of the territories of the Church, he urged that England had a wealthy clergy, well able to contribute largely.

From the income of the clergy we may turn to the outgoings and ask what were the chief demands upon it beyond those of their personal needs.   The Crown laid the needs of the State before them and left them free Charges enforced. to vote in Convocation the subsidy which they could grant, relying on the influence of its ministers, themselves ecclesiastics commonly, to urge and justify the requirements of the State.   Once, indeed, and once only, Convocation ventured to deny formally the duty to tax itself for the necessities of the Crown on the ground of a papal prohibition.   The attempt, as has been seen, was a disastrous failure (*v.* p. 33).

The Papacy issued its demands in more imperious style for tenths, and Peter's pence, and procurations for the cardinals and others sent on diplomatic errands. The Registers abound in letters on the subject; mandates, notices of arrears, instructions to collectors, threats of sequestrations, fill page after page and prove that to these aliens English churchmen were not cheerful givers. The officials of the national Church had to be reckoned with besides. There were subscriptions for newly appointed bishops, hard pressed by fees at Rome and payments to the Crown (*v.* p. 223), the expenses of the visitation rounds of bishop and archdeacon, and the maintenance of the proctors sent to Convocation.

The duties of hospitality were frequently insisted on as a natural charge on the parochial income. Not only should the clergy have "a fairly constructed mansion in which bishop, archdeacons, and other officials might be fitly entertained," but they were expected to take in travellers of all degrees. Regard was had to this requirement when the vicar's portion was ordained. Parliament objected to non-residence on the ground that the beneficed clergy ought, by old custom, to keep up hospitality.

Hospitality.

Systematic alms-giving was also specially looked for at their hands. When a license of non-residence was given, the bishop constantly insisted that a part of the income of the benefice should be applied to local charities; a fat portion (*pinguis*) was the rule of Peckham, to be attested by four parishioners of credit. It is stated often as an unquestionable fact that the parochial endowments were of old intended partly for the poor. Thus Peckham orders a neglectful rector of Lyming to give 200 shillings to the poor; another is required to compensate for the lack of his own ministrations by liberalities "to be left to our discretion." The tripartite division of the tithes for clergy, poor, and fabric fund, which has been so often quoted in recent discussions on the subject, belonged indeed to an earlier period of Church history, before the parochial system had been organised upon its present basis. But the old tradition lingered on, and on all hands it was admitted that the poor ought to receive their share in the benefactions of the past, and a third is even mentioned as their due in a

Charity.

petition of the Commons under Henry V. as if the old rule were morally still binding. It should, however, be remembered that many sources of income were then titheable which are so no longer, and that tithe-owners now pay largely to support the poor, though the money passes perforce through other hands.

A large number of parishes were appropriated to religious houses which had managed to get hold of the rectorial tithes on grounds which are stated in another chapter. Bishops could insist that the care of the parish should not be entrusted to the services of temporary deputies, and that an adequate part of the endowment should be set aside for the maintenance of a permanent vicar. The Registers specify the various forms of lesser tithes, the extent of glebe, the fees and offerings and buildings to be handed over in each case ; they adjust the local burdens and determine the respective duties of the parishioners and the incumbents in providing the service-books, the vestments, and the fittings of the church. The bishop modifies from time to time the earlier conditions, deciding that the vicar's portion is too scanty, and insisting on a fresh division.

The vicar's portion.

The unbeneficed clergy formed a large class, which was needed in consequence of the pluralities and dispensations of which there were so many, as well as the foundation of the chantries, to be mentioned presently. For these the normal stipend was for a long time about five marks, increased probably to some extent by offerings and fees. When the plague had made havoc in their ranks, it was natural that better terms should be desired and secured, and a limit of eight marks is mentioned under Henry V. Unwilling to accept the legalised pittance while prices of provisions were on the rise, many declined to bind themselves to settled posts and hoped to do better for themselves in other ways. Some hired out their services for memorial masses, which they eked out by occasional duties. Others hoped for better things from the liberality of rich merchants, especially at the seaports, or from county squires, whom they served as household chaplains. The beneficed clergy felt aggrieved, and begged the bishops to come to their relief, for surely, they thought, these clergy unattached were

Stipendiary priests.

bound to take parochial work when adequate payment was secured them. The bishops thought so too, and insisted strongly, and in some cases with success, that definite offers must be at once accepted. There was friction between the two classes sometimes on other grounds. An order of Winchelsey (1305) insisted that the stipendiary priests should bind themselves by oath to do nothing in the parish to prejudice the interests of the rectors, to stir up the ill-feeling of the parishioners against them, or claim any of the offerings in the church.

The subordination of the clergy to the bishops was for the most part very real and thorough. At the beginning of our period, as has been seen, a vigorous effort was made *Residence not enforced.* by Peckham to force the beneficed clergy to reside. Though it failed to touch the king's clerks (*v.* p. 22), it might have succeeded with the rest, but the movement was short-lived. Pestilence, nepotism, and court favour, and above all the provisions of the Papacy, combined to disorganise the parochial system. Stringent rules might be made indeed and published in the synods, but they were not long enforced, such as that of Bishop Woodlock (1308), that no parish priest should absent himself from his cure for a single night without provision for any sudden call. The presentments made at the visitations in the fifteenth century insist much on this neglect : " Mr. Vicar abydes not emange us as a curette awght to do." The belief is not expounded to the parishioners three times in the year, though it is noted also that when sermons are preached "the most part of the parishioners cummeth not at all."

The bishops spoke in peremptory terms to non-resident rectors who farmed their tithes and houses with a view to *Strictness on some points.* profit only. Disorderly persons, they complained, occupied the parsonages with their wives and children, turned them even into taverns, and disturbed the peace to the discredit of the Church. They insisted that the tithe produce should be stored on the glebe land and not sold in advance before the end of harvest, or put beyond the reach of sequestration, for the object of the order was in part to strengthen their own coercive powers.

There is little evidence as to the conditions under which

the parish churches were originally built, but it is quite clear
that the responsibility of providing for repairs,
enlargement, or rebuilding when required, fell _{Repairs of churches.}
upon the whole body of parishioners.   The bishops
sent peremptory mandates which specified the work which
should be done, the limits of the time allowed for it, and the
penal consequences of neglect.   Town councils sometimes
portioned out the work among the people, getting some to
dig the stone, others to cart it from the quarries, sending
collectors round, and reporting the niggardly to the archdeacons.   Of course it was often recognised that the parishes
might be too poor to bear the burden unassisted.   Appeals
were made to the benevolence of a wider area, indulgences
were offered to stimulate reluctant charity, subscriptions
authorised in popular centres, agents (*quæstores*) licensed to
receive the funds.   At times penances were commuted into
fines to be handed over to the fabric fund, confessors were
urged to press the good work upon the notice of the dying,
and estates of intestates were devoted with episcopal sanction
to this work of charity.   The Corporation of Plymouth, which
had the charge of the vestments of St. Andrews, ruled that
the second best copes only might be used for the funeral of a
parishioner who left the Church less than twenty shillings in
his will.   And at Rye, when stray animals were found in the
churchyard, a fine was levied on the owners for Church uses.
Another way of raising funds was that of a "Church Ale,"
which was held not only as of old on the annual village
festival, but at other times for special purposes, and thus
became the mediæval equivalent of a bazaar or public dinner
for a charity ; the difference being that it was a general
merrymaking for the whole community, following a brew of
ale on a large scale, when people drank their heartiest for the
benefit of the Church, and sympathising neighbours came
from the parishes around.

So churches rose, and grew to statelier dimensions, and it
was a matter of local pride and pious joy to watch their
progress.   In ages when the peasants' homes were _{Local pride in the churches.}
miserable hovels, and manor houses judged by our
modern standards must have been comfortless and
dreary, the parish church, often beautiful in its proportions

and details, seemed to welcome them at all times under its roof and let the humblest feel that it was his.   To adorn and beautify the buildings thus erected was a labour of love, in which every class of society took part.   In wealthier communities the gifts flowed freely in, painted windows were put up by prosperous burghers and enterprising guilds ; silver chalices, embroidered copes, costly hangings, banners, pyxes, lamps, were stored up in many a town parish, to say nothing of famous shrines like those of Walsingham and Canterbury, where countless pilgrims left some token of their visit.   The richer churches had their watching chambers where clerks could be posted on the look-out above to guard the treasure.   Seldom a will passed through the Courts of Probate which had not some bequest, however modest, in favour of the parish church, and the poorest who had no other means could leave at least some homely ewer of which use might be made.   All this indeed has wholly disappeared, swept away in the havoc and the plunder of the Reformation ; only the bare inventories now remain to show how vast were the accumulated stores which bore their witness to the pious liberality and local pride of many generations.

As population grew in the hamlets of a widely scattered parish, little chapelries were raised for local needs, and occasional ministrations were supplied.   Then, as the Registers of Exeter bear witness, came heartburnings and disputes, and the bishop had frequently to regulate the relations of these chapels to the mother church, the claims for rights of burial, the offerings and dues which might not be too much diverted from the centre.   On the great festivals the people from outlying hamlets thus provided were expected to attend service in the mother church, and to go thither in procession once a year, just as in Whitsun week they went from neighbouring parishes to the cathedral, to keep alive the sense of union in the whole Church, falling out, however, sometimes by the way.   Oratories were fitted up in wealthier houses, from love of ease, or pride, or on grounds of health, but the sanction of the bishop was only given when the interests of the parish church had been secured.   Formal monitions even were addressed to villages where the parishioners had de-

Hamlet chapels.

serted their own churches to attend early masses at some chapel near.

The rights of sanctuary could be asserted only for a consecrated building, and the occasional neglect of the rite of dedication might have grave consequences in a turbulent age.   Thus in a case which is reported in *Rights of* a Year-book of the first Edward, a man brought up *sanctuary.* on a charge of robbery pleaded that he was dragged away by violence from the church of N., where he had taken refuge, and claimed it as his right to be restored to the sanctuary again.   He was told that the church had never been dedicated by a bishop, and a jury decided that it was in fact an unconsecrated building, for which no such immunity existed.

We hear most of course upon this subject in connection with the abbeys and cathedrals with which history is most concerned.   Thus the Frithstool, or seat of peace, to which men fled of old for safety, is still shown at Hexham.   From this, old records said, it was an inexpiable crime to drag a fugitive away.   The knocker on the north door at Durham is thought to have been used by those who fled from their pursuers to rouse the watchmen, who were in readiness in the rooms above to let them in at any hour of the night, and toll the Galilee bell as public notice that some one had come in for sanctuary. At Beverley any who sought refuge had food provided for them with a lodging in the precincts for thirty days, after which the privilege secured them as far as the borders of the county.   Sometimes, indeed, the pursuers braved the spiritual censures and laid violent hands upon the run-away. But it was a dangerous thing to do, and they commonly kept watch outside in the hope that he might venture forth. Nicholas the porter had helped to seize some who had taken refuge in a church at Newcastle, and who were put to death afterwards for their crimes.   He could only obtain pardon by the influence of the pope's nuncio, and was whipped at Durham publicly for three days by the curate of the church whose privileges he had thus set at nought.   Yet this privilege of sanctuary, like "the benefit of clergy," was no real gain to the interests of the Church.   Both shocked the common sense of an Italian visitor (1496), who saw in them encouragement to ruffians and highway robbers, and thought the prevalent insecurity of the roads must be largely due to their abuses.

There were indeed outbreaks at times of sacrilegious violence by which the churches were despoiled. We read in Gregory's *Chronicle* a curious story which illustrates the alternations from bold irreverence to religious awe. Many churches were robbed of the boxes which contained the sacramental elements, and "sad men deemed that there had been fellowship of heretics associate together." But it was found out that the copper had been mistaken for silver gilt. A company of the thieves were sitting at their supper, and one of them talked profanely of the elements which he had eaten, and thus "shamed some of them in their hearts." A locksmith who had made the robbers' tools was present at the meal, and on the morrow he went to church to hear a mass, and "prayed God of his mercy," but could not see the Host at its elevation. "Then he was sorry, and abode till another priest went to mass . . . and saw how the Host lay upon the altar, and all the signs and tokens that the priest made, but when the priest held up the blessed sacrament, he could see nothing of that blessed body of Christ, and then he deemed it had been for feebleness of brain, and went into the alehouse and drank an *ob* (halfpenny worth) of good ale and went to church again, but in no manner might he see that blessed sacrament, . . . then both he and his fellowship lacked grace."

But withal the habits of the age show a curious medley of irreverence and respect in the uses of their churches. Bishops and archdeacons might be disturbed by armed rioters at their visitations (*v.* p. 64); other scenes of turbulence have been described already. Apart from such spectacles, churches were put often to incongruous uses ; parsons stored their grain and straw within the nave, or for some small payment allowed their parishioners to do so ; it was requisite for synods to repeat the warning that markets were not to be held inside the church, for at Exeter the mayor bore witness that the traders were "wont to lay open, buy and sell divers merchandise in the said church and cemetery, . . . as at Wells, Salisbury, and other places more." The mummery of the Boy-bishop spread in later

middle ages from the cathedrals to the parish churches with
sportive scenes and broad burlesque of episcopal dress and
ministrations, in which choir-boys and singing-men took part.
Grandisson complained that the masquerading and buffoonery
of the vicars choral at the feast of the Holy Innocents discredited their dignity and profaned the sacred building.
Wykeham thought it needful in his statutes to insist that his
schoolboys should not play at ball or disorderly games inside
the chapel to the destruction of the stalls and windows.
At St. Paul's each serjeant-at-law had a pillar in the nave
where he met his clients and did business ; stalls were set up
for merchandise inside, and people amused themselves with
the game of fives, and the motley crowd that strolled, chatted,
and bargained up and down Paul's walk, in the centre of the
old cathedral, showed scant reverence for consecrated ground.
Indeed, in most parishes the church was treated as a place of
business as well as worship, for auditing the town accounts,
for justices to try cases of assault, and for the election of a
mayor.   At Ramsey the priest paid the Corporation not to
hold their meetings in the church at the very time when
High Mass was going on.   Then, as now, idlers gathered
round the church in noisy groups, to be warned off—not by
county bye-laws, but by mandate of the bishops—while boys
broke the windows with catapult or ball.   There was one
use, however, to which in our island home it was not often
put.   In Southern lands there were many churches built like
castles, as havens of refuge for the weak, with frowning battle-
ments and fence of solid walls, but here their memories are
all of peace, not of civil feud or corsairs' raid.

In close connection with the parish churches there was a
large number of endowments, commonly called chantries,
which were founded during the fourteenth, and *Chantries.*
still more frequently in the last half of the
fifteenth century.   The primary object of most of these was
that masses might be regularly sung for the souls of the
founder and his family or friends at some altar in the parish
church, or a side chapel adjoining it.   The founder, after
license from the Crown to grant lands in mortmain, commonly
bound the chantry priest to take part in the ordinary services
of the church, in addition to his special work, and the clerical

staff was strengthened by his help. He was required also sometimes to keep a grammar-school for a certain number of free scholars, and these little foundations formed the nucleus of much of the secondary education of after times. But the lists drawn up at the time of the legalised dissolution of the chantries include a number of them in outlying hamlets of scattered parishes, which served the purpose of chapels of ease to the mother church, where many sick and aged were too far distant from the centre. Some of these were endowed by men of wealth, but others were due "to the benevolence of the parochians for their own ease," "to pray for the prosperity of the parochians living, and the souls of the departed." The special reasons for their usefulness are added here and there : "having raging waters there ofttimes, we can in no wise pass to the parish church." Sometimes they were intended for the convenience of travelling folk, or as a resource in case of plague. When so many of this class disappeared, or lost their endowments in the general pillage at the Reformation, they must have left a considerable blank in the ministrations of the parishes concerned.

The local pride and zeal of the inhabitants, which have been already spoken of in connection with the buildings of the churches and the hamlet chapels, showed *Church-wardens' accounts.* itself in a variety of other forms. Happily a number of the churchwardens' accounts of early date have been saved here and there from moths and damp, both in town and county, and they bring before our fancy some features of interest in the common life of a mediæval parish. It there appears as a free republic, organised on a purely religious basis, with no civil functions or responsibilities, no poor, highway, or school rates, subject only to the control of bishop or archdeacon. It cut across manorial lines, including as it did sometimes several manors, sometimes a fraction only of a large one. While the manor court insisted on the distinctions of free and servile status, and tended jealously to preserve the burdens and disabilities of base tenure, in the parish all sorts and conditions of men were on the same level of privilege and service. The lord might, if he pleased, be buried within the church ; his lady might sit "y-paroked (enclosed) in her pue," but payments must be made in each case to the churchwardens for the honour or convenience involved. Fees for "lairstalls," or graves within the church, as well as pews inside it, were frequent in the fifteenth century, as 3s. 4d. for a grave, and as much for having the name put on the bede-roll. The wills of the period contain bequests for the expenses of the "seats called puinge" which might be turned into a source of income. In the meetings for the auditing of the accounts, which were held in church, any of the parishioners might be present; young women even appeared to bring their offerings, and the warden's post might be filled by either sex. We can hardly fail to be impressed, as we turn over the pages, by the abundant evidence of hearty zeal and liberality in all classes which the accounts furnish. There is nearly always money in hand, to be handed over to the incoming wardens, sometimes to a considerable amount. In one case, that of Bridgwater, we read of a compulsory rate, or an assessment, as early as 1383, and elsewhere there is mention of proceedings threatened against defaulters who had promised but not paid their contributions. But commonly they are free-will offerings that we read of; not the large benefactions of the rich, which were funded rather as endowments, and did not pass through the churchwardens' hands, but a multitude of little gifts from those who had comparatively little to bestow. Sometimes the minutes of the meetings, as at Croscombe, are entered in dramatic form. Various guilds are represented as appearing by deputations or officials to present the sums which they have gathered; the young men and the maidens make their collective offerings, for each have taken possession of the road at Hock-tide and made the passers-by pay toll; "there comes in A. B. with the church money that he had in his hands a year ago," and reckons up the increase of it. The various benefactions and payments are recorded: the silver marriage rings which were often promised or presented, the "vyolet long gown in graine," the "vestment of flowery satin," the "kerchief of sypers" (Cyprus silk), the "ewer" or "great brass pot," or "3 silver spoons," which may be turned into money for the church's good, or fourpence from a poor man for the bells; the "money of the Croke" (the processional Cross) which was collected at high feasts, the revenue of the lands, buildings, or livestock which belonged already to the parish. The town-parish of St. Michael's, Bath, had a flock of sheep, of which the wool and lambs were brought into account, or else it was let out at a money rent. At Pilton there was a distinct keywarden, or "guardian of the cows," belonging to the church, for the hire of each of which one shilling a year was paid, and each had its surety to be responsible for its good treatment. Even a swarm of bees might be included in the livestock.

We may read in the same records the detailed accounts of the building of a church-house for Croscombe in 1481, the bills of the carpenter and masons and "diverse things" amounting to £12:2:11, which was all paid out of the savings of the fund. Such parochial halls were usual at this time. They often grew out of, or superseded, the bakehouse, "holy bread-house" and brew-house which had been long used before for parish needs. They were employed on general holidays for entertainments, the proceeds of which figure in the accounts, as the "wives' dancing" or the revel, or the Church Ale, and in these neighbouring parishes sometimes took their part, and liberally paid their quota. The house might be let out for the uses of the guilds or others as at Palton, where we find the entry "six hirings of the church house for 16 pence each, and two for hire of the Chetyll (kettle)," even Egyptians (gipsies) and Jews being allowed for special purposes to rent the hall.

At St. Peters-in-the-East, in Oxford, the wardens not only made profit, as elsewhere, by the sale of the ale and bread which were brewed and baked in the church house, but they also kept a stock of garments and stage properties, which they let out for hire (v. p. 372), and supplied torches to be used at the funerals of the students, while at Stogursey they went so far as to let out at a rent the very "Juells of the church," whether silver plate or vestments adorned with precious stones.

From the accounts of the expenditure we gather that nearly all the work required for the fittings of the church was done upon the spot. If the parish wished to beautify the building with a new roodscreen, it paid the expenses of a small committee who visited some neighbouring town or village famed for a model work of art, which might suggest details for imitation. They bought the timber as it stood and had it carted home, and the local artists set to work with the fine results that in some cases still remain. Strong local pride. The items of the expense are then minutely stated, even to the twopence for two pounds of "talowe for the carpenters." One such work at Yatton we can watch throughout its progress, as we read page after page of the outlay on the rich carving, and the eighty images or more with which it was adorned, the local carpenter's account alone amounting to £31, or more than £300 in our modern value. So when new mass-books, psalters, and processionals were needed, the parchment was bought, the scribe engaged, and when his labours were completed to the satisfaction of the clergy, the bookbinder was brought in to do the rest. The various duties connected with the care of buildings, land, and livestock, where they were held, the trading ventures at the church house, the sale of the miscellaneous gifts presented, must have made large demands upon the time and thought of the officials. At St. Michael's, Bath, there was an occasional allowance of twelvepence to the warden as a stipend; there is also reference to some feasting at the audit which does not appear so nakedly in other records. Commonly the duties of the office seem to have been undertaken freely and discharged in a hearty spirit.

In attendance on the incumbent in the church and also in the visitation of the sick was a "clerk," generally called "the carrier of the holy water," and required to be in minor orders, who was paid partly by funeral and Parish clerk. marriage fees, and partly by the parishioners or the common fund. He had little to do with the vestments or the furniture, and in one case we read that "he shall be charged with nothing save one chalice, and with the church door key, this to keep and hide as he will do for his own." At a Synod of Exeter a rule was made in 1289 that where there was a school within ten miles of the parish some scholar should be chosen for the office, which might thus serve as a sort of exhibition for a deserving student. The care of the vestments, the scouring of the candlesticks, the melting down of the old wax were paid for by arrangement, and once the washerwoman made a free-will offering of her work.   The use of organs was exceptional, but clocks and bells were very general in the fifteenth century and involved much expense and local interest, though at Lambeth it required a monition from the bishop to provide the bells. So long as this hearty spirit for the public good was strong there was little need of such a warning as we find that parishioners must go to their own church only, though curiosity might take them to the sermons of a friar of repute. It is not easy to believe that such good feeling could have been long lived and strong if the clergy on their side had been slothful and unworthy.

At Exeter, in 1289, boxes (*trunci*) had been set up outside the church by some parishioners that money might be given Almsgiving. there rather than into the hands of the officiating clergy.   It was peremptorily ordered that such alms-boxes should be speedily removed, and the old customs revived. The dispute seems to have turned upon the rival claims of the clergy who benefited by the offerings in the church, and of the wardens' fund, for which special offerings were made. In neither case was it a question of almsgiving in our modern sense.   Not that the necessities of the poor were disregarded, for the duty was brought prominently forward in another social movement with which we have now to deal.

Industrial and commercial motives had long since drawn men together to further the special interests of a great Guilds. variety of trades and crafts.   Guilds had been formed which not only kept in view the welfare of the whole union, but acted as provident societies to relieve the sick and indigent among the members.   By the side of these, with which we are not now concerned, a great variety of others came into being from the end of the fourteenth century onwards, in which the religious and charitable aspects were more marked.   They were often named after a church festival or patron saint, and their rules laid stress on the devotional objects, and on the good works which were to take many other forms besides those of mutual help.   Thus the Guild of Corpus Christi at York found " 8 beds for poor people being strangers, and one poor woman to keep the said

beds, by the year 14 shillings and 4 pence." At Beverley
the Guild of St. Helena was bound "to maintain two, three,
or four bedridden poor folks while they live, and when they
die they must bury them, and choose others in their places."
It was a common feature in their rules that age, mis-
chance, and infirmity on the part of any of the members
should give a right to help. Brethren cast into prison were
to be visited, dowry provided for poor maidens, pilgrims to
be lodged and "a woman found to wash their feet." Some
made a point of contributing to the repairs of bridges and
highways ; some provided free schooling for the young ;
many charged themselves with the support of churches.
The larger guilds frequently had chaplains of their own,
whose duties and stipends were carefully prescribed.

The regulations insisted often on the decorum and
courtesies to be observed ; unruly speech was to be silenced,
quarrels and suits-at-law discountenanced among
the members, and friendly arbitration was to take Disciplinary rules.
their place. We may take, as an example of the
moral influence desired, the ordinances of the Guild of St.
Ann in the Church of St. Lawrence Jewry. "If any of the
company be of wicked fame of his body, and take other
wives than his own, or if he be hold a common lechour . . .
or rebel of his tongue, he shall be warned of the warden
three times ; and if he will not himself amend, he shall pay
to the wardens all his arrearages that he oweth to the
company, and he shall be put off for evermore."

Orderly as they would have their brotherhood, they
loved social merriment in season. In splendid pageant and
procession they acted out before men's eyes, on
their anniversaries, the story of their patron saint, Pageants.
or the devotional associations of their common name. At
Norwich it was their custom that "a knave child innocent
shall bear a candle that day, the weight of two pounds, led
betwixt two good men, tokenning of the glorious martyr"
(St. William). At York, on the Friday after Corpus Christi
day, the Guild, which was called after the holy day, "kept a
solemn procession, the sacrament being in a shrine borne
in the same through the city of York," and in this festive
show, in the year 1413, "96 separate crafts took part,

and no less than 54 distinct pageants were prepared and presented in the procession by these crafts, while ten more made the show the more glorious by bearing a vast number of blazing torches."

In the face of such merrymakings, of which examples might be multiplied, and the good cheer of their anniversaries, it seems fanciful to connect, as has been of late suggested, the devotional character of these brotherhoods with the deeper earnestness caused by the shock of the Black Death. Nor, on the other hand, is it likely that many of the guilds were intended as a protest, as has been also thought, against the austerer doctrines of the Lollards ; but they may serve to prove that the great mass of the people was minded to walk in the old paths, and take part in the ancient usages of the Church, in which gorgeous ceremonial and symbolic forms were wont to stir the reverent fancy as the memories of the past were acted out before men's eyes.

AUTHORITIES.—Besides the illustrations of clerical conditions and parochial life to be found in episcopal Registers and the Reports of the Church Councils, we may refer to the *Churchwardens' Accounts*, ed. Bp. Hobhouse, 1890 (Somerset Record Society) ; *Somerset Chantries*, ed. E. Green, 1888 (Somerset Record Society) ; *English Gilds*, ed. Toulmin Smith, 1870 (E. E. T. S.) ; *Records of the Sanctuaries of Durham and Beverley*, 1837 (Surtees Society) ; *Yorkshire Chantry Surveys*, ed. W. Page, 1888-92 (Surtees Society) ; Gregory's *Chronicle* in the *Historical Collections of a Citizen of London*, ed. J. Gairdner, 1876 (Camden Society) ; *Chapter Acts of Ripon*, ed. J. T. Fowler (Surtees Society) ; *Parish Priests and their People*, E. S. Cutts, 1898 (S.P.C.K.).

CHAPTER XIV

THE MONASTIC LIFE

THE development of the conventual system under the
Benedictine rule belongs to an early period of Church history.
Succeeding centuries witnessed the rise and wide-
spread extension of other great religious orders, *The decline of the convents.*
but in the later middle ages progress had ceased
for all alike ; their popularity had waned ; at best in favoured
cases there were signs only of arrested growth, the rest were
moving on the downward road of disorganisation and decay.

In earlier days, indeed, the monks had done good service
in many forms of social work. Though retiring from the
world in the enthusiasm of a spiritual ideal to a haven of
peace and house of prayer, they had inspired by their example
respect for the steady industries of manual labour. They were
pioneers of agricultural progress, they had also fostered art
and learning, storing in their libraries the literary treasures of
the past, and preserving in their chronicles the story of their
times. But this many-sided activity had now become for
most of them a tradition rather than a present fact, and
spiritual fervour had not gained in strength when their
secular interests were narrowed. Time after time, indeed, new movements spread in favour of a stricter rule
and more ascetic practice ; the Cluniac and Cistercian and
Carthusian systems one after another with their higher
standards raised for a while the tone of cloistered life, and
braced its energies afresh. In England from early days the
convents had been numerous and large ; the reforming
movements that came across the Channel had been warmly

welcomed, but the enthusiasm of such revivals seemed to
have spent its force ; passionate aspirations ceased to disturb
the calm of the old religious houses, and there was little
talk of founding more, or of establishing new orders.

At the close of the thirteenth century notices constantly
recur of the financial straits in which the convents were
involved ; so grave, indeed, were these at times
that the inmates of Meaux, near Beverley, were
thrice dispersed by poverty. The crisis often
was so urgent as to call for the intervention of the
Crown. Impoverished communities were secured by formal
grant against the natural consequences of their mismanagement or misfortune, and the monks were treated tenderly
like wards in Chancery, too feeble to make provision for themselves. So frequently was this the case that a customary
form with little variation was adopted for the king's writ
which was issued on the subject. It described the community
in question as overwhelmed with debt, and in imminent danger
of destruction. To save it from such ruin the king granted
his protection, named special guardians of the estates, who
were to make reasonable provision for the monks, and apply
the balance of the income to pay off outstanding debts.
Meanwhile no sheriff or king's officer should demand admittance to the house.

Royal intervention sometimes, though rarely, took a
different form. When St. Augustine's at Canterbury was hard
pressed by debts incurred at the papal Court, the king appealed
to the tenants of the convent to raise a feudal aid for its
relief. To the Abbot of Cluny he complained that a prior
of a dependency in England had saddled his priory with
heavy debts caused by bribes and litigation on his own behalf,
and these, the king insisted, he should be called on to refund.

To ascertain the causes of these financial straits we
must refer to the chronicles which deal with the details
of cloistered life. Some convents by their broad
lands and seeming wealth had tempted plunderers
who could not be resisted. The Papacy and the Crown by
turns had drawn from them subsidies to fill their coffers.
Great nobles, jealous of their state and power, had used
favour at court or local influence to their hurt. Sometimes

*Financial
straits.*

Many causes.

the monks had overbuilt themselves. An ambitious abbot with architectural tastes or love of splendour had used his paramount influence to push on the building of a stately church or large refectory, and left the convent burdened with a debt, which grew steadily when the Jews or other money-lenders appeared upon the scene. Sometimes they had been too eager to add to their estates, had bought hastily but not wisely, and had bound themselves to provide annuities, of which under the name of "corrodies" more must presently be said. Some houses, or their ruling powers, had a marked taste for litigation, which was indeed often needed to defend their interests from grasping neighbours, but was pushed very far at times at grievous cost. The greater houses which had purchased dearly the privilege of exemption from episcopal control had to spend largely when they sent their abbot-elect to sue in person for the papal sanction. Some complained that the duties of hospitality had overtasked their means, if they were near a great highroad or noble mansion, where travellers were always passing to and fro. Here we read of extravagance and wanton waste; there of the sloth or favouritism of an easy-going prior which had wrecked the interests of the brotherhood he ruled. The special causes differed widely, though the net result might be the same.

But one general reason may be given, combined indeed in varying degree with any of the rest, but often of itself enough to account for the straits of which we read. The monks could not live at the old rate on their lands alone, and other sources of income mainly ceased to flow.   No new endowments. Great nobles and landowners had built their houses or endowed them; queens had been their nursing mothers; but there had also been a steady inflow of liberal gifts from year to year. The titled visitor who spent a night with them as guest or pilgrim presented his offering at the altar; pious neighbours left in their wills some token of respect, bought at a price the privilege of their prayers, or of interment in their holy ground. There were many benefactions given by sympathising friends to provide more comfort for them in their sickness, to furnish them with better clothes, and improve, as three times happened at St. Alban's, the quality even of their beer. On the strength of such support the standard of expenditure was raised, new buildings rose, lay brethren and servants were liberally housed, and though there were still some working bees, the life was mainly ceremonious and costly. In later days the gifts came scantily and slowly in; other interests displaced them in the popular fancy; friars, chantries, collegiate churches, hospitals, and schools appealed more to the sympathies of the generous and pious, and hard times set in for the old religious houses of shrinking income, failing numbers, and discredited repute.

We cannot but look with interest for some answer to the natural question how we should explain this difference of sentiment as regards them. Was it a mere shifting of religious fashion, a change in the popular ideal of the spiritual life, or was there enough to justify it in the demoralised conditions of the communities of later days? That much of the contemporary literature paints them in unfavourable colours is quite certain, but its evidence may be questioned as the utterance of prejudiced and one-sided critics. Satire exaggerates and distorts. The vehement attacks of controversialists like Wyclif cannot be accepted as fairly representing actual facts, for the darker side only is described and all the better features are omitted. There is no lack, however, of evidence of a weightier kind. The letters of the bishops and the records of their formal visitations abound in information on the subject, but they deal for the most part with the smaller houses, and in them only with the shortcomings of discipline and order, and are wholly silent as to all besides. They must be used therefore with caution, lest we lose sight of the balance and proportions of the truth. The monastic chronicles, however, were written by men who were in perfect sympathy with the theory of conventual life, and had intimate acquaintance with the practical details; their personal references betray of course the bias and antipathies of ordinary human nature, but the general description of what passed within the convent walls may be relied on as faithful studies from the life. They represent, without disguise, the interests which stirred the current of their daily thought, the ebb and flow of spiritual zeal, the grave anxieties and petty bickerings, the

[marginal note: Monastic chronicles.]

methods of administration and the expedients of finance. They are of widely different character, and their value varies from place to place, and still more from age to age. Some, like the famous records written at St. Alban's, contain first-rate historical materials for the larger interests of social life, as well as for the special details of the conventual system. The earlier writers combined some critical insight with their literary tastes, and enjoyed what were at the time unique advantages for the work which they were authorised to carry on. There were facilities of intercourse with correspondents in the distant houses of the order to which the monastery itself belonged ; the noble traveller who sought a passing welcome was often making history himself in the great world, and had much to tell of courts and council chambers ; the abbot was a peer of Parliament and conversant with the main questions of home and foreign policy ; the pilgrims who were entertained brought with them news of foreign lands ; and royalty itself did not disdain to give encouragement and help to an historiographer of note.

But the abler of these writers with their wider outlook belong mainly to an earlier age. It is a great change to pass from the variety and picturesque detail of Matthew Paris of St. Alban's to the narrowed themes and duller style of his successors, and in most of them the stream of monastic history flows feebly on during some part of the fourteenth century and then commonly ceases altogether. It was not merely a change in the direction of their studies ; the monks did not devote their energies to other forms of literary work, or become theologians and preachers. The great schoolmen had no successors in the cloister ; the revival of ancient culture found little sympathy from them, and Gascoigne insisted bitterly on the decline of scholarship among them.

It is an obvious objection that to judge convents by this utilitarian standard is to apply a rule that was not thought of in the early days when they were founded. It was to save their own souls that the monks sought the cloister, not to be useful to society at large ; the enthusiasm of the noble founders who endowed the convents was stirred by the sense of the ascetic aims of the recluses, and by some hope to gain

the merit of their prayers. Their many services to the cause
of social progress were indirect results, and no part of the
original intention of the system. If the early Benedictines
drained the fens and cleared the forests, it was to provide
healthy discipline for their own lives, and not to inspire in
rude breasts respect for steady toil. In a later age, however, when a large part of the soil of England was held
by the "dead hand," the question forced itself upon
men's thoughts, what was there to show for all this vast
expenditure of the resources of the nation ? Were the monks'
lives so holy and the potency of their prayers so great that
nothing further need be asked for at their hands ? To monks
the early Christianity of England had been largely due ; how
were they helping now to spread the faith ? Were their
libraries being used as storehouses of learning for divines,
and their schools as seminaries for parochial preachers ?
Something no doubt was done in this respect. The inmates
of the larger monasteries did realise perhaps their obligations
in the matter, for in 1452, when Whethamstede was re-elected
Abbot of St. Alban's, he heard loud complaints of the want
of adequate grammatical instruction, the scanty numbers of
monastic students at the University, and the want of able
preachers in the pulpit.

The larger religious houses commonly had grammar
schools for the education of their younger members, to whom
some command of Latin was an indispensable
condition of promotion, and the lack of such
instruction was referred to in the injunctions of the bishops.
The chroniclers, however, do not speak with pride of
their theologians and scholars, but of skilful administration
and finance, and notwithstanding the advantages of ancient
libraries and ample leisure there is too little evidence of any
enthusiasm for learning or care for interests beyond the
routine of the conventual life. Nor was the monks' zeal
for the religious welfare of their neighbours very marked.
They had used steadily for many years their influence with
the landowners to get into their hands the advowsons of
the parish churches, but bishops had found it needful to
insist on some fixed provision for a permanent vicar, and had
readjusted it from time to time in cases where it was found

Scanty zeal.

to be inadequate. The episcopal Registers abound in the
formal details of such arrangements, and they point often to
grudging payments and unkindly pressure by the monks.

It may be said perhaps that at least their social action
was of undoubted value, in their charities for the
sick and poor, and their open-handed hospitality   Charity.
to passing guests.

The Benedictine system included an Almoner among the
officials of a convent, and it was his duty, as ruled by
Archbishop Lanfranc, to ascertain where the infirm or sick
were lying, and to visit and console them with such offerings
as he might have to give, but limiting his ministrations to
those of his own sex. According to the rule of the Austin
Canons again the almoner should be "pityful and God-
fearing . . . old men who are decrepid, lame, and blind or
bedridden, he should often visit and suitably supply." At
St. Swithun's, Winchester, the Manor of Hinton provided
for this purpose both money-rents and produce, but the
accounts show that the expenses of management were large.
At St. Peter's, Gloucester, the archbishop found it needful
to insist in 1301 that all the proceeds of the Manor of
Stanedisch should be spent as by rule upon the poor, and
that there should be no general entertaining with good cheer
at their expense. The Manor of Alton had been set aside
(1080-87) by the Abbot of Hyde with the assent of the
brotherhood for the maintenance of the pilgrims and the poor,
and the deed of gift expressed the wish that any one who
robbed the poor of this " might have his portion with Dathan,
Abiram, Judas, and Nero." But in the injunctions of William
of Wykeham to the abbey it is stated that the poor and the
infirm had been defrauded of their portion, notwithstanding
the pious intention of the donors, and like complaints were
made elsewhere, when the broken meals and cast-off clothes were
no longer distributed, to say nothing of more costly gifts.

At Winchester, Abingdon, and elsewhere, there were
hospitals maintained out of the abbey funds, but they consisted really of almshouses, for which there were commonly
trust funds, and the infirmary of the convent did not, of
course, receive sick folk from the outside. At some of the
greater monasteries, indeed, a few poor boys and clerks had

board and schooling provided for them freely, and it is pleasant to read in the will of a wealthy merchant of York that he bequeathed ten marks to the convent of Durham in return for the " sustenance which he had there in the days of his youth." Generally the monastic almsgiving of which we have details was due to the bequests made by pious donors for gifts on the anniversaries of their death. Thus at Meaux, among the list of donations for special purposes made to the abbey eighteen grants are mentioned for alms to be given at the gate. On the whole it must be said that the charity took the worst form, of doles spread broadcast from time to time, provided for the most part by special benefactions, and not to any great extent out of the common fund, which had been itself given originally in "free and perpetual alms."

It may be urged, however, that the convents showed in their relations to their serfs a generous spirit above the level of their age. Certainly manumissions, which were before occasional, became frequent in the fifteenth century.

Serfs manumitted.

At St. Swithun's there is an average of one every year; at St. Alban's many are recorded, and the fine varying from 3s. 4d. to 13s. 4d. for the whole family, which was at first noted in the margin of the Rolls, disappears entirely after 1467. But it is probable that the action of the monks was not so benevolent as it at first sight appears. There had been often discontent and friction in the past. The serfs at Risborough tried to throw off their bondage, and Christ Church, Canterbury, had a lawsuit which dragged on for fifteen years before the convent could make good its rights. The story was repeated in many another scene. After the insurrection of the peasants it was hard, if not impossible, to maintain the multifarious and vexatious incidents of forced labour, the details of which extend sometimes over half a page of a manorial custumal; serfs could slip away and soon make good their freedom in the town, and as land rose in value there was little to be gained by enforcing the conditions of the old servile tenure.

The duties of hospitality were fully recognised in early rules, and the qualifications of the hosteller (*hospitarius*) were carefully defined. He should have "facility of expression, elegant manners, and a respectable bringing up." A never-ending stream of travellers of all

Hospitality.

degrees flowed in through the doors of the monks who were
near the great highways. Kings and nobles sought a welcome
as a matter of course ; the visit of Edward III. and Queen
Philippa to St. Swithun's was marked by a heavy deficit in the
year's accounts ; the prior of Clerkenwell explains a large
excess of expenditure one year by referring to the "hospitality
offered to members of the royal family and other grandees of
the realm who lodge at Clerkenwell and remain there at the
cost of the house." So in the Hospitallers' Accounts for
Hampton the list of the guests ends with the words "because
the Duke of Cornwall lies near.' Many indeed forced themselves upon the monks, and poorer pilgrims suffered from the
exhaustion caused by such exaction. Edward I. therefore
prohibited the importunities of such intruders, and bade magistrates to institute inquiries on the subject, but the question
which was also asked, if any had revenged themselves
because of the refusal of the welcome, shows that it was
dangerous to enforce the rule.

At St. Alban's, towards the end of the fifteenth century,
it seems that hospitality was quite dying out. The abbey,
which of old had stabling for 300 horses, granted a license to
the landlord of "the George" to have an oratory and low
mass for the great men, nobles and others, who should be
lodged at his hostelry, for they came no more to stay within
the abbey walls. So too at Abingdon, while travellers of
rank were entertained at the abbot's table, there had been a
hospice attached to the abbey for the meaner guests, but in
1414 this was superseded by a "new hostelry" leased out by
the convent at a yearly rent as a public inn, in favour of
which a writ of Henry I. forbade any one to be housed in
the town except with the abbot's license. We hear of like
conversion of the hospice into a public inn at Glastonbury
and at Burcester, in the latter case soon after 1379, and the
Pilgrims' Inn at Gloucester points perhaps to a like change.

The conventual life, then, was becoming more earthly and
self-centred. The monks had no missionary enthusiasm ;
stirred no thrill of admiration by the ascetic rigour
of their rule ; their estates were leased to tenant Self-centred
life.
farmers ; they had ceased to introduce new methods,
or import fresh products. Their interest in history was dying

out; their hospitality was being shifted on the landlords of the neighbouring inns; their almsgiving took the most wasteful and unwise forms of indiscriminate doles. They did very little, in a word, for the service of the outer world.

But in the greater houses the routine of daily life was still marked by a calm dignity and stately order. The management of the whole had been divided into separate departments, over each of which was set a different monk, or "obedientiary" as he was often termed, as appointed by the abbot to whom he owed obedience, with distinct estates assigned to each, and personal responsibility when the annual account of income and disbursements was produced for audit. The organisation was methodical and complete, providing for many of the inmates special interests in the daily supervision of the different forms of work connected with church and buttery, cellar and kitchen, from each of which an official took his special name of sacristan, hordarian, cellarer, and many another. Each was charged with the book-keeping of the accounts connected with his own department, and many of these rolls drawn up by them are still remaining to illustrate the fare and cost of a great mediæval household, as well as the scrupulous care of the accountants. The centre of the conventual life was the consecrated building in which the daily round of prayer and praise went on. No cost was grudged, no efforts spared to enlarge, adorn, and beautify the church, which in the larger abbeys rivalled the cathedrals in magnificence and splendour. Many of the greatest of them have wholly disappeared, but others, as Westminster, Selby, and Tewkesbury, remain, like the cathedrals, to show on what a grand scale the Middle Ages planned and built. Their noble proportions and their lovely tracery still challenge admiration, though too often despoiled by sacrilegious hands of all the accumulated wealth of storied windows, costly vessels, and embroidered vestments, which had been the work of centuries of reverent devotion. The cloisters on the south side of the church were the busy scene of the home life of the brethren. Here the monks sat in their hours of leisure; through them, silent and lifeless as the arcades are now, they were always passing to and fro. On one side school was held for the young novices or singing-

Order in large convents.

boys; near at hand was the scriptorium where the materials
of their chartularies and the monastic annals were compiled,
where MSS. were copied and illuminations painted with
marvellously patient skill.   Meantime, many of the brethren
were abroad on the estates; the obedientiaries themselves
were often on the move in the interests of their departments,
for tenants and retainers needed constant supervision, and the
convent was a great co-operative household to be fed and
clothed by the produce of its own estates and the labours of
its own dependents.

The old renown, the vast estates and splendid minsters
of which they were the guardians caused some of these great
houses to fill a large place in contemporary thought.
Parliaments were held within their walls, as at *Evidence of
Gloucester in 1378, when the convent was thronged decline.*
with councillors and guests of all degrees, who held their
sports even in the cloister, as the monks complained, and left
not a trace of green upon their grass plots.   Their numbers
made it easy for them to choose strong men to rule them,
who could hold the reins with a firm hand and guard the
ancient order; the stately services went on without a break;
the monks lived their common life in refectory and cloister
with little change of outward form and in the full blaze of
publicity irregularities were rare and grave scandal little
known.   Their books were still guarded with fond pride, even
if they did not read them so much as of old, and it seemed
to the chronicler of St. Alban s an abominable thing when
a careless abbot offered to transfer some of their classics to
a famous book-collector.   Yet even then, under the most
favourable conditions, the tone of the records clearly shows
that a change had passed over the spirit of conventual order,
which was gradually settling into complete decrepitude and
decay.   At Christ Church, Canterbury, the stern disciplinarian Peckham at the close of the thirteenth century was
grievously disturbed by the dissensions, rising almost to
mutiny, which forced themselves upon his notice, and called
for repeated intervention.   At St. Alban's the change of
tone is unmistakable in later days.   Without much evidence
of open scandal till the end of the fifteenth century, it is clear
long before, that life moves on a lower moral plane; the aims

are meaner and ever more self-centred; quarrels and petty bickerings recur; while the abbot pays obsequious court to the ruling powers in Church and State, and traffic in patronage fills a large place in his thought.

Grave danger lay in the practical independence which some Orders, like the Cistercian, and of other Orders many great abbeys had secured, for it was a far cry to Rome when episcopal control had been removed.

Independence of control.

To meet the danger of increasing laxity, attempts were made to draw closer federal ties, and to have representative councils of the houses which belonged to the same Order. For the Benedictines a constitution was drawn up in 1334, and chapters were regularly held at fixed intervals. In several cases we have detailed reports of the proceedings, and they point to a real reforming movement in favour of a stricter rule.

Most frequently the disorder of a house could be traced to the vices or the weakness of its head. Sometimes he was only indiscreet, trying too hastily to tighten the bonds of discipline, and so provoking a defiance from insubordinate monks; sometimes recklessly wasteful in ambitious schemes, burdening the community with debts which recourse to usurers made absolutely crushing, as at Ramsey where the monks refused to sing in choir unless secured against the extravagance of the abbot. Sometimes he was domineering and self-indulgent, diverting the common funds to his own uses, starving the poor monks and letting the buildings go to ruin, as notably in earlier days at Evesham. More often the superior was weak, easy-going in his own personal habits, unwilling therefore or unable to restrain the rest, who drifted into lax ways, and hunted and hawked and took their pleasure like their country neighbours. In 1422 Henry V. summoned the abbots to meet him at Westminster and to debate with him on the reforms which seemed most pressing. Stress was laid on the ostentation and extravagance that were so rife, and on the necessity of better examples in high places. The abbot, or the prior where in a cathedral chapter the bishop took the place of abbot, was a feudal lord who had distinct estates and separate quarters and retainers. The Abbot of Glastonbury had ten manor-houses ready to

Misrule.

receive him with his train. When he journeyed abroad or visited his manors it was in stately guise with numerous attendants, and with hounds often or falcon at his side.

This pride of state and self-indulgence was not confined entirely to abbots. The Council of 1422 not only ruled that in their case the train of horses should not exceed the maximum of twenty, but went on to censure the growing extravagance in dress and diet, and the roving habits which were complained of in the monks at large. At Bury St. Edmund's the staff of retainers was divided among four departments with strict order of precedence; "the first cook and the gatekeeper were magnates who held office by hereditary succession and were enfeoffed with considerable estates." At Glastonbury there was like state; the butlership was vested at one time in a girl; sixty-six servants were employed in the domestic work besides the farm men on the home estate. At St. Mary's, York, the porter in 1404 disposes in his will of forty-four cows and four hundred sheep; he had lands also of his own, and refers to a dispute—perhaps a lawsuit with the convent which he served. In earlier days, indeed, many lay brethren (*conversi*) were admitted to help the monks in agricultural work and in the service of the household. But when the monks, drawn as they seem to have been mostly from the middle class, shrunk from hard work themselves, the lay brethren toiled less willingly and were more difficult to manage. On the farms they were superseded by a new class of tenant farmers, and in the house itself it was found convenient to replace them with hired servants, though at greater cost to the common fund. So popular literature describes the inmates of the cloisters as easy-going country gentlemen, not more self-indulgent than their neighbours, but not less inclined to the pleasures of the chase or of the table. Chaucer's satiric pictures of them, which would have been impossible a few generations earlier, probably did not shock many of his readers.

The outlying cells and chantries in districts far away from the parent monastery were not infrequently the cause of embarrassment and disrepute. When distant estates were acquired by gift or purchase, sometimes with the obligation to

^{Self-indulgence.}

provide religious ministrations on the spot, it was found needful to send a few monks, under a prior, to look after the cultivation of the land or attend to the chapel services. In early days, indeed, these cells were looked upon as places of banishment to which the refractory or unpopular among the brethren might be sent. The occupants of these cells might easily become engrossed by secular interests and the pursuits of country life, and drift into scandalous courses. It might be long before the discreditable rumours reached the ears of their superior at home ; if heard, they were not believed perhaps at first ; friends and neighbours used their influence in their favour ; or it was thought dangerous to recall discontented men who would unsettle quiet spirits in the convent, and who were most reluctant to return to the seclusion or routine of their old life.

The out-lying cells.

The allowances for board, called corrodies, had an unsettling influence on conventual order, and often proved a heavy drain on its resources. Those who profited by these were pensioners who either shared the common food or received fixed rations daily at the buttery and kitchen. Among the Hospitallers the pensioners, if of gentle blood, fared with the brethren. At Clerkenwell some were treated on a more liberal scale even than the members of the Order. The records of other houses state exactly the nature and value of the corrody, even to the quality of the beer allowed, with the sop to be dipped into it (*companagium*), and the nails with which the shoes were to be studded. It is pleasant to think of the old squire, hankering in his declining days for the calm and religious privileges of some neighbouring abbey, and making over to it a part of his estates on the condition that he should be welcomed as an inmate while he lived, and buried in its precincts when he died. Such cases are recorded, but men sometimes changed their mind, wearied of the monotony which had seemed so attractive at a distance, and turned back to the old life again. Thus Sir Ralph Wedon came to St. Alban's and proposed to remain there till his death. He gave a manor to the abbey, and no time was lost in selling it to avoid the risks of "mortmain" ; but he may have resented the haste with which the monks parted

Corrodies.

with his land, or if we trust the chronicler who calls him vain and fickle, he wearied of the quiet life which seemed so pleasant till he tried it, and so impatient was he to be gone that, being too weak to ride or walk, he hired a cart even, unseemly as it was thought, to take him off.

The corrody was sometimes given as a reward for long and faithful service to an advocate or agent who had defended the convent's interests in the law courts or at Rome— at Bath even to a plumber and glazier as a sort of retaining fee. It was often a compliment bestowed upon a patron or influential neighbour who wished to see an old retainer provided with a pension which could not safely be refused. Kings frequently made such demands, and that which had at first the semblance of a free gift was claimed afterwards as a right, especially in the houses that had royal founders, and when the pensioner died the Crown named another to succeed him. So the Bishop of Lichfield demanded a corrody for his cook, but Peckham would not let the Prior of Tutbury in Staffordshire consent to it. Even the high-minded Grandisson of Exeter made the same demand at Launceston for his own servant.

It was also a familiar method of finance when the rulers of a religious house wished to round off its estates or raise ready money to meet urgent needs. To take one case out of many, at St Swithun's, Winchester, a *A financial method.* pensioner paid down fifty marks for certain allowances of food and clothing, and bound himself to give the convent the benefit of his services as physician. In later days, when many of the houses were in financial difficulties, recourse was had to this expedient with ruinous results. Improvident priors pledged the resources of the future in order to raise petty sums, which they squandered or misapplied, and the bishops at their visitations found it needful to insist that the dangerous practice should be checked.

There were other reasons for discouraging the practice. In the smaller houses the presence of a few such boarders may well have had a disturbing influence upon the household. Their habits probably were not ascetic, *Moral dangers.* their requirements might lead to needless luxury, like the fine beds and costly vessels at Muchelney, which shocked Ralph of Shrewsbury, the Bishop of Bath and Wells. Their conversation with the anecdotes of camp and field, their amusements, however harmless, might not be such as stern disciplinarians would approve. Episcopal visitors gravely ruled that the monks must not play games with the pensioners; chess and draughts had a demoralising effect, it seems; nunneries must not have paying guests or boarders, for their frivolous gossip might lead the nuns' thoughts all astray and rudely jar with their devotional routine.

The rival interests of houses even of the same Order led at times to most unedifying scenes. Disputed boundaries, or a no-man's land between neighbouring estates, uncertain rights of patronage, questions of the dues at fair or market, these and the like caused long-standing disputes, coming to a climax now and then when sturdy monks gathered with their armed retainers to make good their claims with open show of violence and broken heads. The right of precedence in Parliament had been matter of dispute between the abbots of Westminster and St. Alban's; in 1417 they transferred the quarrel to land in dispute between their several estates. One erected a gibbet on it as a token of his feudal rights; the other had it levelled to the ground "by force of swords and axes." Set up once more, it was again demolished, while the tenants of the neighbouring manors, "for fear of their hides," stealthily made perambulations of the disputed ground and played thus at hide-and-seek for many years. This may be explained, perhaps, by the dramatic usages of feudal law, but disputes were carried further when the Abbot of St. John's at Colchester sent, in 1399, a party of monks to Snape in Suffolk, who broke into the prior's house and burnt the deeds that were found there, and then lay in wait outside, wounding his servants, burning his crops, and carrying off his stock.

Feuds between convents.

The spirit of faction and disorder within the conventual household was far more fatal to its usefulness and health. Such dissensions had not been unknown in earlier years, for the monks could not leave behind them at the cloister gate their natural infirmities of temper, but they became more frequent and intense as life grew more self-indulgent and discipline more

Factions within.

lax. At St. Alban's, towards the close of the fifteenth
century, the abbot twice applied to the Crown, at an interval
of sixteen years, for the arrest of an "apostate" monk, and
in the same terms: "Like another son of perdition he goes
about from town to town, and from market to market, more
like a vagabond and an apostate than a monk, and causes in
his travels the greatest scandal, as well to the Order as to
religion in general." Each of the two had been prior of a
dependent cell; each had been sent as a commissioner to
inquire into the conduct of the other; both were deposed
and reinstated, and one at least confessed that he repented
of the false charges he had brought. There are many
illustrations of such discord and intrigues in the annals of
the smaller houses, as notably in Meaux in 1353. Except
in the Carthusian Order there was no chance of privacy for
moody or impatient tempers, and the necessity of daily intercourse with uncongenial tastes and habits must have sorely
strained the powers of self-control. Dislikes grew more
intense with constant friction, till the mutinous or factious
spirit flared into a blaze, and wrecked the happiness of what
professed to be a pious brotherhood drawn together to help
each other to work out their own salvation.

The litigation in which the convents were so frequently
involved was a common result of the embarrassments of their
position. It was not only that in troublous times
with high-handed neighbours it was hard to   Litigation.
maintain their rights to the estates which they had long
enjoyed, but free gifts of lands had almost entirely ceased,
and in their place there was much bargaining and
questionable traffic. Estates held on doubtful tenure
were transferred on easy terms by timid owners, threatened
with a lawsuit or embarrassed by the feudal charges.
The convent with its powerful connections and experience of the chicanery of law might hope to keep its hold
on what it bought. Sometimes lands were acquired by
timely advance of ready money to spendthrifts hard pressed
by money-lenders, or on specified conditions for the maintenance of an orphan child, or in purchase of an annuity
in the form of bed and board. Misunderstandings and
disputes resulted often from these bargains; even free

donations made in earlier times were liable to be called in question, violence and threats were freely used, and the monks could only meet open force by forms of law. But they could appeal by turns to pope and crown; they could bide their time without surrendering their claims; they retained standing counsel to defend their interests, had recourse to bribery and favour when their cause was weak, and their pertinacity often won the day when their purse was long and patience great. Striking examples show that the monks did not neglect their opportunities to use influence with high-placed officials, and did not rely alone upon the justice of their cause.

It has often been remarked that the monks were the worst enemies of the parish churches and the local clergy, since Appropriations of churches. they pursued a steady policy of appropriating the rectorial tithes, when they held or could acquire the advowsons. In many cases the tithes, or a fixed portion of them, had been assigned by a specific grant of the landowner, while the usages and rights respecting the parochial endowments were still fluid and ill-defined. In the following centuries they managed to secure a large number of others, either for some definite object or for the general support of the community. In each case the formal sanction of the Crown, as also often of the Papacy, was needed, and bishops lent a helping hand, though afterwards they had to interpose to secure an adequate portion for the vicar. The petitions presented to the papal Court illustrate the variety of pleas that could be urged. To repair their buildings, and make good the ravages of fire and flood, to provide more generous hospitality, and brew better beer, to meet the expenses of a General Chapter of their Order, or relieve financial strain caused by the great plague—these among other reasons are set forth in much detail. Sometimes piteous poverty was the plea, as at Wood Church, Herts, where each inmate had only two shillings a year for clothing, and one farthing weekly to find food. The wishes of the parish whose interests were most at stake were entirely ignored in the negotiations. The acquisition was, however, often a doubtful gain, and the expenses of procuring it enormous, as in a remarkable case at Meaux, too long to be described.

When the monks were merely patrons they did not always realise aright their responsibilities of fitting choice. At St. Alban's, for example, in the fifteenth century there were frequent shiftings in the abbey livings. There is reason to believe that there was unseemly trafficking as regards them, as there was also with some of the lay offices of the convent.

Patronage.

Much of the growing laxity of discipline was due to the greater freedom of communication with the outer world. In earlier times we often hear of the yearning for a more ascetic rule, which caused the inmates of one house to quit it for another of austerer type, like those of the Carthusian or Cistercian Order, or of the brotherhood of St. Francis, but now monks slipped away to Rome to get exemption from the cloistered rule. The Benedictine houses combined to keep a proctor at the Curia to arrest any of their Order who went thither without license for such personal object. A prior of Canterbury appealed even to the civil power to issue a writ of *præmunire* against a restless monk who had managed to procure papal letters of exemption from monastic discipline without having first submitted it to the king's council. But the hands of authority were sometimes weakened by the interested action of the papal agents. Thus the Carmelite friar, Walter Disse—confessor of John of Gaunt—was empowered to sell for Urban VI. fifty appointments to the office of papal chaplain ; these secured exemption from conventual control, and even liberty to take a rich rectory as well. A monk of St. Alban's, William Shapeye, begged or borrowed money to buy one of these, and gained thereby his freedom. Many years afterwards he returned in broken health and spirits to plead for re-admission to the convent, and Amundesham in his fantastic style describes the prodigal's return and the welcome he received in words that read like an offensive parody of the parable of Scripture. The same chronicler describes the migration of another monk to Christ Church, Canterbury, to which he was attracted by his love of music, "waxing fat with the fatness of music, he no less anomalously than apostately migrated." The archbishop, it seems, had interceded for him, and the abbot allowed him to depart.

Migration.

It was a cardinal feature of the old conventual system that the property of professed monks should be merged in the common fund, and stories were told which served

Private property.

to deepen the sense of obligation and impress the sensitive fancy. One is said to have appeared after death to a brother monk and complained of the pains from which he suffered because he had hid his old shoes when new ones were distributed among the household, intending to give them to his father. The shoes were found and put back in the common store, and the spirit came back to thank his friend for the care which had released him from his pains. At Canterbury a rule was made that the "vice of appropriation" should be punished even after death, the bodies of offenders disinterred, and cast out of the monastery. The famous robbery of the royal treasury by monks of Westminster in 1303 showed that even in the cloister money could be used as well as hoarded. Suspicion fell on one of them because he dressed so finely and boasted of his wealth. After the imprisonment of many of them in the Tower, the sacrist and sub-prior were found guilty, and after their death the robbers' skins were fastened to the doors of the treasury beside the Chapter-house, to be a warning to the evil-doers of the future.

The practical freedom from control enjoyed by the occupants of distant cells, and the secular business in which many were concerned outside the cloister, implied as a matter of course financial dealings which it was difficult to check. Suspicions were frequently expressed that some of those in office used their opportunities to hoard up for themselves. While the theory of poverty remained the same the practice evidently became relaxed. Thus at St. Swithun's, Winchester, there is an entry in the accounts of 1337 noting the expenses for the funeral of a brother, of whom it is remarked that he had no means of his own out of which they could be paid. It appears that it was the custom to make an occasional distribution of pocket-money to the monks, and that they might retain also other means. In several of the convents of the diocese of Norwich complaints were made before the visitor that the customary payments were irregularly made. At Archbishop Warham's visitation the inmates showed most

interest in the amount of pocket-money which was to be
distributed among them, and one statement made was "that
no one will join the house because the pension was given in
kind and not in cash." The poet Lydgate, monk of Bury,
often alludes to his "heart heavy and purs light," and thanks
his patron for his "bounteous largesse."

One or other of these disturbing causes proved fatal in
the long run to the usefulness and reputation of many of the
monasteries of the later Middle Ages The alien
priories were among the first to fall into disorder. ^{Alien priories.}
As these were merely dependencies of foreign abbeys, and
ruled by their nominees, who were often aliens themselves,
there were many signs of incompetence and discontent.
Bishops interposed to little purpose; they insisted on the
disorders caused by the rule of ignorant priors, on the abuse
of their rights of patronage in parish churches. Complaints
were urged in Parliament of the large sums sent abroad as
tribute to the mother-houses. The Crown laid its hands
repeatedly upon their funds, seized their estates, and removed
the inmates from the coasts during the French wars. At last
they were all handed over to the Crown to be dealt with at
the royal pleasure (1414). Some paid a heavy fine, and were
ranked as English convents; others with their lands were
annexed to loyal houses that were in pressing need of help;
mostly their property was farmed by contractors, who paid in
the rents to the exchequer. The estates of Eton College
and of All Souls, Oxford, came largely from these sources.

Other steps were taken ere long in the same direction.
Bishops whose patience was exhausted by hopeless mismanagement or criminal waste and license, obtained _{Convents of}
the necessary powers to close the houses which _{bad character}
were bankrupt in character or means, removed the _{dissolved.}
few inmates to some other convent, and transferred the poor
remnant of endowment to some worthier object. Selborne
Priory, a small Augustinian house founded in the thirteenth
century, had been liberally endowed. It fell, however, into
debt, and after repeated visits William of Wykeham issued in
1387 a lengthy series of injunctions relating to the various
shortcomings of the inmates. There had been culpable mismanagement; buildings had fallen into disrepair; the convent

plate was pawned ; property had been disposed of without
due care and sanction ; the poor had been defrauded of their
alms, perhaps even of the six pairs of shoes left for the
parishioners of Selborne, the only charitable endowment made
there. Meantime the brethren roamed abroad and hunted,
dressed foppishly, had pocket-money, took their meals apart,
and even, in defiance of their rule, stripped off their under-
clothing when they went to bed. The kind bishop gave
them something more than good advice ; the year before he
had paid their debts, and again he gave them a hundred marks
before he died. His solemn warnings were not heeded. In
1417 Martin V. heard that grants were being made of their
lands on leases for long terms, and sent them a peremptory
notice that they must cancel such agreements. In 1462, when
the numbers of the house had been reduced from fourteen to
four, and the buildings were in ruinous disrepair, their estates
were sequestrated by Bishop Waynflete, and at last, despairing
of any permanent reforms, he suppressed the convent in 1485
with the sanction of the pope, and appropriated what was left
of the estates to the College of St. Mary Magdalen, which he
had founded at Oxford many years before. Other colleges
also benefited by the suppression of decayed religious houses,
as Peterhouse and Jesus College at Cambridge ; others were
merged in larger monasteries, as Alcester in Evesham and
Deerhurst in Tewkesbury.

But short of such drastic measures there was frequent
need of episcopal control. The censures and injunctions
addressed by William of Wykeham to the Abbey of
Hyde spread over many pages, and imply that the
neglect of the ancient Order was carried very far.
From the visitation of the diocese of Norwich in the fifteenth
century we see that the state of some monasteries was very
bad. The editor of the Reports says of the priory at
Wymondham that in the whole course of its history we
hear little or nothing to its credit. Of Walsingham
he summarises thus the evidence which was given at
the visitations : "The prior was living a dissolute and
scandalous life ; he robbed the treasury of money and
jewels ; he kept a fool to amuse himself and his friends with
his buffoonery ; he was commonly believed to be keeping up

Others warned and corrected.

an illicit connection with the wife of one of the servants ; he
behaved towards his canons with the utmost violence and
brutality ; and the result was that the canons themselves were
a dissipated, noisy, quarrelsome set, among whom the very
pretence of religion was hardly kept up. . . . Of course the
servants were insolent, the boys in the school mutinous, there
were evil reports everywhere and not without foundation ; for
the canons frequented the taverns in the town and worse
places, and hawked, and hunted, and occasionally fought, and
scaled the walls, and got out of bounds at forbidden hours ;
some broke into the prior's cellar and stole his wine, and some
sat up all night drinking, and rolled into chapel in the early
morning and fell asleep and snored."

It is true that in most cases the complaints in this diocese
refer to mismanagement and laxty, in which no grave immorality is implied. But still there is too much evidence
of scandals of the gravest kind, and those not only in
the less important convents, withdrawn from the notice of the
world ; Archbishop Morton, acting in 1489 under powers of
inquiry sanctioned by Pope Innocent VIII., brought a terrible
indictment against the Abbot of St. Alban's, in which with some
of its dependent cells and nunneries, dissipation and license
of the grossest kind had been openly encouraged. But the
abbot was not deposed, as many had been by Grosseteste—
the *malleus monachorum*—in an earlier age, but merely advised
to mend his way.

It is impossible to set such evidence aside, as in the case
of the commissioners of Henry VIII., on the ground of sinister
bias or foul play. We may believe that the grave
scandals were exceptional, but still they were too
numerous to be lightly treated, and the general level
of conventual life was certainly not high. We need not speak
of the monasteries as "dens of gluttony and vice," as a
jaundiced critic of ample learning called them, after much
painful study of their accounts and bills of fare, but they
cannot be regarded as, in that age at least, homes of
high thinking and devotional calm, though of course here
and there they might be tenanted by men of learning, like
the Greek scholar William Sellyng, Prior of Christ Church,
Canterbury, or Abbot Bere of Glastonbury, whose advice

Evidence of general de-cline.

Erasmus sought in his translation of the Scriptures, or by men of cultivated taste like the poet Lydgate, who left his priory of Hatfield Broadoke to be monk again at Bury. Unpopular they were not on the whole—except in times of popular excitement, and even then they had much of the sympathies of the north of England—for the monks were kindly landlords and good neighbours, but they were not respected as centres of piety and light; there were signs on every side of laxity and decrepitude in the whole system, and satirists of course made merry with the lapses which austere reformers passionately denounced.

We hear much less of the nunneries than of the convents of the other sex. Contrary to what might have been expected, they were comparatively small and few, and there was no one to compile their annals and reflect their interests and feelings like the chroniclers of St. Alban's or of Evesham. Their rulers could not take their place in Parliament, or be engaged on papal errands or commissions from the Crown; and though guests knocked at their doors, there was no stream of statesmen and nobles such as those who often brought the news of the great world to the larger monasteries. The little troubles that ruffled the peaceful current of their lives were nothing like the storms that raged when St. Augustine's in its haughty self-assertion defied the authority of the archbishops, or crowds of riotous insurgents gathered round convent walls to redress, as they thought, the grievances of ages.

We know much less about the nuns.

We may gather from the episcopal letters and injunctions that the nuns enjoyed much freedom of intercourse with the outside world, could pay visits in the neighbourhood to their friends, and even stay a night or two abroad. The bishops commonly assume that this was usual, do not treat it as irregular, but only try to fence it round with safeguards which may check possible disorders. The nuns of Godstow, for example, must really be more careful and not chatter or joke with Oxford students; the nuns of Cannington who have leave to stay with their friends in Exeter must not go elsewhere without permission; the sisters of Mynchin Barrow must wear their proper dress when

Freedom allowed.

they go abroad and not stay out too long, and wander in levity from house to house.

It is clear that many besides casual travellers came to them, ladies were often received as boarders, and corrodies were granted to those who wished to buy a safe retirement in old age. The bishops, it is true, do not wish nunneries turned into boarding-houses for the well-to-do, and they see that corrodies are a sorry method of finance, and bring disturbing elements into what should be quiet homes of high thinking and plain living.

Visitors.

The comfort and well-being of the sisterhood depended largely on the choice of the superior who had to rule it, but frequently the due formalities had not been observed, or the lady was found to be utterly unfit. Her bad temper roused a mutinous spirit in the convent, or her mismanagement threatened utter ruin to the house, or she pinched the nuns and spent too freely on herself. Then the bishop as visitor stepped in. Sometimes he named a board of discreet sisters to be a check upon the action of the prioress. Or he deposed the incompetent or self-indulgent; he appointed a guardian of the estates, or he gave her good advice and stringent rules. The abbess of Romsey must not keep many dogs or any monkeys, nor should she stint the nuns' food to provide for her own pleasures. On the other hand, the nuns of Holy Sepulchre at Canterbury, who quarrel so much, must be kept in a dark room till they can agree to live in peace.

Disputes within.

Perhaps these troubles were more frequent because the nunneries were small. A few indeed might almost rival the great monasteries in size and wealth, but most of them were little families, where uncongenial tempers lived too closely and too long together. Houses with many monks and vast estates could provide work for restless natures, and train and test the capacity to rule, but there must have been very often a sad lack of employment for the nuns, and a want of experience for the future ruler. Some, it is true, found an outlet for their energies in teaching. The neighbouring gentry sent their daughters to them for their schooling, and their social usefulness in this respect was all the greater because there was so little educational provision for the girls elsewhere.

In contemporary literature it is implied that this was a common practice. Of the wife of the miller of Trompington we read in Chaucer that—

> Sche was fostred in a nonnerye,

and Langland wrote—

> Abstinence the abbesse, quoth Pieres, myn ABC me taughte.

It has been said that there were houses where "the nuns were nurses and midwives, and even now the ruins of those houses contain certain living records of the ancient practices of their inmates in the rare medicinal herbs which are still found within their precincts." But there does not seem much evidence to show that the nuns found many opportunities of this kind to benefit their neighbours, though hospitals had sisters who tended the sick, and did much of the household work without the profession of strict vows.

Yet the presence of nunneries scattered through a countryside made for peace and mutual goodwill; they offered a shelter to the homeless from the storms of troublous times, and here and there at least the inmates were ready to impart what they could of feminine grace and culture to the daughters of the neighbouring gentry. For though it is hard to say with certainty from what class the monks were chiefly drawn, there seems little doubt that the old county families had a lively interest in the nunnery where their kinswomen took the veil. Its reputation touched them deeply, any rumours of disorder soon lowered the social status of the convent, made it shunned as a home for honourable women, whose lifelong comfort was at stake. Some indeed were specially select, as Amesbury, where Eleanor the mother of Edward I. took the veil, and the wealthy Shaftesbury and Dartford, and probably St. Clement's of York, to which a lady who found shelter there in widowhood left in her will provision for wine and spices for the nuns and the "well-born ladies residing in the house." Nunneries once fallen into disrepute were recruited from a different class; the bad traditions lingered on; pious liberality withheld its bounty, and long embarrassment or ruin followed. For the social reputation of a convent had a marked influence on its finances. Large endowments were indeed a matter

of the past, but it was still a common practice to bequeath
to a favourite house some little token of regard, either to the
whole establishment or to each sister in it.

On the whole the bishops' Registers, when they raise the veil,
rarely disclose gross misconduct, nor does it seem that things
grew much worse as time went on. Immoralities
confessedly there were at times; but when they Little grave disorder.
became known the bishops' hands fell heavily on the
poor frail women. But the lighter literature of the times
deals tenderly with the nuns, and drops its tones of coarseness
and satire in their presence. There are of course unfavourable
pictures, as in the vision of the girl who was bent on convent
life in the old poem entitled, "Why I can't be a nun." A lady
called Experience took her to a house of "women regular,"
which was fair without, but not well governed, for dames
Pride and Hypocrisy were there, and dame Envy too, in every
corner. But Patience and Charity were not within: an outer
chamber had been made for them. Langland, too, had much
to say of "wicked words" and jangling, which wrath could
stir among the nuns. The prioress of Chaucer, on the other
hand, was not only—

> Of grete disporte
> And full pleasant and amiable of port,

but refined and dignified and worthy of respect,—

> And all was conscience and tendre herte.

The monks and nuns lived, as we have seen, a social life,
with few lonely hours for quiet meditation, save in church,
but there were others round them who retired alone
to some cell which they found or built by church or Anchorites.
bridge, and there subsisted on the charity of the passers-by.
There were special rules, according to the use of Sarum, in the
case of such recluses. The bishop's sanction after due examination was required; a public ceremony took place in
church, during which the anchorite read aloud the formula of
his profession; prayers were said in his behalf, after which the
people, headed by the parish priest, went in procession to the
cell in which he was immured. For anchoresses there were
ample directions given by episcopal advisers, such as "the
Rewle of a Recluse that Seynt Alrede wrote to his suster," in

which stress was laid on the government of the tongue, and the temptations to frivolous gossip to which they were exposed by idle folks who loitered near their cells. Piers Plowman speaks of such recluses with respect, but we gather from the poem, as from other sources, that there was a larger class called not "anchorites" but "hermits," which included many of a questionable sort. There was, indeed, one hermit in the fourteenth century who had a wide influence over pious tempers through his writings, some of which have been preserved. Richard Rolle took to an ascetic life in early years and wandered to and fro, preaching even, layman as he was, in village pulpits, till he settled at Hampole, near Doncaster, where he became spiritual guide to a neighbouring sisterhood of nuns, and penned his translations and paraphrases of parts of holy Writ, together with devotional works, of one of which Lydgate wrote—

> In perfit living which passeth poysie
> Richard hermite, contemplative of sentence,
> Drough in Englishe " the prick of conscience."

He passed away in 1349, and his mystic tones of pietism may possibly have found more sympathy in wider circles after the shock of the great pestilence. But there were also many of a different stamp, who chose some bridge or corner of a highway in which to find a cell, and appeal to the sympathy of a credulous public, or passed to and fro between the church porch and the alehouse,—lazy knaves who had thrown up the employment in which they had "long labour and lyte wynninge," dressed like clerks or monks, and at the expense of pious simpletons ate and drank of the best "in ydelnesse and in ese."

For such professional beggars, disguised under the cloak of piety, the Statutes of the Realm showed little tenderness, coupling them with vagabonds and rogues, who were to be lodged in gaol whenever they were caught. The like are with us still, though garb and speech be somewhat changed.

AUTHORITIES.—The authorities to be referred to on the subject of monastic life at this period are numerous. There are, besides the collection in the *Anglia Sacra*, the chronicles in the Rolls series, viz., *Annales Monastici*, ed. H. R. Luard, 5 vols. 1864-69; *Chronica Mon. S. Albani*, ed. H. J. Riley,

1863-73 ; *Chronicon Abbatiæ Eveshamensis*, ed. W. D. Macray, 1863 ; *Chronica Monasterii de Melsa*, ed. E. A. Bond, 3 vols., 1866-68 ; *Memorials of S. Edmund's Abbey*, ed. T. Arnold, 3 vols ; *Chronicon Petroburgense*, ed. T. Stapleton, 1849 (Camden Society) ; or statements of their accounts, see *The Compotus Rolls of S. Swithun's Priory, Winchester*, ed. G. W. Kitchin, 1892 (Hampshire Record Society) ; *The Accounts of the Obedientiaries of Abingdon*, ed. R. E. Kirk, 1892 ; *The Knights Hospitallers in England*, ed. L. B. Larking, 1857 (Camden Society) ; *Inventories and Account Rolls of Jarrow and Monkwearmonth*, ed. J. Raine, 1854 ; *Durham Account Rolls*, J. T. Fowler, 1898 (Surtees Society). For Episcopal visitations, see the *Visitation of Diocese of Norwich*, ed. A. Jessopp, 1888 (Camden Society) ; besides the many letters of the bishops in the Registers referred to in Chap. XI. Many details may be found also in *British Monachism*, by T. D. Fosbrooke.

CHAPTER XV

FRIARS AND PILGRIMS

THE friars, who appeared for the first time in England in the early years of the thirteenth century, belonged to various Orders, each of which had some distinctive features of its own, but all alike formed part of a great spiritual movement, which put aside the old traditions of the monks, and sent its brethren forth in the guise of apostolic poverty into the Home Mission field. Four only were much known in England,—the Carmelite, Austin, Dominican, and Franciscan friars, for others like the Mathurins, Brethren of the Sack, and the Brethren of Bethlehem made little way or disappeared after 1307, when the Council of Lyons limited the numbers of the authorised Orders. Two of them put forward some pretensions to a fanciful antiquity, the Carmelites claiming the prophet Elijah as their spiritual ancestor on Mount Carmel, while the Austin friars found in their name a title to the authority of St. Augustine. But the two Orders of the Mendicants, whose rapid growth threw the rest into the shade, were founded only a few years before they set foot on English soil. The Dominicans and Franciscans within fifty years overspread the whole of Christendom, and long before the close of the thirteenth century stood at the culminating point of their social influence and renown. By that time the primacy of the English Church had been filled in succession by two friars, Kilwardby and Peckham, and the latter saw a member of his own Franciscan Order raised to the papal chair.

Both Orders originally aimed, not at the development

of cloistered virtues, as in the old conventual systems, but at the temporal or spiritual good of other men.

Both turned at first to the poorer and least privileged classes, to the humble townsmen and the artisans, whom other agencies of the Church had often failed to reach; it was among them that mediæval sectaries found most adherents; they had often lent a ready ear to passionate protests at the pride and luxury and sacerdotal claims of the rulers of the Church. The followers of Dominic or Francis would share their dress and fare, would beg even from them for their daily alms, if only so they might find a readier way to win them to the faith or soothe their pains and touch their hearts. They did wonders in that cause; but this is not the place to tell of the indomitable energy of conviction with which the preaching friars of St. Dominic proclaimed far and wide the story of the cross in its most orthodox form, and stemmed the rising tide of incredulity and roving fancy, nor to describe the far more touching scenes of the enthusiasm of charity and the heroism of self-denial with which the first Franciscans spent themselves without reserve in the lazar-house or fever-stricken hovel.

Original aims.

Neither Order was content to restrict itself long to early limitations, or adhere rigidly to its founder's rules. If men's minds were to be permanently guided, the training schools of thought must be controlled; at the universities the intellectual currency was being minted; it was of great moment to gain a preponderating influence there, and to entrust the machinery to the right hands. So the friars betook themselves to Paris or to Oxford, crowded to the lecture halls, seated themselves ere long in the professor's chairs, compiled vast systems of theology, and became the leading schoolmen of the age. The great problem of scholasticism was how to use the Aristotelian logic so as to give philosophic form and method to the doctrines of the Church; it was needful to reassure the world that had been lately startled by the subtleties of thought and pantheistic heresies imported with the commentators of "the master of the wise"—*il mæstro di color che sanno.* To meet this need was the life work of Albert the Great, the Universal Doctor, as

Intellectual movement.

he was called, from the vast learning which gathered up all the knowledge of the times to harmonise it with the Christian truth, and of Thomas Aquinas, the great systematiser, whose *Summa Theologiæ* was to be for ages the divine's text-book of encyclopædic method. Both were Dominicans, calm and precise and orderly in style, as with the perfect self-confidence of intellectual mastery. Such erudite expositions were very different indeed from the homely sermons in the people's tongue which the founder of their Order had in view. But the Franciscans, or the Minors as they called themselves in their humility, diverged still further from their early rule. To St. Francis it appeared that learning, much or little, was a dangerous thing, and books a needless luxury. But they too crowded soon to the homes of general study, and had their great men to show among the doctors. There was Bonaventure—mystic by natural genius, logician only by the fashion of his times. There was Duns Scotus, famous for the subtlety of his fine drawn distinctions, and for the audacity which pushed to its extremest limits the realism of the schools, and claimed for the abstractions of the reason an actual existence in the universe of being, apart from their transient life in thought.

While the tone of the preaching friars was commonly formal and dogmatic, such as became the ministers of the Inquisition, the Minorites showed, as might Franciscans. be expected from the poetic and tender spirit of their founder, more many-sided sympathies, a deeper democratic instinct, and more ardour for the study of nature. From them came the frequent protests at the stately buildings and rich ornaments which seemed to make the friars false to their own rule; from them the reassertion of the ideal of evangelical poverty which provoked strong papal Bulls; from them the Apocalyptic visions of the Eternal Gospel, in which the Christian era ranked only as a pre-paratory stage. Hence the vicissitudes and struggles within the bosom of the Order, as conflicting tendencies gained by turns the upper hand, or acted in defiance of control.

The life of Roger Bacon, perhaps the most pathetic story in the records of mediæval learning, may serve to illustrate one aspect of their interests and aims. That adventurous

and independent thinker was an ardent student of nature, born out of due time, anticipating by flash of genius the inductive methods of the future, and with bold flight of prophecy foreseeing the great advance of science. Roger Bacon.
In an unlucky hour he joined the Friars Minor ; he must have sadly rued the hasty act. His biographer asks what could have been the attractive influence which made him join them, but he does not fully answer his own question. We may find perhaps the explanation in the tendency to experimental study which can be traced more markedly in the Franciscan than in any other Order. Their ministrations to the sick, their special care for the else neglected lepers, naturally led them to the medical studies and pursuits which would be of service to them in that cause. Physicians joined their ranks ; the practice even of medicine is said—doubtless too broadly—to have been engrossed by friars in the thirteenth century. Sent to far-off lands on special missions they recorded their experience of foreign countries ; natural philosophy followed the missionaries' travels. The study of anatomy may be traced in the works of Archbishop Peckham as well as Roger Bacon. Among their brotherhood almost alone could be found the use of the laboratory and the art of distillation. But Bacon's originality and learning, his passionate enthusiasm for physical inquiry, far outstripped the sympathies for natural philosophy which might be found among the members of his Order.

His self-confident criticism had not spared the most eminent authorities in the learning of the schools ; his superiors may have been prejudiced and narrow, and soon his freedom of action was restricted, and the materials of research denied him. Withdrawn from his studies and his friends at Oxford to an uncongenial home at Paris, he watched year after year pass by, bringing him no nearer the great discoveries and fuller knowledge on which he had set his heart in sanguine youth. Ten years of enforced seclusion in the cloister had elapsed before a sympathising pope, Clement IV., could procure him a brief respite from his troubles (1266). Three writings then appeared, in which a sketch was given of the promised triumphs of the inductive science of the future.

He returned for a short time to his studies and experiments at Oxford, and published trenchant criticisms on the dominant men and methods both in the schools and in the Church. But already dark stories, born of ignorant fancy, had gathered round his name, and pointed to unholy dealings with the powers of darkness. It was a time too when the Church was startled by freethinkers, who were boldly handling as philosophers the mysteries of the Faith. Soon the storm burst upon his head again ; condemned in 1278 by a General Chapter of his Order, he lost his freedom and all the materials of study, and regained them only in extreme old age, when it was too late to use them. His works, written under such discouraging conditions in his brief intervals of freedom, shared the fortunes of their author, and remained almost unknown for ages, nailed it is said to the shelves on which they lay, by the fears and prejudices of the friars at Oxford, where he died.

Absolute poverty and the homeliest simplicities of religious service were the primitive ideal of St. Francis, but with prosperity came ease and stately buildings and grand ritual. These were indeed in startling contrast with the associations of their earliest home in London, in "Stinking Lane," near the Shambles. How could they be reconciled with the obligations binding on their conscience ? An accommodating pope could solve the problem ; he and he alone could annul the inconvenient restriction. The austerer spirits of the Order, the so-called Spiritual Franciscans, had never acquiesced in this infidelity to the old standard ; they held sternly aloof from laxer brethren, and unsparingly denounced the worldliness in high quarters. Mystics and visionaries appeared among them who brooded over dark sayings of the Apocalypse or incoherent prophecies of later date. Strange movements spread, which threatened alike the practices of the Church and social order, but were ruthlessly repressed by fire and sword. But not content with stamping out these anti-social and anti-sacerdotal outbreaks, Pope John XXII. went on to condemn the dogma of the absolute poverty of Christ, which had been authoritatively ruled by an earlier pope, and accepted as a cardinal tenet by the Order. A storm of controversy followed, in which the bolder spirits, with Michael of Cesena, the General of the

The ideal of absolute poverty.

Order, at the head, maintained the obnoxious principle and defied the papal Bull.

The strife brought a redoubtable champion into the field, William of Ockham, famous alike in scholastic and ecclesiastical disputes. This great Franciscan, the demagogue of scholasticism, as he has been called, not only forged the weapons of debate William of Ockham. which were to be fatal to so much of the realism and fine - drawn distinctions of the earlier schoolmen, and to discredit even scholasticism itself. He had already plunged into the fray when the struggle between the courts of Rome and France was at its height, and Boniface VIII. launched at Philip the Fair his spiritual thunderbolts, meeting in return with a storm of invectives and ignominious outrage. The manifesto which Ockham had put forth was very trenchant; it denied all temporal authority to the pope, and branded as heretics the champions of the plenary power of the Holy See. Not content with repudiating the claims of Boniface in the temporal sphere, he vigorously impugned the doctrine of John XXIL. His *defensorium* or apology for evangelical poverty was in fact a fierce invective against the luxury and splendour of the papal Court. It was no wonder that he found himself in 1328, with Michael of Cesena and others, brought up to trial at Avignon with prospects of speedy doom. Saved only by a hasty flight he made his way to Munich, where he heard presently that a General Chapter of his Order—under pressure from the princes of the Church—had found him and his brethren guilty of heresy and sentenced them to a life - long imprisonment. He appealed, however, to King Lewis of Bavaria, then in arms against the pope, with the proud words, "Protect me with your sword and I will defend you with my pen."

The progress of the Mendicants had been astonishingly rapid, not only among the classes to influence which they were recruited at the outset, but in the sects of learning and the mansions of the noble. Both the Orders of the Grey and Black Friars met a recognised The jealousy of the monks. want, which other religious agencies had not effectually served. The Papacy, hesitating and cautious in allowing them its sanction at the first, soon realised the value of their service, and found in them commonly its heartiest supporters. But their growing popularity and their enterprising ardour brought them ere long into collision with other powerful interests, by whose loss or disparagement they seemed to thrive. The monks, who felt already that the streams of respectful generosity were ebbing from their walls, could not but look with jealous eyes at the rivals, who pushed their way with such uncompromising zeal (*v.* p. 11). A passage from the history of Matthew Paris gives vigorous expression to the feeling shared by thousands: "In three hundred or four hundred years the monastic Orders have not degenerated so entirely as these friars who, when scarce four-and-twenty years had passed, began to build the mansions which have risen to such palatial height." While the friars on their side welcomed any who seceded to them from the older Orders, they would not tolerate a similar migration from themselves. They had a papal privilege, which pronounced an excommunication, only to be annulled at Rome, against any who harboured an apostate Minorite. In 1290 the Franciscans, supported by Archbishop Peckham, asserted their rights against the powerful Abbey of Westminster. Shelter had been given there to a Benedictine, who had become a Grey Friar and then returned to his old Order. The fugitive and the books which he carried with him were demanded by the friars. After appeal to Rome, judgment was given in their favour; public penances and fines were imposed upon the abbot, and the apostate had to be restored.

It was not only against the older Orders that they vaunted their own superior merits; the Mendicants were also ready to dispute the merits of their own respective Orders. Rivalries among friars. As Matthew Paris writes, "the Preachers asserted that theirs was the earlier Order, and that therefore they were the more worthy, that they were more decorous in their dress, and had merited their name and office by their preaching, and so were with reason distinguished by the Apostolic dignity; but the Minors replied that as they had chosen in God's service a life of more rigour and humility, and one of greater worth because of more holiness, brethren might freely pass over from the preachers to themselves as from an inferior Order to one higher because more ascetic. This the Preachers would not hear of, affirming that though the Minors went about with bare feet and coarse garb and ropen girdle, yet they were not denied the public use of meat, or dainty diet, such as was forbidden to themselves, so that men might not pass from them to the Franciscans as to a worthier or more ascetic order, for quite the contrary was true.

Feuds with the University authorities began at an even earlier date. At Paris they took advantage of a quarrel with the townsmen, followed by a secession of the students, and set up in the vacant place a chair of theology licensed by chancellor and bishop. Their encroachments, as their rivals termed them, provoked in a few years' time an explosion of jealous passion, and edicts of the University intended to restrict their power. These were alternately sanctioned and annulled by papal Bulls, after a long war of angry words, in which king, bishops, and cardinals took part. But the influence of the Mendicants was too great to be resisted, and the commanding reputation of their leading schoolmen did much to justify their triumph in the eyes of scholars. The strife was not confined to Paris, but the experience of Oxford may be more conveniently described in another chapter.

Disputes at the universities.

The secular clergy scattered through the country cannot have always welcomed the arrival of the friars in their parochial cures. If they were negligent themselves and self-indulgent, they resented the rebuke implied in the arrival of more earnest men; if they were conscientious in their work, it may have pained them to see strangers interpose between them and their people, and lead them to mistrust or slight their earlier guides. Thus the parishioners of Colyton in Devon complained at a visitation by the Dean and Chapter of Exeter early in the fourteenth century that their parish priest gave them such instruction as he could, but much too scanty. His predecessor used to invite the friars to talk to them for their soul's good, but he did not care to see them, and would not entertain them if they came. They pray that their pastor may be corrected for their good.

Impatience of secular clergy.

Prelates like Peckham, who was a friar himself, might have no misgivings on the subject, and could command his clergy to welcome and entertain the wandering preachers, but in course of time it was apparent that the parish priests had good reason for complaint. Grandisson of Exeter found it needful to issue repeated warnings to his officials to inhibit the pushing friars, who without any license from himself presumed to hear the confessions of the people.

We cannot doubt on such evidence as we possess that the Mendicants fell speedily away from the high standard of their earlier years; the decadence indeed seems almost *Reserves as to evidence.* as rapid as their rise, but there are some general points to be remembered when we study the pictures painted for us in the literature of the age, and some reserves which should qualify our judgment.

1. They were described for us, for the most part, by unfriendly hands. After the first fifty years the friars themselves left few written memorials of their work; there is nothing to correspond to the notable series of monastic annals. Their ablest thinkers turned to logic and theology where they reigned supreme; but they had no taste for history, and were not careful to illustrate or justify the daily practice of the brethren.

2. The original ideal was so transcendental as to make common-place realities seem poor and mean; high professions unfulfilled might be regarded as mere hypocrisy and falsehood. The critic's task was very easy; the celestial fare proposed was too ethereal an ambrosia for poor human nature's daily food.

3. The friar moved in the full blaze of public observation; not withdrawn, like the monk, into the shelter of the cloister and hedged round with safeguards and restrictions; the passing inconsistencies of practice and profession could not rest long unperceived, or fail to grow in bulk when rumour passed them on.

4. But withal, though the people vented their rude jests and made merry at the frailties about which they freely gossiped, the friars were still popular and thought to be most in sympathy with the toiling masses. When the Black Death swept over the land they died by thousands at their posts of duty, where the fever raged the most, and the people were worst housed. At the peasants' insurrection, when

prelates were in peril of their lives and splendid convents were besieged and stormed, the leaders of the outbreak said that all the machinery of the Church could be dispensed with, for the friars would remain to be the people's guides to heaven. And even later in the century that followed, when the offerings to the older Orders almost entirely ceased, men still left something to the Mendicants in a considerable proportion of the cases known, which include even many of the parish clergy. Thus at York it was usual for both landowner and tradesman to leave a legacy to each of the four Orders of the friars in the town, and in one case all the convents of the mendicants in six different towns had the same sum bequeathed them. Their prayers were expected in return, and it is hard to credit that these could have been valued so highly, if men had thought so meanly of the friars' lives. Their political influence indeed was at times not to be despised. Henry IV. could not affect to disregard their attachment to the memory of the king whom he displaced and, forbearing as he showed himself at other times, he struck sternly and promptly at the disaffected friars. The entries in the Patent Rolls which relate to the gifts to the Franciscans were numerous in earlier reigns, but cease almost entirely during his time.

Some features of their practice which in later days were complained of most bitterly by earnest-minded men, may have been justified by earlier conditions, or have grown out of an excess of zeal. Encouraged *Early influence.* by the rulers of the Church, they passed to and fro among the country hamlets as well as the alleys and squalid suburbs of the towns, which had been the first object of their care. Each Friary had indeed its recognised district within which it had a customary right to beg for alms, and through this its members, "limitours," as they were often called, made their rounds regularly within the appointed "limits." Though bidden by their founder to eschew all show of learning and ornaments of style, their adventurous energy, their practised readiness of speech, their varied illustrations drawn from the wide range of their experience, combined with the natural love of novelty to throw into the shade the homelier addresses of the parish priest, and to bring crowds to the pulpit of the friar. If he were as holy and self-denying as he seemed, he must be a safer spiritual guide than one who lived more like themselves, the ill-paid deputy perhaps of some young rector who was spending his time at Oxford in study or enjoyment, or an old incumbent discredited by household ties, which were frequently believed to exist though not avowed. In any case it was easier to confess their sins to a friar of whom they knew but little, than to a neighbour whom they had quarrelled with perhaps about their tithes, or whose rebukes they had resented. Or, as Wyclif put it in his pungent style, "commonlie if there be anie cursed jurour, extortioner, or avoutrer (adulterer) he will not be shriven at his own curate, but go to a flattering friar, that will assoile him falsly for a little mony by yeare, though he be not in wil to make restitution and leave his cursed sinn."

It required a high degree of delicacy and forbearance on both sides to avoid heart-burnings and disputes. As the fire of enthusiasm seemed to be cooling down, and it was commonly believed that lower motives *Relations with parish clergy.* muddied the current of their spiritual zeal, since their presence at a death-bed led so often to a legacy to their own house, their intrusive action was more and more resented. They did not always wait, it was objected, for the sanction of their own provincial, still less for a license from the bishop, but roving where they would, sought by spicy anecdote or humorous jest to catch the people's ear, and by granting absolution on the easiest terms, tended to lower rather than to raise the moral standard. Boniface VIII., in 1300, had ruled that the Franciscans should not preach anywhere without special leave, and that a fourth at least of all the legacies bequeathed them should be reserved for the parochial clergy. But that these restrictions were not thought sufficient is implied by the complaints of Fitz-Ralph, the Archbishop of Armagh, when in 1357 he pleaded before the papal Court at Avignon, in his *defensio curatorum*, the grievances of the parish priests and the unedifying aggressions of the friars.

Another charge which was developed at some length by the same prelate was urged against them in many another quarter, that in their ardour to make proselytes they worked

unduly on the immature thought and feeling of the young,
and won them over to the Order before they fully knew
their minds, or could measure the consequences of
their action.   They were said to be specially busy   Proselytising
in this way at Oxford, so much so that parents   zeal.
feared to let their sons go there, lest they should fall into the
clutches of the friars, who would not let them go or allow them
afterwards to speak freely even to their parents.   Certainly a
story which is to be found in the Register of Bishop Stafford
in the year 1411 implies, if it be true, that there was too little
scruple in the pressure that was brought to bear upon the
young.   Henry Wytbery, a child under eleven years of age,
had been handed over for family reasons by his father to the
Grey Friars of Exeter, who forced him to assume their dress
and tonsure ; and fearing that he might escape, moved him
about "like a vagabond" for six months, and then lodged
him in Wales.   He told his story there to the superior of his
house, but was shut up for a year, and then made to read
aloud a form of "profession" written out in Latin, which he
did not understand, and told afterwards that he was now a
Minorite "professed."   In his fifteenth year they forced him
to take the order of subdeacon, but he escaped at last, and
petitioned the pope to grant him redress and freedom.   A
papal Bull recited the facts alleged, and ordered inquiry to
be made, and after some delay the young claimant appeared
before the bishop, who appointed a commission for the
purpose.   Its report, however, is not given.

If we may credit the Archbishop of Armagh, the students
of Oxford had other grounds for regretting the influence or
resources of the friars.   "In every convent," said
Fitz-Ralph, "is a grand and noble library," and   Monopoly of
he complained that they bought up so eagerly   books.
the books that came into the market that poor students found
it impossible to purchase any, and that young beneficed clergy
sent with an episcopal license to study at the University had
to return, because they could get no books to read there.
This literary enthusiasm must have faded gradually away, or
in times of depression they were forced perhaps to sell their
treasures, for in a later age Leland says, "In the Franciscan
houses there are cobwebs in the library and moths and book-

worms—more beyond this, whatever others may say, nothing, if you have regard to learned books. The owners, indeed, were to him but 'braying donkeys.'" The author of the *Philobiblon* had complained long before that they were ceasing to care much for their books.

There was another tendency which gave great offence at times to regulars and seculars alike. It has been said already that there were many of the friars in the thirteenth century—the Spiritual Franciscans as they were called—who laid stress on the absolute poverty of Christ and His apostles, and in defiance of any papal Bulls, made this a cardinal feature of their teaching. Some maintained the principle aggressively, and preached fiercely against endowments, as contrary to the spirit of the Gospel. Thus in 1425 William Russell, who was warden of the Grey Friars in London, was summoned before Convocation to answer to the charge of having preached that tithes need not be paid to parish priests, but might be used for any pious objects. After some show of defence, he made submission to the court, but failing to appear to do penance at Paul's Cross, he was excommunicated, and fled to Rome to plead his cause. Imprisoned, however, there, he escaped after a time and made his way back to England, and finally recanted at Paul's Cross. It was long before the heart-burnings and excitement caused by this movement died away, and for some time the University of Oxford required every one who would qualify for a degree to adjure this special doctrine of the friar.

More often, however, offence was given to thoughtful critics by deviations from the earlier practice of the Mendicants, and what seemed to be lower and more worldly aims. Almost from the first, indeed, a relaxation of the rule of St. Francis had been sanctioned. Some of his precepts, like the sublime paradoxes of the Gospel, could not safely be adhered to, in their literal sense, as social circumstances changed. To live entirely from hand to mouth by daily alms, to insist on bodily labour and disallow the use of learning, as well as all forms of property in common—this it was clearly seen must limit their usefulness and arrest their progress. It was decreed that mental labour might take the place of manual toil, that proprietary rights in needful things, as also of the friaries and churches of the Order might be vested in the pope, that gifts and legacies for their use might be accepted and exchanged, though the touch of money was still to be avoided. Further declarations on the rules were made at the Council of Vienne in 1311, but the directions of Clement V., while allowing them more freedom in some respects, were mainly meant to guard against the symptoms of laxity and worldliness of which the Order was commonly accused. The charges were denied, so the pope said, by the rulers of the Order, but they were still widely credited, and the high level of unselfish zeal could not be permanently maintained.

It was not only the Grey Friars who were accused of disloyalty to the old rule. The French chronicle of London tells us that the Black Friars in the troublous times of 1327 took to flight because they were afraid, detested as they were for their haughty ways (*orgelouse port*). A few years before grave scandal had been caused by the stories that were current of disorders in their midst. Complaints were posted on the doors of St. Paul's Church by discontented friars of dark deeds done in secret, of brethren immured in pestilential dungeons, some taking their own lives in their agony, others buried like dogs without a funeral service. Notices of appeal were published, and copies have been found of these, which bear out the detailed statements of the chronicles.

In the next century strife and disorder marred the peace of the convents of the Carmelites. Vexatious appeals from the provincial prior to the General of the Order weakened the hands of discipline, and royal letters were sent to Rome to urge that a deaf ear should be turned to these complaints of mutinous (*dyscolorum*) brethren.

Two movements in the later decades of the fourteenth century illustrate the status and reputation of the friars, but in very different ways. One was a reforming movement from within, like those many proofs of vital energy The Observants. which recur in the history of the older Orders. There had indeed been earlier efforts of the kind; there were the *Fratres de penitentia Jesu*, or the Brothers of the Sack, who dressed themselves in sackcloth, and would tolerate no self-indulgence; there were the Spiritual Franciscans, who would have none of the lax sentiments of John XXII. But there was also a later and more permanent revival. After a General Chapter held at Toulouse in 1373 a number of Franciscan houses drew themselves together under a stricter rule, without separating entirely from the rest. These Observants, as they were called, increased in number, and their statutes enjoined a more ascetic rule of daily life, and much reserve and caution in intercourse with the outer world. Restrictions of early date were reinforced, and evasions and abuses rigorously dealt with.

The writings of Wyclif, on the other hand, bring the mendicants before us in a very different light. He was in perfect sympathy indeed with their primitive ideal, for his own "poor priests" were little else than a copy of the model of St. Francis, and he seems to have long hoped that all true-hearted friars would listen to the voice of conscience and range themselves on what he thought was the side of truth and justice. But the philosophic forms which they borrowed from the schoolmen to explain the doctrine of the Eucharist seemed an unscriptural figment which he did not weary of denouncing. Their uncompromising attachment to the Papacy and readiness to support its mandates; their eagerness to hunt down his persecuted preachers: these features of their thought and action excited in him an antipathy so great that he poured his scorn on them in page after page of the controversial pamphlets of his later years, and lost sight of all restraints of charity and moderation.

Attacks of Wyclif,

When the pen fell from his dying hands, his Lollard followers took up the cause in the same spirit; they, too, in writings hardly to be distinguished from their master's, directed alike grave argument and virulent invective on the so-called "heresies and errors" of the friars. As sturdy beggars, it was urged, they shirked the bodily work to which they were bound by their own founder's precepts, diverting from its natural channels much of the charity which the weak and suffering sorely needed. By evasive shifts they kept the letter and ignored the spirit of their rule, having an

and his followers.

attendant close at hand to receive the money, which they
might not touch themselves.   They sold to the simple-minded,
under the name of *letters of fraternity*, drafts upon the capital
of merit amassed by the prayers and self-denial of their Order ;
they encouraged an idle trust in forms and names in place of
the essentials of a good life, by teaching men "that if they
dyen in Frauceys habite (dressed in Franciscan clothes) thei
schul nevere cum in helle for vertu thereof."   They flattered
the vanity and superstition of the wealthy, inscribing their
names upon their walls, finding a place for their bodies in
their churches, as when Edward II., "for the repose of the
most illustrious Queen Isabella, buried in the choir of the
Grey Friars, repaired the great middle window," or when the
heart of Queen Eleanor was carried for interment there.
Much of this of course may be explained as part of the general
practice and temper of the age, and implying no special discredit to the friars, but the popular literature went much
further still, and often painted their moral character in the
blackest colours.

Chaucer's light-hearted satire plays chiefly with the effrontery
of the religious tramp who trades upon the petty vanities
and credulous fancy of the housewives, assuming a
variety of characters by turns, gossip and boon
companion, father confessor and cheap jack, all
things to all men save what a friar should be.   That Chaucer's
pictures were not quite wanton caricatures may be perhaps
supported by the fact that there is a Franciscan MS. in the
British Museum which is nothing less than a collection of
ribald and profane songs mixed with parodies of the services
of the Church.

Langland, with deeper earnestness than Chaucer, exposes
the demoralised practices of the friars, and paints the vigorous
portraits of the vices of greed, wrath, falsehood, and corruption in close association with them.   "Charity," he says,
"has turned peddlar in their persons, for 'alle the foure ordres

> ' Preched the peple for profit of hem selve,
> Glosed the gospel as hem good lyked,
> For covetise of copis construed it as thei wolde.' "

He speaks in bitter terms of the jealousy and strife between
them and the secular clergy of the deceitfulness of their fair

words ; of their readiness to lull the conscience of the sinners, who built and adorned their splendid churches.

Another poem, called "Pierce the Ploughman's Crede," written by a Lollard in the last decade probably of the fourteenth century, describes them—or the poet's antipathies—at greater length. A plain, ignorant man, who has learnt his Paternoster, wishes to be also taught the Creed. He applies in turn to a friar of each of the four different Orders. Each loudly vaunts the merits of his own brotherhood and dismisses scornfully the pretensions of his rivals : but none of them will teach the poor man his lesson. He comes at last to Pierce the Ploughman, who instructs him in his creed, but first vents a long tirade against the friars. They have all the vices of the Pharisees, none of the graces of the beatitudes. They are but idle drones and flattering knaves. They persecuted Walter Brute, and would murder a man's soul and burn his body. If one of them cannot beg cleverly he is soon made away with,—

> Under a pot he schal be put in a pryvie chambre,
> That he schal lyven ne last but lytell while after.

Austin, Dominic, and Francis were good men, but the father of friars is the devil—

> Of the kynrede of Caym he caste the freres.

The great misfortune was that so potent an agency for good, with so much sterling self-devotion, should have been started here under conditions which made it impossible for it to work in the long run harmoniously with the ecclesiastical machinery around it. While the intrusion of its members tended to disorganise and discredit the parochial system, it was exempted by special privilege from episcopal control, and it insisted on its independence of the only men who could have smoothed away much of the friction, and enabled the zeal of the new recruits to supplement without disturbance the localised forces of the old regime. The Mendicant Orders almost from the first were strongly centralised at Rome, for there the Minister general resided in close connection with the pope ; under him were ranged provincial ministers and wardens down to the superior of a friary or the warden of a convent. The will of Rome could

Difficult position.

be transmitted rapidly through the whole body; frequent
intercourse between distant convents, and the lack of proprietary ties made the friars most serviceable as Papal agents,
and less national in their sympathies and aims.   This sub-
servience to the Papacy, accompanied with full knowledge
by the General of the Order of the utter worldliness and
deep-seated corruptions of the Roman court stands in sad
contrast to the spirit of the life and teaching of St. Francis.
No wonder that it fell away so soon from the grand ideal,
if it could long serve with unquestioning loyalty the "pride of
life" and the "lust of the eyes" that were enthroned in the
high places of the Church.   As regards the imputations of
greed and importunity which recur in the satirists we may
notice that at least the friars were so far faithful to their early
rule, that they never became landowners; the site for a friary
and church, a modest garden, they might have, but there
was little more to seize when the dark days of confiscation
came, and the friars were sent away to fare as they could
without a home or pension.   On the other hand, as they
were thrown upon the voluntary system, in its extremest form,
without any local claims or centralised method of finance, there
must have grown up in course of time some of the unlovely
features which we are now familiar with in the sturdy tramp or
the professional begging-letter writer.   These lent themselves
to caricature, to the disparagement of thousands who did
not share the faults.   Yet the evidence before us does imply
that in too many cases the missionary character had almost disappeared; we see few traces of the loving ministrations among
the sick and poor which had been so marked among the earlier
followers of St. Francis.   The friar of the Paston Letters was, as
has been noted, a man of business, a confidential agent, a
political intriguer; and in his case at least the special meaning
of the institution had dropped out of sight and thought.

The friars were not the only mendicants upon the road.
As in our own days, appeals for offertories in church were
always being made from various quarters.   Bishops
urged the claims of the building funds of their
Quæstors.
cathedrals; licensed collectors (*quæstors*) came with briefs
to ask for help for hospital or church, or for some poor
country side whose "foul ways" or broken bridges should

be mended.   From the ends of the earth came suitors armed with peremptory papal Bulls empowering them to urge claims which must not be shelved on the plea of local wants. The bishops, though reluctantly at times, published the Bulls, and gave the necessary sanction.   But the collectors did not always wait for formal license.   In the fourteenth century complaints were rife among the clergy, and found a voice in their church councils, of the bold importunity with which they thrust their claims upon the public.   Some were disowned by the brotherhoods for whom they pretended to collect.   Others, like the agents of the Hospital of St. John of Jerusalem, were specially denounced by papal Bull.   They professed, said the indignant pope in 1369, that they were privileged, and needed not the sanction of a bishop.   They appeared suddenly in parish churches on some feast day, when people came to make their offerings, reading aloud their notices, and making their collections, and disturbing the ordinary services, to the disparagement and loss of parish priests, whom they had the effrontery to sue before some distant judge, and had them excommunicated even for defending their own vested rights and maintaining order in their churches.

That alms might be given with open hand indulgences were often offered, and as these filled so large a place in the Indulgences. religious language of the age, it is of interest to note to what extent the system was developed, and what were the abuses with which it was attended.   The indulgences offered by the bishops were *ab injunctis* only, that is, they remitted the penances which had been or might be imposed in the Confessional for the period stated by them.   They dealt merely with the outward forms of Church discipline, such as the early Penitentials had prescribed with great fulness of detail.   The papal indulgences, however, went much further and professed to relieve the privileged penitents for definite periods from purgatorial fires.   In course of time a theory had been accepted, that the Holy See was guardian of the treasury of the infinite merits of the Saviour and the superabundant graces of the saints, and that from this inexhaustible capital the popes could draw as on a bank and set such portions of it as they pleased to the account of

those whose loyal obedience or devoted service made them
worthy of the boon.   These might be used as drafts in
payment for the release of souls in purgatory for periods varying at the discretion of the pope.   The power was used
sparingly at first in times of crisis for crusades against the
Saracens or Albigenses, or in the struggles with the Empire.
Then it was vulgarised to serve for sordid methods of finance.

When the dangerous practice had been authorised,
designing knaves and blatant hypocrites swooped like birds
of prey upon their spoil.   These were the pardoners
of whom we read in contemporary satire.   High-   Pardoners.
placed ecclesiastics had set them the example ; like the
cardinal who, says the indignant Walsingham, had his tariff
for every spiritual privilege or dispensation.   In Langland's
"Vision" we read that Falsehood, when driven from the haunts
of common men, was sheltered by the pardoners,—

> Tyl pardoneres haved pite and pulled hym into house,
> They wesshen hym and wyped hym and wonden hym in cloutes,
> And sente hym with seles on Sondares to cherches,
> And gaf pardoune for pens, poundmel aboute.

English bishops in their Pastorals exposed the grave abuses,
and the University of Oxford stated in 1414 in its proposals for
reforms, that "shameless collectors make simoniacal
contracts for their offices, traffic in indulgences in   Protests of
the spirit of Gehazi, and waste in riotous living like   the bishops.
the prodigal their illicit gains, dragging their victims down
with them to hell."

Relic mongering played a prominent part in the bustling
trade of these indulgence hawkers.   Early in the fourteenth
century, when Bishop Drokensford allowed the
"Brethren of the Holy Ghost in Saxia" to plead   Relic
their cause on Sunday in his churches, he forbade   mongers.
them to show their relics, or such trumpery (*frivola*) on the
occasion.   But they soon became a recognised part of the
pardoner's stock-in-trade, and Chaucer made merry with their
gross deceptions :—

> Than schewe I forth my large cristal boones
> Ycrammed ful of cloutes and of boones,
> Reliks they ben, as wene thei echoon,
> Than have I in latoun a schulder boon
> Which that was of an holy Jewes scheep.

Besides friars and pardoners there were others often to be met with on the roads who travelled under the shadow of the Church. The custom of pilgrimage had existed from the early days of Christian England. But the movement had lost in course of time much of its simple enthusiasm and artless faith, and though there was no lack of pilgrims on the road, their motives and their characters were not always of the highest.

1. Sometimes pilgrimage was used as a penitential discipline for great offences. Lawless barons who had enticed nuns from their cloister, parish priests who had been guilty of gross vices were absolved only on condition of some long and weary journey to a distant shrine. Many such cases are noted in the bishops' Registers : they were like sentences to hard labour for a definite term of years.

2. It was abused sometimes as a protest against the action of the ruling powers—a demonstration in favour of a weaker cause whose champion had lately fallen. Thus Thomas of Lancaster — least exemplary of saints — and Archbishop Scrope, virtuous prelate but unwary politician, were raised by popular fancy to the rank of martyrs, and numbers visited their graves, not to do honour to them only, but to show their spleen at a government which they dared not openly resist ; even Lollards crowded to the graves of their own martyrs, though they protested at the fond usages of pilgrimage and relics.

3. Some hoped to get the merit of the hardships and the dangers which they paid others to encounter on these pious errands. Men and women who had no mind to quit their comfortable homes for far-off lands left directions in their wills that volunteers should be engaged to be pilgrims and crusaders for them. The practice seems to have become more fashionable as time went on. Commonly a definite sum was named for their expenses : thus ten to twelve marks were thought enough for the journey to Compostella ; twenty-six shillings and eightpence were assigned to defray the charges of four pilgrimages to Bridlington, Hayles, Walsingham, and Compostella ; but ten pounds was not too much for "a prest to go to Rome to the stacyons and sey massys as is according for a pylgryme, and to abyde in Rome alle

Lenton." The rules of the guilds again sometimes provided that all the members should be ready to pay their contributions when a brother or sister started for Compostella or elsewhere.

There was no falling off in the numbers of the pilgrims, but the ruling powers in Church and State showed clearly by their action that they perceived the grave moral risks, the elements of imposture and disorder that tempted roving and adventurous spirits. Villeins who were weary of their homes, and servants who wanted a fresh master, were thought to slip away on false pretences, and the Statute of Labourers in 1388 enacted that no servant or labourer should leave his home under colour of going far away on pilgrimage unless he had letters patent as a license. To cross the seas they must have passports, to be used only at certain ports where strict inquiry could be made into the objects of the voyage. Bishops too had occasion to discourage the growth of spurious objects of devotion which attracted wonder-loving crowds away from their own parish churches. Thus Grandisson of Exeter was scandalised by the votaries who flocked to see some statue set up in what he called "a house of idolatry," "in honour, as it would seem, rather of a haughty and disobedient Eve, or of a wanton Diana, than of the blessed Virgin Mary." Langland, again—to come down lower in the social scale—does not show much respect for the wanderers of this class :—

> Pylgrimes and palmers plyghten hem to-gedere
> To seke Seynt James and seyntes in Rome ;
> Thei went forth in here way with many wise tales,
> And hadden leve to lye al here lyf after.

In Chaucer's poem they are brought before us as a motley company of excursionists taking their holiday together.

AUTHORITIES.—The subjects treated of in the text may be illustrated from *Monumenta Franciscana*, vol. i. ed. J. S. Brewer, 1858, and vol. ii. ed. R. Howlett, 1882 ; Roger Bacon, *The Opus tertium*, etc. ed. J. S. Brewer, 1859 (Rolls ser.) ; *The Grey Friars of Oxford*, ed. A. G. Little, 1891 (Oxford Hist. Society) ; Fitz-Ralph, *Defensio Curatorum* in Brown's *Fasciculus rerum expet.; Fifty Errors of Friars* in *English Works of Wyclif*, ed. T. Arnold, 1871 ; *Political Poems and Songs*, ed. T. Wright, 1350-56 ; *Testamenta Ebor.* (Rolls ser.) ; *Bury Wills*, ed. S. Tymms, 1850 (Camden Society) ; *Wills and Inventories, Testamenta Ebor.*, 1834 (Surtees Society) ; *Pierce the Ploughman's Crede*, ed. W. W. Skeat, 1867 (C.E.T.S.) ; *Roger Bacon*, par E. Charles, Paris, 1861.

CHAPTER XVI

SCHOOLS AND UNIVERSITIES

IT has often been assumed that not only was the higher education to a great extent in the hands of the regular clergy, but that few opportunities for earlier schooling could be found except within the convents. It may be well, therefore, to inquire what were the actual services to society rendered by the monks in this respect in the later Middle Ages. Undoubtedly, it was still thought fitting that there should be a school in every large religious house. A knowledge of Latin could not be dispensed with in the case of those who were to fill any of the higher posts; the more ambitious who looked beyond the walls of their own convents must have some scholarship to qualify themselves for usefulness abroad. William of Wykeham, in his injunctions both to the Priory of St. Swithun's and to the Abbey of Hyde, laid stress on the danger of ignorance among the monks and the need of proper schooling for the novices and others. Again and again, in the visitations of the convents of the diocese of Norwich in the fifteenth century, complaint was made by the monks that this duty was neglected by their rulers, and it was repeated at a later date by Warham as visitor of Christ Church, Canterbury. Education was referred to, not as a new want, or part of a general social movement, but as a primary obligation, allowed indeed to fall into disuse, but such as the bishop as visitor might insist on.

It does not appear, however, that these schools, where they existed, were freely opened to the laity outside. That others beside the novices and younger monks often were instructed

in the convents—though not together with them—may safely
be admitted. The rule of the Austin Canons of Barnwell
provided that "the clerks who live on charity and
are housed in the Almonry should be set to dispute ^{The admission of outsiders.}
formally by the Almoner or other official, and be
kept under the rod that they may learn the better." There
was similar provision at Durham and elsewhere. We do
not hear, however, that sons of the neighbouring gentry were
often sent for their schooling to the monks, as girls were sent
to the nuns. At Guisborough such practice was discouraged by
Archbishop Wickwaine, and in one case at Norfolk late in
the fifteenth century complaints were made that there was
too little profit from the fees of the lay scholars. But there
is little evidence that the smaller houses, especially in the
days of their poverty and decay, had any schools at all, and
only a few poor boys who waited on the sick or sung in choir
were commonly admitted even to the rest.

There were grammar schools, indeed, administered by
some of the great abbeys for the benefit of the towns which
had grown up around them. Bury St. Edmunds
had one which the famous Abbot Sampson built. ^{Abbey grammar schools.}
At St. Alban's Abbot Eversdon in 1310 ratified
the statutes of his school; the master was to take nothing of
the sixteen poorest scholars, but the rest according to old
custom were to pay their teacher for his trouble. At Evesham,
Bruton, Bridgwater, and other places there were grammar
schools in connection with the convents. The masters were
secular clerks, as at Diss, in Norfolk, where Sampson went to
school, and at Dunstable, where a headmaster wrote a religious
play and borrowed as stage properties some of the copes of the
Abbey of St. Alban's. These unfortunately were burnt, and the
poor master in despair to make amends became a monk, or, in
the words of Walsingham, "offered himself up as a holocaust to
God." For several of these schools certainly, and probably
for most, the monks acted merely as trustees. They were
founded by bishops or other benefactors, and were not
maintained out of the corporate funds. No great stress can
be therefore laid on them as evidence of zeal for education on
their part. Happily there were other agencies at work.

The oldest educational machinery is to be found in the

cathedrals and in the great collegiate churches, such as Southwell, Beverley, and Ripon. These had each its gram-mar school, recognised in the statutes as an integral part of the foundation, though separate endowments may have been assigned it, and exhibitions added at a later date, as by Bishops Gynwell and Buckingham at Lincoln. At York the history of the cathedral school can be traced back to the eighth century. To regulate the studies and appoint the schoolmaster was the duty of the chancellor of the cathedral, who in early times had been himself charged with the function of instruction. His powers of control extended beyond the cathedral school itself to others of the same type in the neighbourhood. The schools in question were distinct from the song schools of the choristers, for which a separate maintenance was provided. They were of a higher grade than for merely elementary teaching. At Southwell in 1484 com-plaint was made by the inhabitants of a master who was so slack in his work as to let the boys talk English in the school instead of Latin, and to give them many holidays, elsewhere a rare indulgence.

Cathedral schools.

At Oxford, in addition to the slight provision made at Merton and Queen's Colleges, there were also grammar schools preparatory to the course of general study. At first probably, as elsewhere, they were subject to ecclesiastical control, but the University soon assumed authority to deal with them, though the first dated statute on the subject in 1306 was passed in the presence of the archdeacon and the official of the bishop. At Cambridge similar schools existed, and a special functionary, called *Magister Glomeriæ*, and appointed by the Archdeacon of Ely, presided over them, and decided all disputes between the scholars.

At the Universities.

In early days the higher ecclesiastical authorities, and the masters whom they appointed, claimed exclusive rights to educate the children of their neighbourhood, as grounded in Canon Law and immemorial usage. Only thus, as it seemed to them, could they discharge their duty to the young, on which the Church insisted, and provide due guarantees of fitness for the teacher's office. After a formal petition by the inhabitants

Exclusive rights.

to the Abbot of Walden in Essex for his leave, a legal document was drawn up with great care to authorise each parish priest to receive "one very little child of each parishioner and teach him the alphabet and the humanities but not any higher learning." The Chamberlain of St. Edmund's had a vested right to nominate a master at Beccles, the Chancellor of Southwell claimed the like at Newark, and the same was asserted in the case of Ripon and Coventry, as by the Precentor for song schools at York, and round Beverley several teachers were excommunicated for keeping adulterine schools "to the prejudice of the liberty of our Church." Both in London and at Gloucester protests were made by the ecclesiastical authorities against the intrusion of unlicensed strangers, "feigning to be masters of grammar," and half a century later the incumbents of four city parishes petitioned in 1447 to be allowed to appoint schoolmasters in their several parishes. It may be of interest to note the grounds of their action as set forth in their own words : "Please it unto the full wyse and discrete comunes in this present Parliament assembled to considre the grete nombre of gramar scholes that somtyme were in divers parties of this realme, beside tho that were in London, and howe fewe ben in these dayes, and the grete hurt that is caused by this ; not oonly in the spirituell parties of the Chirche, where often tyme it apperith to openly in som persones, with grete shame, but also in the temporall partie. . . . Wherefore it were expedient that in London were a sufficient nombre of scholes, and good enfourmers in gramar, and not for the singular avail of II or III persones, grevcusly to hurt the multitude of yonge peple of all this land ; for where there is grete nombre of lerners and fewe techers, and all the lerners be compelled to go to the same fewe techers, and to noon other, the maisters wexen riche in money, and the lerners pouere in connyng, as experience openly sheweth, aynst all vertue and ordre of well puplik." The king assents to the request so it be done with the advise of the ordinary or the archbishop.   One of the schools thus set up in the parish of St. Mary Colechurch still survives as the Mercers' School.

In this period, however, many other schools had come into existence.   The guilds were showing on all sides that lay folk and the trading classes were in earnest also in the cause. Formed for a variety of social objects, they all provided for some consecration of their union by religious services on stated days, and the chaplain attached to each often gave free schooling to the children of the members, and accepted payment from outsiders. In course of time rules to that effect, or to provide entirely free schooling, were embodied in the statutes of the guilds, and the school thus recognised obtained a permanent status.

Guild schools.

Besides these corporate undertakings, prosperous merchants and others founded grammar schools for the towns where they made their fortunes, or passed their early years. Sometimes, especially in the fifteenth century, these were purely lay foundations, for oftener they were in close connection with chantries or collegiate churches recently established. So Thomas Scott of Rotherham, who was chancellor in 1474, remembered gratefully that " by some divine chance a teacher of grammar learning " had come to the town where he was born and taught him in his youth. He founded therefore in 1483 a college in his old home, with a provost and three fellows, who were to teach freely any one who came to them. The masters of these schools were in receipt of the rents of lands which varied in amount from 18s. 4½d. to £13 : 2 : 2 a year, and most of the old grammar schools which still exist began in this way, though many disappeared at the dissolution of the chantries.

Private founders.

Some were called song schools, such as were connected with the cathedrals for the instruction of the choristers. A few were elementary, as at Launceston, where 13s. 4d. was received yearly by one who taught poor men's children their ABC, there being there another schoolmaster of higher grade. Canon Law indeed required that in every rural parish a clerk should be provided to attend upon the priest in church and to "keep school" for the children, but of such "pedagogues of raw lads," as the author of *Philobiblon* calls them, there is little mention made. In larger households boys were taught by the chaplain, or some clerk who served as secretary or accountant. The establishment of a great

Elementary schools.

noble or prelate included often a grammar master, who
taught the pages of gentle birth brought up in the household.
The Paston Letters show that not only that family, but friends
and neighbours, lords commoners and domestic servants had
the art of writing, and that no one of any rank or station in
society was quite illiterate. The chief artisans signed every
page in one set of the royal accounts. One great trouble of
modern childhood they were spared indeed,—there was no
standard of spelling ; they wrote the words in such a form as
represented to their ears the spoken language, and varied it
sometimes from page to page. Thus the word chancellor
is spelt five different ways in a single deed of the University
of Oxford. But in the large majority of the schools of
which we read Latin was the staple of the teaching ; the
accounts even of a bailiff of a manor were written out in
Latin ; in law and diplomacy and every liberal career it was
employed, and for this, though not for the mother tongue,
there were definite standards of orthography and grammar.

In many cases they were free schools, the teacher's
income being wholly found by the endowment, or free to the
poor at least, as in Bishop Langley's schools at
Durham, founded in 1414, or to the choristers, as
at Beverley, though newly-made Bachelors in 1338 Free
schools.
had to give pairs of gloves—eight in all—to the chief officers
of the Church. At York, the Abbey of St. Mary's held funds
in trust to provide a boarding-house for fifty poor scholars of
the ancient grammar school of the town. Commonly the day
boys, if they came from any distance, boarded themselves
in the neighbourhood at their parents' cost, but to the profit
of the place, as it is expressed in one certificate : " The
town of Ledbury is a very poor town, and by the foresaid Sir
Richard Wheeler the inhabitants of the same have not
only had profit and advantage by the keeping of a grammar
school there, as in boarding and lodging his scholars, but
also the country thereabouts in uttering their victuals there
by means of the said scholars." Part of the chantry funds
were often given to meet such needs. In this way can be
explained what at first sight may seem strange, that the
endowments of a hospital included sometimes a provision for
a school, as at St. Anthony's Hospital in London, where Sir

Thomas More and possibly Dean Colet were at school; and at the Hospital of St. Nicholas in Salisbury, to which scholars with a warden were attached, under the authority of the chancellor of the cathedral. For the "spital" of the Middle Ages was more often an almshouse for the poor than a hospice for the sick ; and thus among the many who were fed daily at St. Cross there were thirteen poor scholars, named by the master of the High School at Winchester, and each of them entitled to three quarts of beer a day. At Pontefract St. Nicholas Hospital was bound to find forty loaves a week for the scholars of the town. At the Hospital of St. John Baptist at Ripon there were exhibitions to be held by poor scholars at the grammar school.

It may seem a long step to pass from these miscellaneous and often petty schools to the magnificent foundations of Winchester and Eton. These, however, were really chantries or collegiate churches of a larger type and more enduring usefulness, far more ecclesiastical indeed than many of the schools that were being established at the time. Founded in the special interest of the Church, they reproduced some of the familiar features of the old conventual type. Wykeham's desire was to make provision for the supply of an educated clergy, and he had already maintained a number of poor scholars at his own expense before he applied to Pope Urban VI. for leave to found a college. The Bull bore date June 1, 1378, but the royal license and the charter of foundation were not published till October 1382. A warden and seventy scholars were incorporated by the name of " Seinte Marie College of Winchester," to study grammar and live together in collegiate fashion "to the honour and glory of God and our Lady." In later Bulls indulgences were offered to all who should visit the college chapel and lend a helping hand to its completion. Certain English manors and advowsons belonging to French convents, which were assumed to be in schism as in obedience to a rival pope, were transferred to it with Papal sanction, but compensation was to be made when they returned to their allegiance. Wykeham, however, paid over at once the price which was asked for the estates, and was no party to an act of disendowment.

Forty years afterwards the statutes of Wykeham in their final shape were transcribed without material alteration for another great foundation. The Parish Church of Eton was constituted a collegiate church, consisting of a provost   Eton.
and ten priests, with clerks and choristers, and a grammar master who was to teach freely twenty-five poor scholars, as also twenty-five poor bedesmen. In his letters to the pope Henry VI. speaks of this undertaking as " the first earnest of his devotion towards God." It took several years to arrange for the ample privileges that were conceded, and Vincent Clement, his agent at the Papal Court, found it no easy task to satisfy the impatience of the king, who had set his heart upon the speedy attainment of his object. " His daily inquiry is this," it was reported, " When shall we have news of Master Vincent ; when will letters reach us concerning his designs ? " The spiritual immunities indeed which were thus conferred were swept away ere long, but happily the educational objects which he had at heart were more enduring, and through them, feeble as he was, he had a potent influence on later ages.

These great schools, with others founded on their model, —seminaries as they were meant to be at first and of un- doubted service to the clergy—have gone very far to stamp a robust and self-reliant character upon the laity of England. They have done this indeed because they have developed largely what was quite a secondary feature in the founder's scheme. Like most of the grammar schools of early date, they were primarily intended for the poor, not of the lowest social strata, but of the middle class of burghers and of yeomen. But a small number of other boys, sons of men of noble birth and standing, were to be admitted into Wyke- ham's college, to be taught there on the condition that they should be no burden to the trust. The great increase of the number of such commoners not on the foundation, there and in other schools since formed on the same lines, has largely added to the breadth and variety of their social influence, and determined the character of the public school life of England.

It seems then, on a survey of the whole evidence, that in the fifteenth century the monastic schools were doing scanty work, and that there was little show of readiness on their part to educate the society around them, but that there was a great variety of grammar and song and ABC schools in connection with cathedrals, collegiate churches, chantries, and guilds. It is confidently stated by the editor of the certificates under the Chantry Acts that for higher education the provision was actually larger, relatively to the existing population, than in 1865, as given in the Schools Inquiry Commission Report. It is not easy to reconcile this estimate with the complaint of the incumbents of the city parishes in 1447 of the exceeding need of schools in London, or with the language of William Byngham, Rector of St. John Zachary, who petitioned for permission to found God's House, afterwards developed as Christ's College at Cambridge, with the words: "Youre poure Besecher hathe founde of late over the est part of the weye leding from Hampton to Coventre and so forth, no ferther north than Rypon, seventie scholes voide, or mo, that were occupied all at ones, within fiftie yeres passed, because that there is so grete scarstee of Maistres of Gramar."

(marginal note: Much schooling for which monks did little.)

If the scarcity of teachers was indeed so great as is implied in both these documents, it may be accounted for in part perhaps by the distraction of public interest in the long debate of war. Certainly it cannot justify the statements that have been made that instruction in Latin was not easily to be had away from the two great centres of learning, or that the creation of new schools was systematically discouraged. The number of teachers may have been restricted by the fear described at Norwich of the schools of Lollards in the English tongue, or by the jealousy that was felt when peasants aspired to learning, but in few towns of any size does the supply of teachers appear to have been wanting, though it might be true in some of them, as Langland wrote, that few could "versifie faire" or "construe what the poets sung." Still some thought that there was too much popular instruction—

> Now mot ich soutere (cobbler) his sone setten to schole,
> And ich a beggars brol on the book lerne.

Lay teachers, however, were now more frequently appointed, as at Sevenoaks in 1432, where it was ruled that the master must not be a priest, and in Dean Colet's school at St. Paul's, where Lily, whom he appointed, was a married layman. The innovation reached a climax when at Bridgenorth in 1503 order was made by the town council that "there shall no priest keep school, save only one child to help him to say mass, after that a schoolmaster cometh to town, but that every child resort to the common school on pain of forfeiting to the chamber of the town twenty shillings of every priest that doeth the contrary." On the other hand, soon afterwards, in Starkey's poem, in which compulsory education was proposed, and idle children were to be in dread of the inspector and the stocks, the plan suggested was that the clergy were to be paid for teaching.

The students of the universities at the beginning of the fourteenth century were very numerous. Without accepting the startling estimate of 60,000 made by Wyclif—if it be not a copyist's mistake—or of 30,000 gowns- *Oxford.* men reported by Gascoigne, and given also on the authority of Fitz-Ralph of Armagh, or even that of Rishanger, who tells us that in 1264 the names of 15,000 clerks were inscribed on the Registers of the masters, there is ample evidence that Oxford was at the zenith of its European influence and reputation. It had risen to the level of the famous University of Paris, and of late surpassed its rival in the intellectual weight and number of its leading schoolmen. Though at first a mere copy of the older university, it had shown its originality in two characteristic features: first in its collegiate system, and secondly in the great extension of its privileges and jurisdiction.

As far as can be ascertained, there was no ecclesiastical influence in the conditions of its origin or early fortunes beyond the general control claimed by the Church over all forms of education. Teachers brought to- *Not of ecclesiastical* gether, we know not how or when, formed them- *origin.* selves into a teaching guild, and, with license from the Ordinary and the Crown, defined the rules of their own union, and the conditions of admission to their body, and so became a corporation recognised by law or a university in the earlier meaning of the term. Its members lectured where they could, and the degree which they were entitled to confer carried with it the right and obligation to teach within a pre-scribed range of study. So any guild of craftsmen gained from the civil power certain exclusive rights to ply their trade and to fix the limits and conditions of the supply of ap-prentices whom they taught to do work like their own. But at a time when a clerical status was attached to literary pur-suits of every kind, scholars enjoyed the privilege of clergy ; ecclesiastical names and interests were closely associated with them, and their vicissitudes formed part of the history of the English Church. It is important therefore to describe in some detail their relations to the different orders of the clergy.

First as to the monks. When in 1426 the graduates of Oxford applied to the Benedictine Order for a grant towards Not monastic. the expenses of the divinity school they did not hesitate to say that the university sprang from a monastic origin, and it has been assumed that the universities of Oxford and Cambridge first arose out of, or in close affilia-tion with, the schools that are said to have existed in con-nection with the priory of St. Frideswide or with Oseney Abbey at Oxford, and with the conventual schools of Ely. There is little evidence that such schools ever existed in the two former, nor are there distinct traces of monastic influences in the early conditions of the professors and the students ; the chancellor was licensed under diocesan and not conventual authority ; the right of control was exercised by the Bishop of Lincoln, in whose vast diocese Oxford was included, and monks are seldom mentioned in its earliest annals.

But in 1281 a monastery was founded for an abbot and fifteen brethren of the Cistercian Order in North Oseney, Convents sent members there. and this Abbey of Rewley is spoken of as their place of study at Oxford. In 1279 a Benedictine chapter held at Abingdon decided to tax the revenues of all their houses in the province of Canterbury for the support of an establishment at Oxford where their students might be housed, and a few years later Gloucester Hall was founded by John Giffard for thirteen Black Monks under the Benedictine rule, who were at first drawn only from St. Peter's, Gloucester, but afterwards from other houses of the Order. Unusual interest was shown by the great Benedictine houses

when one of the students took his degree as Doctor of
Divinity, and the abbots of Gloucester, Abingdon, Evesham,
Winchester, and Malmesbury, with many other dignitaries, rode
up to be present at the ceremony. Various convents of the
Order built rooms at Gloucester Hall to house their students,
and "Worcester College can show the quaint old lodgings,
with their original doorways and separate roofs, which were
cells to different Benedictine Abbeys." As early as 1286 the
prior and convent of Durham sent some of their younger
brethren to a house which was built for them by Canditch in
the north of Oxford. For their use the literary enthusiast
Richard de Bury proposed to leave his books and to endow a
separate foundation, but the work was left for Bishop Hatfield,
his successor (1345-81). The Order, spurred perhaps to action
by the commanding influence of the friars, showed a praise-
worthy zeal for higher education. The Bull *Benedictina* of
Pope Benedict XII. directed in 1337 that one monk in twenty
was to be sent up to a university with an allowance for his
maintenance, and the Chapters General that were held during
the fourteenth century in order to make a closer federal union
for the whole Order devoted attention to the subject. Lectureships were founded for them in both houses. One of the
monks, chosen by the rest, was to be made prior, and each
student was to pay six shillings to him. Christ Church,
Canterbury, had its hall in 1331 for three students, and
among the records of the convent we may read of three who
started with fifty shillings in their pocket, and after spending
thirty-seven of them on the road arrived at Oxford with
thirteen only left for the expenses of a term. One is bidden
to use his opportunities to find promising recruits for his own
house ; another has permission given him to stay up for the
Long Vacation. In 1442 the prior of the students formally
complained in a chapter of the Black Monks that some large
houses had neglected to recruit the number of the students,
or to pay for their expenses, and the protest was repeated
after a few years. In 1432 a college of St. Bernard was
founded, with the help of Chichele, where St. John's now
stands, and the old statue of the patron saint still remains
in view in a niche in the square tower. Shortly afterwards the canons of St. Augustine acquired St. Mary's College

for the use of all the houses of their Order, and there they received Erasmus while he remained in Oxford.

At Cambridge the earliest college was connected with the Hospital of St. John the Evangelist, which was administered by Augustinian Canons. Hugh Balsham, who And to Cambridge. became Bishop of Ely in 1257, obtained the necessary powers to extend and re-endow the old foundation, intending to combine secular students with the monks. But they could not live in harmony together; perhaps "the scholars were too wise, and the brethren possibly over-good"; and the two elements were parted in 1284, the former to become the separate College of Peterhouse, while the others retained their monastic character but lived as in a house of learning. This did not thrive, however; and it was at last dissolved, or absorbed in the college which still bears its name. There were other conventual establishments of course within the town, as that of Barnwell, for example; but though monks were sent from Ely and Croyland in compliance with the constitution of Benedict XII., the religious orders do not seem to have made special provision for their students on any considerable scale, or at least in separate halls in Cambridge before 1428, when Benedictine students were established in what was known afterwards as Buckingham College, where Magdalen now stands, the prior of the students having lately begged for some such central hall where they might live. At a later date it is said that "all the great monasteries of East Anglia seem to have had several of their younger members in training at Gonville and Caius College."

The friars had settled themselves down at Oxford early in the thirteenth century, as they had also done at Cambridge,— the Black and the Grey Friars very soon after they The friars at Oxford. arrived in England, the Carmelites and Augustinians somewhat later. Between them they took confessedly the leading part in that brilliant intellectual movement which, at the beginning of the fourteenth century, had raised Oxford to the first place among the schools of mediæval thought. No land could boast of such a company of illustrious schoolmen as those whose fame was specially associated with the lecture-rooms of Oxford. "None can show," says Brewer, "three schoolmen like the English Roger Bacon, Duns

Scotus, and Ockham, each unrivalled in his way, and each working with equal ability in opposite directions." These were the most eminent ; but besides them there were others, famous for their logical acuteness and their widespread influence, though they are little more than names to us, for the subjects of their keen debate have lost their interest for our times.   Such were Alexander Hales, the Doctor Irrefragabilis ; and Richard Middleton, the Doctor Fundatissimus ; and John Baconthorpe, the Doctor Resclutus ; and Robert Holcot, besides secular priests, such as Walter Burley and Thomas Bradwardine, the Doctor Profundus.

Of the friars, the Franciscans had done by far the most to raise the University to the front rank.   Not only had they by the writings of their Scotists challenged the supremacy of Aquinas, but by the mouth of Roger Bacon they pleaded for the claims of mathematics and experimental science.   Following Ockham they demolished the figments of realism and disputed the papal pretensions that had been based on the forged Decretals.

The pre-eminent reputation of the friars and their rapid advance in influence and numbers could not but cause some jealousy in the seculars among whom they lived, and at Paris the two sets of interests were soon brought ^{Jealousy of them.} into collision.   At Oxford the peace was preserved longer, and when it was disturbed there were technical grounds for the dispute.   The main question at issue was whether a student should be allowed to graduate in theology without passing first through the faculty of arts.   The principle long recognised was that a training in logic and philosophy—the course that is in the arts school—was a needful preparation for a systematic study of divinity, and such training might be only given by a licensed teacher a regent master of that school.   The friars on their side would not allow their novices or brethren to graduate in secular studies, but claimed the right to give such instruction in them as they thought good through their own teachers.   These candidates, however, were technically disqualified from graduating in theology, unless the chancellor and regents exercised in their favour their dispensing power.   Graces seem to have been freely given for many years.

But the attitude of the friars generally must have grown more aggressive, or the seculars became more impatient of the influence and privileges which they enjoyed. In 1303 the voting power of the Faculty of Arts was so much increased by statute that it was possible for it to override the opposition of the theologians and doctors of Civil and Canon Law, among whom the friars were strongest. About the same time the trial sermons required for a B.D. degree were transferred from the Dominican convent to St. Mary's Church. In 1310 the disputations on the eve of the degree were transferred in the same way to the same place, and the Biblical exegesis of a lecturer was disallowed unless as B.D. he had already dealt with the dogmatic theology of Peter Lombard.

Statutes to their prejudice.

The friar preachers appealed against these changes to the Holy See, including in their list of grievances the disqualification imposed sixty years before, which required a special grace unanimously passed to allow one of the students to graduate in theology without proceeding through degrees of arts. They further urged that the attitude of the seculars had grown more hostile, that graces were refused, attendance at their professors' lectures actively discouraged, and scholars and others dissuaded from the use of their confessionals and churches. The case dragged on for years, and judgment was ultimately given against the friars, though with a few trifling concessions to their interest. The lengthy documents connected with the case illustrate alike the clamorous pertinacity with which the mendicants pushed their claims and the general hostility which was stirred in other circles. These points are brought out in a somewhat comic shape in the proceedings of the proctor of the friars, when he tried to serve notice of appeal against the action of the University authorities. He went first to the chancellor's school, but being refused admittance by the servants, he waited till after lecture, and then presented the copy of the appeal, pushing it even into the folds of the chancellor's gown, only to see it thrown down with "offensive words." Again, the next congregation day, he went to St. Mary's Church to serve his notice, but he had hardly begun to read it when he was hustled out of church by some of the

Appeal.

masters who were there, and the doors were shut against him. Unwilling to be baffled, he mounted on a tombstone near the wall, and in the presence of a " copious multitude of persons " loudly read his notice of appeal through an open window to the congregation gathered in the choir inside, announcing also that a copy of the process would be found nailed to the church doors. He did not leave the scene till this was done, in spite of a volley of abusive words from the scholars' servants, who were standing round about.

We may notice that, though the interests of all the friars were affected by the action of the University, the Dominicans alone took a prominent part in the appeal. It had been so, long before, at Paris, where the quarrel had been fought out much on the same lines. But the different result in the two cases shows that in the interval their influence had waned as their encroachments became more apparent. At Paris the Papal Bull of 1255 (*Quasi lignum vitæ*) deprived the University of all control over the degrees of the friar-doctors. At Oxford this precedent was urged in the appeal, but the tide had turned, and the award was given in the main against the friars, and though the pope intervened in their behalf, and they kept up the struggle for a few years longer, in 1320 they finally submitted to the terms on which the University insisted. But the feeling of resentment lingered on and found expression in a bitter attack on the University as being in its dotage, for it encouraged monks even to come up to Oxford, and get a little learning, that they might turn their preaching skill against the friars.

The secular clergy had not looked on with indifference at the long dispute ; they made the interest of the University their own and sympathised deeply with it in the struggle ; both Convocations agreed to a tax levied Sympathy of the clergy. on the ecclesiastical property of the realm to defray the costs of litigation, for at that date Oxford had no corporate funds, as it had also no buildings of its own. The troubles with the friars at Oxford were not, however, over. The dispute broke out in another shape when Fitz-Ralph, Archbishop of Armagh, pleaded at Avignon against them (*vide* p. 318). His protest there was unavailing, but the University itself passed a statute in 1358 which forbade the houses of the mendicants to receive boys under eighteen years of age under pain of exclusion from the schools of all the members of the offending house. This, however, was disallowed by the king in the Parliament of 1366, while on the other hand it was ordered that the friars should not use their influence at Rome to the prejudice of Oxford.

The friction still continued and showed itself in occasional quarrels, as in 1358, when Friar John was condemned to read publicly a recantation at St. Mary's Church after the Sunday sermon, and to pay 100 shillings, and to lecture no more on theology, for having declared in his lecture room that the University was a training-school for heretics, and that tithes would be paid with better reason to the mendicants than to the rectors of the churches. Another had to apologise for attacking "Sophists" in his sermon, being thought to refer to the faculty of arts, whose students bore commonly that title. He excused his hasty words by saying that he did not mean to speak slightingly of studies which were "the door of admission to all learning."

Continued friction.

Though Convocation helped to pay the expenses of the litigation with the friars, there was little in the early history of the universities or their attitude to episcopal authority to identify them very specially with the interests of the Church; indeed at times they appeared to be the only safe refuge for heterodox opinions. The appointment of the chancellor, their chief official, required at first the sanction of the bishop whom in theory he represented. But before long claims of independence were asserted for his jurisdiction, delegated though it was; practices tolerated from indifference hardened into customary rights, and after some debate Bishop Sutton of Lincoln in 1280 finally conceded to the court of the Chancellor of Oxford the powers of probate of scholars' wills and the right to deal with the contracts and immoralities of the members of the University. The bishop's confirmation of the chancellor's election was for a while a matter of dispute. In the language of Capgrave, "in the year 1287 the Universite of Oxforth chose a Chauncelor, Maister William Kingeston. Thei sent on the Bischop of Lincoln for his confirmacion : the bishop seide it was his deute to com himselve. Thei answerd that

Oxford freed from control of the bishop.

this was her (their) elde privylege ; and this wolde thei kepe.
The bischop was inflexibil and thei were obdurat.   And so ot
malice thei left her redyng, and her teching.   Many scoleres
went away, thei that abode were evil occupied.   But at the
last the bischop condescended to her elde custome."   The
confirmation became in course of time a pure formality, and
on the refusal of the bishop to proceed with it in 1350,
Archbishop Islip issued a commission for the purpose, and
in 1368 it was dispensed with altogether by the pope.

At Cambridge also the chancellor was at first subject to
diocesan authority, but Hugo de Balsham, Bishop of
Ely in 1275, generously extended the chancellor's   Cambridge
jurisdiction to all suits in the University, and re- also.
stricted the powers of his own court and that of the archdeacon.

The refusal of the chancellor to take the oath of obedience
to the bishop in 1374 was not allowed to pass by Bishop
Arundel, and the dispute was decided in the Court of Arches
in the bishop's favour.   But in 1430 Martin V. delegated to
the Prior of Barnwell and a canon of Lincoln the examination
of the claims of independence asserted by the University on
the ground of certain ancient Bulls, of which the copies only
—"rank forgeries," as Baker calls them—existed in their
archives, and the prior finally gave sentence in favour of the
privileges claimed.

As the forms of self-government of the universities were
won at the expense of episcopal authority, so the organisation
of their studies showed no marked regard for the
special requirements of the clergy.   The ruling   No special
faculty was not that of theology but arts : the course   training for
  clergy.
of study did not profess to give any special preparation for the
pastoral office.   The friars might train men to be preachers, and
encourage the literal study of the Scriptures, but the regent
masters chiefly cared for the subtleties of logical disputes, for
controversial questions of philosophy which had no immediate
relations to the future work of the confessional or pulpit.   The
ecclesiastical courts required and rewarded the study of the
canon law, but for the humble duties of the parish priest
there was no direct provision.

The absence of professional training for the clergy could
not but be felt in the discharge of their parochial duties, but

on the other hand the secular studies of the Faculty of Arts, together with the free intercourse of different nationalities, and the frequent passage from one school of "general study" to another, fostered an enthusiasm for liberal culture, a wider outlook, and a freedom from intellectual narrowness which made the English University a most valuable training-ground of national temper, and a counterpoise to the dominant influence of Rome.

It was with a true instinct, therefore, that the bishops felt that Oxford was, as Matthew Paris calls it, "the second school of the Church, or rather the Church's foundation or support." They gave their dispensations freely to the young incumbents who asked for leave of non-residence to carry on their studies; they proposed to the councils of clergy to vote subsidies in case of pressing need or for the endowment of a professorial chair at Oxford—as the grant of one farthing in the £ by Rigaud of Assier for the study of Greek and Hebrew. They appealed to Crown or pope in its behalf when encouragement was needful to reward its scholars with preferment, or to secure for its degrees a wider recognition, like that which Paris had enjoyed.

Favour of bishops.

With its system of self-government they had no wish to interfere: but they could not look on with unconcern when the currents of free thought were moving in what seemed a dangerous course, and Archbishop Kilwardby in 1276 and Peckham in 1284, in solemn visitations of the University, condemned various theses which had been maintained by the Dominicans and might soon be taught authoritatively in the schools. The voice of the rulers of the Church was listened to with respect, but a century later the assertion of authority to stamp out the influence of Wyclif could only be carried through with the use of force, which must for many years have marred the intellectual vigour if not the prosperity of Oxford. At Oxford the authorities had gone so far in 1411 as to appeal to the pope to grant them once more exemption from all episcopal authority, a privilege which they had renounced in 1397. The step had laid them open to the charge of a breach of the Statute of Præmunire, which Archbishop Arundel speedily pressed against them. The danger was a real one, and the University was forced to

Archbishops as visitors.

apologise humbly to the archbishop and sue for the intercession of the Prince of Wales.

The introduction of the collegiate system in the later half of the thirteenth century, which influenced so markedly the future development of the English universities, did much also to connect them more closely with the Church. The movement was in favour of the studies of the secular clergy, for whom no separate provision had been made, like that for the regulars around them. *The college system.*

Shortlived attempts indeed were made to combine the two classes under the same roof, as at Cambridge by Hugh Balsham (*v.* p. 342). The experience of Archbishop Islip at a much later date was perhaps much the same. He proposed to bring together in Canterbury College, Oxford, secular priests and monks from Christ Church, but first the monks were expelled by Islip, and then the seculars by his successor Langham, by whom the monks were reinstated. The incompatibles could not be fused, though the experiment was tried again by Bishop Hatfield, who directed that eight secular students should be admitted to wait in Durham College on the regulars at table. *Attempts to combine regulars and seculars.*

The statutes of Walter de Merton, given in 1274 in their final shape by him when bishop-elect of Rochester, furnished the model for most of the colleges of Oxford and of Cambridge. It was not, of course, entirely original in its object or its methods. Provision for poor students at the University had been already made in various forms, by the occasional bounty of the rich and even by permanent endowment, as, but a few years before, by William of Durham and Sir John de Balliol. *Merton and other colleges.*

Collegiate churches had existed long ago, where secular priests could live together under rules which contemplated piety and learning. But educational objects were now to be combined with the corporate life in forms that were suited to the age, and the rapid extension of the system showed that the experiment was felt to be successful. Ere long, indeed, discipline was grievously relaxed at Merton, and Archbishop Peckham had to intervene to repress the mutinous scholars and assert the authority of the warden. But the college passed through its troubled waters into a period of prosperous fortunes, during which it could proudly point to a succession of the most distinguished scholars of the age among its members. Peterhouse, at Cambridge, followed soon afterwards on the same lines, and in the first half of the fourteenth century Exeter, Oriel, and Queen's at Oxford, and Pembroke, Gonville Hall, and Trinity Hall at Cambridge, were in the main developments of the same leading ideas, though with many variations of details.

The colleges were ecclesiastical in their outward forms, modelled as they were on the conventual type, which was familiar to the experience of the age. To the monks' vows corresponded in less rigid forms the rules of college discipline, the celibate life required of all the members, and the charitable endowments coupled with the restrictions of the personal income. In place of abbot and obedientiaries there was the head, known by various names, with dean, bursars, tutors, and chaplains for the varied work of the establishment. Like the convents they were self-governing corporations, with landed estates held in mortmain, and were to have instruction within their walls provided for the younger by senior members of their body. The monastic aspect was maintained by the common meals in hall, during which a Latin author was to be read aloud, and by a year of probation for the scholars like the novitiate of the monks. The ecclesiastical character was enhanced by the provisions for prayers and anniversaries for the founders, as in the collegiate churches, by the obligation to take holy orders enforced commonly, but under various conditions, on the fellows ; by the preferments in the form of college livings, which Walter de Merton set the example of securing for the objects of his care.

The statutes of nearly all the colleges show that it was the intention of the founders to encourage general culture in the first place rather than professional studies. General culture. The arts course was to come first, a literary or philosophic training, such as the universities always had prescribed as introductory to theology or law. A few only of the fellows were commonly to be allowed to go on to the canon or the civil law. But during the disorders of the earlier years at Merton one of the irregularities complained of was that the scholars cared only to acquire such learning as would prove useful and remunerative, and they forsook the liberal arts for medicine and law.   Roger Bacon had already, in 1271, made a like remark.   One founder, indeed, and he a bishop, designed his college of Trinity Hall at Cambridge in 1350 only for students of civil and canon law, but William Bateman of Norwich had held office in the court of Avignon, had risen by his legal skill, and thought little of the culture that could not speedily be turned to profit. Generally, however, the old University tradition was maintained that a liberal education in the School of Arts must take the first place in the academic course of study.

All that we read of University life before the foundation of the colleges shows how great was the need of more effective discipline than was elsewhere to be found with such inadequate powers of control as chancellor or Need of discipline. mayor possessed as guardian of the public peace. The motley multitude of hot-headed youths gathered from all parts of England, or even from foreign lands when the English universities were better known, scattered themselves at first over the town wherever they could find a lodging, then grouped themselves in halls or hostels, where each little community of scholars elected its own principal and made its own rules, with scant control from chancellor or masters. There had been little effective check on license and disorder ; riotous frays frequently occurred, and were carried to alarming lengths at times.   Northerners and southerners often came to blows.   Irish scholars broke the peace in desperate encounters, which led in 1422 to a petition in the Commons against the "wilde Irishmen at Oxford"; the spirit of clanship moved Welshmen and Scotsmen to take part in the fray. Jousts and tournaments were forbidden in 1315 in the neighbourhood of Oxford, where there was already too much danger of excitement.   As Fuller says, "so many war-horses were brought hither that Pegasus was himself likely to be shut out, for where Mars keeps his terms there the Muses may even make their vacation."   Much more frequently, however, the scholars made common cause against the laity around them.   Quarrels were constantly occurring between the townsmen and the petulant scholars, who treated local

interests and customs with contempt ; one such, already mentioned (*v.* p. 71), has found its historian and poet.   If worsted
in the strife which they provoked they could retire from Oxford
and set up a "general study at Stamford or Northampton,"
where schools founded by the Carmelites and others were
already in repute ; they could invoke the sympathy of
friendly bishops or Papal legates, who threatened to excommunicate the townsmen ; they could move the Crown
to interpose in defence of a famous seat of learning.   So
time after time the University forced the burghers to submission, gaining fresh privileges as the price of peace, and
wresting even powers of self-government from the humiliated
town.

The new colleges not only bore witness to the sense of the
need of a more effective discipline for student life than had
been hitherto provided ; they also pointed to the
ravages of the Black Death among the clergy.   In
default of fitting candidates men of scanty learning
and low social status were accepted for the ministerial office.
The statutes of Trinity Hall and Clare Hall at Cambridge
refer to this pressing need.   Archbishop Islip in endowing
Canterbury College was moved avowedly by the desire to
meet it, and Wykeham's statutes say the same for New College.
A little before this it seems that Oxford reached the
highest point as regards both its numbers and its reputation.
The writer whose literary enthusiasm found a high-flown and
fantastic utterance in *Philobiblon*, after speaking of the
pleasure with which in his youth he visited at Paris the
"paradise of the world, with its delightful libraries and luxuri-
ant parks of all manner of volumes," implies that Oxford had
completely surpassed her as a seat of learning.   "Minerva
having passed by Paris has at length happily reached Britain,
the most illustrious of islands."

Oxford, however, had work enough to do to raise the learning
of the clergy to its proper level, if we may trust the same writer's
lamentations.   In his pages books are represented
as complaining, "We are expelled by force and arms
from the homes of the clergy which seemed to be
ours by hereditary right. . . . For our places are now occupied by hounds and hawks and sometimes by that biped beast

[margin note:] Colleges founded after the plague.

[margin note:] Decline of learning.

. . . from which we have ever taught our nurslings to flee, more than from the asp or cockatrice; wherefore she always jealous of the love of us . . . spying us at length in a corner, protected only by the web of some dead spider, with a frown abuses us with bitter words . . . and advises that we should be bartered away forthwith for costly head-dress, cambric, silk . . . and furs."

But the need of books must have been sorely felt by many in their studies, if we may trust the statement of Archbishop Fitz-Ralph about this time, that many who came to study returned home ill-instructed, because the mendicants had bought up all the books. Indeed there is ample evidence that books were scarce and dear, and we can appreciate the liberal forethought with which a few were specially bequeathed for the use of a kinsman in his studies, to be passed on—so the wills at times directed—to some younger member of the family when he went up to Oxford. It was one of the marked services of the newly-founded colleges that they had at least some little store of books— chained often to the desks, where all might use them. The supply was small at first. In 1343 the scholars of Balliol, who were so poor that they   College libraries. had to seek a living by manual labour (*mechanice*), had an allowance of twelvepence a week, and the books of the divers faculties in common, by the grace of William de Felton, who wished, however, for a grant of tithes to save his pocket. At Queen's College in 1389 there is an entry in the accounts of twenty-six shillings and eightpence spent on "chains for the books," and as twopence was enough for a like chain at Exeter the expense may point possibly to many books at Queen's. Exeter indeed had been so hard pressed at times, that it was obliged to pawn the few it had to one of the "chests" founded for the purpose, or even to "our barbour," who lent four marks on a Bible pledged to him. Oriel in 1375 had about one hundred volumes, the catalogue of which has been preserved. William of Wykeham gave 240 to form a library for his great foundation. On some of these a price was fixed, to be paid in case of loss or damage, and most of these represent a value which must have been quite beyond the means of poorer students, who could do little more than fill their note-books at the lectures, unless they belonged to a friary or college.

The same conclusion may be drawn from the prices put upon the books of Bishop Gravesende, early in the fourteenth century, when they were valued for purposes of probate. A Bible there is marked at £10, and a book of Avicenna at £5, sums to be largely multiplied to give the prices in our currency. So too in other documents for probate the *Revelations of St. Bridget* are valued at £3 : 6 : 8, and a *Pupilla Oculi* at £1 : 6 : 8, though a French Mandeville was worth only 2s. ' Neither of the college libraries referred to contained much in the way of Latin classics ; philosophy was of most account, and civil law of least ; the supply of theology was largest.

Prices of books.

Such colleges as were already in existence were having their little store of books increased by special benefactors, and a liberal provision was made, as has been stated, for New College, which was established by formal charter in 1379. This noble foundation of the munificent and large-minded William of Wykeham was on by far the largest scale of the colleges hitherto endowed, and the leading motive in the founder's thought was the encouragement of the studies of the clergy. The characteristic feature of his scheme, suggested perhaps by experiments on a humbler scale elsewhere, and copied afterwards by Henry VI. and others, was the establishment of two great educational systems, the school for boys at Winchester, the college for men at Oxford, to be worked in close connection with each other, and to provide the best possible training and culture from their early years for the working clergy of the Church, whose interests Wykeham had so much at heart.

New College.

The prosperity and reputation of the English universities, which had been so marked at the beginning of the fourteenth century, were passing away before its close, and there followed a long period of discouragement and decline. The pestilence had made fearful havoc among the narrow streets in which the students' halls were crowded. The convents, which owned many of the halls where the clerks were lodged, could find no tenants, and a fatal blow was given to the interests of liberal study, or,

Fewer students.

as an old writer says, " arts and learning did degenerate, and
the empty babbling of sophisters did everywhere make a
noise in the schools." During the fifteenth century the
complaints were frequently renewed, that the old prosperity
had not revived ; halls were deserted or occupied by townsmen only ; and Oxford and Cambridge were but shadows of
their former selves.

Various reasons have been, or may be, given for this
decline. One explanation would connect it with the stern
measures of repression which silenced the partisans
of Wyclif, and arrested the movement of reform at <sup>Causes alleged
—coercion.</sup>
Oxford. The heart-burnings and excitement were
intense, and the decisive triumph of the rulers of the Church
reacted certainly on the whole tone of Oxford thought for
many years to come, causing grave loss of dignity and independence. But there is no evidence of active discontent in
the form of a secession ; nothing to connect it with an
immediate fall of numbers ; none of the older writers regard
it in that light, and all that can be inferred safely is that
the freedom and self-confidence of philosophic thought was
hampered by the ecclesiastical restrictions, and no succession
of brilliant teachers, like those of an earlier generation,
attracted students to the lecture-rooms of Oxford.

On the other hand, the University authorities themselves
seemed to have no doubt as to the main cause of the decline ;
students ceased to come, they said, because the
rewards of study were precarious and scanty ; a <sup>Abuse of
patronage.</sup>
disinterested love of knowledge might have brought
enthusiastic students round the chairs of the great schoolmen
of the past ; but in this later age, it seems, men reckoned up
the chances of advancement, and sought a livelihood as well
as learning. The constant burden of complaint was that
graduates did not get their fair share of ecclesiastical preferment. Even in happier days they had appealed time after
time to Avignon and Rome, so long as popes could dispense
their patronage without control. Thus we have copies of
petitions sent to Pope John XXII in 1322, to Benedict XII.
in 1334, to Clement VI. in 1342 in behalf of the poor
masters who were hungering after livings. A roll of deserving graduates was sent to guide the Papal choice, and letters

were written in pressing terms to cardinals and king to ask for their support.

When popes seemed backward in their bounty the impatient masters moved king and Parliament with protests at the practice which filled so many English benefices with alien rectors. But after the Statutes against Provisors were enforced, patrons at home seemed even slower than popes abroad to recognise the claims of learning. Then the cry was that government should not enforce the statutes rigidly, but allow poor clerks to sue for favours at the Papal Court and pick up such crumbs of apostolic provisions as they could. In 1390 Parliament took up the cause, requesting the king to keep "tenderly at heart" the state and needs of the universities of Oxford and Cambridge, and the lords of the Council to deliberate as to how the statute might be modified for their relief. As little came of this an appeal was made to Convocation. A stringent rule was made in both provinces that ecclesiastical patrons should present only graduates of either university to such benefices as they might have at their disposal. The order was treated, however, as a counsel of perfection, for the old complaints were still renewed in the spirit, if not in the actual language of Wood's remark, "all things were so corrupt that virtue and learning went barefoot, while asses and fools who had money or friends rode in pompous array." The appropriation of a large number of the churches to religious houses, which allowed a pittance only for the vicars, narrowed still further the chances of preferment. Nor was this all; bishops lived at court, spent largely, and did little for poor scholars either in their own households or by exhibitions at a seat of study.

The reason which the graduates gave themselves for the discouragement of liberal studies was certainly more pertinent than that which the townsmen of Oxford urged on their side. It is the want of apprentices, they said, whom we are forbidden to engage unless their parents have a certain income, which keeps the numbers of the industrial population down. We cannot please the clerks and satisfy their wants, if we have not apprentices to do the work, and so men do not come up to study as of old.

The fear of the seductions of the friars, on which Fitz-

Ralph laid stress at Avignon, might pass muster as a
rhetorical device, as one of many arguments against
them, but was not probably of much account in the ^{Proselytising friars.}
narrowed numbers of the students.

A far more potent cause is to be found in the disturbing
influence of war.   The free intercourse between the Universities of Oxford and of Paris which was provided
for in the terms of peace in 1360, was again sus- Wars.
pended on the renewal of the war in 1369, and during the
long strife between the two countries what Wood calls "the
loving knot of communication" between English and foreign
scholars was often broken.   Men's minds were diverted from
the arts of peace and liberal studies, and coarser interests
prevailed amid the turmoil of foreign and domestic strife.
The restlessness and party spirit that were so rife in the
society at large reacted on the scholars, and deadly brawls constantly disturbed the peace and discredited the scenes of study.

No single cause then need be singled out; it was the
spirit of the age that was at fault, its turbulence and military
passion, the selfishness of its prominent ecclesiastics, the
decline and rivalries of the great religious orders, the lowered
ideals and deep-seated corruptions.

But the universities declined in moral dignity as well as
numbers.   They spent their energies in petty squabbles about
precedence : thus the doctors of the faculty of
civil law were up in arms at the pretensions of the Decline in dignity.
faculty of physic, and begged Archbishop Chichele
to interpose in their behalf and be "the Ebenezer of the
suppliants," for, as they urged, "the waiting-maid Hagar
rears her neck in contempt of her superiors, the care-taker of
a carcass claims the honour due to the guardian of a state."
Congregation again voted graces and conferred degrees with
scant regard to literary merits, relaxing the rules as sordid
interests or favour prompted.

As time went on and numbers dwindled, efforts were
made to court the favour of the rich and noble, and the
honour of welcoming a young prince as scholar
was sought with eagerness and urged even with Cringing letters.
indecent haste.   Letter after letter was written
about the king's nephew, Edward Pole, when it was hoped

that the Bishop of Salisbury would soon come "to lay the noble infant on his mother's lap." For many years the official Registers consist largely of begging letters, addressed to noblemen, bishops, and heads of religious houses. St. Mary's Church must be repaired, for the masters are drenched with the rain that pours through the faulty roof; new schools of theology and law are sorely needed; a library building is a pressing want; but the funds of the University are quite exhausted, for the fees are very scanty, now that the numbers are so low, and Oxford is, like Rachel, mourning her lost children. Surely the generous will come to its relief; the nurslings will not fail their *alma mater;* a debt from the Bishop of Chichester is still unsettled, but he will doubtless by speedy payment take his name off from their books that it may be written on the Book of Life. Poverty is the constant theme of their complaints. The Benedictine scholars refuse to pay the six shillings and eightpence due to the master whose lectures they attend: the loss of this would be a fatal blow. The poor students must be allowed to make their own clothes, though no one else must trespass on the privileges of the tailors' guild. The Chancellor even of the University must resign his office, which he has not means enough to fill with credit. It was no wonder, therefore, that in the great ecclesiastical debates of the fifteenth century the English universities played a very secondary part; when invited to send delegates to the general Councils they appealed to Convocation to supply the necessary funds, but their voice carried no great weight, in spite of the compliments of Gerson; the University of Paris took the first place again, and the commanding influence of her orators and divines eclipsed completely the representatives of theology in England.

But though the fortunes of learning had sunk very low, a movement had begun, feeble and ill-supported at the first, in favour of that keener sense of literary grace and classical refinement, and that broader human interest to which the name of the Renaissance is commonly applied. The first step in this and the primary condition was the revival of the study of Greek. The clergy read the Bible only in the Vulgate, with at best a Greek Father or two in a Latin dress. The early schoolmen,

Greek studies.

busy with interminable debates on their problems of meta-
physic, knew little at first hand of the "Master of the Wise"
to whose authority they bowed; their Aristotelian lore was
mainly drawn from the Arabian commentaries, based themselves on Syriac renderings from the Greek. Later still the
translations to which the great theologians had recourse,
such as those of Michael Scot, were clumsy and inaccurate,
while Plato and the Greek poets and historians were a
treasure wholly sealed.

In the middle of the thirteenth century indeed the outlook in Oxford seemed to brighten; Grosseteste, confessedly
its foremost scholar, exerted his influence in favour   Grosseteste
of Hellenic studies, and himself translated Aristotle's   and Roger
Ethics, while Roger Bacon, not content with point-   Bacon,
ing with prophetic insight to the future triumphs of inductive
science, insisted also on the pressing claims of linguistic and
literary culture. A student himself of Greek, Hebrew,
Arabic, and Chaldæan, Bacon could not speak patiently of
the sorry translations which were used around him, and of
the stores of literature, both sacred and profane, of which
there was as yet no Latin version. He had himself spent on
his experiments and books £2000; surely prelates and
princes might stretch out a helping hand to introduce the
classic models of good taste and sober method in place of
the arid dialectic and fine-drawn distinctions of the schools.
The humanism of the fifteenth century seems antedated in
Bacon's flights of fancy, but his age would not listen to its
boldest thinker: the new learning made no way, and grace
of style was a forgotten art. As regards literary form, the
fourteenth century went backward and not forward. The
later monastic chronicles are heavy, laboured, and diffuse
compared with the vivid descriptions and word-painting of
Matthew Paris; a John of Salsbury could write in the
twelfth century like an accomplished man of letters, but the
Latin of Wyclif, the last of the English schoolmen, was
detestably uncouth.

Popes indeed gave good advice. Innocent III. proposed
that scholars should be sent from the University   and popes.
of Paris to learn the language of Constantinople;
Clement V. pressed the chief universities of Europe to found

professorships in the four languages which Bacon recommended.

The friars, as they spread themselves in distant lands, acquired foreign languages, and something of Greek among the rest, and Byzantine scholars occasionally sought a refuge in the West from troubles at home.

The author of the *Philobiblon* again had a real enthusiasm for learning, though his affected verbiage shows little influence of good models. " Ignorance of the Greek language," he writes, " is at this day a great hindrance to the study of the Latin authors, without which the doctrines of the ancients, whether Christian or Gentile, cannot be understood." Richard de Bury, Bishop of Durham (1333-45), whose name was connected with the book, though probably he did not write it, had some intercourse in Italy with Petrarch, who shared his enthusiasm for learning and reverence for Greek MSS., which neither of them could read, and hoped indeed, though vainly, to get information from him about the *Ultima Thule* of the ancients. De Bury went home again, and died in poverty; the books which he had destined for the University of Oxford seem to have never reached it, and a dark cloud settled for many a long year on the prospects of scholarship in England.

Petrarch meantime had stamped upon the social thought of his own age his love of classic purity of style, his horror of scholastic quibbles, and his broad interest in liberal culture. Enthusiasts like Boccaccio and Lionardo Bruni learnt from him to take up with ardour the new studies; Greek scholars like Chrysoloras were invited to fill new professorial chairs; old libraries were ransacked for their literary treasures, and ere long Italy was known in Europe as the fountain-head from which the streams of the new learning must be drawn. It was long before the influence was felt in England. Here and there indeed, but very rarely, a book of Petrarch mentioned in the inventory of a scholar's library at his death shows that some breath of the revival had been felt by a Church dignitary or a nobleman of taste. But early in the fifteenth century Italian scholars began to look for encouragement to English patrons: Titus Livius of Forli came here to write a life of Henry V., and

The friars.

R. de Bury.

Italian scholars.

found a liberal protector in Humphrey, Duke of Gloucester. Others dedicated to him their translations of the *Politics* of Aristotle and the *Phædo* of Plato.   Poggio Bracciolini, one of the most learned scholars of his time, though not, as has been fancied, the author of the *Annals of Tacitus*, spent several years in attendance upon Cardinal Beaufort, receiving a benefice of 120 florins for his pains, "the birth of the mouse after the labour of the mountain," as he angrily complained.   Bernard Andreas and Polydore Vergil were foreign scholars of a later date, who found a home and welcome in high circles, and repaid the debt with works on English history.

So far the influence was only felt by a few noble travellers of taste, but the gift of Duke Humphrey's books to the University of Oxford opened the new studies to a wider circle.   Four distinct donations by him are   Gifts of books. recorded between 1435 and 1443, and these were in all 280 volumes.   The graduates hailed the timely gift with ardour; "no prince had ever made to them so splendid a donation," they write after the first instalment was received. "Our right special lord and mighty prince hath late endowed our University with a thousand pound worth and more of precious books to the loving of God, increase of clergy and cunning men, to the good government and prosperity of the Realm of England without end."   This was not all, for shortly before his death he promised by word of mouth in the presence of a large number of masters in the Congregation House to give them all his Latin books, and he actually bequeathed them in his will.   But the books were long in coming—if indeed they ever came at all—though letters of entreaty were despatched from Oxford to the king and House of Commons, to the duke's executors, and men of rank and influence to beg that the claims of the University might be respected.   Others, however, followed the example of the duke.   A grocer of London sent his copy of Josephus; a literary abbot of St. Alban's presented his *Propinarium*: the University did not fail to remind the friends and executors of men of letters that their books would find an appropriate home at Oxford, and the collection steadily grew larger, till a new building was required to house it.   The duke's library had included some of the Latin poets and translations of parts of Aristotle and Plato, five books of Boccaccio and seven of Petrarch, but there was nothing of Greek but a vocabulary among those presented by him. A letter of thanks for them addressed to him from Oxford speaks, however, of a flowing stream of literary works translated from the Greek and dedicated to the duke, and of the consequent revival of Greek letters, which had lain buried for so many ages.

The new movement spread but slowly, but we now begin to hear more frequently of Englishmen with taste for liberal culture, who brought books with them from Italy and turned to good account the literary stores which they had gathered there. The library of Balliol College was enriched in this way by William Gray (Bishop of Ely, 1454); that of Lincoln College by Robert Fleming; and John Tiptoft, Earl of Worcester, gave to the University Manuscripts of value, which he had collected in his travels. William Sellyng, student of Oxford and Prior of Christ Church, Canterbury (1472), brought back with him from Bologna, after a long stay in Italy, some Greek MSS. which he gave to his convent, and a knowledge of the language, which he taught to Thomas Linacre at home; and Chandler, Warden of New College, Oxford, who "wrote remarkably well in prose and verse," appointed Cornelio Vitelli prælector in his college.

From the lecture-rooms of Vitelli came probably the instruction in the elements of Greek which was turned to such account by William Grocyn of New College and Magdalen, who became confessedly the first scholar of his age in England, a man, said the great publisher Aldo Manuzio, "of exceeding skill and universal learning." After spending two years in Italy in the continuous study of Greek under Demetrius Chalcondylas and Poliziano, he returned to Oxford in 1491 and lectured publicly in Greek, as did Linacre of All Souls, who had studied in Italy a few years before him, having accompanied Sellyng in his embassy in 1486. Colet and More were Grocyn's pupils, and Erasmus, who came to Oxford to learn Greek in 1497, said that it was no longer necessary to go for it to Italy, since it could be learnt as well at Oxford, and in the company of men of accurate and polished culture.

Grocyn, Colet, and More.

Unlike the humanists of Italy, there was no vein of sceptical reserve or moral indifference among them ; Grocyn and his friends were earnest and devout, and there was nothing to arouse religious fears in the early stages of the Renaissance in England, little even of such blending of the language of heathenism and Christianity as in the epitaph on John Claymond, the first President of Corpus Christi College, Oxford, in which Phœbus and his sister, gods and goddesses, one and all, were referred to in the same breath with " Mary's son." Nor was Colet, when he lectured on the Epistles of St. Paul, minded to act upon Bembo's advice to Sadoleto to avoid the Apostle's letters, "lest his barbarous style should spoil your taste."

But the little company of Oxford scholars soon dispersed : Colet to the Deanery of St. Paul's, More to the bar, Grocyn to St. Lawrence Jewry ; Erasmus quitted England. The intercourse with the humanities was renewed indeed in London, where the lectures even were resumed from time to time, as by More on the *De Civitate Dei* of St. Augustine, and by Grocyn on the *Ecclesiastical Hierarchy* of Dionysius. William Lily, who had spent some time at Rhodes, was with them, but at their university the new movement soon found itself in troubled waters : ignorant fear and narrow prejudices raised their threatening voices. Was not the Greek Church itself in schism, it was urged ; were there not heresies in the old Greek Fathers ? To spread their influence must tend to shake the authority of St. Augustine, and the very dogmas of the Church. Grave doctors even preached, says Wood, against the study of Greek as " devilish and damnable." But the students on their side were handier with clubs than logic, and thought broken heads a very sound conclusion. The young " Trojans " were soon masters of the streets, and drove the " Greeks " within the college walls of New and Magdalen and Exeter, where the new studies found their earliest homes. It needed finally a royal letter on the subject, and Wolsey's intervention with a readership in Greek, to enforce peace, and reconcile the academic mind to the statutes of Bishop Fox's College of Corpus Christi, in which Greek was allowed as an alternative for Latin for ordinary talk in hall and chambers, and lecturers in theology were

Troubled waters.

bidden to refer directly to the ancient authors rather than to mediæval commentators like Nicholas de Lyra or Hugo de Vienna.

The new learning reached Cambridge somewhat later and was more tranquilly received. The great influence of John Fisher, Master of Michaelhouse in 1497, and finally Bishop of Rochester, was exerted in its favour, and lectureships in Greek and Hebrew were founded by his fostering care. Erasmus on his return to England was induced to settle there awhile to give lessons in Greek, which he had been studying meantime with ardour. He complained indeed bitterly of languid interest and scanty recompense from the pupils whom he taught, but the great scholar was querulous and hard to please. His studies on the text of the New Testament may well have startled prejudiced readers, though Wood exaggerated possibly when he reported that at Cambridge " it was appointed under a great mulct in a certain college that no fellow should be so vile and impious as to bring Erasmus' text of the Greek Testament within the gates." Otherwise we read of little ferment, and the efforts of Richard Croke, the cultivated reader (1519), seem to have gone far to secure the future interests of Greek at Cambridge.

New learning at Cambridge.

AUTHORITIES. — Evidence as to the monastic schools is scattered over many of the volumes of the list given in Chap. XIV. Much information is to be found in the certificates under the Chantry Acts, which have been carefully edited and discussed by A. F. Leach, *English Schools at the Reformation*, 1896 ; see also *Early Yorkshire Schools*, ed. A. F. Leach, 1899 (York. Arch. Soc.). For University questions at Oxford reference may be made to Wood (A. E.), *History and Antiquities of Oxford*, ed. J. Gutch, 1786-96 ; *Munimenta Academica*, ed. H. Anstey, 1868 (Rolls ser.) ; *Epistolæ Academicæ Oxon.* ed. A. Anstey, 1898 ; *Collectanea*, ed. M. Burrows, containing *Friar Preachers of the University*, p. 193, H. Rashdale ; Linacre's *Catalogue of Grocyn's Library*, p. 317 (Oxford Historical Society) ; see also *History of the University of Oxford*, by H. C. Maxwell Lyte, 1886 ; *The Universities of Europe in the Middle Ages*, by H. Rashdale, 1895. For Cambridge, which was then of far less importance, there is less documentary evidence available. The general history is given in *University of Cambridge*, by J. Bass Mullinger, 1873. The quotations from the *Philobiblon* have been taken from the edition of Mr. E. C. Thomas, 1888. On the question of its authorship see a paper by Mr. Thomas in *The Library*, vol. i. p. 335.

CHAPTER XVII

THE INFLUENCE OF THE CHURCH ON SOCIAL LIFE

It only remains now to consider briefly the influence of the Church on the social life of the Middle Ages ; to bring, that is, under one general view some of the thoughts which must have passed before us in various aspects of the subject. We cannot doubt that that influence was intense and many-sided. The great body of Christian doctrines, of which the Church had been the guardian for ages, was accepted in the main with unhesitating faith ; the scholastic doctors might dispute about the philosophic forms in which they should be developed or explained, but these problems were not vital, and scepticism had hardly begun to lay irreverent hands upon the central dogmas.

The influence of the Church on social life.

The Church itself, as a visible institution, stretching through Western Christendom in her yet unbroken unity, appealed with overpowering force to the imagination of her children. Her ceremonies were associated with every important phase of private life from the cradle to the grave ; her cathedrals and parish churches were the only public buildings to which every class had the same rights and opportunities of access ; in a society deeply scored with the lines of class distinctions all could meet there on the same common level. Only through her service could men of low degree rise to the highest offices of State ; her sanctuaries alone could give a passing shelter to the hunted criminal or outlaw ; her holidays alone brought rest and freedom to the serf.

Let us dwell a little more at length on some of the channels through which the Church diffused her influence on common life, while busy also with her special mission to make men realise a world unseen, and live in faith and hope of a nearer union with a Father in heaven.

The kindly sympathies of charitable hearts found expression in a great variety of institutions called by the general name of Hospital or God's House. The earlier of these were

Hospitals. intended for the most part as permanent homes for lepers, or for the entertainment of pilgrims on their way, and were founded on a grand scale by noblemen or high-placed ecclesiastics, like St. Leonards at York, which had 206 bedesmen on its roll, or Sherburn, where 65 lepers found a home. In later days they were endowed by merchants and townsmen, as almshouses for widows and orphans, poor and aged, blind and lunatic, as well as worn-out clergy. Besides the warden and the brethren of the house there were often sisters also, to wait upon the sick and bedridden and attend to household duties. A certain number of poor applicants were in many to be fed daily at the gate, and a night's lodging was often given to those who were too weak to travel far. Where orphans or other children were received within the walls a schoolmaster was also sometimes reckoned on the staff (*v.* p. 335). The hospitals were also to be houses of prayer, with religious ministrations for the inmates, and regular intercession for the founder and his kin. This last condition was a fatal one to many of them in the evil days of dissolution, when they were swept away on the ground of the superstitious uses to which the funds had been applied. But some of them have lasted on from early days, with their mediæval features still preserved, like St. Cross at Winchester, while others like St. Bartholomew's and St. Thomas' in London have been enormously enlarged and entirely recast to meet the wants of a great city. There is evidence enough to show that in the fourteenth century many of the earlier foundations were in disorder or distress. Some had been imperfectly endowed; some had suffered by the hard times through which the landed interest had passed; more had been mismanaged or robbed even by their wardens or trustees, and the old rules had often been ignored. There were signs enough of abuses in the past, and charity might need to change its objects and its methods. Leprosy was happily more rare, and there was less danger that passing travellers should be "devoured by wolves and evil beasts," as the foundation deed at Flixton phrased it, but sympathy was very keen and active for distress of every kind. Bishops often led the way, as Grandisson at Exeter, Greenfield at York, and Hethe at Rochester, but the townsmen heartily took up the cause. Convents or their abbots had often founded some alms-houses near at hand, but as their sympathies for outsiders grew more languid, citizens like William of Elsing and Whittington took up their work and built homes for the aged and the poor. Their foundations were still under the shadow of the Church, and the statutes which they framed spoke throughout in the language of religion.

The streams of benevolence were also flowing constantly through many other channels. Scarcely a will was made without some charge on the estate in the interest of the needy, and religious motives were appealed Other forms of charity. to and pious language always used by the clerks who drew up the deed. Commonly a definite sum was to be given in doles on the day of the funeral, or immediately before or after, and the amount was often very large. John of Gaunt's body was not to be buried for forty days, and each day 50 marks were to be distributed and 500 on the last day. Bishop Skirlaw desired that £200 might be given away be-tween the hour of his death and the time of his interment, and that a thousand poor folk might receive a mark apiece to buy beds or other comforts. At the funeral of Bishop Gravesende more than 30,000 applicants received a dole in money, and one in bread was given to 10,000 for Bishop Bytton. Traders gave also with no niggard hand. A draper of York provided 100 beds with necessary furniture for as many of the poor. Thirteen people in each of twenty-one distinct parishes received a dole left to them by a mercer. A cloth-maker desired that thirteen poor folk dressed in suits of his own cloth should sit round his coffin for eight days, and keep the clothing for themselves. Another would have no one invited to his funeral feast, but all men made welcome, and the poorest served the first. Besides the sums definitely given it was customary to instruct the executors to lay out the residue of the estate in such forms as might be best for the soul of the testator, that is, for religious and charitable objects.

John de Kineton, remembering the words, "if thou wilt be perfect sell all that thou hast and give to the poor," bids his executors distribute all his property in alms. It might be thought, perhaps, that the words would have been more aptly quoted if he had done this himself in his own lifetime. But, indeed, large liberality was very commonly not put off till death was near. Bishop Drokensford, for example, in 1313 gave formal instructions to his steward that 200 poor should be fed daily at his various manors at his expense.

Thoughtful generosity was not content with the rough and ready forms of indiscriminate largess. Directions were given in many of the wills that prisoners should be cared for in the gaols, pittances given to the lepers and old folks in the hospitals, that "feble waies and brigges" should be mended, king's taxes even paid awhile to lighten civic burdens, books provided for the use of students in the grammar schools, food and clothing found for young scholars to help them on the road to learning. It was a common thing for bishops and wealthy laymen to pay the expenses of a student at a University (*exhibere*). Another frequent form of help to the same class was to endow a "chest," or hutch as it was called, a special fund named after the donor from which money might be borrowed on the security of valuables pledged, such as books or silver cups. The relief seems to have been prized by struggling scholars, and many such chests were founded in both the universities, which had the benefactors' names recorded in their public prayers. The guilds have been already treated in connection with parochial life, and it has been seen that they were not merely a form of mutual insurance or the outcome of self-interest, but that they insisted on the brotherly sympathies which should unite the members, and they softened the asperities of competition among rival traders.

It will of course be noticed that many of the forms of mediæval charity are now replaced by municipal or State control. Poor Law Guardians, Highway Boards, County and Town Councils feed our poor or mend our roads or make our bridges, and provide for what seem now the primary conditions of our civilised progress. The expenses are charged upon the rates; blue-books and official papers make no appeal to our religious feelings, for all perforce must pay.

But it was the Church's function to quicken and inform the sense of public duty, which can now pass on to a multitude of other tasks, and have leisure to solve more complicated problems.   Slowly and painfully men learned the lesson that for almsgiving, as for other precepts of the Gospel, "the letter killeth but the spirit giveth life."   For the sloth and hypocrisy of sturdy vagrants were not the less but more unlovely when they put on a religious dress, and appealed not only to real tenderness of heart but to superstitious hopes and fears.

The subject of education has been discussed at length above.   The schools, as has been seen, were mainly under ecclesiastical control, and only rarely and late was a desire shown for independent action.   The uni-   *Education.* versities, indeed, were more jealous of their freedom ; though largely used for the training of the parochial clergy, they insisted on the priority of the course in arts with its round of secular study, and questionable theses were propounded, and heterodoxy aired its doubts there under the shelter of a tolerance which was unknown elsewhere.   But the students ranked as clerics : the professional classes bore the same character, and some superficial influence of the Church was stamped thereby on all liberal pursuits and culture.

Mediæval literature of course was shaped and coloured by the conditions of its growth.   The monastic chroniclers compiled the annals which were to serve as the materials of our national history; the philosophy of the school-   *Literature.* men, while indulging here and there in daring flights of fancy, consisted in the main in one long attempt to marry the forms of Aristotelian logic to the dogmas of the Church.   The favourite study of ambitious clerics was the canon law ; the popular poem which gave expression to the deepest feelings of the people was the " Piers Plowman," saturated with the sentiments and traditions of the clergy, even while it appealed to the moral instincts of a wider circle.

There were plays written in the English tongue to be acted on the stage, but these Mysteries and Moralities were almost wholly drawn from Scripture and the legends of the saints. The homely satires and the pasquinades that passed in the streets from mouth to mouth were, many of them, full of the quarrels between the Lollards and the friars, or complaints about the shortcomings of the clergy. There were poems indeed, like those of Chaucer, which breathed a freer air and were written for a gayer public, but ecclesiastics and their doings figure largely in the "Canterbury Pilgrims," and though the handling is secular enough it shows how large a place they filled in contemporary thought.

If we turn to the wills, which deal in great detail with all the valuables to be bequeathed, we find indeed books often mentioned as objects to be prized and separately given, but they are Bibles and Missals and religious works. Only very rarely come such gifts as those of translations of French books, "called Tristram and Grace Dieu," though in the fifteenth century works of Petrarch are more often named.

Not only could the clergy control the education of the governing classes, but much of the administrative power was in their hands. The spiritual lords formed a large proportion of the upper House of Parliament; the chief Ministers of State were great ecclesiastics; in all the departments of the State most of the skilled work was done by clerical officials; to be rewarded after long years of faithful service by preferment in the Church. The monopoly, indeed, was often challenged and disputed. Great nobles looked with jealous eyes on the ambitious prelates; sweeping ministerial changes were brought about by court intrigues; laymen gradually displaced the clergy in the law courts; secular interests grew stronger in the liberal professions. Lollard discontent, which honeycombed the industrial strata, called attention to the danger and abuses of the ascendency of the privileged caste, diverted from its proper work, and, as was loudly urged, demoralised by the secular duties and distractions forced upon it. In the fifteenth century the higher clergy were too often self-seeking time-servers and political intriguers. The evil example must have influenced others below, whose coarser lives and lowered standards weakened their hold upon the national conscience. Nevertheless the associations of the past were potent still; the links of union indeed were being slowly loosened, but it had taken centuries to forge them, and they were strong enough, as it seemed, to bear the strain of many changes.

Political power.

While literature and political power and the higher education had a meaning only for the few, the influence of the ecclesiastical courts was widespread and strong. Their competence as Courts of Probate and their matrimonial jurisdiction brought in course of time every household in the land within their range of action. They had also a wide sphere of authority over the everyday concerns of human life. For the canon law, "by its jurisdiction *pro salute animæ*, entered into every man's house, attempted to regulate his servants, to secure his attendance at church, to make him pay his debts, to make him observe his oaths, to make him by spiritual censures, which by the alliance with the State had coercive force, by the dread of a *capias excommunicatum*, keep all the weightier matters of the law, not only justice, mercy, and truth, but faith, hope, and charity also." There was obvious overlapping therefore in the provinces of the common and the canon law, and consequent friction between the agents of the rival courts. It was much to be deplored that the Courts Christian were generally mistrusted and disliked. Their methods of procedure were complained of as inquisitorial and vexatious: their scale of charges seemed excessive, their sompnours and apparitors overbearing and corrupt. The stronger of the archbishops tried, but ineffectually, to correct the abuses of the ecclesiastical tribunals, and the popular discontent grew more intense.

If the Church laid a heavy hand upon her children, and vexed them with her discipline, worked by questionable agents and in irritating forms, on the other hand she showed her sympathy with the people's pleasures, and did what she could to give brightness and gaiety to the social life of the humblest and the poorest. Her holy days became the people's holidays. While the manorial custumals formulated the long catalogue of the forced labours which every serf in old time rendered to his lord, so many days to plough, and reap, and cast and spread manure on the lord's land, the Church's almanac prescribed her days, not of rest only but of innocent enjoyment: the village festival in honour of the patron saint in the one building in the parish where all could meet as equals; the

[margin: Ecclesiastical courts.]

[margin: Popular amusements.]

solemn seasons of the year on which she claimed for them
a brief respite from their workday cares.

The manor courts, as their rolls testify, were chiefly
occupied with the penalties imposed for infringement of the
lord's customary rights, and fines exacted from the tenants;
the Church spoke to them only of a Master " whose service
was perfect freedom." In the towns of course there were far
more opportunities for spectacles and pageants to vary the
monotony of commonplace life, and to these the Church
gave encouragement or sanction. There was the procession
to the coronation service, in which the Primate bore a leading
part; royal visits to the city, like that of Richard II. in 1393,
when a forest scene was exhibited at Temple Bar with wild
beasts, and John Baptist in the desert and angels showering
their flowers from above. There was the opening of Parliament
in state, with a sermon from the Chancellor with Scriptural
text and divisions in the pulpit style; there were frequent
processions of the various guilds, with much show of symbolism
and brave apparel, on their way to Church or to Guildhall,
when the annual festival came round, of which something has
been said already (*v.* p. 277).

The most notable of these spectacles and the most professedly religious in their character and object were the
sacred dramas of Scriptural or legendary matter
which were acted on the stage for the instruction
and amusement of the people. There were many
of these Mysteries, and we can still read some of them which
were acted at Coventry and Chester. The stage was on
the upper floor of a theatre on wheels, which could be shifted
from one street to another, so that each part of the town
might be entertained in turn. Sometimes a prosperous guild
bore the whole cost of a play, which was chosen to illustrate
the special interest of the craft, as when the shipwrights
represented the building of the ark, and the wine merchants
the marriage at Cana; or a town council defrayed the
expenses of the whole show out of the civic funds, but found
an appropriate scene for the characteristic feature of each
craft, which appeared in succession on the stage or in procession through the streets. The Grey Friars, who were most
in touch with the industrial classes, took a special interest in

The
Mysteries.

these exhibitions, and one of whom we read at York in 1421 as "professor of holy pageantry," recommended publicly the Corpus Christi play, but warned the people against the abuses of "revellings and other insolencies," which had degraded what was meant to edify a reverent public. There was no lack of distinguished company at times. Henry IV. sat at Clerkenwell four days with queen and prince to see the parish clerks act out a long Bible story, which only ended with the day of doom.

As we read these mediæval dramas we can find anachronisms and absurdities enough. Annas and Caiaphas appear as "busshoppys"; Herod and Pilate strut like braggarts on the stage, and talk with scraps of French or Latin to indicate their rank; Noah's wife is a scolding shrew, and we pass abruptly from the most solemn subjects to broad farce. The stage directions and accounts treat the mysteries of the faith and sacred names in terms the most irreverent and grotesque. Payments are entered for the "repairing of hell's mouth," or making a suit of buckram for the Spirit of God, or mending of Herod's head, or the white and black souls are measured for their coats. But we must not therefore underrate the moral influence of these pageants, or their power of appealing to the imagination of the people, or lifting them awhile out of the dull routine of selfish cares.

They do not satisfy the standards of our modern taste; there were elements, it may be, of gross and superstitious fancy; but we cannot doubt that through them the Church brought her influence to bear upon the people's lighter moods as well as their religious thought. The poetry might be sorry doggrel, and the acting somewhat rude, but possibly they did as much for the deeper interests of human life as the music halls, dancing saloons, and pantomimes of our civilised days —the secular equivalents of the mediæval pageants.

If it be true, according to a famous phrase of Bacon, that the philosophy of the Middle Ages was subservient to theology, it may certainly be said that art was then the handmaid of religion. Unquestionably the cathedrals *Art.*
were her noblest work. Compared with them the stateliest baronial castles were but great piles of masonry, showing no lack of constructive skill, but with few elements of beauty,

while on the former their designers lavished all their wealth of fancy, and powers of harmonious proportions, and mastery of imaginative symbolism. The Manor-house of those days would seem to us now but comfortless and rude, while the parish church hard by was often richly decorated with the offerings of many generations.

Architecture, however, was not the only art whose early stages felt the sway in England of religious motives. Scriptural scenes and the legends of the saints occupied here the painters' thoughts, as much as in the schools of Giotto or Van Eyck elsewhere. Frescoes for the walls or triptychs for the altar were in request for countless churches while other forms of the pictorial art were little known. The illuminator's skill was lavished almost exclusively on missals, books of hours, and Bibles. The sculptors' hands were busy with the figures needed for crucifix and rood screens, and they carved in monumental forms the passages of Bible history, and long lines of apostles, patriarchs, saints, and kings were crowded round the Minster walls in numbers which almost seemed to vie with the assembled multitudes within, as if to represent alike the Church triumphant and the Church militant below.

Nor was it only in the buildings set apart for sacred uses that the artists' work was full of the associations of a reverent fancy. The burgher's house and the Guildhall bore the same witness to the Church's creed; just as still in the richly decorated mansions of old German towns Scriptural texts are blazoned on the outer walls and Scriptural symbols meet the eye on every side.

Nor was this all. The humbler and more industrial arts followed the same lead; the choicest tapestry lined the chancel walls; the finest embroidery graced the altar; bell-founders and silversmiths found their best patrons in the pious donors who vied with each other in their offerings to the house of God. An Italian traveller, familiar with the works of art in Florence and in Venice, marvelled at the riches to be seen here on every side in the ecclesiastical ornaments and holy vessels. The churches were the museums of mediæval art; their contents far exceeded probably in costliness and splendour all that could be found elsewhere, except here and there in the king's palace or great noble's mansion.

But there came a stormy time of pillage and of desecration, and the colourless pages of an "inventory of Church furniture" are commonly the only traces of the accumulated wealth stored up in the course of ages by the fancy which designed, and the cunning hands which wrought, in the service of the mediæval Church.

APPENDIX I

SOME PRINCIPAL EVENTS

APPENDIX

KINGS OF ENGLAND	Accession.	ARCHBISHOPS OF CANTERBURY	Accession.
Edward I. . . .	1272		
		John Peckham . .	1279
		Robert Winchelsey .	1294
Edward II. . . .	1307		
		Walter Reynolds . .	1313
Edward III. . . .	1327		
		Simon Meopham . .	1328
		John Stratford . .	1333
		Thomas Bradwardine .	1349
		Simon Islip . . .	1349
		Simon Langham . .	1366
		William Wittlesey . .	1368
		Simon Sudbury . .	1375
Richard II. . . .	1377		
		William Courtenay .	1381
		Thomas Arundel . .	1397
		Roger Walden . .	1398
Henry IV. . . .	1399	Thomas Arundel (restored)	1399
Henry V. . . .	1413		
		Henry Chichele . .	1414
Henry VI. . . .	1422		
		John Stafford . .	1443
		John Kemp . . .	1452
		Thomas Bourchier .	1454
Edward IV. . . .	1461		
Richard III. . . .	1483		
Henry VII. . . .	1485		
		John Morton . .	1486

OF

ARCHBISHOPS OF YORK	Accession		POPES			Accession.
			Gregory X.	.	.	1272
			Innocent V.	.	.	1276
			Hadrian V.	.	.	,,
			John XXI.	.	.	,,
			Nicolas III.	.	.	1277
William Wickwaine .	1279					
			Martin IV.	.	.	1281
			Honorius IV.	.	.	1285
John le Romayne .	1286					
			Nicolas IV.	.	.	1288
			Celestine V.	.	.	1294
			Boniface VIII.	.	.	,,
Henry of Newark .	1298					
Thomas of Corbridge .	1300					
			Benedict XI.	.	.	1303
			Clement V.	.	.	1305
William Greenfield .	1306					
			John XXII.	.	.	1316
William of Melton .	1317					
			Nicolas V. *	.	.	1328
			Benedict XII.	.	.	1334
Willlam de la Zouche .	1342		Clement VI.	.	.	1342
John Thoresby .	1352		Innocent VI.	.	.	1352
			Urban V.	.	.	1362
			Gregory XI.	.	.	1370
Alexander Neville .	1374					
			Urban VI.	.	.	1378
			Clement VII. *	.	.	1378
Thomas Arundel .	1388		Boniface IX.	.	.	1389
Robert Waldby .	1397		*Benedict XIII.* *	.	.	1394
Richard Scrope .	1398		Innocent VII.	.	.	1404
			Gregory XII.	.	.	1406
Henry Bowet .	1407		Alexander V.	.	.	1409
			John XXIII.	.	.	1410
			Martin V.	.	.	1417
			Clement VIII. *	.	.	1425
John Kemp .	1426		Eugenius IV.	.	.	1431
			Felix V. *	.	.	1439
			Nicolas V.	.	.	1447
William Booth .	1452					
			Calixtus III.	.	.	1455
			Pius II.	.	.	1458
George Neville .	1464		Paul II.	.	.	1464
			Sixtus IV.	.	.	1471
Lawrence Booth .	1476		Innocent VIII.	.	.	1484
Thomas Rotherham .	1480		Alexander VI.	.	.	1492

* Antipopes.

INDEX

THE END